THE PEOPLE'S RAILWAY

OTHER BOOKS BY DONALD MACKAY

The Lumberjacks
1978

Anticosti: The Untamed Island
1979

Scotland Farewell: The People of the Hector
1980

Empire of Wood: The MacMillan Bloedel Story
1982

Heritage Lost: The Crisis in Canada's Forests
1985

The Asian Dream: The Pacific Rim and Canada's National Railway
1986

The Square Mile: Merchant Princes of Montreal
1987

Flight from Famine: The Coming of the Irish to Canada
1990

THE

PEOPLE'S RAILWAY

A HISTORY OF CANADIAN NATIONAL

DONALD MacKAY

Douglas & McIntyre
Vancouver/Toronto

For my great-grandfather, conductor George McCully, and my grandfathers, Jack MacRae, locomotive engineer, and Jim MacKay, station agent, all of Nova Scotia, and for railroaders everywhere.

Douglas & McIntyre
1615 Venables Street,
Vancouver, British Columbia V5L 2H1

Canadian Cataloguing in Publication Data

MacKay, Donald, 1925-
The people's railway

Includes index.
ISBN 1-55054-062-9

1. Canadian National Railways – History.   I. Title
HZ2810.C14M32 1992   385'.06'751   C92-091463-2

Editing and design by Robin Brass
Cover design by Barbara Hodgson
Cover illustration of the *Continental* from a Canadian National advertisement (courtesy CN)
Maps by Anthony Clegg
Printed in Canada by D.W. Friesen & Sons Ltd.
Printed on acid-free paper

CONTENTS

PREFACE &
ACKNOWLEDGMENTS

MANY BOOKS HAVE BEEN WRITTEN about the Canadian Pacific Railway but relatively few about Canadian National and its predecessors, many of which predated the CPR by many decades. To help fill the gap, *The People's Railway* continues the Canadian National Railways story, published in two volumes in 1960 and 1962, begun by the late G. R. Stevens, who dealt with CN's predecessor companies in the period 1836 to 1922.

The original plan was to confine *The People's Railway* to the period from 1923 through the mid-1970s. However, to understand the forces that coalesced in January 1923 to form Canadian National Railways, the starting date was moved to 1902. For similar reasons of completing the picture, the narrative has been continued to present times, though since this is obviously venturing into current events rather than seasoned history, there is not the same depth of documentation available.

Like the Stevens books, this volume is for the general reader rather than the specialist. It is, however, part of a larger history project, begun three years ago by a dozen independent researchers and writers – professors, social historians, archivists and others – working at arm's length from CN to produce monographs of a specialized nature that will be published by McGill-Queen's University Press. They will range from such people-oriented subjects as "railway culture" in its various aspects, and a demographic study of the railway community of Point St. Charles, Montreal, and the railways' role in immigration, to such matters as technological change, and CN's merchant navy.

This volume, like the monographs and the Stevens books, was commissioned by CN, which has been scrupulous about the independence of the writer. Thus the contents are solely the responsibility of the author, as are interpretations or errors of fact.

A great many people have helped. Many of them appear in the text as the story unfolds. I would, however, especially thank historian Ken Mackenzie, former CN archivist, now of Salt Spring Island, B.C., for making the project and this book possible and providing so much generous assistance. I am grateful to Lorne Perry for supplying the photos and opening many doors at CN, Dorothy Webb, now of Ottawa, for contributing the foundations of the epilogue and reading the text, Jim Davidson of Ottawa for the research on the war chapter, and Anthony Clegg for his work on the maps and graphs.

J. Norman Lowe of Brockville, Ontario, whose historical knowledge of CN railroading is unexcelled, kindly volunteered to instruct me in technical matters and read the text. Peter Murray in London, England, instructed me in CN overseas. Thanks to an inspired suggestion from Roger Cameron and Marie-Andrée Vaillancourt at CN, Bill McNeil, the Toronto broadcaster, shared with me one of the delights of the project, which was interviewing veteran railroaders, nearly all of them now retired, around the country. Among them was Ron E. Lawless, who has taken a personal interest in the history project.

I was grateful for information from E. G. Abbott of the Canadian Railway Labour Association, J. M. Hone of the United Transportation Union, Margaret Mattson of the National Archives, and generous helpings of immigration research from Prof. Brian Osborne and Susan Wurtele of Queen's University, Kingston, and insight into technology from E. F. Bush of Ottawa and into railway culture by Prof. Allen Seager of Simon Fraser University.

I wish to thank Normand Paiement for ably translating the book into French and Hélène Jacquaz for reading the result. I should also like to thank Gloria Pratt, Carol Paterson and Julia Matusky of Montreal for much patient research, Fred R. Wallet for his assistance, and Sherri Mason for transcribing so many interviews. Richard Brown and Carl Vincent of the National Archives of Canada, Ottawa, eased the path of research for both this book and the project as a whole, and the staff of the CN Library in Montreal have been unfailingly helpful.

Finally, as on so many of my past eight books, I wish to thank editor Robin Brass of Toronto, who has once again raised editing to an art form.

DONALD MACKAY
Montreal, June 15, 1992

INTRODUCTION

"Does the railway exist to serve the people or the people to serve the railway? We must seek the answer to these questions in a study of railway history." E. B. Biggar, *The Canadian Railway Problem*, 1917.

A LATE-COMER IN THE ANNALS OF RAILROADING, Canadian National Railways was born of the turmoil of World War I and a marriage, unique among railways of the time, between private and public enterprise. The CNR (later CN) was one of Canada's first crown corporations, a commercial business and an instrument of government all in one, but whether it existed to serve the people, or the people were there to make sure railways were profitable, depended on your view of how society should be conducted. As the country grew, the need to serve government policy diminished.

Had the infant CN sported a coat of arms, its emblems might well have been a silver spoon and an albatross, for while it could count on the federal treasury to make up its annual shortfall, it had to carry the mountainous financial obligations of its debt-ridden ancestors. Though half of the railways that went to make up CN were built between 1850 and 1880, our story begins at the turn of the century when the forces that created the "People's Railway," as CN was called in the 1920s, began to coalesce.

Emerging more or less in final form on January 30, 1923, CN was a mosaic of mismatched parts which included all but one of the four great railways of Canada's industrial revolution. Though it was the youngest, it had a pedigree that went back to Canada's first public railway, the Champlain and St. Lawrence Railroad Company, which opened near Montreal in 1836.

Because of Canada's size, sparse population, lack of private capital, and need to improve communications to develop the country, railways attracted more public concern than in most countries, including the United States, which had private capital to count on. In pre-Confederation years, railways were constructed as public works or in partnership between government and a private company. Building railways being notoriously more profitable than running them, Canada in 1900 had 19,000 miles of track. All the major systems – one owned by the government and three by private enterprise – had depended on government handouts, and if modern cost-benefit analyses had been carried out it is doubtful if half of them would have raised the financing to lay steel. But with so many leading politicians doubling as railway promoters, governments were there to help. So much so, it is not always clear which came first, the nation or the railway, for while Confederation depended on railways, the railways needed Confederation to assure their viability.

The eldest, the Grand Trunk Railway of Canada (GTR), though conceived as a public project, was built in the 1850s by private British capital with Canadian government assistance in an era when cabinet ministers thought nothing of serving simultaneously as railway executives. It was built to compete with the waterways in southern Quebec and Ontario and to give Montreal access to trade with the American mid-west and compete with American railways and canals. It was run, at a loss in its early years, by absentee directors in London, which contributed to its downfall, and their uninformed pursuit of profit clashed with the needs and desires of the country it was built to serve. Its role in nation building included such projects as the 1860 Victoria Bridge across the St. Lawrence, which assured Montreal's place as Canada's industrial and commercial capital for another hundred years.

"The Great International Route between East and West," as the Grand Trunk called itself, had a north-south aspect, to the chagrin of Halifax and Saint John. For though the Grand Trunk ran through southern Quebec and Ontario to the Michigan border at Sarnia, Ontario, one foot was planted in the stockyards of Chicago, where it picked up a third of its income, and the other in tidewater at Portland, Maine, which competed with Maritime ports in commerce with Britain.

The Grand Trunk, to its lasting regret, refused a government invitation in 1880 to build the first transcontinental railway to the West Coast, a timidity that consigned it to playing catch-up for the rest of its life. While the Canadian Pacific Railway took up the challenge, raising the spectre of railway monopoly in the West, the Grand Trunk raised equal fears in central Canada in 1882 by swallowing its arch-rival, the Great Western Railway, which served southern Ontario and linked with U.S. tracks at Niagara Falls and Windsor. Sixteen years later the GTR extended its U.S. track, buying into the Central Vermont Railroad, which had 125 miles in Quebec and 382 through Vermont, Massachusetts and Connecticut, to New London, whence it fed New York City.

Canada's second oldest system, the Intercolonial Railway (ICR), from which CN derived the motto "The People's Railway," was an exercise in state ownership pure and simple. Completed in 1876, the Intercolonial, as much an incentive for Confederation as the CPR drive to Vancouver nine years later, was the fulfillment of a forty-year-old Maritime campaign to secure a government railway into central Canada.

Created at a time New Brunswick was threatened by American annexation, the Intercolonial followed a thinly-populated, roundabout route from Moncton up the northeastern shore of New Brunswick, far from the Maine border, and snaked across the neck of the Gaspé Peninsula and up the south shore of the St. Lawrence River to Rivière-du-Loup. Its chief engineer, Sandford Fleming, had not set out to build a commercial railway – it was a political and military project – but at least he built to such high standards that much of the ICR infrastructure is still standing strong.

As a department of government, managed by the minister of railways and canals, the ICR was burdened with low freight rates designed to aid farmers at the expense of railway revenue. Politicians got votes by assuring jobs on the railway for their constituents, and in an age when patronage was commonplace, critics called the ICR less a public investment than a public sinkhole. For half its life at least, the ICR was managed better than it was given credit for, but like its smaller cousin, the government-owned Prince Edward Island Railway, it thought itself fortunate to cover operating expenses. When the third eldest line, the glamorous Canadian Pacific Railway, was completed in 1885 from Montreal to Vancouver and subsequently extended to Saint

John, New Brunswick, through Maine, the ICR was criticized for a poor comparative showing, but the CPR, for all the gifts of government money and land bestowed upon it for the public good, had been designed for profit.

The youngest and most precocious, the Canadian Northern (CNoR), began in Manitoba in 1894 with two engines, two second-hand passenger cars and fifty freight cars. A country that had lived off furs and lumber had begun to export wheat from "the new Canada beyond the Lakes," and CNoR was a farmer's railway backed by local government to counteract the CPR monopoly. The most unusual aspect of this unusual railway was its two sole owners, Sir William Mackenzie and Sir Donald Mann, Canadian originals in an era when railway bosses were American or British. Backwoods boys from southern Ontario who had made their millions contracting for the CPR, they exploited an innovative system of railway financing based on provincial, municipal and federal loans and bond guarantees, which left the railway's financial structure vulnerable when hard times hit.

Mackenzie, with a genius for raising money, and Mann, with a flair for laying low-cost steel where it could pick up the most grain, built piecemeal as traffic demanded, with a promise, that did not always materialize, to improve the track as traffic warranted. They opened a 438-mile line from Winnipeg to Port Arthur (Thunder Bay), built grain elevators, undercut CPR freight rates, and shipped wheat down the Great Lakes or via the Duluth, Winnipeg and Pacific Railway through Fort Frances, Ontario, to Duluth, Minnesota.

At the turn of the century the rare optimism sweeping Canada attracted capital into mines, dams, mills, and of course railways, which had played such a part in the new prosperity and looked forward to an even brighter future. The Grand Trunk had acquired Charles Melville Hays, its most dynamic manager, who insisted on running things not from London but from Montreal. The ICR was managed by a minister of railways, A.G.Blair, who had reformed the People's Railway and was determined to prove that a public system could be as good as a private one. The Canadian Pacific had survived years of difficulty to achieve the constant profits for which it became famous. The upstart Canadian Northern nursed visions of rivalling the CPR. All four railways, running east and west as they did, played their part in maintaining Canada's integrity as a society distinct from the colossus to the south.

It seemed in those halcyon years that good times would flow on forever like the rippling wheat. The railway scene, as Canada entered the 20th century, could hardly have seemed more promising – or been more deceptive.

BOOM AND
BUST

"For half a century the clamour against railways after they had been constructed has been almost as vociferous as the clamour *for* railways before they were constructed." Sir John Willison, Editor, Toronto *Globe,* 1921.

URING THE FIRST TWELVE YEARS OF THIS CENTURY, Canada's enthusiasm for railways reached heights we were not to see again. In fifty years of deals honourable and scandalous, four railway systems, equal in the mind of the times to all our present transportation systems combined, had brought a magic unity and prosperity to a country of hopelessly vast distances. By 1900, 19,000 miles of steel had been spiked down — more rail per capita than anywhere else on earth — most of it operated by the Grand Trunk Railway of central Canada, the government's Intercolonial in the Maritimes, and the Canadian Pacific Railway and Canadian Northern Railway in the West.

Financed by taxpayers as well as private investors at home and abroad, the luscious pickings of railway building spread wealth across the land, creating railway millionaires and adding a new dimension to pork-barrelling.

Confusing technology with democracy, the civil engineer and railway philosopher Thomas C. Keefer had believed in the 1840s that better communications would deter the baser political instincts. This, of course, was asking too much, as he later admitted, though Keefer's "restless, rushing, roaring civilizer" did bring comfort and enlightenment to a country emerging from backwoods pioneering.

The black monsters that panted and whistled across the lonely landscapes, scaring horses and thrilling children, delivered your food and mail, carried your family, brought the world to your door and hauled your crops to market. They even brought weather reports, having "weather discs" on the side that gave country people the forecast – a full moon for fine weather, a crescent for showers and a star for rain. Rough-hewn communities condemned to build their own amenities and light them with oil lamps were treated to a glimpse of "hotels on wheels," a world of plush, damask and polished mahogany. Passenger coaches were lighted by electricity (since the 1890s), heated by steam and cooled with fans blowing over blocks of ice; dining cars glittered with snowy tablecloths, polished crested silver and waiters in white coats serving six-course meals.

"There used to be a passenger train through Stratford, Ontario, every night," recalled J. D. Cryon. "I would hear the whistle as it was coming in and run for blocks just to see this thing shooting by. That was a real thrill when I was a kid." Cryon grew up to become a CN conductor, and other small boys dreamed of sitting at the throttle in an engineer's blue denim and red bandanna, tooting the whistles that were more than haunting folk music. Two long hoots meant a train was pulling out; one long, thrilling blast and clanging bell announced it was coming into the station in a perfume of steam and warm oil.

The station, with its prize flower beds and the name of the community picked out in white stones, was the place where small-town Canada came for the latest news from the telegrapher and to talk crops and hockey over a hot stove. Webb Vance of Moncton remembered the little station at Macann, Nova Scotia, crowded every night, "where everybody came, the main meeting place in town." Railwaymen, like cowboys and seamen, smacked of adventure and far places, and in towns across Canada the engine driver and the conductor were part of the well-paid elite. In the village of Ashern, a hundred miles northwest of Winnipeg, the only link with the rest of the world was the Canadian Northern Railway. "They had the only telephone in the village and you could use it only in an emergency," recalled John Whitney "Jack" Pickersgill, who grew up there. "The whistle of the locomotive was what connected people, especially on the Prairies," said the future minister of transport.

In the second half of the 19th century Canadian railways fashioned themselves after the American lines, which themselves had borrowed from older industries (the duties of a conductor were not unlike those of a merchant marine captain) and the army, with its tradition of seniority, discipline and semi-autonomous regional operations. Railways followed their own codes of conduct, ran their own police forces and controlled time, having organized four time zones across the continent in the 1880s for their operating convenience. Their rules had the force of law, railway debates were major events in Parliament, and the words of a senior railway official were front-page news in a way they are not today. The "railway vote," large blocs of people influenced to vote for company favourites in hundreds of railway communities across the nation, played its part in electing governments.

With their massive infrastructure of rail, rolling stock, stations, round-houses, coal depots and freight sheds, railways were Canada's most visible industry. The Grand Trunk shops at Point St. Charles, Montreal, were a virtual steam city, sprawling over thirty acres, with iron foundry, rolling mill, wheel mill, smithy and thousands of boilermakers, machinists, electricians, moulders, pattern makers, pipe fitters, metal workers and carpenters. The shops at Hamilton, Ontario, built by the Great Western, which had produced North America's first real sleeping cars, repaired thirty locomotives a day in a "general hospital where the sick giants were disposed in long rows and supported at a considerable height on wooden blocks and beams."

The railways owned tracts of land as big as European countries, as well as hotels, ships, docks, grain elevators, coal mines, and the telegraph companies that had evolved from their own communication systems. But at the turn of the century they wanted more and governments and money lenders were eager to oblige them as a rare optimism swept the country like a happy contagion. In the conviction that good times would roll on forever, capital was flowing into mines, lumber woods, dams, mills and cheap steel rails to serve them.

It is hard today, after two world wars, a depression and several cycles of boom and bust, to imagine those days when bankers, merchants, and speculators smelling money took Prime Minister Sir Wilfrid Laurier's hopeful notion that "the 20th century belongs to Canada" so literally. Though in hindsight it would have been wiser to extend branch lines to serve the West rather than creating new railway companies, the obsession with railways had its own compelling logic. Eastern Canadian waterways were virtually useless in winter, the range of a horse and loaded wagon was a dozen miles a day, and motor vehicles were as rare as good roads. Building more railways in 1900 made sense in a world where steam was king and the government was prepared to pay.

"We want all the railways we can get," said the *Manitoba* (later *Winnipeg*) *Free Press,* "for Manitoba's proper policy is free trade and we have got to have more railways if the crop of this country is to be moved out in a reasonable time." With immigrants arriving in their tens of thousands from Britain, Europe and even the United States, the monopolistic young Canadian Pacific Railway, like the weather a source of farmer frustration, was simply not enough. Fast-growing, frost-resistant Marquis wheat had pushed the agricultural frontier 200 miles north and doubled the arable land far north of the CPR line, and with the American grain belt filling up Canada offered the "last best west."

Steam railways, symbolizing all that was efficient and up-to-date, were a breeding ground for visionaries. A. G. Blair, Laurier's minister of railways and canals, returned from a trip through the Prairies in 1892 convinced there was room for three transcontinental railways. A former premier of New Brunswick, Blair dreamed of extending the ICR, or a reasonable facsimile, a "public highway ... run under government control," to the Great Lakes to give the ports of Saint John and Halifax wheat traffic from the West. Defending government ownership of the patronage-ridden ICR, despite Laurier's aversion to it, Blair insisted that the ICR was not as bad as it had been painted and "if other than high state considerations had influenced its location it would now be enjoying a most successful career." The race to build a transcontinental railway to rival the CPR really began, however, when the Grand Trunk Railway, which had spurned a government offer to build a transcontinental line in 1880, and thus gave the honour (and a bonanza of government funding and land) to the CPR, began to have second thoughts.

Those who argued that Canada, having one twelfth the population, should not emulate its rail-hungry neighbour were no match for Charles Melville Hays from Rock Island, Illinois. Hired as Grand Trunk general manager in 1896 to pump American know-how into a British-owned railway in whose ornate Montreal headquarters everything stopped for tea, Hays ordered double track between Montreal and Toronto, bought powerful locomotives and installed air brakes in place of the hand brakes that had maimed so many trainmen. He reorganized the American leg of the Grand Trunk and called it the Grand Trunk Western. He increased earnings, eliminated the deficit and for the first time in thirteen years paid interest on preference stock. Recalling how many American railroads had failed because of timidity, "the little American" regretted that his predecessors had not beaten the CPR to the Pacific. He felt "bottled up," for though the Grand Trunk controlled a third of Canada's rails, all of it lay east of North Bay, Ontario, and the GTR, which might have been the first in the West, had to depend on the CPR for western freight.

It was Hays as much as anyone who pushed Canada toward a second transcontinental railway when even the railroad-mad United States had no single line across the continent. Hays had a bold plan. When he heard that Laurier wanted a transcontinental railway identified with the Liberals as the CPR had been identified with Sir John A. Macdonald's Conservatives, he created a subsidiary, the Grand Trunk Pacific Railway (GTP), and secured Laurier's backing for his bonds. On November 24, 1902, he announced that the GTP would build from North Bay through northwestern Ontario, the Prairies and the Rockies to tidewater at Prince Rupert. Being 500 miles closer to the Orient than the CPR stronghold of Vancouver, Prince Rupert would attract business, or so he thought, and for good measure he would launch ships to challenge the CPR fleet that traded to the Orient.

As the CPR had done, he would use the Prairies as a land bridge between Britain and the riches of the Orient, the latest version of the old imperial dream of an "all-red route" by ship and rail from London to Tokyo. "To my mind," he told Grand Trunk directors in London who raised awkward questions, "it is difficult to conceive that there can be any objections to this scheme, which promises so much to the Grand Trunk Railway, and which links its fortunes to the government of Canada in a way the two must work together…. The question is not what is going to happen to you if you adopt this enterprise, but what is going to happen to you if you do not adopt it."

Newspapers across the West agreed with the Calgary Board of Trade that the "time is now ripe for another transcontinental railway" and even the former president of the CPR, Sir William Van Horne, thought it a good idea. "We would hail with delight a parallel route from the Atlantic to the Pacific to help us develop the country," said Van Horne during a stopover in Winnipeg. "There is enough of it up there for all of us." The current president, Thomas (later Lord) Shaughnessy, who frequently disagreed with Van Horne, opposed the plan, as did the owners of the Canadian Northern Railway, William Mackenzie and Donald Mann, who called it "unnecessary and wasteful."

The five-year-old Canadian Northern, which had begun life as the Manitoba government's counterweight to a CPR monopoly that was doing more to alienate than unite west and east, was now operating 1300 miles of track, mostly in Manitoba and in Saskatchewan, serving thousands of farms and 130 communities that the CPR had never reached, and was preparing to head west into Alberta. Convinced it had Laurier's support if a second transcontinental railway were to be built, the Canadian Northern abandoned all pretence that it was a regional line, moved its head office from Winnipeg to the Railway Chambers in Toronto, and got government authorization to lay rail from Port Arthur to Ottawa.

Given the Canadian Northern's expansion plans and the existence of the CPR, said the Vancouver *Province*, why build another transcontinental railway? Blair, the minister of railways, agreed, running athwart his laissez-faire leader in insisting that any new transcontinental must be government-owned all the way. In London, where the Grand Trunk directors were suffering the same timidity they had shown in 1880 when they passed up a chance to go west, their chairman, Sir Charles Rivers Wilson, sensibly considered merging the Grand Trunk Pacific with Canadian Northern and making Mackenzie president. This opportunity to avoid "Canada's Railway Problem," as the press had taken to calling it, was lost when Mackenzie, on a visit to London, delayed contacting Rivers Wilson until the latter had to leave for an extended visit to Rome. It seems likely the delay was deliberate, for Mackenzie and Mann had been caught up by visions of spanning the nation themselves. At all events, Hays wanted to buy CNoR outright, as did the CPR, under the impression that Mackenzie and Mann, having become millionaires, would be ready to sell. "Both companies wanted to buy us out and neither was friendly," Mann said. "We were too young and ambitious to sell out at that time."

Amalgamation being the sensible course, Laurier called the Grand Trunk and Canadian Northern to his home in Ottawa but failed to break the deadlock, which he might have done by withdrawing federal aid. Whatever the reasons – disagreements in cabinet, refusal to entertain Blair's suggestion that the ICR be pushed west, fear his own dream of a northern railway was at risk, failure to see Dominion transportation policy as a whole – the ranking proponent of laissez-faire Liberalism opened the future to a third transcontinental railway – and too much railway for too few people.

Encouraged by a thriving economy, the Grand Trunk and Canadian Northern each set out to build its own transcontinental line, deaf to warnings they were building one railroad too many. "You know," said Mackenzie, "we expected at one time to be the favoured people to build this new transcontinental road. Now we must go along as best we can. It may take a little longer than it otherwise would." In the end it took too long and cost too much and Mackenzie, like Hays, would be caught in forces beyond his control.

Compared with what was to come, Hays' proposal had been modest. Canada being such a regionalized country, the politicians naturally made regional demands, as they had since the Colonial Guarantee Act of 1842 had thrown government and capitalist into a symbiotic relationship in which Fathers of Confederation doubled as railway entrepreneurs and conflict of interest was so little regarded that a cabinet minister could moonlight as a railway official.

Why terminate at North Bay? Two thirds of Canada's grain was being diverted to American ports, so why not build to Quebec City or even to the Maritimes? As the political pressures grew, a timorous Grand Trunk board in London agreed to a departure from the traditional partnerships in which the government provided money and the capitalist laid the rails. Ottawa would build the eastern half of the system and the Grand Trunk would build the rest.

Eighteen years after completion of the CPR, Laurier stood in the House in July 1903 to serve notice that Canada was to have a second coast-to-coast system based on the "need for increased transportation facilities for the forwarding of our grain and other products to the markets of the world." As a Quebec politician he had been pressured by the Roman Catholic Church to build a railway through the north and open land for French Canadians who had migrated to the New England mill towns for work, and by businessmen who wanted to bring northwestern grain and timber down to the slumbering wharves of the Saint Lawrence. From Halifax and Saint John came pleas for a share of the grain that was going to American ports on its way to England. The prime minister, more poet than economist, had been ill and some thought him feverish as he launched into one of his glittering speeches.

> To those who urge upon us the policy of tomorrow and tomorrow and tomorrow, to those who tell us, wait, wait, wait; to those who advise us to pause, to consider, to reflect, to calculate and to inquire, our answer is: No, this is not a time for deliberation, this is a time for action.... I am well aware that this plan may scare the timid and frighten the irresolute. But I may claim that every man who has in his bosom a stout Canadian heart will welcome it as worthy of this young nation.

The system would be twice the size of the original Hays proposal. The government half, the National Transcontinental, would run east 1844 miles from Winnipeg through the northern wilderness of rock and conifer forest to Quebec City and then follow a more direct and populated route than the ICR, cutting down the St. John Valley to Moncton, with links to Halifax and Saint John over the ICR. Once complete, the National Transcontinental was to be leased to the Grand Trunk Pacific in return for a percentage of construction costs and other considerations. The *Montreal Star* called it "that mad route, unknown, unsurveyed and uninhabited, through the North country, over granite ranges, from Winnipeg to Quebec."

The western half, 1944 miles from Winnipeg to Edmonton and through the northern British Columbia wilderness to Prince Rupert, would be built and operated as the Grand Trunk Pacific, with Ottawa guaranteeing bonds covering 75 per cent of construction. In London a clairvoyant Grand Trunk director resigned, in the belief these terms could only lead to the death of his railway. In Ottawa, Blair resigned as minister of railways, foreseeing that the National Transcontinental would take business from the ICR, which laboured under the disadvantage of being in the wrong place. Denouncing "one of the most indefensible railway transactions which has ever taken place in this country," Blair called Laurier's scheme an unhealthy compromise between two antagonistic principles, private and public ownership, thereby anticipating CN's woes in the years ahead. Politics being a balancing act, Laurier appointed Blair chairman of the Board of Railway Commissioners (later the Canadian Transport Commission and later still the National Transportation Agency), which, after complaints from the West and the Maritimes, Blair had established to regulate freight and passenger rates, safety standards, express services and telegraph companies, and the opening or abandonment of branch lines.

With Blair out of party politics, the case for building a government railway to the Pacific was taken up from, of all places, the Conservative benches.

As a reformist, Robert Borden, leader of the Conservative Party and MP for Halifax, eastern terminus of the ICR, had to satisfy a divided caucus which included free enterprisers such as Senator Mackenzie Bowell, the former party leader. "If we are to take the Intercolonial Railway as an example to guide us in future," Bowell said, "God protect us from the financial results that must follow if the government are to own and run many other roads in future."

Borden, like Blair, favoured pushing the ICR westward to the Great Lakes or even beyond but, given the opposition to public ownership in his caucus, at first suggested only that better use be made of private capital. He urged the government to purchase the tracks the CPR had been compelled to build through the barren stretch between Sudbury and the Lakehead and give running rights to all, which, had the idea been adopted, would have linked the Canadian Northern in the West with the Grand Trunk Railway and rationalized railway building.

On April 5, 1904, convinced he had public support, Borden came out firmly for another People's Railway, telling the House that the second Canadian transcontinental railway should be "entirely owned by and under the control of the people of Canada." He saw no reason, whatever the history of ICR, why a public railway could not operate free of party pressure. "Can any better use be made of the excessive taxation wrung from the people of Canada," he asked, "than a thoroughly national system of railways extending from the Atlantic to the Pacific?"

In the 1904 general election, public ownership, largely due to Borden, had become the Conservative alternative to the policy of subsidizing private railways. Playing on public distrust of large corporations in the States, Borden claimed the Liberal government's contract with the Grand Trunk Pacific was far too favourable to the company. Since taxpayers were underwriting 90 per cent of Canada's railways, he said, they might as well pay the extra and own the whole thing.

There was ample support for the government's right to control its investment. "If the government is to build and own the road from Moncton to Winnipeg, and guarantee most of the money for the balance of the road from Winnipeg to [the Pacific], why not build and own the whole?" asked the *Guardian* of Charlottetown. "Of course it will be a stiff proposition and a costly one, but the feeling in favour of government and municipal ownership of public franchises is undoubtedly growing rapidly." Stating that "Mr. Borden irrevocably committed his party to the principle of public ownership of railways," the *Weekly Sun* of Toronto, an organ of Ontario farmers, called it the most important issue since Confederation. "Our railway policy has met with warm approval from many quarters, some quite unexpected," Borden said. "It is simple, easily comprehended, and not only interests but appeals to the people." Nevertheless the public voted the Liberals into power and Borden, who lost his seat, berated voters for a "verdict against themselves in favour of corporate interests."

In September 1905 Laurier turned the first sod for the National Transcontinental in a ceremony at Fort William (Thunder Bay), Ontario, which he predicted would become the Chicago of the North. A heroic era of railway building had begun. The following spring 2000 men were clearing a right-of-way through the forests, muskeg, swamps and brûles in northern Quebec and Ontario and 5000 were laying track and building bridges through the buffalo grass on a survey line between Winnipeg and Edmonton. With the exception of the Panama Canal, it was the greatest construction project of its time. "Perhaps no more comprehensive plan of railway structure was ever conceived," declared the *Canadian Magazine*. "It rivals the great Trans-Siberian Railway, undertaken by the Russian government, and the famous Cape to Cairo Railway to connect the two ends of the continent of Africa."

In 1905, the year Saskatchewan and Alberta became provinces, both William Mackenzie and Charles Hays came west, Mackenzie covering the last few miles in a bouncing automobile following the Canadian Northern right-of-way into Edmonton, cheered by the promise of a federal bond guarantee. The bearded, energetic Hays drove a horse and buggy 700 miles through the Prairie heat over the Grand Trunk Pacific route, which lay between the CPR to the south and Canadian Northern.

"I think it is very generally admitted we are going to have the best transcontinental road this side of the Atlantic," said Hays. "Certainly nothing heretofore done in Canada will approach it." Like the National Transcontinental, the Grand Trunk Pacific would be built to high standards, unlike the Canadian Northern, which had been built frugally with a view to improvement when traffic demanded. Stations were spotted every dozen miles to encourage communities to grow around them and given names in alphabetical order, Atwater to Zumbru. But unlike its rivals, the GTP received no gifts of land, so Hays formed the Grand Trunk Pacific Development Company, buying 45,000 acres and laying out 120 "towns-made-to-order."

In the summer of 1908, 21,000 men were at work on the National Transcontinental–Grand Trunk Pacific and thousands on the Canadian Northern, which Mann boasted to Laurier would build "in the true sense of the word a great national highway." Taming the mountains was expensive, as the CPR had discovered, but having received funding, bond guarantees and land from the Prairie provinces, which got them as far as Edmonton, Mackenzie and Mann could look forward to help from Premier Richard McBride of British Columbia to get them to the coast in return for more control over freight rates. McBride called the Canadian Northern a "thoroughly Canadian system controlled by Canadians," a reference to the Grand Trunk's absentee directors and the CPR's shareholders in Britain.

By 1911, the year Mackenzie and Mann were knighted, Canadian Northern ran from Lake Superior to Edmonton, had created 500 communities, served half the grain elevators on the Prairies, but still had no rail to central Canada – the mirror image of the Grand Trunk which had been "bottled up" in the east. "Driven by the laws of self-preservation," having tried and failed to purchase the ICR, Mackenzie and Mann had acquired 1600 miles of railway in eastern Canada: 350 miles in Nova Scotia, 600 in Quebec and 650 in Ontario. Arguing that a transcontinental Canadian Northern would be good for Canada, Mackenzie used these scattered lines as bait for federal funding to build 1000 miles of track across the wilderness from Port Arthur to central Ontario. Having once turned him down Laurier now agreed, concerned perhaps in an election year that Canadian Northern would divert grain south to the United States. He lost the election to the Conservatives, partly because of the national railway policy he had formulated a decade earlier, but his concession to Canadian Northern guaranteed that not only a second but a third railway would cross Canada.

In 1912, the Canadian Northern, which had tracks into the little Moreau Street station in east Montreal, began to invade the city centre, headquarters of the Grand Trunk and the CPR, by tunnelling three miles through volcanic rock under Mount Royal and laying double tracks. (It was the second longest tunnel in the country, after the CPR's five-mile Connaught Tunnel in the Rockies.) At the southern end CNOR bought fourteen acres and planned a terminal where the Central Station stands today, and at the northern end it built a garden suburb, the Town of Mount Royal.

In the West, Canadian Northern was racing the Grand Trunk Pacific through Yellowhead Pass, two sets of tracks running together on a coveted route where grades were much easier than the CPR's 150 miles to the south.

"The outlook up to 1912 was all that could be desired," CNoR general manager David Blythe Hanna wrote in his memoirs, though this was the last time he could display such optimism. "There was no cloud in the sky; everything was beautifully blue; western development was going ahead, immigration was entirely satisfactory, and there was plenty of money." The clouds began to appear that autumn when farmers complained there were not enough box cars to move their grain crop.

The Grand Trunk Pacific had been less euphoric. Construction in the mountains cost twice as much as building through the Prairies, and though the GTP continued construction of the Fort Garry Hotel in Winnipeg and the Macdonald Hotel in Edmonton it abandoned hopes of turning Prince Rupert into a port to rival Vancouver, scrapped plans for a deep-water Pacific fleet, and concentrated on a coastal service. Despite massive transfusions from its parent and the federal government, the Grand Trunk Pacific was in such trouble, pulling the parent down with it, that Hays made another of his trips to London, apparently carrying a plan to fob off the GTP on a government already hopelessly involved in the eastern or National Transcontinental half of the system. What Hays might have done to rescue the Grand Trunk Railway we shall never know, for he was one of the 1513 who died when the *Titanic* went down on April 15, 1912.

In little more than a year the wheat boom came to an end, the flow of money and immigrants dried up, and the two new railways were left with neither sufficient traffic nor funding. Both had reached the point where interest on capital expenditure must be met out of earnings but neither was a profitable operation. Canadian Northern still had 1420 miles of track to lay – between Edmonton and Vancouver and between Port Arthur and central Ontario – but in the prewar recession railway bonds were a drug on the market.

So long as Canadian Northern had remained a regional line it had prospered. Now questions were raised about government subsidies and bond guarantees that permitted Mackenzie and Mann to control the stock. The *Grain Grower's Guide,* the strident voice of Prairie farmers, complained that the government had been giving cash without retaining control. The *Winnipeg Free Press,* describing Mackenzie and Mann as "wonder workers in the magic arts of modern high finance," suggested the government "take a determined stand in support of the principle that before another dollar of public aid is granted to the Canadian Northern there should be an uncovering of Canadian Northern's finances." "Day by day they are getting into a financial corner that will not be easy to escape," said Shaughnessy, who accused them of recklessness. If Canadian Northern should fail, he said, the government would be obliged to take it over and confront the CPR with a competitor subsidized by the taxpayers.

By 1915 CNOR had nearly 9000 miles of track across the country and when Mackenzie drove the last spike near Kamloops Junction, B.C., the one-time school teacher from Ontario was one of the richest men in the country, with interests in Canada, South America (Brazilian Traction, now Brascan) and elsewhere, but the centrepiece was about to become the greatest business failure in Canadian history, threatening to haul down the Bank of Commerce, a major backer. "We hung on to the job of making the best of a heart-breaking, never-ending crisis," said Hanna. "It has been a nightmare for several weeks," admitted Borden, "not so much by reason of the fate of the Canadian Northern itself as on account of our concern for the stability of a large financial institution." Laurier, who had been as responsible as Mackenzie for the crisis, told Parliament that Canada must on no account permit Canadian Northern to collapse. "We have too much money in it – not only the money of the country but of the provinces and [private] bondholders." The government agreed to increase its stake from 10 to 40 per cent and become co-owner.

Railway construction had far outpaced population. In the fifteen years since 1900, mileage had increased by 130 per cent but the population had grown less than 40 per cent and Canada possessed a mile of track for every 250 inhabitants, an uneconomic ratio compared with the mile for 400 in the United States and for 2000 in the United Kingdom. Nearly 12,000 miles of the total was operated by two virtually bankrupt companies, Canadian Northern and the Grand Trunk Pacific, and another 3500 by the Grand Trunk Railway, which was in trouble itself.

Nor were the government railways much healthier. The National Transcontinental, completed in 1915 except for the bridge across the St. Lawrence above Quebec City which had collapsed twice with the loss of about seventy-five lives, was earning barely half its operating costs. With two thirds of its track running through wilderness, the National Transcontinental had been built to extravagant standards, costing three times the original estimates, which gave the GTP an excuse to renege on leasing it.

"The Grand Trunk Pacific Company have practically thrown up their hands," said Borden, "and the Grand Trunk management are thoroughly sick of the Grand Trunk Pacific and are intensely desirous of being rid of the whole enterprise." Borden himself was fed up. "I would personally prefer to resign and let the Grits clean up their mess," he told his diary, regretting perhaps that railway failures could not be handled as they were south of the border where the solution was harsh and simple. When a railway got into a jam in the States, it declared bankruptcy, and while shareholders suffered it usually emerged, phoenix-like, from its ordeal of reorganization and refinancing. But with World War I increasing the national debt, finance minister Sir Thomas White was convinced that allowing Canadian Northern to declare bankruptcy would destroy Canadian credit – federal, provincial, municipal and industrial. Nor would the government abandon the scores of communities that must moulder into ghost towns without the railway.

As the "railway problem" festered, Borden's vision of public ownership was supported by Sir Joseph Flavelle of Toronto, a millionaire meat packer, chairman of the wartime Imperial Munitions Board, financier and, as it happened, a director of the imperilled Bank of Commerce. In a letter to Borden on June 18, 1915, Flavelle anticipated the nationalization to come:

> If you were [he said] to create a "National Railway System of Canada" and acquire the Grand Trunk Railway System, the Grand Trunk Pacific, the Canadian Northern Railway, and add to them the Intercolonial Railway, would you not present a constructive policy of commanding importance and to the permanent advantage of Canada?
>
> Do not the very difficulties of the situation create an opportunity for the establishment of a State-controlled national railway system under the circumstances of exceptional advantages, in which the country, out of its necessities owing to various guarantees, and out of the crippled position of the railway corporations can enter into possession of great properties and for all time control the railway policy of Canada?

The government temporized. Tired of keeping Canadian Northern and the Grand Trunk Pacific afloat with subsidies disguised as loans, it fell back in 1916 on that antidote to government perplexity, the royal commission. The chairman was A.H.Smith, president of the New York Central Railroad, aided by A.H.Acworth, a British railway economist, and Sir Henry Drayton, a Conservative Toronto lawyer who had succeeded Blair on the Board of Railway Commissioners. Before the proceedings began, Borden's finance minister gave the commissioners a nudge toward government thinking, suggesting they "might conceivably recommend the amalgamation of the Canadian Northern, the Grand Trunk, and the Grand Trunk Pacific into a system in which the government might be interested to a certain extent."

"The Canadian Northern is weak in the East," said the commission report in 1917. "The Grand Trunk with the inadequate prairie branches of the Grand Trunk Pacific would be almost powerless to compete in the West with the Canadian Northern and the Canadian Pacific. The natural tendency of the Grand Trunk and Canadian Northern organizations, if left separate, would be for each to invade the territory of the other." Reflecting Canadian fears of railway monopoly, Drayton and Acworth rejected CPR assimilation of the weaker railways and recommended that the "people of Canada" take control and combine the Grand Trunk and Canadian Northern with the Intercolonial and National Transcontinental and operate them as "one united system on a commercial basis." Though none of the privately owned lines had been able to pay interest on their government guaranteed bonds, and it was unlikely the new railway could yield a return on investment for years to come, Drayton and Acworth contended that a commercial operation similar to the CPR's would stimulate efficient and profitable management. Rejecting the ICR system under which the minister was responsible for oper-ations, they proposed a non-political, self-perpetuating board of trustees, which, apart from staving off political interference, would provide buffers between the Canadian and U.S. governments over a thousand miles of track in the States regulated by the Interstate Commerce Commission.

In a minority report that anticipated the trouble to come, Smith pointed out that his colleagues had not solved the political problem. "My friends," he said, "seem to avoid government ownership and operation, in fact condemn it as inadvisable, but propose a plan which contains so many elements of danger in the direction which is sought to be avoided that I am unable to join them." As a free-enterpriser he would have left the private railways in private hands to work out their own salvation. For a maximum of efficiency with a minimum of expense he would have the Grand Trunk operating in the east with its own lines plus the eastern lines of Canadian Northern. The Cana-dian Northern would confine itself to the West, incorporating the Grand Trunk Pacific.

By this time Canadian Northern's difficulties had become urgent. Though it had managed to fill in the missing links in its cross-Canada sys-tem, including the gap down B.C. to Port Mann, near Vancouver, the war closed money markets at the most expensive and difficult time of its history.

Over the years, governments had paid for half of Canada's railway construction, including the CPR's, by subsidies, loans and bond guarantees, but now
the well had gone dry. When Mackenzie turned to his old friend, Borden, the
prime minister had an unhappy task:

> On July 14, 1917, I had an interview with Sir William [wrote Borden]
> and I definitely informed him that the Government could not grant any
> further aid and must take over the Canadian Northern in its entirety. Sir
> William was a man of iron nerve and this was one of only two occasions
> on which I saw his self-control desert him. Knowing my decision was fi-
> nal, he was silent for a moment and then completely broke down with
> audible sobs that were most distressing.

Even then Mackenzie did not give up, as Gerard Ruel, Canadian Northern vice-president of legal affairs, recalled. "I suggested to him then two
things," said Ruel. "First, to make a joint operating arrangement with Lord
Shaughnessy for a period of years (I suggested ten) and I thought that at the
end of that time with the savings effected by the joint operation the company
might reestablish itself. The other alternative was to sell the enterprise to the
crown with the option to buy it back at a stated price. Both of these proposi-
tions fell down, the former because Lord Shaughnessy would not consider
any such proposition (it was a matter of personal animosity) and second
because Sir William knew that there were many provisions in the Canadian
Northern Act preventing him from dealing with the CPR and he felt that the
sentiment in the west would not permit any cancellation of that legislation."
A member of Parliament suggested that the Canadian Northern and Grand
Trunk Pacific be sold to the CPR for the traditional token dollar and was told
that this would leave the government with the immense railway debt but
nothing with which to convert it into an asset.

With half of Canada's railway system bankrupt, Borden grasped the
Drayton-Acworth report as a practical way out, support for public ownership
having grown – not least in Ontario because of the popularity of the ten-
year-old Hydro-Electric Power Commission. Moreover, Borden's new Union
government, a coalition of Tories and Grits, included monopoly-shy western
Liberals who hoped public ownership would lower freight rates and prevent
the CPR from swallowing the Grand Trunk.

The Grain Growers Association and the United Farmers of Alberta
favoured nationalization, as did the influential Canadian Council of Agriculture. The Toronto *Globe* called it the "logical and courageous solution of the

railway problem," a view shared by many newspapers across the country, though the Canadian Northern fought to the last to preserve its independence. It cited a report by reputable engineering consultants, retained by a Wall street syndicate interested in backing Canadian Northern, that the railway was sound and if allowed to go on would become solvent in time. But things had gone too far. Already part-owner, the government announced on August 14, 1917, that it would take over Canadian Northern completely, paying $10 million to investors (10 per cent of the par value of capital stock), and run it "on behalf of the people of Canada." Three weeks later Mackenzie and Mann resigned into obscurity, taking with them one hundred shares each as mementoes of twenty years of labour unexcelled in the annals of railroading. David Blythe Hanna, third vice-president and CNOR's general manager, was left in charge.

Against all odds Canada had built three transcontinental railways, but in little more than a decade the scene had changed from manageable cost and moderate expansion to over-extension and confusion. The cost of fuel, equipment and labour had shot up while freight rates remained too low to cover them. Trackage had been doubled, to a total of 38,000 miles, though with insufficient planning and financing.

The time had come to seek order in the chaos. With the money already spent, the tracks in place, and no going back, nationalization was invoked to protect Canada's credit and more than half of its railways. For this reason Canadian National Railways has been seen as a child of necessity, but it was also a child of Borden's conviction that the country could benefit from a mix of private and public railroading. Since Confederation, governments and railways had been so entangled, and so much tax money had been spent, that nationalization was logical if not inevitable.

Borden said there must be no patronage or interference, a warning that has echoed down the decades whenever the government has taken a hand in running what is, when all is said and done, government property. The insistence of Drayton and Acworth that CN be commercial failed to acknowledge that CN's importance to national growth must inevitably generate political pressure. And when legislation to incorporate the new national railway eventually appeared, instead of a self-perpetuating board of businessmen concerned solely with CN's health, regional representatives were to be appointed by the government. Unfortunately, neither Borden nor other architects of CN who came later were able to provide clear and unequivocal guidelines to govern the relations between politicians and the People's Railway.

2

PUBLIC
PROPERTY

I T WAS FATED," David Blythe Hanna wrote in his memoirs, "that we
should carry through one of the strangest phases in the history of transportation – to change two great systems of privately projected and privately controlled railway into public ownership properties." There had
long been state railways in Europe and Asia, and Britain and the United
States had briefly nationalized their railways during World War I, but the
hybrid system in Canada, half business and half public service, was unique.

As befitting a giant, the gestation of Canadian National Railways took
five years, beginning in September 1917 when a Canadian Northern board,
with Hanna as president, assumed command of Canadian Government Railways – the collective name for the National Transcontinental, ICR, the Prince
Edward Island Railway, and the Hudson Bay Railway, which was being built
to Churchill, Manitoba, so that wheat could be shipped to Britain by the
shortest route.

Whatever their individual merits CNOR and the government railways had
never been created to work as one and Hanna took on the thankless task of

fitting a head to an octopus, while believing in his heart that his Canadian Northern should never have been nationalized. "The conviction remains," he said long after he had retired (to become chairman of the Ontario Liquor Commission), "that if it could have been kept as a separate entity, it would have made a small profit during [the next] four years, with the small exception of the abysmal 1920, and its emergence into an entirely self-sustaining system would have been immediately in sight."

Hanna may well have been right. He knew his railway better than anyone, and the booming economy of the mid-1920s would have been in his favour. Perhaps the CNOR and the Grand Trunk could have been saved if the government had controlled costs during the war as well as it controlled rates, but the truth was the ailment was much older than the war and went back at least to 1903 when the Grand Trunk and Canadian Northern failed to join forces. Since then the growth of the railways (an additional 13,000 miles in a decade) had far outstripped growth in population (less than two million).

Once CNOR was nationalized, Hanna, whatever his private views, gave his all to making the thing work, stumping the country in support of public ownership. Typical of so many Scots who made good in Canada, Hanna was the son of a factory foreman, had worked as a teenage ticket agent in a railway station near Glasgow, and came to Canada at the age of twenty-four to the auditor's department of the Grand Trunk. He joined Canadian Northern at Winnipeg in its first year when CNOR boasted only two engines, fifty freight cars and two second-hand passenger cars, and a staff which totalled thirteen people. Though he worked all his life in an office he regarded himself as a "simple railwayman." "Service was our motto," he recalled. "We had more stopping places to the ten miles, I think, than any other railway in the world."

Given the record of government involvement in the ICR and the National Transcontinental, where money had been ill spent, Hanna's first letter from the government in late 1917 was reassuring, reflecting the spirit of Drayton and Acworth. "The board must operate the railways without any interference or influence from anyone connected with this department or outside it," wrote the minister of railways, J.D. "Jack" Reid. "The operation should be carried on the same as a private corporation keeping in view at all times economy and the interests of the shareholders, who of course are the Canadian people."

Borden and his successor, Arthur Meighen, did not falter from that principle and chose a competent board of directors consisting of A.J. Mitchell and E. R. Wood of Toronto, Dr. A. P. Barnhill of Saint John, New Brunswick, Maj. Graham A. Bell, the deputy minister of railways, Col. Thomas Cantley of New Glasgow, Nova Scotia, Robert Hobson of Hamilton, Ontario, Sir Hormisdas Laporte of Montreal, and R. T. Riley of Winnipeg.

"Not one of them was considered because he had any political influence," said Hanna. "Every one of them was chosen for his potential value to the board as a man of wide experience in business, in most cases as a large shipper of freight and in one case because he was one of the foremost financiers in the Dominion. Every man hated the idea of political influence being injected into railway business. We were a real board of directors and I think no more harmonious body of business men ever worked together – I don't mean in the sense that there were no differences of opinion; but in the sense there was unity of aim, and a single-minded desire to do the best that was in us for vast properties, in the success of which the national prosperity was very heavily at stake."

Since CNOR was the flagship, Hanna felt free to bring his fellow vice-presidents, Samuel J. Hungerford, R. C. Vaughan and Gerard Ruel, which did not endear him to the government railways or the member of Parliament who said, "We are still leaving this whole business in the hands of the Canadian Northern crowd, the same people who have been filching money from this country for years." Under two general managers, the new system was organized into an eastern region, from the head of Lake Superior to the Atlantic Ocean, and a western, directed out of Winnipeg, which ran to the Pacific. The eastern region was divided into three districts and the western into four, subdivided into divisions averaging 500 miles.

Though Canadian Northern brought twice as much mileage to the new system (9400 as opposed to 4775 by the government railways) there were inevitable jealousies between Canadian Northern, based in Toronto, and the Intercolonial in Moncton, which complained that Canadian Northern had kidnapped its best rolling stock to replace inferior equipment in central Canada. Boxcars might take a month to travel from one end of the country to the other, and occasionally disappeared completely. When Hanna and his directors paid their first visit to Moncton they received a cool reception.

The difficulties were immense in the years after the war. The Spanish influenza epidemic in the winter of 1917–18 killed tens of thousands and crippled railway operations. The McAdoo award in the spring of 1918, which was named for the wartime controller of the temporarily nationalized U.S. roads and granted the eight-hour day and wage increases to employees of U.S. railways, doubled Canadian railway wages over prewar levels, the unions being common to both countries.

Visible unification occurred on December 20, 1918, when the various railways, still known by their original names, were authorized by order-in-council to call themselves by the "collective or descriptive designation" Canadian National Railways. Canadian Northern passed out of the picture as a separate entity, though for the sign painters it was an easy transition, the "National" replacing the previously familiar "Northern" but the initials remaining CNR – the initials used up to the early 1960s when CN was adopted. The parliamentary act that gave CN statutory basis came six months later when the Canadian National Railway Company was incorporated on June 6, 1919, for the purpose of consolidating Canadian Northern and the Canadian Government Railways.

The Grand Trunk Pacific announced it was bankrupt and would have to shut down and the minister of railways took it over in receivership. By 1920 the government had brought the GTP into Canadian National and the long task began – it was still going on years later – of consolidating staffs, rearranging train schedules, negotiating joint use of terminals and closing duplicate workshops, stations and roundhouses.

While these measures reduced operating expenses, Hanna foresaw that welding the railways into one and replacing rolling stock and tracks worn down in wartime would need vast public funding "which in turn would mean the declaration of huge, and to the short-sighted, terrifying deficits." While neither CNoR nor the Grand Trunk system was in a position to incur the capital expense of rehabilitation, the government was prepared to do so as a makework project for war veterans.

Many of CN's 130,000 ubiquitous ruddy-brown freight cars and nearly two thousand locomotives were so old Hanna was authorized to purchase 8450 new cars, 163 locomotives and 200 passenger cars. "They knew we were not going to spend it on any tomfool things," Hanna said, "but were going to spend it on the road for the purpose of getting freight traffic." Though insisting the government would never interfere with management, he took the precaution of adding that all costs should be charged against revenues so there could be no mistaking that CN was a business and not a branch of government.

While not the first public business of its kind (harbours, canals and the ICR being much older), CN was the first on a national scale. As a proprietary crown corporation it could engage in competitive business and, unlike a department of government, was expected to conduct operations without parliamentary appropriations though government funding was available if needed. "In the event of a deficit occurring at any time during any fiscal year," said the Canadian National Railways Act of 1919, "the amount of such deficit shall from time to time be payable by the Minister of Finance out of any unappropriated moneys in the Consolidated Revenue Fund of Canada...." CN directors, "not less than five and not more than fifteen," were to be chosen by the government and all stock was vested in the minister of finance.

Once the Grand Trunk Pacific was swallowed, it was only a matter of time, as the royal commission had urged, before the parent company followed, though in 1920 the Grand Trunk was still operating on its own and the idea of its joining CN upset Shaughnessy so much that he came up with a surprising proposal. Fearing that a nationalized railway would reduce freight rates and lower CPR profits, he said the CPR could live with the Grand Trunk but uniting it with the government-owned railways posed a threat. Nationalization in some form being inevitable, Shaughnessy was prepared to have his own company nationalized so long as it was on his own terms and there were safeguards for investors, of whom 80 per cent lived outside Canada. "There would appear to be but one course for the government to adopt," said the CPR chairman, "and that is nationalization of most railroads in the country. The public mind in almost every country in the world where private ownership exists has been gradually centring on the nationalization of these essential arteries of commerce and nowhere else is there such opportunity or are there so many reasons for adopting this policy as in Canada today."

Despite the popular opposition to railway monopoly, Shaughnessy suggested that CPR's Canadian railway operations – though not its hotels and steamships, telegraph system and nearly 5000 miles of track in the U.S – be combined with the lines operated by the government but was careful to ensure that the private railway would lose nothing by nationalization. If earnings failed to pay costs plus CPR dividends, Ottawa would make up the deficit and pay CPR investors their due. "With the exception of the Canadian Pacific, the share capital of no Canadian railway company is worth a penny," said Shaughnessy. "By combining the earning power of the Canadian Pacific with the weaker lines, the annual deficit would be substantially reduced, to the advantage of the Canadian people, and in time the whole property might

be put on a profitable basis." Borden found Shaughnessy's proposal "imperti-
nent," but the voice of the farmers, the *Grain Grower's Guide,* which was all
for nationalization in whatever form, welcomed the proposal. "If the people
of Canada are to become proprietors of the two lean railways," it said, "there
is all the more reason why they should take over the fat one at the same time."

Many believed, with Shaughnessy, that the Grand Trunk Railway could
have survived once it no longer had to keep the GTP afloat. Its equipment was
evidently better than Canadian Northern's, independent assessors having
found its locomotives and coaches in above-average condition. Though it
carried a substantial debt, the Grand Trunk served the industrial heart of the
Dominion and its operations in the States had been profitable. President
H. G. Kelley, the Grand Trunk's former chief engineer, claimed the road was
in such good shape it could carry half again its current traffic without large
capital expenditure, but the government took the view that if it had to digest
the bankrupt western offspring it would swallow the parent as well.

On St. James Street in Montreal business leaders fought a final battle to
keep the Grand Trunk out of government clutches, but the Conservatives,
under Borden's successor Arthur Meighen, rammed through the Grand
Trunk Acquisition Act late in 1919. "We are at the penalty stage of railway
development in this country," Meighen said. "A price in some form has to be
paid by the people of Canada. We are now at the point where an awakening
bitterness follows a night of intoxication; an ebb of retribution now follows
in the wake of a flood-tide of railway construction." The Montreal tycoons
called Meighen a socialist, though his support for nationalization had been
less than ardent. The Toronto *Globe* asked what all the fuss was about. Canada had owned the ICR for half a century without suffering serious loss of
credit, said the paper, adding that government ownership was a "merciful
way of liquidating the failure of private ownership."

In May 1920, the government assumed financial responsibility for the
Grand Trunk Railway, though it was technically the property of the shareholders in England until an arbitration board could rule on its assets and
more than two years would pass before it became an integral part of CN. Its
direction was shifted from London to Montreal, where it was run for a year
by a board that included men from Canadian National. Then in the spring of
1921 the government appointed an interim board under Sir Joseph Flavelle,
who told Meighen that Canada's railway problems could not be solved by
merely reducing mileage, but only by increasing population "and consequent

THE PEOPLE'S RAILWAY

increased tonnage of commodities for movement by the railways, and increased passenger, express and other revenues." This mirage of a population that would support a healthy passenger service, as in, say, England, was to cause CN to throw good money after bad right up to 1968.

1920 was a terrible year for all North American railways. As prices dropped across the country and the Board of Railway Commissioners reduced freight rates, the gulf between earnings and expenses was the worst the railway had known. An arbitration board appointed to determine the value of GTR stock declared preferred and common shares worthless and no compensation would be paid, to the lasting dismay (and litigation) of 80,000 British investors. The judgment was based on evidence that a huge sum would be needed to bring the Grand Trunk up to standard, though former U.S. President William H. Taft, acting for the company, insisted Grand Trunk earning power had been grossly underestimated.

With the Grand Trunk an orphan, neither in nor out of the CN system, pro-CPR senators made an unsuccessful effort to shove it into the arms of the CPR. Nationalization, said one, encouraged the "destruction of private initiative, the frightening of capital and the undermining of our political and social organizations." Sir Vincent Meredith of the Bank of Montreal said, "Canada today has a very large National Railway system which is being operated at a heavy loss, thereby increasing the load on the already heavily tax-burdened country. Sooner or later some means must be found to relieve this situation.... My own view is that the proper solution will be found if the government, at the earliest feasible time, divests itself of ownership and operation of the roads and places them under corporate [i.e. CPR] control...."

Even Flavelle had doubts and declined Meighen's invitation to take over permanent leadership of the new railway. As head of Grand Trunk he had been collaborating with Hanna at CN "to clear any of the things which may enable this ragged, broken system to operate as much as possible as though it were one system," but he wondered if anyone could successfully run "the most difficult business enterprise ever undertaken in Canada" or cope with "the political influences in the various ridings, the strained position of governments having narrow majorities in the House; the ignorance of public men over the nice problems associated with a great business." Flavelle believed, with Meighen, that the job should go to a Canadian but nothing came of his suggestions, his most prominent candidate being W.N. Tilley, chief government counsel during the Grand Trunk arbitration.

While all this was going on, Hanna dedicated himself to running a rail-way whose operating deficit was $33 million, due to so much unprofitable track, compared with the CPR's profit of $33 million. His achievement in cut-ting costs by two thirds and cobbling together CN's various parts had been such that no one could justly suggest he was a poor manager, though one MP saw fit to say that while Hanna was a "just and honourable man" he was sus-pect through his association with Mackenzie and Mann, whose early suc-cesses and unusual methods had raised suspicions of irregularity. Hanna, defending them in his memoirs, conceded they could not have built and acquired ten thousand miles of railways by preaching altruism and despising the money market, but added, "They could not have done it if their sole pro-pulsion came from love of money for money's sake." Hanna also expounded a recipe for relations between Parliament and CN that was soon forgotten. While defending Parliament's right to control expenditures, he called for com-mon sense: "Parliament's attitude to a national railway must be based on one of two assumptions – that the management is worthy or is unworthy of confi-dence. The efficiency of its management, like that of any other public man-agement, is to be judged from the methods employed to carry on its business."

For every CN problem there were self-appointed experts prepared to point to the CPR as the ideal railway. Shaughnessy's place as president had been taken in the autumn of 1918 by the forty-one-year-old Edward Went-worth Beatty, the aggressive little CPR general counsel and a dyed-in-the-wool capitalist, and though Hanna avoided conflict with Beatty, whom he admired, CN was the target of Beatty's displeasure. "The National Railway's slogan is, I understand, patronize the People's Railway and save taxes," said Beatty. "Imagine a man being compelled to travel on any railway system, simply to relieve his neighbours, who might not travel, of a fair share of their country's obligation! In this era of state socialism and prohibition there should be some personal freedom left to the individual." "Personally," Beatty said, "I have no fear of the competition adversely affecting this company or its interests, and the reason why I have a right to that confidence is to be found in the organization itself and the character of the officers and men who comprise it – officers and men who, I think, can be relied upon to play the game of transportation competition as it was meant to be played – adroitly, persistently, aggressively, and fairly."

Nor did Beatty have cause to be pleased when in 1919 the Canadian Gov-ernment Merchant Marine (CGMM) was entrusted to CN, confronting the

CPR with government-funded competition at sea as well as on land. "The government was perplexed as to what to do with the ships," explained R.C. Vaughan, the CN vice-president who supervised the vessels, "so they thought the easiest way out was to put the boats under the jurisdiction of Canadian National Railways." The Canadian Northern was experienced in deep-sea shipping, having achieved a fine record with the crack passenger liners *Royal George* and *Royal Edward,* which had won the Blue Riband for crossings to Canada and carried the trans-Atlantic mail.

Ranging in size from 2500 to 10,500 tons, the CGMM ships had been built in Canadian yards for wartime needs, though the first had been launched two weeks after the war ended. C.C. Ballantyne, minister of marine and fisheries, believed a national merchant fleet in peacetime would provide a "great advertising medium for Canada, and for our products generally" and under the management of R.B. Teakle, who had been hired from a shipping company, sixty-three ships were commissioned, manned and assigned routes to England, Europe, the West Indies, South America, Africa, Asia and Australia. In their first year they completed 144 voyages, bringing in money which, as Teakle said, "previously went into the pockets of outside carriers [and] now finds its way into the Treasury of Canada." Canada was now competing on the high seas with its own merchant navy, under the slogan "Carrying Canada's Flag to the Ports of the World."

At sea or ashore, the 1921 recession reduced traffic. "Though 1920 was bad enough, 1921 excelled it in horror," wrote Hanna. Though operating ratio, the ratio of operating costs to revenue, is a blunt instrument when comparing two different companies, it is useful in gauging changes in a company's health. Between 1918 and 1920 the CN ratio shot up from 95.6 per cent to 114.5, which meant that it now cost nearly $1.15 to make a dollar. The government had no hope of reducing the losses on the Grand Trunk Pacific and Transcontinental but did hope losses on the other portions of the road could be reduced.

F.B. Carvell, K.C., chairman of the Board of Railway Commissioners, who believed the CPR was the "finest system on the American continent," was, as usual, outspoken in complaining that it had cost $40 million more to run the CNR during the past year than it had brought in. Certainly the financial record since 1918 was daunting. Operating deficits averaged $12 million a year, four times that figure after interest on investment was paid, not to mention $28 million of unpaid interest on government loans to cover deficits and reconstruction. "It is a heartbreaking affliction," Hanna wrote, "to have to go on month after month with the results of a ceaseless endeavour written monotonously in red ink. To any Scotch soul, the continued outlay of more than a dollar to earn a dollar was to feel very much like predestined doom."

Had he been left alone, Hanna would have sensibly based his formula for recovery on increasing freight – the products of agriculture, forestry and mining. Passenger service, on the other hand, was labour-intensive, heavy with overhead, a money loser, and he would have left passengers to the CPR.

Having failed to find anyone else to head the railway, Meighen was reconsidering Hanna when the Conservatives were ousted in December 1921 by William Lyon Mackenzie King's Liberals. The incoming minister, W.C. Kennedy, wanted neither Hanna nor Kelley of the Grand Trunk, believing neither commanded public confidence, or at least the confidence of politicians.

Kelley had been so uncooperative, trying to derail nationalization, that Flavelle regretted not having got rid of him. Hanna had made enemies when he issued an edict that CN employees, and for that matter CN directors like Col. Cantley, must not run for political office on pain of dismissal. In Ottawa he informed Conservatives that prices CN paid for supplies, equipment and services were none of their business. "I took the position," he said, "that it would be against the public interest to disclose prices, which, I knew from experience, were apt to be taken by certain firms desiring the business … and a tender put in for a few cents per ton below the price obtained by absolutely strict competition." Now he annoyed the incoming Liberals as well. "Letters soon began to arrive from parliamentarians, the substance of which was 'Now that we are in power, of course, our friends will have consideration.' Hundreds of such letters went on file, some of them from men high in the nation's service. Surprise was great when it was found that the talk about [abolition of patronage] wasn't merely gas."

When Hanna had dismissed three employees who ignored his ban on running for public office, Mackenzie King, then leader of the opposition, had reacted as if democracy itself were at risk, though George P. Graham, a Brockville journalist who was soon to become Liberal minister of railways and canals, had been urging the same thing for years. Now heading the government in the spring of 1922, King took it upon himself to force cancellation of the CN president's edict banning employees from political office. Hanna's staff rallied around with a testimonial expressing "united loyalty, devotion and affection" to the down-to-earth Scot who had kept Canadian Northern running for Mackenzie and Mann and had started the long task of repairing the wreckage of the pre-war railway boom, but at the age of sixty-four his days on the railroad were ending.

Along with the rest of the board Hanna had submitted his resignation when the government changed, agreeing to stay on until a new board was chosen in the autumn, temporarily hiding whatever bitterness he felt at how he had been treated. "Heaven preserve me from expressing political opinions," he said in his memoirs.

That summer so many people refused the post of president (including A.H. Smith of the royal commission) that Starr Fairweather, a young assistant at the Department of Railways in Ottawa who would later head CN's research and development department, was reduced to thumbing through *Who's Who* to prepare a fresh list. The delay had turned into a political issue. King wanted a president unconnected with any of CN's predecessor railways though it seemed he would have to settle for a little-known officer from Canadian Northern, Samuel J. Hungerford, vice-president of operations, who at least had the advantage of political anonymity. "If we cannot get anyone worthwhile to take it," Kennedy told King in a revealing statement on August 17, "there is nothing left to do but to go ahead and form our board and place Hungerford in charge."

"But then," recalled Fairweather, "Sir Henry Thornton burst on the scene."

SIR HENRY THORNTON

ARLY IN JUNE 1922 Mackenzie King received a letter which was to change railroading in Canada for years to come. Having heard that the prime minister was seeking a president for the national railway, J.H. "Jimmy" Thomas, British Labour MP and general secretary of the National Union of Railwaymen, recommended his friend Sir Henry Thornton. Writing from London, he said Thornton had transformed the world's busiest commuter line, the Great Eastern Railway in England, from "one of the worst to one of the most efficiently conducted railways in the country."

Having never heard of Thornton, and treating the matter as highly confidential, the PM asked Thomas for further information to be delivered by hand to the high commissioner in London, Peter Larkin, who was so poorly briefed that a misunderstanding ensued. With his penchant for ambiguity, King did not identify Thornton by name; Larkin, a Toronto tea merchant new to his job, somehow got it into his head that King was referring to Sir Eric Geddes, who was overseeing the unification of England's independent railways. With his amateur attempts at headhunting rapidly getting out of control, King abandoned stealth and cabled testily, "Thornton, not Geddes, person referred to...."

Henry Worth Thornton was hardly a typical railroader. Born in 1871 at Logansport, Indiana, where his father was a lawyer, he attended a private school in New England and was graduated from the University of Pennsylvania with a degree in civil engineering. As one of the new breed of college-educated American railwaymen, he became a draftsman in Pittsburgh for the Pennsylvania Railroad, served in many departments to gain experience, and at thirty became the youngest division manager in an industry that valued age. At forty he was general superintendent of Penn's subsidiary, the Long Island Railroad, directing America's greatest crush of commuters through Manhattan's Penn Station.

In 1914 the chairman of the Great Eastern, Lord Claud Hamilton, invited Thornton to become general manager and announced to the press that an American had been chosen because no Englishman was capable of restoring the tarnished glory of a system that served 76 million people in its railway, hotels and steamships every year. Thornton's first task was to placate patriotic Englishmen who had taken Hamilton's remark as an insult to the nation that had invented railways.

Ignoring hierarchy and bureaucracy, Thornton endeared himself to union leaders by treating them as equals. At their first meeting Thornton won their gratitude simply by having chairs brought in so all could sit down, something previous managers apparently had not bothered to do. "Sir Henry is one who does not believe that success can be achieved only by the man at the top," said Thomas. "He believes, and gave us ample evidence of it, that the humblest worker has a share in the success of any enterprise, that success lies not only in individual effort, but in team work. Sir Henry met us workers on our own ground when others were too proud to notice us. He accepted us as men, and he dealt with us man to man."

A young draftsman, who provided Thornton with graphs instead of old-fashioned columns of figures, said he brought fresh air into the office. "The conservative methods that then pervaded the general manager's office suffered a considerable shock. I remember my first entry into the great man's room, to be greeted with a friendly 'Come right in! Sit right down!' uttered with a typical American drawl, but putting me completely at my ease."

Four months after Thornton's arrival World War I began, Britain nationalized railways for the duration and Thornton was drafted to speed troop movements in England and France. By war's end he was inspector general of transportation with the rank of major general, had become a British citizen and had been knighted.

Back at his desk at Great Eastern he demonstrated that successful processing of millions of commuters depended less on the frequency and speed of trains than on the speed of emptying coaches at station platforms. He taught his staff American-style public relations and to deal quickly with grievances. "In fact," said London's *Railway Gazette,* "we have heard him described as an ideal publicity agent … a student of labour problems, a good engineer, and a train operating officer; he can talk in the vernacular on any of these subjects."

When the Great Eastern was merged with other railways, Thornton sought a new job and Thomas wrote the letter that parachuted the Anglo-American railroader into Canadian history. Western Australia Railways was interested, warned Thomas, so Canada should move swiftly. On September 13, 1922, the Montreal *Gazette* reported that two more Americans had declined the CN job. King concluded that Thornton was his man. "My thoughts turn to Sir Henry Thornton, as one who has received English recognition, done good work during the war, and still has knowledge of U.S. conditions & methods & American point of view," King wrote in his diary September 18. He invited Thornton to Ottawa and the two met in the prime minister's apartment at the Roxborough – King careful, pudgy, introverted, Thornton tall, athletic and hearty. Having gone to an Ivy League college and worked as a labour consultant for John D. Rockefeller, King liked Americans and as former deputy minister of labour he was partial to Thornton's enlightened views on employee relations. The two formed a friendship that endured some questionable actions on King's part through the vicissitudes of a decade.

Thornton had two conditions: no political interference and a five-year contract at $75,000 a year. The first was easy to promise, if difficult to achieve, and King agreed, but he balked over salary, protesting that neither the governor general nor the president of CPR made more than $50,000. Thornton suggested $50,000, coupled with a $25,000 bonus if he succeeded in making CN pay its way. With deficits of tens of millions of dollars each year because of interest on debts, it was hardly likely that Thornton could earn a bonus, but the cautious prime minister turned that down as well, whereupon Thornton signed for three years at a straight $50,000, almost double his English salary.

"I shook hands and congratulated him and extended my best wishes," said King. "He said he hoped it would be for the best and believed it would." In his hurry to fill a politically embarrassing vacancy, King was content with Jimmy Thomas's assessment, his own first impressions and those of George Graham, acting minister of railways during Kennedy's illness. Apparently they did not question the suitability of a candidate whose expertise lay mainly in commuter traffic. "It was an exceedingly interesting situation," Thornton said, "so I took the job. I like a good fight. Here was certainly the place to have it."

That evening King took Thornton to dinner at the Country Club, introducing him as "the man who is going to head Canadian National Railways." In London, where Thornton had become the first executive to receive honorary membership in the National Union of Railwaymen, his appointment made such headlines as "England to Lose Superman."

Hanna, who had bequeathed his successor a better railway than the one he came to five years earlier, received a thank you note from the acting railways minister for his many years of service: "...your position has been very onerous," it said, "but I desire to assure you that you have come through that difficult period with enhanced reputation." Hanna had built "wisely and courageously," said the Ottawa *Journal.* It now cost less than a dollar to make a dollar – 98 cents to be precise – and the railway in 1922 had produced its first slim operating profit. His management style and his conviction that CN had no future in hotels or even in passenger service were far removed from the ideas of his free-spending successor. "The future success of the Canadian National Railways depends on one thing, and on one thing only," Hanna said. "That one thing is to keep it out of politics." He hoped his successors would be allowed to demonstrate "that public ownership may still be consistent with good management."

On October 4, 1922, Flavelle and his Grand Trunk board resigned and a Canadian National Railways board was chosen; six days later Thornton was appointed chairman and president – and heir to the debts, problems, assets and opportunities of a railway with a third again as much track as the CPR: 22,000 miles (1300 in the United States), nine hotels, real estate, oil deposits, a coal mine, 50,000 miles of telegraph wire and fleets of ocean steamships and coastal ferries. Within the next four months the Grand Trunk would officially join CN.

Unlike his predecessor, who had taken over in the bleak end of the war,

Thornton arrived when Hanna's efforts were bearing fruit; crops were boun-tiful, government finances were improving and the country was moving into the Roaring Twenties. "I can recall no appointment in years which has evoked such general and enthusiastic approval," said Mackenzie King. Bor-den and Meighen had promised freedom from political interference, and King could hardly do less even if it was difficult to define, being one thing to a railwayman and something else to a politician.

King himself came as close as anyone to describing how interference worked, when asked by a prospective minister. "I said he knew how that operated," King confided to his diary, "not directly but indirectly." It usually came in three types, not only from Ottawa but from individual MPs in the CN regions or lobby groups with the government's ear. Patronage usually took the form of jobs or contracts in exchange for political support; ICR old-timers recalled having to call on a senator in Dorchester, New Brunswick, when they sought work. Intervention while less obvious was more perni-cious, as when the railway was directed to do something it would rather not or should not do – such as purchase railway ties from a supplier other than one of its choice. In the third type, the railway was required by the govern-ment to assume an unwanted and usually money-losing task, such as salvag-ing a derelict regional railway.

Some system of accountability was obviously required for a public enter-prise and various schemes to insulate CN from politics were mooted and dis-carded: joint trusteeship by Commons and Senate; a mixture of directors chosen from provincial governments, boards of trade, manufacturers and farmers' organizations. John Dafoe, editor of the *Winnipeg Free Press* and a supporter of Liberal government and public ownership, declared there was little chance of "keeping politics wholly out of the administration of the Canadian National Railway system while the board is appointed directly by the government and liable to dismissal at its hands."

While in opposition, the Liberals had demanded that CN divulge its business on demand. Once in power, the party's position changed and the minister of railways said, "It is the intention of the government that the board in its exercise of its duties and functions shall be free from interference, political or otherwise." The Conservatives were sceptical and Meighen prophesied that a railway containing elements of both public and private enterprise was fated to suffer forever from politics. Borden, now on the side-lines, was more optimistic. "It is clear," he said, "that for some years it will involve direct burdens, although these will be compensated by the indirect benefits. In the end that system will become a great national asset, unless our anticipations as to progress and development are wholly falsified. Above all let it never be made the football of party politics.... Every man who seeks to bring the business administration of the peoples' system of railways into the sphere of party controversy is an enemy of public ownership, and, therefore, of the people."

With sceptics referring to public ownership as "an experiment," Thornton went to work on December 1, 1922, on the sixth floor of the Jackson Building, Bank Street, Ottawa, his proximity to Parliament Hill alarming those who feared government intervention. He met with Mackenzie King, beginning the series of private talks the two were to have over the next ten years, and on the morning of December 5 he entrained for Montreal. The occasion was a formal dinner of the Montreal Board of Trade in the Rose Room of the Windsor Hotel, where the 650 guests included Flavelle and president Beatty of the CPR, who had dominated the railway world for four years since taking over from Lord Shaughnessy. Sir Arthur Currie, a war hero and one of those canvassed for the CN job, was there along with senators, MPs, and the financiers and bankers of St. James Street who opposed public ownership.

The newcomer they met that snowy night, chosen for one of the most important jobs in Canada, was in his prime at fifty-one, confident, sociable, with the build of a football tackle. In a welcoming address, Flavelle recalled that CN and the Grand Trunk between them had met operating expenses that year, though failing to pay interest on debt. Beatty, who had been asked to introduce his rival, hoped the two railways could cooperate for the good of the public, and allowed that if Thornton were given a free hand CN could be managed as well as a private company. He raised a few wintry smiles when he said that as Canada's biggest taxpayer CPR had a vested interest in seeing CN succeed, crown corporations not then being required to pay income tax.

Most of Thornton's speech was as bland as the postprandial cigar smoke drifting through the Rose Room. Final amalgamation with the Grand Trunk would improve CN's outlook as would CN's immigration program to build the west and provide much-needed traffic. Unimpressed by the state-owned railways in Europe, nevertheless he was undaunted at the prospect of running a publicly-owned corporation and, still new to the job, believed the only difference between CPR and CN was that one was owned by thousands of shareholders while the other was owned by one, the government on behalf of the people.

Adopting the ICR motto, the People's Railway, he made a brave stab at warning politicians to keep their distance. "Let it be emphatically understood, now and for once and for all," Thornton said, "that there is to be no political interference, direct or indirect, in the administration and working of the Canadian National Railways. I cannot put it any more forcefully without transgressing the rules of polite speech.... The prime minister has solemnly assured me that there is to be no political interference, and it was with this distinct understanding that I accepted the post.... It is vital to the success of our railways, and any other procedure spells inevitable disaster." Someone must have warned him of the disruptive tendencies of Canadian regionalism, for he added, "Perhaps no less dangerous than political interference is what may be called pernicious sectional pride."

The *Gazette* reported that he won his audience "by his kindly smile." The Toronto *Globe* ran a cartoon showing him on Parliament Hill posting a sign: "National Railways of Canada – notice – Politics or Politicians not allowed on Railway Premises." Flavelle, who had turned down the CN presidency himself while opposing an "American appointment," had been expecting a bombast offensive to a Canadian audience and was pleasantly surprised. "He is very simple and unassuming, speaks little of himself and stresses the value of team play," he said, "nor does he attempt to create a favourable impression of what he may do in the future by finding fault with the present systems. He is an excellent mixer and has quite won the hearts of all who have met him. If he is as good in action as on dress parade the government has made a wise choice."

Reaction to Mackenzie King's promise to keep hands off was less optimistic. "Unfortunately," said *Canadian Railway and Marine World*, "the prime minister's record in this respect is very unsatisfactory," King having admitted that the government would not hesitate to "make known the attitudes, which in its opinion, should be taken by the board of directors." The Conservative Halifax *Herald* reported it had already detected cases of "intermeddling" by the Liberal government and that cabinet ministers had been "promising to make deals for contracts" between CN and industries, "thus usurping Sir Henry Thornton's control of management...."

Flavelle was concerned at the government effort to keep a hand on CN's shoulder by putting Maj. Graham A. Bell in charge of finances. "The appointment of the deputy minister of railways and canals as vice-president of the National Railways and his retention of both offices is in my judgment playing politics in a direct and fairly mischievous manner," Flavelle told

Dafoe. Bell's vice-presidency had been meant to be temporary and he stepped down; since no one knew more about CN's tortuous finances, Thornton was relieved when he stayed on as a director.

There were other able directors on the Canadian National Railways board appointed late in 1922: James Stewart of Winnipeg, former chairman of the Wheat Board, was expert at moving grain; Gerard Ruel, CN general counsel, brought his years of experience with Canadian Northern, though like others from the predecessor railways he would have preferred private enterprise; Tom Moore, president of the Trades and Labour Congress of Canada, brought union representation to the crown corporation for the first time.

The rest were known for service to the Liberal Party rather than for knowledge of railways. Frederick C. Dawson of Prince Rupert, B.C., was a wholesale grocer; Richard P. Gough was a Toronto financier; John H. Sinclair, New Glasgow, N.S., had been an MP for seventeen years; Ernest R. Décary of Montreal was a former city official and owner of a real estate business. Meighen complained that apart from Bell, Ruel and Stewart they were "party henchmen." "If railway terminals were voting booths and time tables voters lists, they would no doubt be eminently fitted as directors of the National System," he said.

Dafoe at the *Winnipeg Free Press* preferred the CPR's pragmatic method of choosing directors exclusively from men who brought new business or expertise rather than people with regional political interests. "I think the present system of appointing the board of directors quite hopeless," he said. "It is bound to keep the system in politics and the result will be upon the whole more detrimental to the political parties than to the railway."

Thornton agreed and wanted the CN board open to all political parties, not just the one in office. "As long as the directors are purely political appointees they will come and go as the government changes," he said. "Such a board excites no respect, nor is it capable of constructive work. So long as the opposition remains without representation on our board of directors, they will suspect, in spite of every effort to the contrary, that, in some mysterious way and secretly, if not openly, the railway is being used for political purposes." Instead of waiting for the far-flung members to meet once a month, he appointed a four-man executive committee that met once a week and received $40 per meeting in addition to their director's stipend of $2000 a year.

Whatever his views on the board, Thornton was pleased with the senior staff he inherited, railwaymen who had started as apprentice machinists like

Hungerford or W.D.Robb, who had been the first Canadian to work up to a vice-presidency of the Grand Trunk and was now vice-president of a catch-all department embracing insurance, lands, express, telegraphs, pensions and colonization; Montreal-born J.E.Dalrymple started as a clerk and became vice-president of traffic (freight and passenger service) at Grand Trunk; Robert Charles Vaughan, who had begun as a CPR messenger, was vice-president of the purchasing and stores department. In Walter S. Thompson, a Briton who had started his newspaper career on Fleet Street before going to work for the Grand Trunk in Montreal, Thornton had arguably the best public relations man in the country. To rationalize the operations of the railways that now made up CN, Thornton founded a bureau of economics under R.A.C.Henry from the Department of Railways and Canals. Henry and Starr Fairweather, who succeeded him, were university-trained engineers and economists.

Convinced that CN had been playing Cinderella for too long, Thornton had hardly got his size eleven shoes under his desk when he went off on a cross-country tour to practise lessons learned from a pioneer of modern public relations, Ivy Lee of the Pennsylvania Railroad. On the road, Thornton's style was more glad-handing politician than brass-bound Victorian railway official, and he sometimes seemed to be reaching for public support over the shoulders of his political masters as if doubtful they would keep their promises. "If Sir Henry Thornton should ever transfer his activities from the railway to the political field his success in the latter is assured," said the Montreal *Gazette*. "Indeed the aptitude he is showing in the art of pleasing the public is quite remarkable."

In Toronto on December 11 he told the Empire Club his aims were to gain the confidence of the people of Canada and arouse the enthusiasm of CN employees. In Halifax on December 13 he promised relief from such chronic Maritime complaints as high freight rates and trade discrimination. Four fifths of Canada's grain was still shipped out of U.S. ports. In Saint John, a CPR town, he promised a fairer share of western grain shipments, which had been flowing down the tracks from Montreal to Portland, Maine. In Quebec City on December 21, he apologized for neglected facilities and promised the grain shipments that had been a prime reason why Laurier built the National Transcontinental.

Soon after Christmas, Thornton was off on a twenty-two-day ride through the West in his business car, *Bonaventure*, having endeared himself to employees by rescinding the "Hanna Order" that had barred them from political office. At Winnipeg he announced plans to bring in immigrants to satisfy the demand for farm labour. To delegations in Edmonton, Drumheller and Calgary demanding branch lines, he confounded critics in the east who insisted there were already too many by agreeing that more were needed to get grain to market. With trucking in its infancy, no one imagined that branch lines would become obsolete within a generation.

"On and on we went, across the country, along the main and branch lines," he said. "There were speeches, speeches, speeches, questions and answers, and the incessant demand that Canada look to its own future and make it a rosy one through sheer force of will and faith." In Thornton's view, a successful CN would be patriotic as well as commercial. In Regina he promised to develop western resources and complete the Hudson Bay Railway. He told the CPR strongholds of Vancouver and Victoria they could count on CN to increase trade and carry grain to West Coast ports.

He questioned the Crow's Nest Pass Agreement of 1897 under which the CPR had received a federal subsidy to build from Lethbridge, Alberta, through the Crowsnest Pass to Nelson and the mining country of southern British Columbia. In exchange the government claimed the right to reduce freight rates on grain and flour shipped east or exported to Britain, and on farm implements, livestock and furniture coming west from central Canada, which made the Crow rate important not only to the West but to eastern merchants as well. Freight rates having been an issue since the CPR first appeared, the agreement reassured Prairie farmers, who saw it as protection of regional rights against greedy capitalists in Montreal and Toronto. Nor was it particularly onerous on the CPR, for the government allowed it to increase rates when wages and costs shot up during the war. But when the government made a move to eliminate "the Crow," western opinion forced it to compromise and merely suspend the rate. When Thornton arrived in the West, the Crow rate had been suspended for three years and there was controversy over whether and when it would be reinstated and if it would also cover CN.

"Because the CPR and the government twenty-five years ago engaged in a horse-trading proposition it does not follow that the results of that agreement should be adopted as determining the freight rates of today," said Thornton. While agreeing that rates should be low enough to enable farmers to market their produce in Canada and abroad, Thornton urged the government to change a system that gave the railway such a poor return.

At the end of his tour, Thornton returned across the Prairies on the tracks built by the Grand Trunk Pacific to Winnipeg and took the National Transcontinental through Cochrane in northern Ontario and Amos in Quebec, and down the frozen St. Maurice River through the logging and pulp and paper region to La Tuque and Shawinigan Falls. He was impressed by the quality of the line and, clad in a long sheep-skin coat, hat and boots, he had a cheerful word in English or French at every stop.

On January 30, 1923, Parliament approved amalgamation of the Grand Trunk Railway with Canadian National Railways, which contributed 4775 miles of Ontario, Quebec and U.S. track and so much debt someone compared CN with a toddler required to carry a fifty-pound pack. More than 220 companies, not all of them railways but shipping companies, hotel companies and a wide variety of others, had gone into making CN. With the 1919 incorporation act brought up to date, this final step in creating Canadian National Railways made Canada unique in having a publicly-owned railway competing with a privately-owned one, the two providing over 90 per cent of the rail service of the country. CN was now the second-largest railway in the world, after Russia's Trans-Siberian Railway.

"We have a task this year exceedingly difficult," Thornton told employees. "This is our test year, and it is my most anxious year." Having decided that CN's salvation lay in expansion rather than in penny-pinching, he said, "Our problem is building up our business on bigger lines to support the large mileage and the moment our gross reaches a certain point we can make money."

A site for CN's headquarters, which at the time was split between the Canadian Northern building in Toronto and Thornton's office in Ottawa, had to be decided. Winnipeg and Port Arthur-Fort William (Thunder Bay) each wanted the honour on grounds they were midway across the continent. Thornton favoured Montreal, headquarters of the Grand Trunk and the CPR, and Canada's commercial and financial capital and major summer port. In Ottawa, he would be too close to the politicians, and after eight years in Europe he preferred cosmopolitan Montreal to the subdued evenings of 1920s Toronto.

But when Thornton proposed Montreal, regional interests bumped heads. The board that had been chosen for geographical representation split predictably with two directors voting for Toronto, two for Ottawa and others favouring Montreal. This being a political plum (under the 1919 act), the decision rested with the government, and railways minister Graham chose Montreal "from a purely business standpoint." Before spring, hundreds of

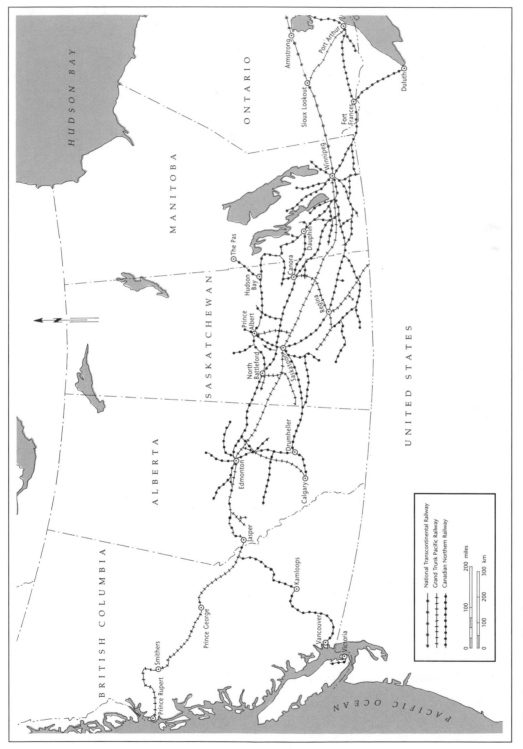

CN lines in western Canada, 1923.

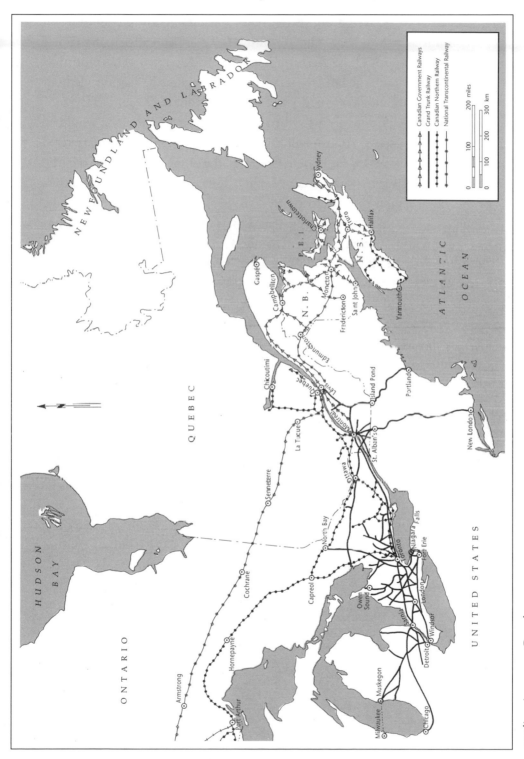

CN lines in eastern Canada, 1923.

employees were moved from Toronto to the Grand Trunk building on McGill Street in Montreal. The Toronto *Mail* complained that the choice was purely political. Once the prize had gone to Montreal, Thornton trod carefully in defining the boundaries of the three regions he had decided on: Atlantic, Central and Western, divided into forty-four divisions and 120 subdivisions. The Maritimes were soothed by assurances that Moncton would be regional headquarters, and though they wanted the western boundary fixed at Montreal, they settled for Rivière-du-Loup, the original railhead of the ICR.

Toronto was somewhat mollified when Thornton made it headquarters of a Central region that stretched from Rivière-du-Loup to the Lakehead, though Quebecers were unhappy that Protestant English Toronto should control the line through Roman Catholic Quebec. The largest region, the Western, with headquarters in Winnipeg, stretched 2000 miles from the Great Lakes to the Pacific, and the problem there was the demise of a three-year plan to build twenty-six branch lines, all but one in the West. It had been proposed by Hanna, passed by the Commons and rejected by the Senate, which objected to the expense, in what the *Canadian Annual Review* called "one of the sensations of 1923." It took another year before the branch lines – or nineteen of them – were approved one by one.

Writing in a script that seemed too small for such a big man, Thornton got into the habit of confiding his problems to Mackenzie King and the prime minister would reply with insights, disappointments, hints as to what the government expected of the CN or a request for favours for his Saskatchewan riding of Prince Albert, which was on the CN line. Thornton's reports ignored the valuable groundwork done by Hanna.

"The first three months have not been satisfactory," Thornton told King in April. "In contemplating results for 1923, it is only fair to sound a word of warning, in that we shall be working with an organization newly created, untried, and, in some ways, inexperienced. It is hardly likely that the new organization will be able to develop the full stride of its efficiency before the first of the year.... I have been obliged to create in four months a complete organization for the administration of 22,000 miles of railway and to provide, without much acquaintance with them, officers for highly responsible posts ... it is evident that the remaining months of the year will be fully occupied in bringing our organization to a maximum of efficiency. For these reasons, although I feel confident that our financial showing will be favourable, too much must not be expected."

Freight business improved that summer though passenger traffic was disappointing to a man who had run passenger railways in New York and London. Like many people in a new job, Sir Henry brought ideas and attitudes in his luggage, and Europe was on his mind when he addressed his first board meeting. The CPR was well known in Europe, he said, but CN hardly at all. This was a pity, as there was business to be had – tourists, immigrants, freight and parcel express. Having inherited the imposing Grand Trunk office on Cockspur Street off Trafalgar Square, he said, CN should have offices in Paris like the CPR. Though he told only Bell and Ruel, Thornton had a building in mind and a plan to buy it without making the matter public.

The building in the centre of Paris was a reasonable investment, and having accepted King's assurance of no political interference as carte blanche, Thornton started the negotiations that were to land him in his first serious trouble. It began with the hiring of Arnold Aronovici, a multilingual Romanian who had been Continental agent for the Great Eastern. As CN agent general in Paris, Aronovici was to develop European business and find a Paris office, and when he heard that the sixty-year-old building named for the librettist Eugène Scribe, and currently home to the Jockey Club, was available, he told Thornton that two other companies were preparing to bid and speed and secrecy were vital.

Thornton envisaged the building as a centre for Canadian activities in Paris, with CN occupying the main floor and government trade and immigration departments and a cinema to show tourist films in other parts of the building. He invited Aronovici to Montreal to discuss a plan that would bypass the federal finance department and Parliament and thus avoid publicity that would drive the price up. Having advanced Aronovici $200,000 for a down payment, CN would deposit the purchase price of $2.6 million in a Toronto bank as security for a transfer of like amount to Aronovici, who would acquire the Scribe in his own name and at an appropriate time turn ownership over to CN in exchange for a commission. At least that was the idea.

The press got hold of the story as the parliamentary Committee of Supply was sitting to consider CN's appropriation of $73 million for 1923, and Arthur Meighen pounced with all the relish of a Prairie lawyer confronting Parisian sin. "Where are we today?" he asked. "Mr. Aronovici has the title and has mortgaged the property to us. As everybody knows this course is merely a substitute for having it in the name of Canadian National Railways." Warming to his subject, Meighen tried to make Thornton's "subterfuge" to secure a CN office in Paris into an international scandal. "There was revealed last night," Meighen thundered, "the most extraordinary transaction, I think, ever disclosed to this Parliament." CN had no business pledging taxpayers' money without the authorization of Parliament, he said. "This thing is a scandal. This is outrageous, and when this became known to the minister, Sir Henry Thornton should have been called to book at once...."

No law had been broken, replied the minister of railways, adding that the head of a crown corporation had discretionary powers of which this was one. Unused to Canadian parliamentarians, Thornton grew fearful that his effort to give CN an office in Paris might topple the government. "I have been through the most anxious time in my life and I am not yet done with it," he wrote in mid-June. He apologized to the prime minister and promised to get a syndicate, which included another wartime acquaintance, George A. Gaston of New York, to take the Scribe off Aronovici's hands. Aronovici, however, refused to part with it.

"I have reason to suppose that Aronovici is not disposed to play the game with us," Thornton admitted to the prime minister. "It is with great regret that I say this, as my opinion of him, based on a long acquaintance, would have led me to think otherwise." However reluctantly, King came to Thornton's defence. "He took the action without any knowledge on the part of the government," King insisted. "But while he is president of the CN and we are representing the people of Canada in the House we propose to give Sir Henry in this and every other transaction precisely the same degree of latitude and freedom as the shareholders of the Canadian Pacific would give to Mr. Beatty."

By October Maj. Bell had taken over the messy affair and a financial agreement with Aronovici was worked out to relinquish title to CN in exchange for 150,000 francs ($7,500), which gave him a total of $33,041.46 for the year, a large salary at the time. It was discreetly announced that this was "in lieu of notice" and that Aronovici had been let go because of a departmental "reorganization." Years later, he came to haunt Thornton in Montreal with demands for more money, which Thornton apparently paid out of his own pocket.

In a private company Thornton's methods might have passed without comment but at CN the Scribe affair provided the Conservatives with ammunition to fire at the government. Though a sideshow in the business of running a railway, it did reveal that Thornton was not above cutting corners, a habit useful in wartime France when men and supplies had to be rushed to the front but unwise in a quasi-governmental body in peacetime.

The Scribe affair had hardly died down when the government's fiscal and railway policies came under attack from the *Montreal Star* in a series of articles bearing the melodramatic headline "The Whisper of Death." To rescue Canada from ruin, said the newspaper in boldface type, it was time to come out and say the thing that people were whispering behind their hands: "This unspeakable thing which threatens the life of the nation is the fact that, though the war has been over for nearly five yours, our national debt is still rising by the hundred million – that our railways, built to serve twenty million people are piling up deficits at the same ruinous rate – that the floods of immigrants who will stay in the country, use our railways and pay taxes, constitute the only conceivable cure for this desperate condition – and, yet, so little is being done to get and keep these immigrants that it is hard to credit we are not being sacrificed by a policy of deliberate neglect." Both the CPR and CN came under fire. One article commended Hanna for having cut CN expenses and lectured Thornton for being too free with taxpayers' money.

The articles were "deliberate propaganda of a political character," Thornton told King, but they did not worry him as much as his brushes with the minister of finance, W.S. Fielding, former premier of Nova Scotia, veteran of the Laurier cabinet, and King's unsuccessful rival for Liberal leadership. Fielding believed CN should have become a functional arm of the Department of Railways and Canals, like the ICR, and disliked Thornton's independence. When he heard of the Scribe he questioned whether Canada had the legal right to buy property in France and suggested the government stop the purchase even if it meant losing money.

Thornton's biggest clash with the stern old finance minister came that summer while CN was trying to raise money in London to buy rolling stock. Fielding, who understandably regarded Thornton as a greenhorn at finance, rejected his plan, and when Thornton advanced a second wherein he and the finance minister would jointly seek financing, Fielding unceremoniously refused him again and there were hot words. "As long as he is minister of finance, I am tied hand and foot," Thornton complained to King. "I told him I did not propose to be reduced to the position of a little boy and made an object of ridicule in the railroad and financial worlds." Only when Thornton threatened to resign did Fielding agree to cooperate.

A new pitfall was revealed when a CN director, R.P. Gough, asked Maj. Bell if CN would deposit $1 million in the Home Bank in Toronto. Since CN got traffic from regions the bank served, there seemed at first glance to be no objection to giving the bank some CN business. (Neither Bell nor Thornton seemed to remember that Gough was a vice-president of the bank.) Pending a final decision by the CN board, the money was deposited, only to be withdrawn hastily when the conflict of interest was discovered along with the fact that the bank was on the verge of bankruptcy. In the end Gough and seven other Home Bank officers were found guilty of negligence in the affairs of the bank and sentenced to terms in the Ontario Reformatory but the convictions were quashed on appeal. Another CN director, Frederick Dawson of Prince Rupert, was accused by Conservative MPs of bootlegging, a charge apparently arising simply from Dawson's position as a wholesale grocer empowered to distribute beer by the provincial government.

Throughout these troubles Thornton could count on King's support. "I have meant to let you know how splendidly Sir Henry Thornton has measured up to the high expectations we entertained of him," the prime minister told Jimmy Thomas. "What impressed me most in your commendation of Sir Henry was the emphasis you placed on his ability to gain the confidence of all parties to the industry, and to secure their loyal cooperation.... It is what, more than anything else, is required to make a success of the many factors which have to be coordinated in our national railway system."

But King developed doubts when his friend Alistair Fraser, a CN lawyer who later became lieutenant governor of Nova Scotia, came to lunch late in 1923 with rumours from Montreal. In an entry in his diary for Thursday, December 13, King wrote: "He tells the most amazing stories which he says are current in the office, of graft, etc. e.g. Thornton determining the price at which ties are to be bought, also coal from U.S. etc. at prices above competitive rates and against the wishes and advice of his purchasing agent [R.C. Vaughan] who has had to resist him; of getting company's [sic] formed to dispose of certain properties of Merchant Marine [the CGMM]; of his keeping a mistress and ward at Jasper Park; giving a ball for Conservative organizer at Winnipeg at cost of $600 to Company, having money for all purposes without vouchers, of great graft on Paris Bldg., of promising [to erect] buildings at Regina [hotel] and Victoria [elevator] etc. In short behaving like a drunken sailor. I am afraid there is ground for much that he says. That Thornton is getting himself into deep water."

Allegations of price-fixing in the purchase of railway ties were a serious matter. Millions of ties were bought each year by the vice-president of purchasing and stores but a few weeks after Thornton arrived he had issued orders that half the ties were to be bought, on a twenty-year contract, from a new supplier with plants in northern Quebec, Ontario and B.C. Vaughan protested, and when Mackenzie King summoned Thornton to Ottawa two days after Christmas, Thornton sought to reassure him. The purchase of three million ties had been divided as usual between companies competing for the contract, said Thornton. As for the other complaints, the prime minister had all the facts about the Scribe and the building would increase in value, the party in Winnipeg merely returned the hospitality of a local bigwig, and twenty-seven of the smaller CGMM ships were losing money and the board had considered selling them but offers were too low. As for rumours of a dalliance, he told King the woman referred to may have been an "inspecting hostess" hired to report on the CN hotels from the woman's viewpoint and had now left the company. Whatever was said, King let the matter drop; as he said in his diary, he hated confrontations.

At last the "test year" was over. Moving the biggest grain harvest in history had been a profitable exercise despite low rates and helped bring down the operating ratio to 92 per cent; the incorporation into CN of the Grand Trunk, with its profitable operations in southern Ontario and Quebec and the U.S., helped as well, and CN was able to pay a third of that year's interest on its debt. "The year went by," said Thornton, "to the accompaniment of the unscrambling of a jigsaw puzzle of railroad trackage and the beginning of something tangible in the form of a true transcontinental railway."

The *Canadian Annual Review* decided, however, that Thornton had failed to capture undivided support. "A very influential section of the press opposes government ownership in principle," it said, "and this is also true of a considerable element of public men. Nor can it be said that Thornton has the sympathetic assistance of the opposition although it was a Conservative government that had been responsible for the consolidation of the railways under national control and ownership."

There had been mistakes – a tendency to forget he was working for an enterprise answerable to Parliament. He sometimes said things better left unsaid, as when he boasted he would double net profits by the end of his second year. "Those offhand statements which Thornton has the faculty of making," Hanna told a friend, "will come home to roost some day with embarrassment for the railway and the government."

RIDING THE
WHITE
ELEPHANT

WHEREAS HANNA HAD SOUGHT to concentrate on freight and a tight budget, the expansive Thornton favoured an all-purpose system with passengers, hotels, ships and whatever else it took to rival the successful CPR. CN, he said, had to be merchandised like a department store.

Fortunate in joining CN at a time the Canadian economy was about to soar to new heights, Thornton brought qualities the young company needed, instilling an *esprit* oldtimers remembered long after his death. "Stand up for the company," he told them. "We have reached the stage in our career when we may maintain a considerable degree of self respect."

His first concern was rolling stock. "No one feeds oats to a crippled horse," he said. CN needed better engines, bigger freight cars, stronger rails and stouter bridges. Someone in the Public Relations department had figured that if you hooked CN's 3353 locomotives, 129,500 freight cars, and 3580 passenger cars together they would stretch a thousand miles, which was certainly impressive until you took a good look. At a time North American railroads were entering the last great age of steam, too much equipment was obsolescent or obsolete.

In the next few years CN bought almost twice as many locomotives as its rival, starting in 1923 with Mikado types, the workhorses of CN's predecessor companies. With their wheel arrangement (2-8-2, or eight driving wheels, two guide wheels in front and two in back for boiler and firebox) they had been a favourite in Japan, hence the name. Next the company modernized by purchasing 286 Mountain-type locomotives, fourteen-wheelers that reduced costs on long, heavy hauls; equipped with the latest automatic stokers, super-heaters that increased the efficiency of steam, and protection in the cabs from Canadian winters, they became standard equipment on both passenger and freight trains. Within a year they were joined by powerful Santa Fe (2-10-2) freight engines fifteen feet tall, ten feet wide, weighing 300 tons and, like many CN locomotives, built at Canadian Locomotive Company of Kingston.

"In the very first year," Thornton recalled, "ninety-seven engines went to the junk heap. In the next year a hundred more. The next year 144 gave up the ghost; then ninety-nine and ninety-seven and forty-nine. If one can visual-ize more than seven solid miles of useless, discarded locomotives, one may also visualize the motive power that it has been necessary literally to throw away."

Most of the 3500 new freight and passenger cars were manufactured in Canada, but when CN purchased special cars in the States to carry automo-biles it was criticized by the Canadian Manufacturers Association for not buying in Canada. Seizing this opportunity to assert CN's independence, Thornton said that the railway sought the equipment in the U.S. because it would be used over American lines. If made in Canada it would attract a 30 per cent duty on crossing the border. "The time has come," he said, "when it must be clearly laid down that a dissatisfied contractor cannot dictate how we run this railway system. A thousand cars have been ordered to be built in the U.S. and they are going to stay ordered."

In Canada CN was operating nearly 21,000 miles of track – 2803 miles in the Atlantic region, 7669 in the Central and 10,407 in the Western. Shaping CN's incompatible ancestors into a single network was so difficult that some-one likened it to stitching five spider webs together. Almost 4000 miles of mainline was reduced to secondary line and cutoffs were built to connect previously competing lines and reduce operating milage. As lines were joined, a town might find itself with one railway, two stations, and perhaps two repair shops and too many workers with nothing to do. Rails built by

Canadian Northern and Grand Trunk Pacific paralleled each other in the West for hundreds of miles and business sense demanded that one set be torn up. "It cannot be done," Thornton replied. "People trusted those railroads. They built their homes along them and founded their farms. They have invested their savings and their labours; the roads must stand."

People called CN a white elephant, that prestigious Siamese beast whose upkeep costs more than its worth. The human problems were immense. There were three employees for every staff job and loyalty to one or other of the old systems – the Grand Trunk, Canadian Northern and government-built railways – subverted loyalty to the new. With 108,000 employees, CN had become the biggest industrial employer in Canada, and counting relatives nearly half a million people, an eighth of the population of Canada, depended on CN pay packets.

Though Thornton cut 9000 jobs in his first three years, his concern for employees made him more popular than any president before or since. "Last night, after dinner," he wrote in 1924, "I visited the Montreal yards as I never get a chance to see the men who work at night. I took about three hours and visited all offices and engine houses. I found everything in good shape and the men on the alert. It was rather a shock to them as railway presidents have been rare visitors, but they obviously were delighted to see me." In his travels of fifty or sixty thousand miles each year he rarely missed an opportunity to shake hands here with a dining car chef, there with a veteran yardman. After passing through Rosebud, Alberta, and hearing that the young daughter of an employee had died in an accident, he had the train back up twenty miles to express his sympathy.

In labour relations he was ahead of his time. He abolished the unpopular system of piecework and in place of an inadequate pension scheme inherited from the Intercolonial, Canadian Northern and Grand Trunk (the first railway in North America to have one, in 1873) laid the foundations of a modern pension plan. He established a company-union cooperative, an idea borrowed from the Baltimore and Ohio Railroad, to improve the lot of non-operating staff who were less privileged than the people who actually ran the trains. Most of them belonged to the Brotherhood of Maintenance of Way Employees and the Federated Shopcrafts. Thornton explained that he had five objectives: Continuity of employment, better employer-employee relations, improved output at less cost, use of the ideas of employees and a better idea of each side's point of view.

Whereas management and unions had sat down to talk only after prob-lems had arisen, now joint shop committees met before trouble arose; they analyzed jobs and studied standardization and better use of raw materials, and even how to secure new business. "Every employee will in a sense become a partner in the enterprise," Thornton said when the Union-Management Cooperative Movement made its first appearance in Canada at the Moncton shops in 1925. When it spread to the maintenance of way, express and tele-graph departments and the Chateau Laurier Hotel, it cut grievances in half and increased productivity. (Grievances were heard by the Employees Board of Adjustment No. 2, an arbitration body established in 1925, and wage nego-tiations were conducted as before between management and unions.) Apart from maintenance and shopcraft unions, which included machinists, car-men, boilermakers, blacksmiths, etc. of the Railway Employees Department, Division No. 4 of the American Federation of Labor, CN unions consisted of the following: the Brotherhood of Locomotive Engineers, Brotherhood of Locomotive Firemen and Enginemen, Order of Railway Conductors, Broth-erhood of Railroad Trainmen, Order of Railroad Telegraphers, Order of Commercial Telegraphers, Brotherhood of Signalmen of America, Order of Sleeping Car Porters and Canadian Brotherhood of Railway Employees.

"Thornton brought in a means of good relationship," recalled R. W. "Dick" Worraker of Montreal, a general foreman. "For example when I started working at CN there were no paid holidays except things like Christ-mas. No week's vacation in those days. It was Sir Henry who started them, through the Union-Management Cooperative meetings."

Another Thornton innovation was the broadcast service launched on July 23, 1923, as a novel way of attracting passengers away from the CPR, which had nothing like it. As early as 1902 Sir Ernest Rutherford at McGill University had transmitted radio signals to a moving Grand Trunk train, the *International Limited,* between Toronto and Montreal, but no one had fol-lowed up until Thornton had music and information transmitted from a rented studio in Montreal and picked up on a CN lounge car speeding west with an influential group of American tourists.

CN is credited with the first network radio in North America. On December 30, 1923, the company created a rudimentary hookup using the transmitters of Northern Electric in Montreal and an amateur station in Ottawa, which were linked for a broadcast of live music. The *Ottawa Citizen* on February 5, 1924, said, "The Canadian National is making brilliant use of broadcasting to keep the nationally-owned system before the travelling public." In March 1924 CN broadcast the first network hockey game, Montreal Canadiens vs. Ottawa Senators, from Ottawa. The railway's growing number of stations were hooked together as occasion suggested and extended across the country to be received in trains and CN hotel rooms and by anyone who might pick up the signal. In Ottawa, Moncton and Vancouver the stations were owned by CN and the other nine were operated under a "phantom lease," wherein private stations were rented to broadcast programs with CN call letters.

Sixteen mainline passenger trains were equipped with radios, earphones and uniformed operators to twiddle dials and act as mediators among passengers demanding different programs, whether prize fights, symphony concerts, hockey games, opera, the Hart House String Quartet of Toronto or that comic favourite, Amos and Andy. "The radio-equipped observation cars had an aerial right around the roof," recalled Jack Carlyle of Toronto, one of the first employees of the radio service. "They installed thirty-two headphones at the seats and also the radio loud speaker operated by the attendant. They put in radios in the United States later but they didn't have an attendant so everybody used to operate it and it was not a success."

On its first anniversary station CNRO in Ottawa received six thousand telegrams and twenty thousand encouraging letters, a third of them from listeners in the United States. In 1925 the CN station in Moncton made the first Canadian broadcast to Britain and CN became the first railway to broadcast from a moving train, CN No.2, which was steaming through Redditt, Ontario, at the time. By 1927 CN Telegraphs had introduced the "carrier system," which allowed it to transmit programs at varying frequencies over the same wire at the same time.

A highlight of CN's venture into radio came on July 1 of that year when it celebrated Canada's Diamond Jubilee by arranging the first nation-wide broadcast carried over the airwaves and 23,000 miles of telegraph and telephone circuitry to millions of listeners. "Never before," said Mackenzie King, "was a national program enjoyed by citizens of any land over so vast an area." The Vancouver station began broadcasting to schools that year and the station in Quebec City broadcast in French.

"We used to try to get Canadian shows," said Carlyle, "and we also brought up the famous singer John McCormick from the States and gave him a pass and $500. I did the Dempsey-Tunney fight from the studio in

Montreal. I had a telegraph operator at ringside in New York and one in the studio and we broadcast the action two minutes behind the actual fight."

To communicate with employees across Canada, Thornton arranged for them to buy radios on an instalment plan. "By coming into the homes of our men of an evening," he said, "by talking to them in human fashion, by inspiring in them the thought that the railway is a joint enterprise in which they have a stake I believe that we shall be able to excite a degree of human contact and get in return an efficient and loyal service which could not be reached by any other instrument."

He used radio as a weapon against CN's opponents. "Certain interests are determined to prevent the ultimate success of the People's Railway," he said. "By constantly stirring up turmoil and bringing malicious charges they hope to discourage the administration, the officers and the employees." It was evident that little in Thornton's career had prepared him for Canada's regional politics or the rivalry of the CPR.

"The hostility of the CPR to the CNR had to be experienced to be believed," Starr Fairweather said in his memoirs, CPR's attitude having emerged unmistakably in mid-1923 when Beatty called CN and public ownership an "extremely hazardous adventure" in an address to London financiers, the very men CN might go to for capital. Beatty was convinced CN could succeed only at the CPR's expense.

Sir Joseph Flavelle demanded fair play:

> I am concerned [he told Meighen] at the persistence of the critical attitude of the Conservative Party towards the Thornton administration. I am even more concerned at the willingness to bring the administration of these railways into the field of party politics. This criticism and opposition commenced immediately following Thornton's appointment....
>
> I have been anxious, as I am sure others have been anxious, at the heavy expenditures by Thornton. It may be that he is a man of vision and capacity, who plans these heavy expenditures in the belief that the return will come in increased business which will warrant them. If he is right, and gives a demonstration of his wisdom and courage in the results secured, there will be general satisfaction and there will be no political credit to his premature critics. If he is wrong and makes a mess of it, or by reasonably common consent does not succeed, the opportunity for the opposition to score against the government will be present. An alert opposition can sufficiently indicate the danger signals without being committed to antagonistic relationship with an administration which the country prays may succeed.

In CN's defence, George Graham, the minister of railways, went so far as to say the railway was attacked not because it was poorly managed but because "it is altogether too efficiently managed to suit its enemies.... Every movement made by the Canadian National Railways which makes for the betterment of its financial position, brings forth an avalanche of protest from members of both parties." Interestingly, the same protests were heard half a century later when CN began to show a profit for the first time in decades.

One of CN's loudest detractors was Sir Henry Drayton of the 1917 royal commission. Now the railway critic on the opposition benches, he proposed a parliamentary committee to monitor CN estimates, capital commitments and the sale of property and assets. This threatened to erode CN independence, said Thornton, and would open the railway to the prying eyes of commercial competitors; the public railway would obviously be at a disadvantage in having to disclose business information while the privately-owned CPR did not. Nor did he wish to give such power to a committee "whose composition will change in harmony with political fortune, thereby surrounding the system with a purely political atmosphere which is generally admitted as fatal to successful administration."

The *Winnipeg Free Press* said, "If the Canadian National Railway is to become a mere department of the government, with all its officials ranking as civil servants, there can be no objection to the proposed procedure; but it has been the policy of the country, with the hearty approval of the great mass of people, to operate the railway on the basis of a corporation with a minimum of political interference."

Nevertheless, the Standing Committee on Railways and Shipping Owned and Controlled by the Government, to give its full name, was established June 4, 1924. In the course of testimony covering fifty pages, Drayton, a lawyer with an adversarial style, tried to squeeze more juice out of the Scribe affair but the committee found that Thornton had committed no serious wrong though his methods were questionable. It recommended the building be sold; CN instead negotiated a forty-year lease with a French hotel chain, Société des Hôtels Réunis, under which it would get a return of 5 per cent on its investment and free office space on the ground floor. "All our friends are chuckling," said Thornton, "and those who were our enemies are busy assuring us that they always felt sure I knew what I was about."

When the committee approved an appropriation of $54 million for the year, Thornton's opinion of the committee improved. "The committee is friendly and I think wishes to be helpful," Thornton told Dafoe. "I am hopeful that I can, perhaps, steer the thing in such a direction as to use this committee as a buffer between the railway administration and the politicians. I am getting along very well with them, but it will take at least two weeks, time which ought to be spent on railway problems and efforts to reduce our expenses."

Both CN and the CPR complained in July 1924 when the Crow rate was made statutory and extended to cover both railways. After a three-year hiatus it confirmed Canada's position as the country with the lowest freight rates, a reflection of the country's vast distances and scanty population. Since grain accounted for half of western Canadian railway traffic, the artificially low Crow rate meant the railways were losing millions they might otherwise have earned. "Our present freight rates," Thornton protested, "have evolved as the country grew, and now they have grown inconsistently, unsatisfactorily...."

At Thornton's request the Board of Railway Commissioners began a general freight rate investigation in which economic issues were joined with social and political considerations, as they would be increasingly from now on. After these hearings, statutory grain rates were extended from the Prairies to Vancouver, and in what was to become the Maritime Freight Rates Act, steps were taken to make good, in effect, on Laurier's promise that grain should flow to the St. Lawrence and Maritime ports rather than to American ports.

Thornton's first effort in bringing in an outside aide having been a disaster with Aronovici, his second was somewhat more successful, though not everyone at head office was pleased when he hired Lee V. Hummel, a small, thin and opinionated railroader of the old school, to be his executive assistant. Hummel had been his chief clerk at the Long Island Railroad, and though he was not sure what CN was, confusing it with CPR, he contacted his former boss and got a key job. Starr Fairweather complained that Thornton's "chief cook and bottle washer" was hard to deal with, though Maynard Metcalf, who like Fairweather was destined to rise to a vice-presidency, had a milder assessment. "I regarded him as a man of action, with a good background in the business of railroading," said Metcalf, adding that Hummel "got in over his head" when he dabbled in the purchase of railway ties.

At the end of 1924 Canada entered the five boom years of the Roaring Twenties. Wheat prices were high, crops were good and mineral production was setting new records. American capital, fuelling investment at a rate even greater than in the U.S., pumped money into the mining, steel and newsprint industries. Sir Herbert Holt, president of the Royal Bank and a leading industrialist, said, "At no time in the past has the outlook been more favourable than at the present for the prolonged prosperity of Canada."

Travelling twelve miles from Ottawa one summer afternoon in 1925 to Mackenzie King's hideaway at Kingsmere, Thornton told the prime minister that railway earnings had improved and service increased. The two men, so different but tied together by the railway, sat talking companionably for three hours on King's veranda before going in to dinner. There was a lot to discuss, such as the latest effort to form one big Canadian railway.

Influenced by senators partial to the CPR, a committee of the Senate had decided the two railways should be merged, CPR dividends should be guaranteed by the government, and any surplus above that should be divided between the government and the railways. George Graham, who preferred cooperation to amalgamation, effectively laid the committee's recommendation to rest by invoking the gods of capitalism. "Nothing should be done to frighten capital invested in Canada," he said. "There appears to be a concerted effort being made to unload the Canadian Pacific on the people of Canada," wrote Sir Clifford Sifton, the former Liberal interior minister. "I do not think the Canadian Pacific has ever been as active in propaganda as it is now."

King hinted to Thornton that perhaps the time had come for a merger. The old lords of the line, Van Horne and Shaughnessy, were dead. Beatty, said King, was more lawyer than railroader, and when he went who was to take over? If King was hinting that Thornton take command after a merger, Thornton either missed the point or ignored it. He replied that he would welcome voluntary cooperation, joint use of facilities and pooling of earnings on certain routes – but nothing more.

King raised the question of Thornton's future and Thornton replied that the Chicago and Milwaukee Railroad had offered him a presidency at more money but he would prefer to stay at CN. He asked King for $75,000 and a five-year contract, and after some bargaining accepted $65,000 for three years, on being promised, as King delicately put it, "greater latitude in making up his statement of expenses." "Were he to leave the National Railway at this time it would be disastrous to the system," King wrote in his diary.

The upsurge in the economy improved the operating ratio but revenue fell far short of covering fixed costs represented by the interest on government loans and government-guaranteed bonds, which totalled more than a billion and a half dollars ($10 billion in today's money) and equalled a third of Canada's national debt. Some of the debt dated from the 1850s when the Grand Trunk was built, and by the time Thornton joined CN the government had spent $937 million on CN's predecessor companies, plus interest on amounts owing to investors. Nearly $430 million had been spent on building the original government railways, $299 million on Canadian Northern, $124 million on the Grand Trunk Pacific and $84 million on the Grand Trunk Railway. In addition the government had assumed responsibility for public bond issues totalling $800 million, plus interest.

"There is now almost unanimous agreement that CNR capitalization should be reduced," said the *Free Press*. "It is not fair for a national railway to be shackled by an utterly unreasonable load of debt simply because it is publicly owned." The Saskatoon *Daily Star* said, "The vast sum of losses incurred long ago with interest compounded should not be fastened on the national system."

For all his professional optimism, Thornton was heard to refer to the railway as a white elephant and to question the competence of his predecessors in permitting a debt so far beyond CN's earning capacity. "I have been going into it somewhat myself and discovered it is simply chaotic," he wrote. "We hardly know ourselves what some of our capital obligations involve. I think it will take a couple of years to work it out. Deficits in the past in some cases were concealed and in other cases pushed off on the government. You have no idea of the mess. I certainly had no idea of it. Fortunately my skirts are entirely clear. It is only since I took hold that affairs have been honestly administered. I think we have caught it just in time. There are going to be some anxious moments and hard fighting ahead of me and I shall need all my physical and mental resources. But I am going to pull this country out of the mire and finish the job."

In the privacy of his diary Mackenzie King agreed. "The whole railway business is one horrible mess – waste, waste so vast that no one can intelligently grasp the whole situation." Certainly the government was in an unusual position – both owner and creditor of CN – for it loaned money year after year at the prevailing rate of interest and persisted in treating the loans as an asset on government books though receiving no interest payments. Interest owed to the investing public could not be so easily ignored but since it averaged $40 million a year, CN could pay only part and had to depend on the government to pay the rest.

"Not one single error of financing or vision has ever been wiped out," said Thornton. "When the government took over the roads it took over their debts. The transfer was simply a turning over of assets and liabilities from private to public ownership. There had been no stepping down of stock and bond valuations to permit lower interest charges. Every handicap of bad financial judgment, overexpansion, building into non-paying territory, excessive cost of construction, and the hundred and one other burdens which throw a business into bankruptcy had remained."

Despite a responsibility to provide an adequate national transportation system, Parliament had no long-range plan, voting the money Thornton wanted without much question except in 1924 when the Commons Committee on Railways and Shipping questioned estimates in detail and drew attention to unnecessary competition. Mackenzie King persuaded Thornton to hire a qualified vice-president of finance, G.C.Grant of the Bank of Toronto, to tackle corporate reorganization and recapitalization, and Thornton also reached into his past for a special assistant, hiring George A. Gaston, whom he had met during the war when Gaston was selling American trucks to the British army. A midwestern American like Thornton, Gaston had trained as a lawyer but apparently never practised. He now ran his own financial consultancy and had figured briefly in the Scribe purchase.

Mackenzie King, who heard of Gaston's mysterious activities when a CN director told him the American had popped up in London seeking a bank loan, sent Thornton a testy query. Why had the prime minister not been informed? Thornton assured him that while it was true CN was seeking money, Gaston had been dispatched on a fact-finding tour, and King's source of information was trying to make trouble, but there was trouble anyway when the Conservatives heard that Gaston was making $62,000 dollars a year, the second largest salary in the company after Thornton's. Metcalf, who played golf with Gaston, doubted if he was worth it: "He may well have been an expert in corporate organization accounting, but for Thornton it would have been better if he had engaged an experienced and able Canadian, to come up with a plan for simplifying the corporate structure."

Confounded by the CN debt, Thornton turned to other ways of securing the future. "We must always remember that our railway in the last analysis has only one problem," he said. "In fact Canada has only one problem, and that is the problem of development. If we had twice as many people in Canada as we have, I do not think we would have anything like the problems that confront us."

Immigration had fuelled the turn-of-the-century boom and Thornton, who had seen the effects of immigration on the American midwest, was convinced it was the key to CN's future and Canada's growth. Whereas the railway needed 400 persons per mile to be economically viable, there were barely 300 on average and often fewer than 200. Believing a population of 25 million would double CN's earning capacity, he established a semi-autonomous Department of Colonization and Agriculture to serve regions not covered by the CPR. As European commissioner he hired Dr. W. J. Black, the former federal deputy minister of immigration.

The government had long relied on the railways to develop immigration and formalized this in the Railways Agreement of 1925, signed in Mackenzie King's office by Beatty and Thornton. It gave the two railways authority to select, transport and locate "immigrants mentally, morally and physically and industrially fit and of a type suitable for permanent settlement in the Dominion."

CN's "Col and Ag" department opened its head office in Winnipeg and district offices in Saskatoon and Edmonton and the U.S. midwest, and began working with the British Immigration and Colonization Association and the German Lutheran Immigration Board, and steamship companies such as Cunard. Overseas Col and Ag operated from CN offices in London, Glasgow and Liverpool, with branches in Oslo, Gothenburg, Copenhagen, Rotterdam, Warsaw, Prague and Zagreb. In Canada 400 field agents surveyed settlement possibilities, met immigrants and assisted in getting them located, calling for help when necessary from 2000 station agents across Canada – 700 in the Prairie provinces, where most of the immigrants settled. CN settled 4200 families under the Railways Agreement in the years 1926–1930 as well as thousands of farm workers, many of them in northern Saskatchewan where CN branch lines were opening the 8000-square-mile "park belt." Mackenzie King, who had been under pressure to get French Canadians from factories in New England back to the land, had reason to be grateful because CN helped 850 Quebecers settle around Lake Abitibi or in New Brunswick, and another 550 in western Canada.

Apart from people from the United Kingdom, CN colonization focused on Poles, Ukrainians and Germans. Often placed together by nationality in one region, the newcomers would attract friends and neighbours from the old country. Most went west in colonist cars, which also carried the annual harvest workers and provided minimal comfort for minimal cost. A car accommodated more than fifty people, who brought their own bedding for bunks that were thinly-upholstered seats by day, and their own food to cook on the stove that stood in each car. Those who had a bit of money might opt for the so-called tourist cars, which were more comfortable, with more padding on the seats and an attendant to make up the berths.

Eighty-five per cent of CN's passenger business from the United Kingdom and the Continent consisted of immigrants. Although it is difficult to ascertain the income the immigrants provided the railway once they were settled on their farms, CN's annual report for 1927 predicted there would be an extra $1 million in yearly revenue from grain transportation because of the ground broken that year. "Once families are settled along the 32,000 miles of the Canadian National system," said a CN report, "they need building supplies, farm machinery, fertilizers, seed, livestock, feeds, and a thousand and one other goods and services. It is the railway's concern to ensure that as much of this volume of agricultural traffic as possible travels via CNR."

Canada was growing and CN would grow with it. Trains were faster and usually on time. Prestige services such as the *Montrealer* and the *Washingtonian* linked Ottawa and Montreal with the American capital. "A railroad is never finished," said Thornton and sent vice-president Hungerford and C.E. "Ned" Brooks, the young chief of motive power and car equipment, to study diesel engines, which were little known in North America. Because of the abundance of cheap coal, railways in the States were only beginning to investigate diesels, the first experimental version being a switching engine tried out by the New York Central in 1924, but none had appeared in Canada. At the William Beardmore works in Glasgow, Brooks found a diesel with possibilities (originally developed to power the propellers of lighter-than-air dirigibles). Starting in 1925 fourteen self-propelled diesel-electric rail cars, which looked more like trams than locomotives, were built for CN, each hauling one or two coaches at moderate speed to compete on branch lines with buses. "One would say that steam locomotives are the ultimate as freight haulers," said Thornton. "Maybe they are. But we've already found something to take their place on branch lines in the oil-electric engine which generates its own electricity from self-contained diesel engines and operates at a great saving as compared with steam cost. The time may come when they will cross the continent without a necessity for additional water, fuel, or anything, in fact, except the taking on of crews at the different divisional points. This can be accomplished with a 50 per cent saving in the fuel bill."

CN's history-making self-propelled run across the continent came sooner then Thornton expected. In what was part publicity stunt and part test, on November 1, 1925, No. 15820 slid out of Montreal (as a CPR steam train had forty years earlier on the very first transcontinental journey) and had a phenomenal run to Vancouver of 2937 miles in 67 hours. A normal passenger run, with all its stops, took more than 87 hours, even thirty years later.

The secret of reducing expenses, Thornton maintained, was to move as much freight as possible, preferably high-tariff goods, over as few train-miles as possible. But one of CN's chronic problems was that 40 per cent of its steel ran through unpopulated areas that generated little business – only 5 per cent of the railway's total. There were signs the lonely miles of track in northern Quebec and Ontario were coming into their own, however. "It is at the stations on this road that prospectors gather to jump off for the new gold fields," said Thornton. "One of its feeders is the tremendous copper camp of Rouyn. The dog teams took off from it for the gold fields of Red Lake, Pickle Lake, Crow and Woman Lake. It is the steel backbone today of tremendous endeavour. French-Canadian pioneers, filtering west through northern Quebec, have conquered its bush for farms; thousands of settlers are there now where a decade or so ago there were only hundreds. Tremendous power and pulp mills dot its route."

The Rouyn-Noranda branch that CN built at this time was an example of how the People's Railway could be caught up in provincial as well as federal politics. When Toronto financiers showed a desire to spread their mining interests across the border into northwestern Quebec by extending the Ontario-owned Temiskaming & Northern Ontario (Ontario Northland) Railway, Premier Louis-Alexandre Taschereau was determined to keep exploitation of the area out of Toronto hands. He was successful in convincing Thornton, who had at first questioned whether the line would be profitable, to build a branch south from the old National Transcontinental route. The T&NO also built into Rouyn, but CN had ensured that Toronto's effort to become the financial capital of northern mining did not extend to northwestern Quebec.

On the Canadian Northern line in Quebec hydro-electric plants appeared; at Arvida the Aluminum Company was building a plant and a town; pulp and newsprint mills were springing up. To test economic potential and help new industries along its tracks, CN established an Industrial Department, which offered help to industries or entrepreneurs.

In 1926, CN earned enough for the first time to pay the year's interest of $41 million to public investors. "This is a remarkable achievement," commented the *Ottawa Journal.* "It would have taken a bold prophet indeed to predict that in such a short time the road would be taking care of all interest owing the public." In the U.S. the *Locomotive Engineers Journal* said the CN balance sheet "must make sorry reading for the paid propagandists who deluge us with misinformation [about] public ownership."

"The railway has turned the corner and is steaming ahead," Thornton declared, as he travelled the country preaching a united, prosperous Canada. If Canadian freight rates were like those in the U.S., he added, CN's earnings would be doubled. "If this railway is to progress in the future as it has in the past three years," he told the Canadian Club of Toronto, "it must not be expected to carry goods without a fair margin of profit." At the railway town of Cochrane, Ontario, he told the Board of Trade he hoped to wipe out CN's deficit within three years. In Edmonton he promised a new railway station. At Prince Rupert, which waited in vain to turn into a second Vancouver, the best he could offer was hope. In Vancouver he pointed out that CN had increased its shipments of wheat through that port by 75 per cent since he took over. One of his favourite themes was the role of the People's Railway. "Apart from any question of operating this railway for financial profit," said Thornton, "it must be our first endeavour to benefit the communities that we serve."

Being university-trained himself, one of Thornton's aims was to train university graduates for managerial posts. "Sir Henry's plan for training these recruits was to place them as student observers and assistants," said Fairweather. "I should like to report that they were welcomed by their fellow employees and supervisory officers but in point of fact the newcomers were detested. They were considered interlopers in an organization where advancement was to a large extent based on seniority. Long, limber knives were sharpened to carve them when opportunity arose. It came when Sir Henry resigned. The knives were unsheathed and the slaughter of the innocents began."

The railways insisted that the working language, even in Quebec, be English and had few French Canadians at headquarters. Thornton attempted to recruit francophones and three of his protégés were to go far, one being Lionel Côté, who got his start up the corporate ladder when he was transferred into the Bureau of Economics in Montreal after prejudice had deprived him of a position in the northern Ontario district where he had first been sent to work. Eventually he became vice-president of the law department. Another was Joseph Gibault, a graduate in civil engineering from the University of Montreal, who had a minor job in the engineering department when Thornton had him transferred to the bureau of economics for training under Fairweather. Gibault became a rarity for the times, a French-Canadian divisional superintendent, and later chief assistant to the vice-president of the Atlantic Region and later still assistant vice-president of research and development when, long after Thornton had left, his origin denied him the Atlantic vice-presidency. The third was Jean Lessard, who had won a scholarship to the Harvard School of Business Administration and was taken under Fairweather's wing before he was seconded to the Board of Railway Commissioners, where he came to the notice of Mackenzie King, who named him deputy minister of transport.

1926 was a year of change in Thornton's life. Having obtained a divorce from Virginia, whom he had married in his youth, and with whom he had two children, he was married that autumn to Martha Watriss of New York, a woman twenty-seven years his junior whom he had met in France during the war. After their honeymoon Sir Henry and Lady Thornton were entertained by Governor General and Lady Byng, but even this failed to impress polite society in an era when a CN president's private life was almost as vulnerable as a prime minister's. Metcalf suggests in his memoirs the divorce hurt Thornton's career, and some society matrons of the Square Mile in Montreal dropped him from their parties. Mackenzie King also disapproved but confined his thoughts to his diary because he was more concerned with using Thornton as a stalking horse to divert anti-government criticism in the Maritime provinces. Thornton was willing to take on the role.

Since CN was founded, Maritimers had complained about high freight rates and that two-thirds of Canada's grain was flowing to Britain via American ports like Portland, Maine, rather than Halifax and Saint John. The line built to bring it to the Maritimes, the National Transcontinental, now part of CN, was not serving its purpose. "Over in Portland they are advertising themselves as having the 'Winter Port of Canada' and with good reason," said the Halifax *Herald.*

Maritimers were also charging the CN with perpetuating ICR patronage. "The trail of the political serpent can be seen along the CNR," said the *Herald.* As the centre of CN's Maritime operations, with 3500 employees, Moncton bore the brunt of these charges. When the Liberal government of New Brunswick lost a by-election there, Premier P. J. Venoit complained that Conservative foremen at CN's shops were to blame for refusing to hire Liberals. King evidently found it convenient to let CN take the blame.

"We are held responsible for all the sins of omission and commission on the part of the National Railways yet are powerless in all matters affecting its administration," was King's disingenuous defence. "Your letter helped me to speak to Sir Henry Thornton with a measure of plainness which under the circumstances I should have hesitated to have employed. There is certainly no excuse for anyone in authority permitting the use of the railway for political ends by our opponents when as a government we are rigidly adhering to our policy of not permitting political interference in matters affecting the management and discipline of the Road."

Thornton advised employees not to wear their politics on their sleeves. "Vote as your conscience dictates," said the man who had earlier rescinded the Hanna ban on employees running for office, "but do not appear actively in politics; in other words mind your own business." Like Hanna, Thornton tended to play down government intrusion, whatever its nature, though at times he admitted he had to deal with it. "We tried to keep the railway out of politics," Thornton said of the 1925 general election, "and so far as I am aware no pressure was brought to bear to influence votes, though I was obliged to more than once put my foot down on certain things the government wanted me to do, but that is to be expected and is part of the job."

Thornton began to spend time in Moncton, where he opened an office to study Maritime freight rates. In 1927 the Maritime Freight Rate Act was passed, authorizing Ottawa to pay 20 per cent of all traffic which originated or terminated in the Maritime provinces. The government compensated the railways directly. Rates across the country had developed by now along three lines: one, as in the Crow rate, maintained them below cost with no continuing compensation; a second system set maximum and minimum rates to prevent unfair competition or overpricing; the third system set rates at below-cost levels with government compensation for any losses, as in the Maritimes.

In the spring of 1927 a reporter for the Vancouver *Province* caught up with Thornton in his business car, in which he spent so much of his time crossing the country. The president, looking tired, in his shirtsleeves and sitting in an old-fashioned wicker chair, was asked if CN would have performed better if it had been privately owned. Thornton said no. "The CN railways used to be a menace to the happiness and prosperity of the Canadian people," Thornton added. "They are now a national comfort. The great White Elephant about which a terrible legend grew up during many years has vanished. The railways have demonstrated they can pay their way and a little more and they have given justification for believing that before many years they will be earning a handsome profit."

"What does this mean to the average Canadian?"

"One thing it means," said Sir Henry, "is lighter income tax the last couple of years. It also means lighter business tax, a lighter burden on the shoulders of the individual tax payer, a gentler hand reaching into his pocket, because the railway now is not obliged to ask the government for huge sums of money each year."

Having spent most of his life in the United States and England, Thornton had no experience of the boom and bust cycles of his adopted land, and having had the good fortune to join CN on the surge of a rising economy, he had great faith in the future.

KNIGHTS OF
THE IRON
HORSE

WITH CANADA ENJOYING its most prosperous years since World War I, Sir Henry Thornton set out to beat the CPR at its own game. By the mid-1920s CN was carrying more freight, more express packages and even marginally more passengers than its rival down the street in "Windsor Castle." Though CN's revenue per mile remained lower than the CPR's, which as usual enjoyed greater traffic density because of the more populous regions it served, Thornton had managed to pare operating ratio to 86 per cent. The gap between the two railways was closing. "The CPR no longer bestrides Canada like a Colossus," said the *Canadian Forum*. "Another great railway system has been built up, largely on the strength of government contributions, to curb the giant's power."

Competition during the next six years was a duel between two very different men. Thornton, the midwest American trained as a civil engineer, was a practical railroader with a freewheeling style that frequently got him into trouble. Edward Beatty was a lawyer, Ontario-born of Scots-Irish parents, a reserved, handsome bachelor who worked for the Boy Scout movement and the YMCA and relaxed at his woodland camp north of Montreal playing poker with male cronies. Both were made knights of the realm, though Beatty's knighthood came only in 1935, fifteen years after Thornton's. Both had been college football stars but now their game was Monopoly played over the Canadian landscape.

When Beatty rebuilt the Banff Springs Hotel, Thornton responded by doubling the guest capacity at Jasper Park Lodge. While the CPR built the Lord Nelson Hotel in Halifax, CN built the Nova Scotian Hotel, which gave Halifax more hotel rooms than it needed. When Thornton tried to offset the public image the CPR had cleverly built over the years, Beatty urged his people to step up their efforts. "The National Railways have adopted a very extensive system of propaganda through newspaper publicity," Beatty said. "Their officials, through personal entertainment and in every other way, are daily keeping that system in the public eye. No officer of the CPR, no matter how high his rank, should miss an opportunity to let it be known that our position as a transportation unit in Canada is still first and not second – an idea which the National officials are combating with every means in their power." When Thornton added faster trains, Beatty said CN was trying to reduce the CPR "to a condition of inferiority ... to establish a primacy at all costs, to duplicate and surpass every facility furnished by the Canadian Pacific."

Much of the battle was fought on common ground and under the same general government constraints on their freedom to carry on business. Both railways owned hotels, express companies, telegraph services, steamship lines and vast tracts of land and were obliged to operate under the Board of Railway Commissioners. Under the Railway Act, they were permitted to raise non-statutory rates by an agreed percentage of revenue requirements but had to publish joint tariffs. Traffic on both railways was similar: of CN's revenue 75 per cent came from freight and 15 per cent from passengers. The CPR carried marginally more wheat, CN more forest and mineral products. They had met since 1923 under the umbrella of the Railway Association of Canada, which represented the lesser railways as well in agreeing on strategy for seeking freight rate increases, whereupon the association would present the case to the railway commissioners in Ottawa.

In some ways, however, they were as different as two railways can be. The CPR could pursue success without having to justify itself to Parliament, buy where it wished and finance expansion through common shares, whereas

CN financing was limited to interest-bearing government loans and government-backed debentures. If the CPR failed, shareholders could blame its directors; a failure at CN would be a failure by the government. As a crown corporation with a split personality, CN was expected to spin money with one hand and carry out government social and economic policies with the other. The People's Railway set the pace for public service, leaving the CPR to excel at business efficiency, or so people believed. Though the railway commissioners determined, fixed and enforced what they considered just and reasonable rates, the CPR had become the government's yardstick, as CN, being less profitable, would have invariably justified higher rates.

As Thornton learned, CN had to steer a course between those who wanted a public utility, exempt from profit and loss, and those who believed CN should operate on a purely commercial basis. "The government chose to use the Canadian National Railway as the instrument of acquisition," said Fairweather. "Sir Henry agreed, though he knew the CN deficit would be increased. The day had not yet arrived [indeed was forty years distant] when CN management would demand compensation for undertaking unprofitable operations at government direction." In 1925 the government had CN purchase the Atlantic, Quebec and Western and the Quebec and Oriental railways after lobbying by the Quebec caucus of the Liberal Party. Though Thornton thought the price too high, he accepted it as the "responsibility which a state-owned railway has to the community."

Sometimes rivalry between the railways became bitter, as in the election campaign of 1925. "After Beatty gave me his solemn word of honour that he and his side would not attempt to bring the railway question into politics," Thornton wrote to a friend, "he arranged for the PM to dine at his house in Montreal with Sir Herbert Holt and himself to try to make a bargain with Mackenzie King on the railway position. The PM acting on advice from [railway minister] Graham refused to commit himself and nothing transpired."

Disliking the public railway for what it stood for, Beatty complained that, as he had feared, the CPR as Canada's biggest taxpayer must subsidize its rival, since CN paid no federal income tax (it did pay municipal and sales taxes and in 1952 would become liable, like other crown corporations, for income tax). "It is a peculiar anomaly that the less profitable the operations of the National System, the greater the taxes of the CPR, while if the National Railways prosper through diversion of traffic from the CPR, we lose in revenues more than we gain in taxes," he said.

CN wanted no special privileges. "We do not want business because we are The People's Railroad," Thornton said. "We do not want to be wrapped in cotton wool. We have to stand up and take our knocks the same way as any privately-owned company." He did, however, invoke patriotism in support of CN. "In private concerns," he told a Winnipeg audience, "gain was the end, but in a system like the Canadian National, while profit was an objective, there was a higher motive, a patriotic one. Our only motive is to make our railway the people's railway, to be of real service to the people of Canada."

Whatever the effect of competition on the railways, it pleased the travelling public, for the comfort of Canada's long-distance trains was equal to any in the world. Competition had brought faster trains, grand hotels, high cuisine and European standards of service. Dwellers in small towns, families on lonely farms, enjoyed intimations of worldliness when passenger trains swept through, their lights illuminating a countryside where electricity was rare, the dining cars revealing a luxurious world where men and women dined from shining silver on snowy linen and were off to adventurous lives in Montreal, Toronto or Vancouver. Both railways spent large sums on attractive advertising, and CN's employee publication, *Canadian National Magazine*, founded in 1920, was edited to such high standards it drew readers from outside the railway. Whatever else they did, the rival railways' activities and infrastructure – the chateau-like hotels, beaux arts railway stations, pioneer radio stations, telegraph and shipping services – played a seminal role in Canada's development.

Though Canadian trains were more notable for comfort than speed, the CPR had the edge until Thornton announced in 1924 that CN had the faster passenger service between Montreal and Winnipeg. CN began to advertise such crack trains as the *International Limited,* which was introduced by the GTR in 1900 and as one of the best trains on the continent ran from Montreal to Chicago, via Toronto, in 23 hours. It normally consisted of a diner and parlour cars as far as Toronto, and a sleeper, buffet, lounge, solarium car and coaches to Chicago. At the Toronto stop only 15 minutes, no more, no less, were allowed for servicing. In 1927 CN introduced the *Continental Limited,* which ran between Montreal and Vancouver in 108 hours, 10 minutes. Other CN trains introduced that year were the *Confederation* between Toronto and Vancouver, the *Maple Leaf* between Montreal and Chicago and the *Acadian* between Montreal and Halifax, an all-sleeper train operated in the summer to relieve pressure on the *Ocean Limited* (first placed in service by the ICR in 1904).

Though accounting for only 15 per cent of CN's total business, passenger revenue was still satisfactory on medium-distance trains like the *Capital City* and *Queen City* between Toronto and Ottawa and on the Quebec and Montreal service. As highway traffic increased, CN did its best to secure passenger loyalty with such luxuries as mahogany interiors, armchairs of Spanish leather or dark green plush, and richly-appointed steel sleeping cars divided into twelve sections and fitted with "boudoir dressing rooms," which Walter Pratt, general manager of the Sleeping and Dining Car department, described as "hotels on wheels." Nothing seemed too much bother. When passengers complained of dusty roadbeds, CN fitted locomotives with water sprinklers or laid rock ballast, which added stability and drainage and ensured less dust. Grades and curves were reduced and roadbeds strengthened. When CN's new slogan, "Courtesy and Service," was introduced, Beatty referred disdainfully to "slogans, radio, dog-teams, much boasting, and mob appeals." "Beatty says I am a showman," responded Thornton. "I'll show him a three-ring circus."

CPR for years had been in the forefront, but now CN was spending twice as much as the CPR on design and production of locomotives in its shops at Point St. Charles, Montreal; Moncton; Transcona, Manitoba; and London, Ontario. In 1927 CN introduced the new "Mastodons of the rails," Northern-type (4-8-4) engines of the CN 6100 series, which became the workhorses until the coming of the diesel age in the 1950s. The Northerns could haul 150 loaded freight cars and travel 841 miles from Montreal to Halifax without change of engines, whereas other locomotives might be changed three times.

In 1928 CN introduced Canada's first road diesel, a year before they appeared in the States (on the New York Central). Bigger and more powerful than the self-propelled diesel-electric railcars introduced three years earlier, this locomotive was another of Ned Brooks' innovations and was followed the next year by a twin. They were coupled to produce 2660 hp, which made them the first real challengers to steam locomotives on the main line. Built by the Canadian Locomotive Company, Kingston, and probably the most powerful diesel locomotives in the world at the time, when hooked together as a unit they were ninety-four feet long. Called road diesels to distinguish them from the yard diesels used for shunting, they bore CN numbers 9000 and 9001 and were assigned to the *International Limited*, covering 333 miles between Montreal and Toronto in 7 hours and 40 minutes, with bursts of 80 miles an hour. Brooks also introduced a diesel switch engine for use in the yards, using a Beardmore engine as in the others. CN, it seemed, had a good start toward dieselization, with its 9000 and 9001 units, a 400 hp diesel switcher and a fleet of diesel-electric railcars.

With its modern locomotives and improved passenger equipment, CN possessed more up-to-date rolling stock than its rival. Both railways ran specialized services, CN converting three passenger coaches into travelling schoolrooms, two in the West and one in northern Ontario, which it operated for the provincial governments. Fitted with desks, blackboards and living quarters for the teacher, and flying the Union Jack, they visited areas where there were no schools and sat for five days on a siding before moving on. The service reached its peak in the 1940s when CN was running four school cars and the CPR two. "This unique type of school answers the inarticulate call of the wilderness child for help," said the Ontario Department of Education Report for 1940. "Without it, he had no hope for even the rudiments of education." Other coaches were fitted as classrooms to teach immigrant men how to farm their new land and their wives how to can food and prepare nutritious meals. Some cars were equipped as medical and dental clinics.

Despite competition for freight and passengers, the rivals found reasons from time to time to cooperate, as in their joint use of Toronto's monumental Union Station. A legacy of the Grand Trunk and twelve years in the building, it remained unfinished until the two railways completed the work and the Prince of Wales presided over the opening ceremony on Canada's birthday in 1927. Inspired by the École des Beaux Arts in Paris, as were the stations in Ottawa, Halifax and Winnipeg, its classic style and suggestion of imperial Rome made it an outstanding example of railway architecture.

But there was to be no such cooperation in Halifax, a CN stronghold where no CPR trains were seen, except for those of its subsidiary, Dominion Atlantic Railway, which had running rights on CN rails. Halifax needed a new hotel, and in 1927 a group of Conservative businessmen formed the Lord Nelson Hotel Company and invited both railways to join in building the hotel near the Public Gardens in the centre of the city. "As you are aware," Thornton told the minister of railways, Charles Dunning, "the hotel situation has a strong political aspect and one must always anticipate that politics are at the bottom of practically anything that takes place in the Maritimes." The CPR joined the project but efforts to involve CN were rejected by the

Liberal government, which instructed Sir Henry to build a more costly CN hotel, with an adjoining station in the European fashion.

CN built the Nova Scotian Hotel of sandstone and brick in Georgian style, with 160 rooms, a handsome addition to a dingy waterfront. But since only one hotel was needed, the Lord Nelson suffered financial difficulties, causing Beatty to urge Thornton to consolidate the Nova Scotian, the Lord Nelson and the Admiral Beatty in Saint John (which CN and CPR had jointly financed) into one chain. Fearing this would put the Nova Scotian Hotel at risk, CN declined.

The CPR got its own back by refusing to collaborate in Montreal, where CN had a problem dating back to 1917 when Canadian Northern, having tunnelled under Mount Royal to the heart of the city, was unable to finish the job. The only structure at the end of the tunnel was a two-storey building of reinforced concrete called the Tunnel Station on de La Gauchetière Street, used mostly by commuters. Otherwise CN had to make do with three scattered stations – the downtown Bonaventure built by the Grand Trunk, Canadian Northern's inconvenient little Moreau Street Station in eastern Montreal, and the Montreal and Southern Counties Railway station by Youville Square. Thornton wanted a new terminal to accommodate both railways, as in Toronto, but CPR wanted to convert its Windsor Station into a terminal for both railways for less money than CN would spend to build a new one.

In 1927 Thornton decided to go it alone and bring all CN passenger trains to one terminal at the downtown end of the tunnel, starting years of controversy for all concerned – the railways, the city and the federal government. Mayor Camilien Houde and the Montreal business community opposed CN's plans, but it was Thornton's opinion that Beatty was mainly to blame for the three-year delay in starting work on Central Station. "I am convinced," Thornton told King, "the opposition to our terminal plans originated with the Canadian Pacific Railway, has been fostered by them, and that it is their intention, if at all possible, to keep the Canadian National Railways in a condition of impotence in the city of Montreal – and everywhere else for that matter."

Less conspicuous but equally important were CN's efforts to improve traffic between the Turcot marshalling yard, built by the Grand Trunk in the west end, and the growing industrial area at the east of the island of Montreal. Though the two were only a dozen miles apart in a straight line, a three-mile gap in CN track, which could only be bridged by using the expensive harbour authority line when and if it was available, meant a ridiculous detour of 109 miles via L'Epiphanie on the north shore of the St. Lawrence to get from one end of Montreal to the other.

The Canadian Northern had also bequeathed a problem in Vancouver. In exchange for land, Canadian Northern had contracted to build a hotel, as the CPR had done decades earlier, but the company collapsed before the hotel was started, and when the city threatened to sue, CN was bound to honour the commitment. Thornton believed he could turn the situation to CN's advantage and steal a bit of the CPR's thunder in a city where CPR tracks lined the harbour side, CPR's station dominated the city core and CPR's Hotel Vancouver was the social centre. A 500-room hotel, which CN was committed to building anyway, would enhance the railway's image.

At the same time CN improved the hotels it had inherited: the Chateau Laurier, whose capacity was doubled to 948 rooms; the Fort Garry in Winnipeg; the Macdonald in Edmonton; the Prince Edward in Brandon, Manitoba; and six resorts: Jasper Park Lodge; the Highland Inn at Algonquin Park; Nipigon Lodge at Orient Bay and Minaki Lodge, both in Ontario; the Grand Beach Hotel on Lake Winnipeg; and Pictou Lodge, Nova Scotia, purchased when the Maritimes complained their tourist trade was ignored.

The expense was justified, said Thornton, because hotels were showwindows that attracted freight and express business as well as passengers. Freight revenue, the bread and butter of Canadian railways, was climbing at a reassuring rate. Expansion of the Prairie wheat bowl and the growth of industrialized logging in British Columbia and the pulp and paper and mining industries in Ontario and Quebec had made Canada a major exporting nation. To make sure CN had its share, Thornton strengthened European operations, appointing his executive assistant, C.J.Smith, to the new position of European vice-president, with headquarters in London at the Grand Trunk's handsome building on Cockspur Street, off Trafalgar Square, and branch offices in Leadenhall Street and New Broad Street in the City, London's financial district, and in Glasgow and Liverpool, the most important port for ships bound for Canada. It now opened branches in Manchester, Birmingham, Cardiff, Southampton, Belfast, Genoa, Antwerp and Paris. Its European staff totalled more than 100, including the traffic, or freight sales, passenger, express, industrial, publicity and bookkeeping departments. CGMM vessels ran between Montreal and Liverpool with grain and livestock eastbound and anthracite westbound from Cardiff, but having no trans-

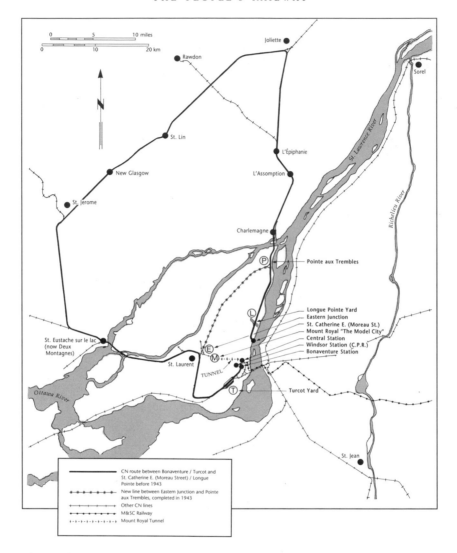

Closing the gap. CN lines in the Montreal area.

Atlantic passenger liners, CN joined with White Star and Cunard to book passengers wishing to travel by CN once they reached Canada.

Charles Thearle recalled that as clerk in Leadenhall Street in the 1920s his job was to make sure CN got the railway passenger and freight business when ships docked in Canada. "You kept in touch with shippers and forwarding agents to see CN got the routing inland. Ships sailed to Montreal and Quebec in summer, Saint John and Halifax in winter, and through the Panama Canal to Vancouver." Thornton promoted European traffic during a trip in 1925 in which he was feted by Prime Minister Stanley Baldwin, Winston Churchill, Ramsay MacDonald, leader of the Labour Party, and Jimmy Thomas. Thomas, whose son worked for Thornton, used his connection with the CN president and his own position as secretary of state for colonies to encourage emigration and to sell coal from his native Wales, to the dismay of the coal communities in Nova Scotia.

CN was also seeking business, if not immigrants, in Pacific Rim countries, where the CPR had enjoyed a monopoly since the 1890s. "We tried very hard to open the door to China and the rest of the Orient for Canadian produce and manufacturers," said August Brostedt, CN's first manager in the Far East, who had been sent from Vancouver in 1921 to sell the services of CN and the Canadian Government Merchant Marine, which was carrying British Columbia lumber to China, India and Australia, where CN had opened offices in Sydney and Melbourne.

CGMM now had sixty ships of seven types and sizes, built in Canadian yards and manned by mostly Canadian crews, sailing to the United Kingdom, Europe, the West Indies, South America and South Africa. The Canadian flag fleet did well in Australia but had a disappointing performance in the Orient apart from the period following the Japan earthquake in 1923, when great quantities of B.C. lumber were sent to rebuild Tokyo and Yokohama.

CN agents in Yokohama, Shanghai and Singapore were responsible for ensuring that, no matter who carried cargo across the Pacific, once it reached Canada it would finish its journey over CN rails. "Our prestige in the Far East is steadily increasing," Brostedt said. "It will be realized that the task of securing business against the very effective competition of the CPR with their splendid ships on the Pacific has been a difficult one. But I think substantial progress has been made." In hopes of capturing passenger trade from the CPR Empress ships, he opened an office in Hong Kong, "considered the centre of the Orient," in 1923.

Hungry for high-revenue traffic, CN captured a share of the CPR silk trade wherein raw silk was brought by fast ships to Vancouver, San Francisco or Seattle and hustled across the continent in special trains for which freights and even passenger trains had to sit in a siding until the "silkers" went by. There were several reasons for speed: the perishability of the silk, the danger of robbery, the uncertainty of a fickle market, and the high insurance premium based on hours in transit.

On July 1, 1925, CN's first silk special, eight sealed baggage cars lined with stout paper and protected by armed guards, left Vancouver on the 2749-mile trip to warehouses at Manufacturers Terminal in Hoboken, across the Hudson River from Manhattan. The shipment was worth $2 million, the equivalent of $18 million today. Most of the silk was brought to CN at Vancouver by the British Blue Funnel line or by Japanese ships. The bales, weighing 133 pounds, were unloaded and put in the train in remarkably short time; one shipment which filled eight box cars was loaded and on its way only two hours and twenty minutes after the ship docked.

During the next six years, CN ran 100 silk trains, the average silker run being about 91 hours, the fastest 83 hours, 56 minutes, or 3 days and 12 hours, which was almost a day faster than the ordinary passenger could expect to make the journey. CN's most lucrative run, in October 1927, consisted of twenty-one cars in two sections containing 7200 bales of silk worth $7 million. CN and the CPR between them carried 30 per cent of the silk bound for New York that year, American railways carrying the rest. Pound for pound, CN made more money from silk than from any other commodity until the trade was killed by the Panama Canal, the Great Depression and synthetics such as nylon. CN's last silk run was made in 1941. Thornton, though he did not like to travel at high speed himself, paradoxically found "silkers" fascinating. "Those mysterious things, silk trains, roaring across the country while everything else takes a siding, are good examples of what speed means to present day freightage," he said. "For here is the heart and soul of railroading – speed, speed, always more speed!"

Less exotic Asian imports were lily bulbs, Mandarin oranges, rubber, tin, jute, tea, rice, copra, spices and nuts, and exports included wheat, flour, pulp, timber, salmon, automobiles, electrical equipment, lead and zinc. "The whole country is beginning to realize the possibilities of trade with the Orient," said Mackenzie King when Japan became Canada's third best customer, after the United States and the United Kingdom. The *Port of Vancouver News* said, "Taken all in all, this is Canada's era in the Pacific.... Vancouver, rather than San Francisco, is now considered the leading Pacific port."

On the Atlantic, CN started a freight and passenger service as a consequence of the 1925 Canadian trade agreement with the British West Indies. CGMM ships had previously served the Caribbean but sailed only every three weeks, had sparse accommodation for passengers and little refrigeration for perishable fruit, and were costly to operate. Thornton, more interested in passengers than freight, called them obsolescent and built five speedy little liners for tropical service: the *Lady Drake, Lady Rodney, Lady Hawkins, Lady Somers* and the *Lady Nelson,* which was the first to take to the seas in December 1928, the year after CN had reorganized its Caribbean shipping arm into Canadian National (West Indies) Steamships Ltd. (CNS) under CGMM general manager R. B. Teakle. The "Lady boats" called at Halifax and Saint John, N.B., and at Montreal in summer, the *Lady Nelson, Lady Drake* and *Lady Hawkins* sailing to British Guiana, with eleven stops among the islands, and the *Lady Rodney* and *Lady Somers* to the Bahamas, Jamaica and British Honduras. Along with six CGMM freighters, they improved ties with the West Indies, though CN ran into trouble when it invested in a Jamaican government project to build the Caribbean's first luxury tourist hotel, the Constant Springs Golf and Country Club near Kingston; the hotel failed soon after it opened.

Thornton then embarked on an ambitious effort to compete with the CPR coastal service in the Pacific. For a generation the CPR had run its Princess ships between Vancouver, Victoria and Seattle, in competition in later years with the Grand Trunk Pacific's bi-weekly service with the *Prince Rupert* and *Prince George,* which also called at the lonely port of Prince Rupert. Having inherited those ships and wanting three more, Thornton was urged by Mackenzie King to build at luckless Prince Rupert but the shipyard was inadequate and orders went out in 1928 for the *Prince Henry, Prince David* and *Prince Robert* to be built in England to a standard more luxurious and powerful than the CPR coastal ships. A grain elevator was opened at Prince Rupert but the railway did not control grain shipments and few freighters called. (The port from which grain left Canada was determined by wheat pools according to prevailing ocean freight rates.)

Thornton's proudest year was 1928 when CN's first quarter earnings stood third among all the railways in North America. Only the Pennsylvania and the New York Central did better, and the CPR was down the list at seventh place. "This is not bad for a railway which five years ago was regarded in many quarters as a White Elephant," Thornton told the prime minister. Though passenger service had improved only marginally, despite all the money spent on it, lower overheads and a bumper grain crop had pushed revenues higher than running costs. Money available to pay off interest, an acid test of earning power, had quadrupled despite wage increases and freight rate reductions. The federal minister of trade and commerce, James Malcolm, told a Board of Trade luncheon in Toronto, "Sir Henry first sold Canadian National Railways to its employees. Now they have sold it to the businessmen of Canada."

In a time of plenty there was little objection to the expensive rivalry Thornton had embarked on. "In conversation I cannot but be impressed with his originality, real ability, broad vision & courage," King wrote in his diary on July 29, 1928. "He is certainly the right man for the present post." The only trouble spots appeared to be in the United States, where receipts were disappointing on the Berlin, New Hampshire, subdivision that connected Montreal to Portland, Maine, via Island Pond, Vermont. In the midwest, the ten railways the Grand Trunk had acquired in Michigan and neighbouring states, including its main line to Chicago, were also in difficulty, calling on the parent in Montreal to cover deficits. Since the lines provided traffic to and from Canada, American offers to buy them were rejected. Though operated as one unit by the Grand Trunk, the ten were separate legal entities and to improve performance were consolidated in 1928 as the Grand Trunk Western Railroad with 1000 miles of track through such manufacturing centres as Detroit, Pontiac, Flint and South Bend. Within a year of consolidation the Grand Trunk had made a small profit. Thornton, who had made such a success of commuter lines in New York and London, wanted to add a rapid transit system between Detroit and Pontiac with twenty-five passenger trains daily but was thwarted, as in so many other plans, by the Depression. (According to Fairweather, Thornton also had a secret scheme to create a new trunk line using Grand Trunk and CN track between Chicago and New York State to compete with the four U.S. railways already enjoying that lucrative route, but this too became a victim of the Depression.)

In Canada CN-CPR competition was taking the form of new branch lines in the West, a process started six years earlier when Mackenzie King made good on an election promise to end CPR's monopoly in British Columbia's Okanagan Valley. Thornton had barely arrived when the prime minister urged him to build an extension from Kamloops to Kelowna, which was opened in 1925 over ninety miles of new track and twenty-six miles of running rights over CPR tracks.

Before World War I the CPR had built 4212 miles of branch lines on the Prairies, though it had only one little branch of about twenty miles (in Saskatchewan) north of the Canadian Northern line from Winnipeg to Edmonton. Starting in 1928 the CPR began to push toward the northerly limit of grain production in Saskatchewan and eastern Alberta, which CN considered its own territory. Since the CPR insisted it was merely taking advantage of its historic land grants, Thornton took a conciliatory tone. The CPR might "assist in the development of the North Country" so long as this did not exclude CN from territory it had colonized or was planning to colonize. Beatty was not appeased. Insisting that CN had no special claim to any part of Canada, let alone the Prairies, he announced a branch line program of 1200 miles and began to build lines between the Peace River country in the west and the Hudson Bay Railway in Manitoba, where CN had run a ninety-mile branch line to the copper and zinc mines of Flin Flon.

Thornton let the CPR go unchallenged until he received a phone call from Charles A. Dunning, the Saskatchewan-based federal minister of railways. "He told me that as a matter of strategy and policy we would have to do something of a similar nature," said Thornton. "Accordingly I went back to the office, had a conference with Hungerford and [C.S] Gzowski [CN chief engineer] and we came out with a program which, as I recall it, involved about 600 miles of new line, which of course we would not have built had it not been for the threat of Canadian Pacific." In 1929 CN retaliated by expanding south into CPR territory with a branch line which ran eighty miles southwest from Unity, west of Saskatoon, and crossed the CPR line. "I then moved from Unity," recalled Maj. J.L. "Les" Charles, "to supervise construction of three branches farther south. I made my headquarters camp by a lake near Mawer, some eighty miles northwest of Regina. The nearest town was Morse on the CPR main line. Apart from the fact there were no trees, the country was pleasant with rolling hills which caused the grading of the railway to be fairly heavy. Supervising these projects during the one summer was a full time job involving driving thousands of miles over prairie tracks and dirt roads."

The rivalry spawned some 3000 miles of branch lines, some of questionable value even then in the days before trucking, of which CN contributed 1895 miles. "The result," said Starr Fairweather, "was a network of railways so extensive that in developed areas suitable for agriculture it would be hard to find a spot more than fifteen miles from a railway line. The cost of moving a ton one mile by a horse-drawn vehicle was at least one hundred times that of moving it by railway, which explains the multiplicity of branch lines." The possibility that trucks would one day make railway branch lines obsolete was not considered.

In Alberta, CN and the CPR reluctantly agreed in 1929 to join forces in operating the Northern Alberta Railway Company, one of eight provincial railways scattered across Canada. Based on Edmonton, it eventually covered 920 miles and ran northwestward to the Peace River country and Dawson Creek, B.C., and northeast to Fort McMurray on the Athabasca River, providing service to a northern frontier where there were no highways. Thornton had wanted the Northern Alberta line for CN alone but found himself in a bidding war. "So we said 'Let us stop this poker game and make a joint proposition,'" Thornton recalled. "It really resulted in the CPR buying the land and offering us half interest."

In the spring of 1929 Sir Henry Thornton was at the top of his career. He had tripled CN's net income and had increased rolling stock by purchasing 500 locomotives and 40 per cent more freight cars and nearly 20 per cent more passenger cars than the CPR had bought. CN and the CPR between them had increased Canadian railway mileage by almost one third in a decade.

In the battle with motor travel, which now accounted for half of all passenger transport, CN's new lounge cars were equipped with barber shops, soda fountains and two-way telephones, the parlour-buffet car *Minaki* on the *International Limited* being the first in the world so equipped. The best train of all, the *Confederation*, which ran to the West Coast, gave sleeping car passengers a choice of single and double bedrooms and lounge cars equipped with showers, gymnasium, and writing desks. The dining cars, which seated thirty-six people, were finished in walnut veneer with inlays of rare woods. The Grand Trunk repair shops at Point St. Charles, the largest in the country at thirty acres and employing 2500 men, were rebuilt and tracks across the country improved with automatic signals, grade separations and steel bridges.

"Sir Henry Thornton has done well since he took over the presidency of the Canadian National Lines," said the *Monetary Times* of Montreal. "This is admitted even by the opponents of public ownership. He has shown energy and resourcefulness and ability in meeting the competition of a privately-owned road which is famous the world over for efficiency, and has accomplished results on the National system which to some must have appeared impossible a few years ago." In a sign that the business barons of Montreal were accepting him, he was appointed to the board of the Royal Bank, though some thought it no place for the head of a quasi-government body.

In the autumn of 1929, even before the stock market crash, Thornton's luck began to turn. The cost of building branch lines had been twice the amount paid by the CPR, higher costs, it seemed, being the price of public enterprise. Losses in passenger service were increasing despite expensive enticements. Hopes of building western traffic through immigration were fading as the number of immigrants began to drop, along with prices for farm products and demand for farm labour. Railways historically show a lower return on investment than most industries, but CN's return was hopelessly low at 2.26 per cent, while the CPR's was closer to 7 per cent.

Seeking a capital structure comparable with the CPR's, Thornton was frustrated by Mackenzie King's unwillingness to write off ancient loans and advances. "Important bankers and reputable journals have described the present financial structure of Canadian National Railways as the prime joke of the financial world," Thornton protested. "I have studied it for seven years and I am not yet quite sure whether I understand the blessed thing or not." He wanted a simplified accounting system and the mass of heterogeneous securities replaced by uniform, readily marketable issues, and a financial structure that reflected the worth of the railway. With George Gaston and Maj. Bell, the deputy minister, he devised a plan to free CN of government aid, but King, concerned as always that eliminating CN debt would invite demands for wage increases and freight-rate reductions, insisted the time was not right to put the issue to Parliament.

Thornton had to agree, for by now financial planning had been "knocked sky-high" by a poor grain crop. Wheat pools were holding grain in hopes of higher prices but Thornton, displaying more social sensitivity than was common at the time, was reluctant to order layoffs. "I have felt that as a state-owned railway we were in a somewhat different position than a private company and owed a rather different sort of debt to the public. That is to say, we should not resort to such wholesale dismissals as would create distress, unemployment, and eventually shake the confidence of businessmen in the welfare of the country, and perhaps eventually provoke a really Dominion-wide business depression."

Troubles of a personal nature were also taking root. When Thornton's contract came up for renewal in 1929, the directors suggested he be given a bonus of $100,000. Thornton's contract stipulated that he would not be paid anything over and above his basic salary, so he refused the bonus but let it be known he would welcome financial help to buy the Frederick Beardmore mansion he was renting on Montreal's Pine Avenue, across from Beatty on the slopes of Mount Royal. He thought this reasonable since he entertained official guests of the railway and the government. "We agreed we could not ask Parliament for a bonus or a house," King wrote in his diary, "but if directors were determined to have a house for him, it was their responsibility not ours. We would advise against it, as not likely to be in accord with wish of public."

In addition to his five-year contract at $75,000 a year and a pension of $30,000 a year upon retirement, the directors voted that Thornton should have his house, which E. R. Décary, a director with real estate connections, was assigned to purchase. In a series of manœuvres to avoid government restrictions on capital expenditure reminiscent of the Scribe affair, CN rented the house from Décary, or rather his agent, and gave it rent-free to Thornton.

Trouble began to pile on trouble as business plummeted by 40 per cent, the biggest drop of any railway in North America. Noting that Thornton was overweight and tired, King said the railwayman had lost his zest. "Three quarters of life, he said, is made up of disappointments; best not to think of them but go on – a rather significant statement from him," King wrote in his diary. The penultimate act of what a biographer called "The Tragedy of Henry Thornton" had begun.

6

"A COLOSSUS
FALLEN"

L IKE MOST CANADIANS Sir Henry Thornton underestimated the virulence of the 1929 Depression. Recalling the cyclical setback of 1924, he believed prosperity would soon return, and Edward Beatty was equally sanguine, telling CPR shareholders that business would likely return to normal within a few months.

"This is not a time for panic," Thornton said in his New Year's message for 1930. "We propose to proceed with courage in those things which relate to the maintenance and improvement of our property." He saw no reason to halt expansion. A crown corporation, he said, should not encourage unemployment.

Ill himself in the spring of 1930, having suffered a mild heart attack at the age of fifty-eight while holidaying in Bermuda, Thornton was unable to give full attention to the ailing economy. Mackenzie King, who had gone to Bermuda on the same Canadian National Steamships liner, the *Lady Somers*, (prompting Conservatives to speculate the two were plotting King's election campaign) confided to his diary that Thornton's illness was due to overindulgence. "He looked like Falstaff and Henry VIII rolled into one," said King. He doubted Thornton could go on but within a month Thornton resumed his trips across the nation, promoting his adopted country, national unity and the People's Railway.

Regaining his zest for new enterprise, Thornton proposed an airline owned jointly by CN and the CPR and began negotiations with James A. Richardson of the Winnipeg grain family, who had consolidated several small companies into Canadian Airways Limited, which was flying 36,000 passengers and four million pounds of express freight a year. The government authorized CN to join the CPR in buying into Richardson's company, each putting up $250,000 of the capital stock and creating the foundation for what was to become in 1936 Trans-Canada Air Lines, and later Air Canada. Thornton and Beatty became vice-presidents of Canadian Airways.

In the West the Depression was particularly bad along the CPR tracks, where the southern Prairies were under drought for the second successive year. CN territory to the north fared somewhat better, but wheat prices everywhere were falling to the lowest level in memory. Two hundred thousand Canadians had lost their jobs, tripling unemployment, and on the eve of the 1930 general election Thornton told King he feared a tragic winter. King failed to take convincing measures and lost the election to R. B. Bennett's Conservatives.

For a Liberal appointee with no reason to expect Conservative favours, Thornton got along comfortably at first with the new cabinet, though there was understandable scepticism the *entente* would last, and one newspaper cartoon showed Bennett and Beatty as the Walrus and the Carpenter preparing a feast of oysters labelled "CNR." Bennett had been careful to distance himself from the CPR, for whom he had worked as a Calgary lawyer, and had coined the campaign slogan, "Competition Ever; Amalgamation Never!" "They say I wish to hand over Canadian National Railways to the Canadian Pacific Railway, to fatten my dividends in that great corporation," he said. "That is not true. When I assumed this task I divested myself of every dollar's worth of securities which I had in the CPR, whether stocks, debentures or bonds.... No man in the country rejoices more in the strength and progress of the Canadian National than I. I love my country and what it has done, and one of its greatest achievements has been the development of this important transportation system of which I believe every Canadian is proud."

Bennett politely asked Thornton's opinion on appointees to the new CN board and Thornton suggested candidates suitably Conservative, eager to establish the same relationship he had with the Liberals. Because the prime minister had no official residence, Thornton offered the seventeen-room vice-regal suite in the Chateau Laurier for a token thirteen dollars a day. The bachelor prime minister accepted and lived there with his sister, though as a millionaire he could easily have paid the normal cost.

Even the pugnacious new minister of railways and canals, Dr. R.J.Manion, a medical doctor from Fort William, seemed friendly at first, though King warned Thornton to be wary. As the Depression deepened, Thornton needed all the friends he could muster; as he admitted himself, if CN had been a private railway it would have been in receivership. Freight traffic had sunk to the lowest level in a decade and passenger travel was the lightest in twenty years. At his first meeting with directors early in 1931, Manion expressed the forlorn hope that within five years CN would no longer need government funding. "Neither I nor the government have any intention of interfering with the internal management of Canadian National Railways," promised Manion, "nor have we any thought but of the most scrupulous fair dealings towards that railway."

Manion even had praise for the CN president: "In the last six months I have learned a great deal about the secret of the *esprit de corps* which he has encouraged on the Canadian National Railways. He has been able to develop this *esprit de corps* and efficiency because he is not only likable but because he is also efficient. Whether or not we always agree with what he says, we have to respect and to like him. When we consider the beginnings which he had, the lines and the staffs, we must admit that he has brought about a magnificent accomplishment in the Dominion of Canada."

Thornton returned Manion's compliments. "I have served under a number of ministers of the crown, but none for whom I have a greater respect and a real affection than for the present incumbent of the office of minister of railways and canals. He is ardently desirous of the welfare of the Canadian National Railways and a really fine friend."

This exchange of compliments, ironic in light of what was to happen between the two men, was made at a gala dinner in January 1931 attended by 400 government officials, CN directors and officers, and union leaders who had come to Montreal for the annual session of Union-Management Cooperative Committees. Judging from the menu, the Depression was forgotten. While the Canadian National Railways orchestra played soft music in a hall decorated with flowers from CN hothouses, waiters served dishes from regions served by CN trains and steamships: Nelson River caviar from British Columbia, a soup made from West Indies turtles, lobster from the Maritimes, lamb from Manitoba, potatoes from New Brunswick, green peas and salad from Quebec, fruit from Jamaica, and coffee brought on CN ships.

H.B.Chase of the Brotherhood of Locomotive Engineers thanked Thornton for the "family gathering." "When you have fair dealings with the officers, it is only natural that loyalty and efficiency should follow," he said. Thornton called the gathering a milestone in labour–management relations and urged his listeners to go forth and disarm criticism. "To those who feel critical I would say 'Examine the position of the Canadian National eight years ago; look at its services; look at its spirit; look at its financial performance; then come to the year 1930 and see if in your judgment there has been measurable improvement in efficiency, in spirit, and in service.' I think there can be but one answer."

Hoping to attract French-Canadian workers, he told a meeting of the Cercle Universitaire in Montreal he did not want CN to be exclusively Anglo-Saxon. Speaking in French, he urged young francophone university graduates to apply, and the journal *Le Canada* said it was high time CN had a French-Canadian vice-president. Thornton's offer was well meaning, but with jobs at a premium the many French Canadians of all ages and classes who applied were sent away disappointed.

By 1931, commerce had sickened, wheat, lumber and pulp prices had tumbled, factories had closed and people were going bankrupt. Even the prosperous CPR found its income cut in half, but as always CN proved the more vulnerable. The CPR had consistently made enough money over the years to pay dividends to its shareholders but CN had been able only twice, in 1926 and 1928, to pay all the annual interest due public investors. Income available for interest payments had varied from 4 per cent in 1922, to 70 per cent in 1928 before sliding back down to 10 per cent in 1931. As for the loans advanced by the government, there was never enough earned surplus to pay any interest at all, let alone capital.

Branch lines were losing millions, one service which cost $1.25 per mile to operate producing a revenue of thirteen cents a mile. Both railways began to curtail passenger services. In May 1931 CN cancelled the *Confederation* between Toronto and Vancouver and the *Acadian* between Montreal and Halifax. Both railways cut wages by 10 per cent, and Bennett urged Thornton and Beatty to cooperate for joint economy. Cooperation had flourished in joint use of Toronto Union station, CN's use of CPR terminal facilities at Regina and Quebec City, and CPR use of CN facilities at half a dozen cities, including Ottawa, and a cost-cutting agreement for foreign traffic whereby Halifax for the first time became a regular Canadian Pacific Steamships port of call, but efforts to cooperate on running rights had been disappointing. CN had rights over only 127 miles of CPR's line and the CPR over 281 miles of CN's.

Among the few bright spots was the completion of the Hudson Bay Railway by 3000 men laying track. In September 1931 the first two ships sailed out of Churchill with Prairie grain for England, to be followed by nine vessels the next year, a tenth being sunk by an iceberg. In Montreal the long-delayed Central Station had become a make-work project that meant hundreds of jobs. "The $50,000,000 Canadian National terminal project is now well under way," said the *Gazette* on March 1, 1931. "It is a big program, this five-year task of giving to the railway system in Montreal terminal facilities which will be adequate for the needs of a growing metropolis." CN also built a hotel in Charlottetown, where the Board of Trade praised the railway for what it had done for Prince Edward Island. "I managed to survive the shock," Thornton said in a letter to Manion, "but I am sorry you were not here to participate in the festivities."

Thornton was trying in vain to establish rapport, for Manion was beginning to take a strong dislike to the big American for reasons that are not completely clear. Fairweather in his autobiography ascribed Manion's antipathy to slights, real or imagined, though Manion himself explained his mounting antipathy as fear the CN president was amassing so much power no one dared to criticize him. They had their first major difference when the new Conservative minister suggested that Liberal supporters, who had been getting 90 per cent of the lucrative railway tie contracts, were still getting the lion's share. He wanted the ratio reversed but Thornton assured him that patronage had been done away with and the Liberals had made no attempt to play politics with CN supplies. Manion insisted that Conservative supporters get two thirds of the contracts and, according to Mackenzie King, Manion got his way: "…the present government have forced the company to buy ties etc. etc. – always interfering – our regime was Heaven compared to this."

To do him justice, Manion also worried about keeping CN afloat. Long-term debt had doubled since Thornton took over and was a third of Canada's total national debt. "We are in much the same position with regard to the railway finances as we were ten years ago when the railways were requiring cash loans of more than a hundred millions annually and guarantees of fifty and sixty millions as well," said Manion. "In the interval there was improvement, but it was more superficial than real, and was immediately discounted and nullified by railway policies that mortgaged the future."

As usual when revenues fell, it proved impossible to cut costs in proportion. Work on the Montreal terminal had to be abandoned, bogged down in disagreements with City Hall, which had sided with the CPR's campaign to have Windsor Station remodelled. Thornton's effort to compete with CPR's British Columbia coastal service with the expensive *Prince Henry, Prince David* and *Prince Robert* had proved a disastrous investment and the service was discontinued at government insistence. The ships had arrived at the worst possible time, in the depths of the Depression, and turned out to be unsuitable for a tourist trade which was confined to three or four months of the year.

For Thornton the world had changed. During the boom years even CN's enemies conceded the railways were giving industry and agriculture the means of achieving progress and prosperity. Now all that was forgotten. In April a Quebec Conservative MP, John T. Hackett, a lawyer for the Delaware and Hudson Railroad, which had ties with the CPR, shot the first volley in a campaign against CN, public ownership and the CN president. "Men fought me," said Thornton, "because they believed it impossible to administer these roads without politics and that anyone who did call it possible was a fool. Sometimes they called me a three-ring circus showman and a four-flusher. They meant it and believed it."

Thornton's ordeal began in June 1931 at the first meeting of the Select Standing Committee since the election. He found the Conservative members hostile, particularly Dr. Peter McGibbon of Bracebridge, Ontario, who said he supported public ownership but felt it his mission to expose graft and save tax dollars, F. R. MacMillan, a lumber dealer from Saskatoon and a supporter of the CPR, and R. B. Hanson a Fredericton lawyer.

Under attack for decisions made when times were better and for failure to cut the wage bill as CPR was doing, Thornton explained his reluctance to fight the Depression on the backs of employees. "They have certain rights that have to be regarded by both the government, and by the railway company itself. You cannot turn a horde of people loose upon the street and merely transfer the burden of their maintenance from the railway company to the city or province or to the federal government."

They let Thornton have his say until he refused to divulge salaries. It had been customary to permit management to follow the practice of private corporations and withhold information not in the company's interest to reveal, but now this practice was discarded. His own salary was a matter of public record, Thornton said, being a contract with the government, but his officers should be protected; otherwise raiders would hire them away. Hanson reminded him that thirty-five CN officers were paid more than the prime minister of Canada.

"It was rather a shock to the members of the House," said Hanson.

"Well," Thornton smiled, "the prime minister of the country is notoriously underpaid. It is one of those unfortunate things. If I were running the show, I would promptly increase the salary of the prime minister." Rubbing salt in their wounds, he unwisely told them that conductors made more than members of Parliament, slyly suggesting the MPs form a union.

At the fourth session on June 16 the hearings got rough. As the law stood, though Parliament was entitled to an annual report from the board of directors as a matter of information, its role was simply to approve or reject any request for funding. Since CN was not a department of government, there was no legal basis for parliamentarians to investigate details of CN's operations, these being the responsibility of the company's auditors. Dr. McGibbon did not see things that way. "This is our property," he argued. "We represent the Canadian people. We have a right to know whether CN is managed economically or not." Insisting that strong medicine was needed to cure the patient, the blunt fifty-eight-year-old surgeon repeatedly dealt in rumours while insisting he did not necessarily believe them. Rumour had it that Sir Henry, whose salary had been set at $75,000, was making twice as much.

"I wish it were true," Thornton replied.

"Well, I am just telling you what the public at large are talking about," retorted McGibbon. He charged CN with "rank extravagance in the way of salaries all the way down from the top to the bottom ... they are talking about it every place, in other words, that the National Railways is a fertile field for graft, to use a common expression. I am not saying these things are true, but it is being said all over the country, and I do say that it is in the interests of the National Railways and it is the interest of the public to have this matter cleared up."

"Perhaps it is unfortunate that a debate of this particular form should go on," said W.D.Euler, a former Liberal minister of finance. "I for one regret that we should use a phrase such as 'fertile field for graft.' I have heard a few little more or less unimportant rumours, that possibly some of the executives are being paid higher salaries than should be paid. I have never at any time heard anybody say that the conduct of the National Railways is a fertile field for graft...."

McGibbon: "If only those questions are answered it will clear the air."

Euler: "That is not so. It can only do one thing, and that is to hurt the National Railways...."

McGibbon was forced into half-hearted withdrawal but, as always, the accusation, not the withdrawal, made the headlines. Reporters who usually suffered boredom during the railway hearings were running to the phones. The Select Standing Committee on Railways and Shipping had become front-page news.

Manion joined the attack, citing rumours that Thornton was getting $300,000 a year, four times his published salary, though as minister he would have known this to be untrue. He did not believe the rumours, he hastened to say, but wanted the salaries divulged. "If the Canadian National Railways were in a position that it did not require guarantees of vast amounts or cash assistance from the government of Canada, then I should say that the question of salaries would never get before a committee of this kind at all...."

"We all know," said Euler, "that rumours are going on throughout the country, most of them false; certainly the one about the $300,000 is so grotesquely false that it is hardly worth considering."

"Are you sure about that?" asked McGibbon.

"Yes, I am sure about that."

"What is his salary?"

"Seventy-five thousand dollars a year."

"Is that all?"

"As far as I know, yes."

"Well then, don't say if you don't know"

"Don't say if you don't know, either."

Tiring of this school-yard exchange, A.A. Heaps, Labour MP from Winnipeg, observed that Conservatives seemed to feel the future of the biggest corporation in Canada depended on the size of the salaries of its senior officials, a tiny percentage of the CN budget.

The Conservatives not only wanted details of salaries; they wanted to change the ground rules and make the salaries public. While insisting he did not care whether his own income was published, Thornton nevertheless did not say how much he really made, which proved to be a mistake. His total pay, as some committee members had guessed, was nearly $50,000 more than the $75,000 officially listed and included $10,000 a year as president of two American subsidiaries, Central Vermont and the Grand Trunk Western, $5000 from the Ontario Car Ferry Company, in which CN had an interest, and a rent-free house worth $18,000 a year, plus $15,000 in expenses for which he did not have to account.

Manion was now openly hostile, saying Thornton "had no realization of the value of money, whether his own or that of the government," and took him to task for "unnecessary capital expenditure" on the construction of the new Hotel Vancouver, which had cost thrice its original estimate. Thornton recalled that the project had been vetted by Manion's own party when briefly in power in 1926. The hotel was needed for the tourist trade, the third most lucrative industry after agriculture and forestry, he said, but since hotels lost money he, for one, would be glad if CN did not have to build them.

Day after day Thornton answered questions until the proceedings filled 500 pages. Though the committee had been summoned to vote on the money to make up CN's shortfall, which this year totalled $68 million, it was turning into an inquisition. "This is exceedingly distasteful to me after all the years I have put in this company," Thornton protested. "I think that some of you may be agreed that I have at least not been lacking in industry, but it is exceedingly distasteful to stand up here and be put in a position like this."

Thornton's achievements seemed to count for little. He was losing his credibility and his friends were dismayed by his failure to fight back, for had he done so he would have won considerable support. "The Canadian National is the people's property," said the Toronto *Globe*, "and has no place in politics." Dafoe at the *Free Press* wrote: "The attacks upon the Canadian National management are unreasonable and palpably partisan." Walter Thompson, CN's publicist, wanted to counterattack. "I don't know what happened to him," said Thompson. "All of a sudden he seemed to clam up." Thornton was tired, defensive and, as it would turn out, ill. To add insult to injury, the committee stripped him of the $30,000 pension the board had promised in 1929.

Like many whose early years have brought only success, Thornton was ill-equipped to handle adversity, though he was capable of surprising his tormentors, and on the last morning of the ten-day hearings he asked to say a "word or two." His thoughts were rambling but he finally came to the point

– he wanted a commission to formulate a badly needed transportation policy for the country – though he was so vague the committee at first failed to understand. Was the CPR to be included in the probe? asked Manion. Yes. Could he say what the commission should concentrate on? No. Nor was it clear that the proposal had really originated with Beatty, who, reviving Shaughnessy's call for amalgamation, convinced the beleaguered CN president that this was the only way out of the gloom. "I had for two years prior been very apprehensive as to the railroad situation," the CPR president said later. "Our traffic had fallen rapidly, our debts had increased, and the deficit of the National lines was great. So I conferred with the president of the National Railways and suggested to him that during the course of his examination by the committee he might advise such an investigation as I had in mind. He readily agreed and made such a recommendation."

Dafoe, Thornton's friend and confidante, was dismayed. "Thornton, who finds the present conditions intolerable, is flirting with the idea of an amalgamation of some kind, in the hope that the matter would be managed so that the Canadian National interests would be protected and the road permitted to function in conjunction with the Canadian Pacific under some kind of control that would eliminate the politicians.... There is no doubt in my mind that there is an understanding between Mr. Bennett and Mr. Beatty that the Canadian National System is to be tied up with the CPR under some kind of control which will really mean control by the CPR officials."

Fairweather, whom Thornton had asked to study the Beatty plan, said: "Beatty thought that a prestigious Royal Commission coming out with a unanimous report in favour of the plan would carry enough weight to release Bennett from his election promise [to oppose amalgamation]. As regards the other obstacles, Beatty was aware of Thornton's popularity with the Prairie farmers and organized labour. It would be Thornton's chore to convince these interests that a nationwide railway system under CPR control would hold no terrors for them. Thornton would be their protector. The prize to be obtained was so enormous that Beatty could be most generous with Thornton. He tempted him with an arrangement in which the two would alternate yearly in holding the position of president. In the off years, each in turn would hold the position of Chief of Financial Affairs. Sir Henry, debt-ridden and bedevilled by political attacks and personal vendetta, took the bait – hook, line and sinker. Having agreed, they proceeded to take steps. Bennett was approached and he approved."

Thompson feared his chief's position would seem a betrayal to the western farmers and the unions that trusted him, as did Dafoe of the *Free Press*. "This would be quite fatal to the Canadian National," said Dafoe, "as it would mean that the publicly-owned road would be systematically looted for the benefit of the private and in five years it would be a mere shell." He described Thornton's state of mind as confused when they met for two hours in the Fort Garry Hotel, Winnipeg, on October 12, 1931. "I was a great deal shocked by his distracted appearance, and the somewhat disjointed character of his utterances," said Dafoe. After a year of the Bennett government, Thornton no longer believed CN could keep free of politics. "I tried to suggest that it was surely too early to abandon the project of maintaining the Canadian National as a separate institution," said Dafoe, "but he had one reply to this and he made it over and over again with a sort of desperate and despairing earnestness. It was useless, he insisted, to try to keep the road as a public utility in the light of the revelation that had been made of both the power and the willingness of the government to interfere and destroy the enterprise by imposed policies."

The public heard of the plan – or plot, as some called it – when the *Wall Street Journal* published a leak attributed to "influential political circles" which claimed the savings from amalgamation would amount to 20 per cent. "The Canadian National has had an ostensibly independent management, while obtaining government guarantees for its financing," said the newspaper, "but its policies have been by no means free from political influences. Directors of the government road, although limited in their power over management, have generally been better known for their political than their business activities. It is generally believed that operating heads of neither Canadian Pacific nor Canadian National would consent to any unification plan, unless the board of directors was recruited exclusively from among Canada's industrial and business leaders, with no consideration given to political factors."

Several weeks later, in November 1931, Bennett established the Royal Commission on Railways and Transportation, headed by Sir Lyman Duff of the Supreme Court of Canada, whose politics in the past had been Liberal. Leonor Fresnel Loree, president of the Delaware and Hudson Railroad, and Lord Ashfield, who as Albert Henry Stanley had worked up from the ranks in American railways and returned to his native England as head of the London Underground, were friends from Thornton's past. A fourth commissioner was the aging Sir Joseph Flavelle, whose knowledge of CN's background was unquestioned, which was just as well since the seven-man commission was rounded out by regional representatives with little experience of railway affairs: Beaudry Leman of Montreal, general manager of the Banque Canadienne Nationale; Walter C. Murray, president of the University of Saskatchewan; and Dr. John Clarence Webster of New Brunswick.

As the committee to enquire into the whole problem of transportation in Canada travelled the rails holding hearings, Beatty insisted amalgamation was the only solution and that no amount of cooperation would solve the problem. In a variation on the Shaughnessy proposal, he favoured leasing CN to the CPR on a profit-sharing basis and keeping the two lines physically separate, a course that would have given CPR the greater share of the profits. He submitted a plan to close down certain stations and abandon 5000 miles of duplicate or little-used lines, including 3258 miles of CN tracks, mostly in northern Ontario, and 1743 miles of CPR tracks.

For the CN, Fairweather, now director of CN's Bureau of Economics, said Beatty could never achieve such savings without a "docile or practically helpless public and an equally docile or helpless staff of employees," and Hungerford argued that cooperation, if given a proper chance, could achieve most of the savings Beatty wanted without compromising the competitive principle. Thornton, who was having second thoughts about Beatty, failed to make any reference at all to the amalgamation he had led Dafoe to expect. Instead, he lamented the lack of a central authority to control competition. "There ought to be somebody to lay down the rules of the game if we are to continue as integral companies," he told the commission. He suggested a government "superboard," an umpire to prevent the railways from invading each other's territory.

Thornton deplored Beatty's lack of cooperation. "Excepting in one or two instances," he said, "the Canadian National never deliberately invaded the territory of the Canadian Pacific. Time and again I discussed cooperation with Mr. Beatty. Commencing in the spring of 1923, I suggested the pooling of our passenger earnings between various centres in Canada, for the purpose of reducing train service with no inconvenience to the public. I offered him trackage rights, under terms to be agreed. I suggested amalgamation of the two telegraph and two express companies, I suggested to him an arrangement to use the Canadian Pacific North Atlantic Steamship service as the ocean agency of the Canadian National, and this last is the only cooperative arrangement I ever succeeded in getting Beatty to accept."

As the hearings progressed it became clear that Thornton had repudiated

Beatty's amalgamation. "After the anxious time I had before the parliamentary committee," he explained, "I had what may be called a bellyfull of government ownership and I think I would have welcomed private ownership in any form. However, after mature consideration and after refusing to allow personal experiences to influence my judgment I stood out for the integrity and entity of the CNR. I was under a good deal of pressure to do otherwise and from Beatty in particular. I felt the chances were that I was signing my death warrant in holding to a fidelity owed to the people of Canada and the West in particular. But I was convinced it was the only course to follow with honour...." Fairweather took a more jaundiced view and believed that Thornton turned against amalgamation when he realized he could not possibly produce what Beatty wanted. Thornton was in no position to influence organized labour and western farmers to embrace a monopoly, even if he was part of it.

As 1931 came to an end, Gerard Ruel, who along with R. C. Vaughan had become the focus of an anti-Thornton faction, wrote a letter that illustrates the split in the executive suite. "At the present time you have a nearly desperate situation with regard to financing in the Canadian National," the vice-president for law said in a confidential note to Manion. Receipts had dropped nearly 40 per cent since the Depression began and a 13 per cent reduction in operating expenses had failed to keep pace with declining revenues. Drastic solutions were needed, said Ruel, "and the country may have to tolerate what might be called a monopoly, or at least absence of competition, for a period long enough for us to emerge from our present situation." Ruel had a new idea: a unified company called the Canadian Railways Company, headed by five directors appointed by the government and five by the CPR.

To those who wanted Thornton to fight, his 1931 appearance before the Railway Committee had been disastrous. Beatty had more or less accused him of being a government lackey, saying that the worst kind of influence "comes from the political attitude of men in publicly-owned institutions." Aware perhaps that he had sometimes anticipated government policy, Thornton let it pass, but there was no ambiguity about his position at the next annual meeting of the committee in Ottawa early in 1932. Amalgamation would be repugnant to the people of Canada and politically unworkable, he asserted, and political interference must be cut to a minimum so CN could behave as a private enterprise while developing cooperation with the CPR "in order that waste in whatever form it is found may be eliminated." Recalling that CN had been formed by politicians rather than businessmen, he said the board of directors should not be chosen for political and geo-graphical reasons, a practice that encouraged the factionalism that was evident in construction of branch lines, purchase of ties and coal, and disputes over freight rates. He advocated a mix of two Conservatives, two Liberals, two Progressives, a representative of the unions and a representative of the minister of railways and canals.

Thornton said Canadians had a choice: low freight rates, a money-losing public railway and increased taxes, or higher freight rates, remunerative operation and lower taxes. They could not have both. Fairweather, pulling out his charts, told the committee that the CPR, not CN, had been the chief offender in branch lines, having siphoned traffic from twice as much CN territory as CN had from the CPR. "I endeavoured to show that Sir Henry had done a magnificent job in creating a unified system from its warring component parts," Fairweather wrote in his memoirs, "notably as regards physical facilities but also as regards the human element. I told them of the massive job of improving the standard of the sloppily built Canadian Northern System and of the cost of repairing the damage done to the Grand Trunk when the company let the property run down to avoid bankruptcy. They pressed me about extravagance. My reply was that in such a wide-ranging program it was only to be expected that some extravagance should creep in, but at worst it was only a small percentage of the whole. I also showed that the CPR had made larger expenditures for hotels and such like than the Canadian National Railways."

Fairweather argued that accountancy alone could never show CN's real value, which unlike a factory could not be easily assessed. "It came to me that some other measure of the value of the railway than balance sheets and income statements had to be found," said Fairweather. "I found it in what I called the fecundity of railways. I took western Canada as an example. I made a study of the capital wealth of the Prairie provinces. Without railway service this wealth would not have been created. I then determined railway investment. The ratio between the two I called the index of fecundity. The fecundity factor was about thirty. Put in another way, for every dollar spent on railway in the Prairie provinces, the national economy reaped thirty dollars. A railway might lose money while the nation grew rich." He used the same principle, in reverse, on closure of branch lines. "The savings to the railway might well be accompanied by loss of productive capacity and collateral capital losses to settlers, developers and merchants, and ultimately people at large."

As before, Conservative MPs were out to publicize Thornton's true salary, and much was made of the fact that he was a director of the trust company from which the CN director Décary had borrowed the money to purchase the Thornton house. Thornton explained how, when Mackenzie King had declined to raise his salary, the prime minister had left the impression that Thornton could expect to be rewarded in other ways for improvements made to the railway. When his contract was renewed in 1929, Thornton understood from the minister, Charles Dunning, that it would be in order to claim perquisites. "Dunning suggested that it lay within the legal power of the directors to deal with such matters and Thornton took this to be consent," recalled Fairweather. "It might be added that a copy of all minutes of the board were routinely sent to Ottawa and that the deputy minister of railways and canals was one of the directors. It is simply inconceivable that Dunning did not know what took place."

Dunning, who had left politics for the time being, was summoned to testify. "I was with Sir Henry when Dunning appeared," said Fairweather. "He stopped to greet Sir Henry and I heard him say, 'Don't worry Henry, you will come out all right.'" But Dunning dodged the question when he came to testify, even when Décary, whose directorship had ended with the change of government, testified that the government knew about the house from the first. But Thornton's problem was this: the extras he enjoyed at CN had been part of a gentleman's agreement with former railway minister Kennedy, and Kennedy was dead and apparently nothing had been written down.

For the Conservatives everything came under suspicion. It would be hard to imagine anyone questioning Edward Beatty's expense account, but Thornton's was fair game. His claims for entertaining Japanese royalty and U.S. senators on behalf of the government were sifted with the same zeal as his bill for having the gift of a moose head cleaned for a U.S. university. Improvements in passenger travel were condemned as extravagant, though when they were made they were reasonable efforts to compete with motor transport. Had the improvements not been made, and the unexpected Depression not come, the same people would have found Thornton remiss. He was accused of hiring Americans at the expense of Canadians, though Americans made up less than 1 per cent of employees. McGibbon, still leading the attack, cited instances of lax accounting and padded expense accounts, though he retreated when Thornton flared up.

"I know of no railway company in any country which is officered by men who are more honest, more capable, or more loyal, more enthusiastic, and more moved by patriotic endeavour than the officers of Canadian National," Thornton said. "And I can say without hesitation that there is not an officer of the company who is pursuing any other course with respect to his expenses than that which is entirely honourable."

"I object strongly to your putting words in my mouth," replied McGibbon. "I did not say such a thing. I said I heard it, and I have heard it. I did not say it was true. I do not think it is. But if we get the details we will know."

Thornton's defiance decreased with the days. "He was no longer the Thornton who had tied four failures together and made a resounding success," said the *Montreal Star*. "He was tamed and dumb and conciliatory before his enemies...." Arthur L. Beaubien, National Progressive party member from Manitoba, was fed up. "If this committee is here to destroy the confidence the people have in the railway," he said, "it is adopting the best method I know of to do so ... surely we are not going to try to discredit the management or the board of directors by delving into these items which to my mind are quite legitimate. You cannot expect a railway official, when he goes out on the company's business, to travel in a boxcar or stay in a boarding house."

The Liberals, the ultimate targets of the Conservative campaign against Thornton, did little to help, apart from one ineffective counterattack in which they accused Prime Minister Bennett of feeding off the CN by living cheaply in the vice-regal suite at the Chateau Laurier. Bennett appeared before the committee, put up a bold defence and escaped unscathed. "I feel our men are not seeking to defend the CNR as they should, nor attacking Bennett as they should," King wrote in his diary while publicly cautioning his followers against throwing mud which might spatter back on the Liberals. "Thornton too is more subservient," wrote King. "It is all a mess, and will probably end in Thornton dropping out with some consideration and the Tories capturing that stronghold." Only when it was far too late did the senior Liberal committee member, W. D. Euler, declare that Thornton got the "rawest deal any man ever received from the Government of Canada."

The newspapers were carrying rumours that Sir Henry was on his way out. To catch up on gossip in McGill Street, King lunched with CN lawyer Alistair Fraser, who told him Thornton was living beyond his means but had been involved in no graft. "He said there is no doubt the Tories mean to get Thornton out and Thornton has made up his mind he is to go," King wrote in his diary. "He is not in good shape physically, has been much upset of late. The committee are giving him a hard examination. The truth is he has been too hoggish. It is another case of power destroying a man, turning his head."

On May 30, Manion sent Bennett the letter that would end Thornton's career. Seeing that Thornton was in personal financial difficulties, Manion meanly suggested the government "could get rid of him cheap" for $100,000. "I am convinced," said Manion, "that because of the publicity and the various exposures during the railway committee hearings, Thornton should go. I believe that the public really are expecting this, though naturally there are exceptions in various parts of the country among newspapers and others who are under favour to him; or who are a bit mad on the idea that we are trying to injure Canadian National."

Dispirited and ill, Thornton had planned to retire in the autumn after the Duff Commission report was tabled, but distrust, dislike, even fear, had reached unusual heights at the Department of Railways. Manion was convinced that Thornton was out to make himself more powerful than the government. "He boasted on some occasions that he was aiming to build up such a powerful organization that no government would dare to interfere," Manion wrote later. "He nearly succeeded in doing this, but the crisis of 1929 was his undoing, as it suddenly placed his much too elaborate expansion program and its extravagant cost in a clear cut manner before the people."

In a six-page memo, Manion listed forty reasons why Thornton should go, including expense accounts for "liquors, flowers, and other questionable items," hiring his architect father-in-law to work on CN hotels (which in fact he had done), "foolish and costly expenditures on train radio, train telephones," and his effort to get the government to purchase Thomas Cook and Sons, the international travel agency, which was going at a good price because of the Depression. While he argued that Thornton had lost the confidence of "his *real* staff and employees and a large majority of the people of Canada," Manion's reasons for firing him smelt of politics. "It appears to me that this man has been and is a menace not only to the CNR but to our whole national position and if he is not removed we will be placed in the position of condoning all his actions, and we will be retaining in our employ one who owes everything to Mackenzie King and who will naturally do everything he can to discredit us and to bring back to power the government which gave him his position and his prominence."

On July 19, having received Thornton's letter of resignation five days earlier, Manion announced that Thornton would leave CN as of August 1, 1932. Thornton's letter offered a half-hearted defence, recalled that money he had been accused of misusing had been approved by Parliament and added that a publicly-owned railway could only be successful if the management had the complete confidence of the owners of the property and this was no longer the case. "…in this period of financial depression," he said, "and in view of the further fact that a royal commission is now investigating the whole railway situation of the country, I feel I should tender my resignation."

To his friends he was more forthcoming. "I resigned," Thornton said "because I was asked to do so by the minister of railways speaking for the government…. I had in some curious way excited the hostility of the government and did not have its goodwill nor support. Under such conditions I was no good to anyone." Thornton was now dealing with the government through his lawyer, and though he asked for a separation payment of $250,000, his pension having been stripped from him, he received half that.

"The board as a whole was, I think, very sorry," said Thornton. "As a matter of fact I had got on very well with them and we had no differences." Their parting gift to him was a gold cigarette case. Hummel, Thornton's unpopular chief of staff, retired the next day with an ex gratia payment of $5000 and some awkward questions about money he personally received from a railway tie company that did business with CN. Gaston, another of Thornton's lieutenants hired out of his past, had already gone after half a dozen years, which had included the executive vice-presidency of the Central Vermont, which he had competently restored after the devastating flood of 1927.

Few mourned Thornton's passing more than the unions. "During Sir Henry's stewardship of the Canadian National Railways, cooperation between labour and management for mutual benefit and public service has been developed to a degree unsurpassed anywhere in the railway industry," said Robert J. Tallon, president of the umbrella labour organization the Association of General Chairmen. "Sir Henry leaves behind him one of the finest monuments in human relations ever erected in large-scale industry."

The day after Thornton's resignation, the *Winnipeg Free Press* asked why the Bennett government pursued Sir Henry with such implacability and concluded he stood in the way of their taking charge of CN. The *Toronto Star* was troubled by the way he was treated. The Conservative Toronto *Telegram* was glad he was gone. The *Montreal Star* put the blame on the Liberals. "Sir Henry's job was to make this national railway an asset. It was not his job to decide how much capital the country could afford to venture on the 'gamble.' He did his own job – not the job of the elected, appointed and paid watchdogs of the Treasury. He did his own job so effectively that things looked better every normal year. No one could be sure that he was not going to accomplish the impossible – to work the miracle."

Sir Henry would have liked another position in Canada, but that was impossible. "I shall leave my reputation to the future, feeling as I do that when the blood lust of political vindictiveness has run its course, justice will be done," he said in a letter to a newspaperman. "At any rate, the successor administration will inherit a hanged sight better property than was given me, and as most of the money necessary to rehabilitate the railway has been spent, they can economize with safety and good results."

No one thing had brought Thornton down. Politics, the ambivalence of CN's mandate and his inability to straddle state and private enterprise, the fact he had been a Liberal appointee when the Conservatives came to power, ill health – all these combined to defeat him. The hardest blow was the one that had ruined so many others – the Great Depression.

"His record for a time seemed to be of failure and disgrace," said Fairweather four decades later, "but like the view of a great mountain which gains in majesty as it recedes in distance, the accomplishments of this strange man assumed proper perspective with the passage of time. The spirit of the man survives to this day in the sense of purpose of a great railway." Vice-president Maynard Metcalf made this assessment: "He was often criticized, but my own humble opinion is that he was the right man in the right place to best serve the needs of the newly-organized Canadian National Railways."

To King's relief, Thornton avoided last-minute publicity. "He chose to bow out with dignity," said Fairweather. "In a last talk I had with him, he told me that had he been so inclined he could have embarrassed many of those who were attacking him, but that to do so he would have to descend to their level." Before leaving, he took his private papers to the basement of CN headquarters and burned them in the furnace. If King was grateful, he did not tell his diary. "He had himself to blame," King grumbled. "He was excellent the first few years. Of late his bad habits have got the better of him and destroyed his judgment. Had he possessed a Christian faith and lived by it he would have been one of the greatest of men. As it is, he is now a colossus fallen."

On the evening of August 1, Thornton said farewell at Bonaventure Station, where the stationmaster, J.C.Webber, gave a brief speech to a small group of friends. Thornton said, "Tell the boys that I'm sorry I can't say goodbye to them all. Tell them that." The train pulled out for New York City.

HARD
TIMES

I N THE SUMMER OF 1932, CN had neither compass nor captain. Having failed to provide for an orderly succession in its haste to get rid of Thornton, the Conservative government appointed as acting president Samuel James Hungerford, vice-president of operations, maintenance and construction.

A lean man of sixty who wore old-fashioned wing collars and shunned publicity, Hungerford was a typical railroader of the time. Born on a farm in the Eastern Townships of Quebec, he had to leave school when his father died. He became an apprentice machinist in Farnham and in a career with the CPR across Canada rose to locomotive foreman, divisional master mechanic and superintendent of locomotive shops in Winnipeg, where he modernized work methods. In 1910 he was hired by Canadian Northern as superintendent of rolling stock.

That Hungerford lacked experience in policy-making – one reason he had been passed over in 1922 in favour of Thornton – hardly mattered. The only policy now was retrenchment. Despite charges that Thornton had gone on spending after the Depression began, CN had in fact made heavy cuts during his last two years and its reduction of 50 per cent in transportation expenditures was more than any other railway in North America had managed. Despite his protestations that he would not fight the Depression by firing people, a third of the work force had been laid off and fifty senior positions abolished.

Many daily branch line services became semi-weekly, stations were closed, and repair shops were reduced from a forty-eight- to a thirty-six-hour week. Advertising, which Thornton had increased as an antidote to hard times, was slashed by 70 per cent. The natural resources department, which explored for minerals, oil and forests suitable for exploitation along CN routes, was cut to skeleton staff, as was the industrial department, since no factories were being built anyway.

Manion listed sixteen economies "mostly made by me," in which a $1.5 million reduction in maintenance-of-way payrolls jostled with such items as "Chibougamau Railway passes, thirty-four of them stopped," which meant Indian youths in the northern Quebec community could no longer commute to school. Manion decreed that the top floors of the CN hotels at Vancouver and Saskatoon be left unfinished. The minister of railways believed these savings provided a "splendid foundation for a structure which will place CNR within hailing distance of a chance of paying its interest requirements when times improve." In the meantime CN was able to pay barely a fifth of the $58 million in interest it owed and the government had to pay the rest, while hoping that the tardy Duff commission report would find ways to ease the burden on taxpayers.

For nine months the commission had travelled the rails in business cars, conducting fifty days of hearings and amassing enough information to fill five large books. Dafoe, who testified in Winnipeg, thought its solemn atmosphere was like "being in church" and the commissioners were too old to have open minds. Flavelle, in his mid-seventies, was boring his colleagues with tales of the Grand Trunk. The railway briefs complained that truck competition had become a serious threat, having increased 200 per cent in ten years. While still the most efficient transportation for long hauls, the railways were losing business on hauls of up to 250 miles and suffering from government's reluctance to increase freight rates and failure to collect highway taxes commensurate with use. A. R. Mosher of the Canadian Brotherhood of Railway Employees advocated nationalizing all transportation, including trucks, while M.J.Patton of the Automotive Transport Association of Ontario said the truckers wanted no regulation at all.

Although Flavelle, Loree and Leman initially favoured a CPR takeover of CN, Duff, whom Bennett was soon to elevate to Chief Justice, convinced them that the public would never stand for it, and the commission report in September 1932 gave CN a new lease on life and rejected Beatty's amalgamation in favour of Thornton's "cooperation," compulsory if necessary.

The commission took both railways to task for "irrational and wasteful competition," pointing out that cooperation could have cut the cost of branch construction by a third. Though Lord Ashfield said privately that "man for man and property for property" CN was superior to its rival, and the commission said publicly that CN had been "energetically administered" and its hotel expenditures had been half those of the CPR, nevertheless, without going to the roots of CN's troubles, the commission felt obliged to aim its sharpest barbs at the public railway, for the very reason that it was public. CN had failed to realize, it said, that Canada "could not afford further capital and maintenance expenditures for unwarranted branch lines, for deluxe services, for unrequired hotels, for the building of ships in competitive service to be shortly abandoned; and, generally, for costly adventures in competitive railways out of proportion to the needs of the country."

It blamed the directors for leaving money decisions to the president and the government for failing to control CN spending. "This left the railway open to political influence and to public pressure exerted by communities and by associations of business and labour interests," it said. The commission found so much government interference that the "ordinary principles of commercial operation were lost sight of."

As to a cure, the commission was timid, offering only a short-term solution, hesitating to "commit future generations and even the present one, to a policy adopted under the stress of difficult circumstances, which may not be best adapted to a new set of conditions difficult to forecast." While recognizing the threat of the trucking industry, it failed to stir the government into seeking a solution to an increasingly serious drain on railway traffic and revenue. Nor did it come to grips with automobile competition, which was already cutting into railway passenger revenues, but placidly maintained that there was really no cause for alarm because Canada's geography and climate had created a complementary relationship between railway and highway. Though opposing the absorption of CN by its rival, the committee consigned the railway to three years of virtual receivership, the board of seventeen replaced by three government-appointed trustees. The commission recommended an arbitral tribunal composed of the chairman of the Board of Railway Commissioners and a representative from each railway, with power to enforce cooperation in running rights, joint use of terminals, abandonment of lines and the pooling of services, but it failed to materialize once Beatty had denounced it as interference and "political expediency."

Thornton, while agreeing with recommendations that echoed his own, such as elimination of political pressures and wasteful competition, was stung by the report's assertion, headlined in the press, that the "red thread of extravagance" ran through his reign. "I think anyone will see that there runs through it a thread of hostility to the Canadian National Railways," he retorted. The CN had been singled out unfairly, he declared, for if anyone had failed to cooperate it was the CPR. He opposed the appointment of trustees, who would have more power than a board of directors, "because such power cannot be safely entrusted to the government."

At CN headquarters, Hungerford cautiously allowed as how the Duff report opened the way to the "utmost economy and efficiency," but Bennett, having been lectured by Flavelle that "cooperation is not a system, or a plan, but a spirit," urged the railways not to wait for legislation. Late in 1932 the two railways met in the CPR board room to appoint a joint committee of cooperation. Within a few months CN and CPR were cooperating on minor chores such as car switching and cleaning, but the only major cooperation, apart from wages and rates negotiations, was the pooling of passenger service on the heavily-travelled lines between Toronto and Ottawa, Toronto and Montreal, and Montreal and Quebec City. Hungerford and Beatty discussed a general pooling of passenger services right across Canada, but on July 7, 1933, Hungerford told the CN board that country-wide pooling was not a good idea "at present," expressing a deep resistance among CN veterans against becoming too closely involved with their rival.

In 1933 the country was in the trough of the Great Depression. One million three hundred people, a tenth of the population, were penniless and on relief and passenger travel was down by nearly half. (There had been more passengers in 1902 when railway mileage and population were half as big.) Instead of tourists listening to Thornton's radios in the parlour cars, tens of thousands of jobless men and women were riding the rails, fifty or more to a boxcar, living on handouts as they moved from town to town. Branch lines rusted, sidings filled with weeds and idle rolling stock. The two regions hard-est hit, the Maritimes and the Prairies, had lost traditional markets, and the Prairies, which normally provided a third of CN's traffic, were providing hardly one sixth. To keep farmers on the land, CN provided free seed and sometimes free provisions and transportation to take crops to market.

Complaints about both railways were never off the front pages of Prairie or Maritime newspapers for long. In Nova Scotia the Halifax *Herald* attacked CN for importing coal from its mine in Ohio, instead of relying on the Nova Scotian product. The "count against the CNR in relation to coal purchases is a long and serious one," it said. U.S. coal was being imported into central Canada because Nova Scotian coal was more expensive and the newspaper said it was "un-Canadian" to use American coal "in this grave emergency."

With revenues halved since 1928, both railways reduced wages again, making a total 15 per cent reduction. The payroll had shrunk 40 per cent in five years. For the first time, the CPR failed to pay dividends; unable to meet fixed charges, it emulated its rival and turned to the government to guarantee a large loan.

Since the Duff report rejected "amalgamation," Beatty was now talking of "unification" (Manion said this was playing with words) and forty clerks were employed at CPR headquarters mailing thousands of letters and pamphlets explaining Beatty's vision. He believed that 5000 miles of track could be shut down though he did not say how many people would be laid off or how many communities abandoned. "By no other means can we secure a sound business administration for our railway undertakings and relief to the taxpayers of Canada," he told the Canadian Club in Toronto on January 16, 1933.

The Conservatives refused to back him. "The solution of the difficulties is not as easy as Mr. Beatty would have you believe," Bennett said. "When he talks of saving $75 million a year, you know, of course, that is ridiculous, unless many miles of rails are taken up. That, of course, is something that the people will not view with any degree of favour."

"Unite them," Arthur Meighen told the Senate, "and you will have a power which, in the hands of competent, shrewd, far-seeing men, could be made an almost insuperable factor in the political life of this Dominion." The *Farmer's Sun,* the weekly voice of Ontario farmers, said the CPR was try-ing "deliberately and boldly" to convert Canada to a policy of private railway monopoly. A generation after Canadian Northern had begun to break the CPR monopoly in the West, most westerners, as always, opposed a CPR monopoly, although the United Farmers of Alberta in Calgary favoured amalgamation under national ownership to lower the cost of transportation. The Manitoba government opposed monopoly of any kind, governmental or otherwise, and in Toronto no one was surprised when the Canadian Brotherhood of Railway Employees came out in favour of public ownership. New Brunswick opted for cooperation rather than unification, but Nova Scotia would accept amalgamation if it improved the economy. In Sault Ste. Marie, a CPR town, the *Star* said taxpayers would support *any* sensible solution that would ease their tax burden. "What other solution is there but a union of the CPR and the CNR either under government or CPR management?"

"Unquestionably," Thornton wrote Dafoe from New York, "there is a definite plot on the boards to turn the Canadian National over to the CPR," but Dafoe felt there was "something phony" about it all. Since the CPR stood so little chance of swallowing CN, what was Beatty's hidden motive? What Beatty really wanted, one heard in the Parliamentary Press Gallery, was to sell CPR's money-losing branch lines to the government, while keeping the lucrative main lines, shipping, real estate and hotel divisions.

Early in 1933 as Parliament began to draft the Duff commission recommendations into law, including the requirement for CN-CPR cooperation, Beatty said the CPR was prepared for voluntary cooperation, though with little hope it would work. David Blythe Hanna, still vigorous in his seventies despite his claim "I am too old, and was worked out ten years ago," testified at a Senate hearing into CN-CPR cooperation that though he opposed Beatty's campaign he saw no reason why the railways should not "get on in harmony." He also revealed his dislike of Thornton. He wondered aloud how Thornton had been able to get money so easily from Parliament. "His budgets were passed with very little criticism. Large amounts – sometimes they represented more than half the debt of Canada before the war – were passed at a single session." He blamed the government for "these annual budget comedies" but favoured keeping the debt intact as a reminder of past mistakes. "One of the officers of the Canadian National recently said that me and my criticisms could go to hell," said Hanna, "that I've always been a piker when it comes to money. That is, I don't understand that to get back returns you have to spend money in a big way. You've spent big money and what have you got ten years later?"

Mackenzie King, leading the opposition, warned that a trusteeship would be CN's death, recalling how in 1914, when CN's predecessors had begun to go under, Bennett had wanted a receivership but was overruled by Borden. Now Bennett's references to trustees as "receivers" made it "clearer than ever the need to oppose this measure, which I am convinced is to lead to the submerging of the CNR," said King.

King, as it happened, was walking down the aisle of the Commons to fight trusteeship on the afternoon of March 14 when he heard that Sir Henry Thornton had died of cancer in a New York City hospital at the age of sixty-two, the day CN unions had chosen to honour Thornton with a gala dinner. "It is sad, the close of a great career," King wrote in his diary. "He has helped to destroy himself, and Bennett has helped to kill him as he has helped to kill others. It is strange death should come just at this time, as we are debating this railway bill, the effort to destroy much of his work. I think he came to regard me, if he did not always do so, as the truest friend he had." Only half a dozen CN people, led by Hungerford, attended Thornton's funeral in the United States, the government being represented by the deputy minister. According to his widow, Thornton died insolvent.

King laboured hard to produce a eulogy that would do justice to a man more sinned against than sinning, while deflecting criticism of his own role in the Thornton tragedy. "What Sir Henry achieved in the period of his administration of the National railways may be obscured for the time being by the existing depression, and by political controversy to which it has served to give rise. As, however, the years go by, and all things fall into their true perspective, Sir Henry Thornton's work in bringing the Canadian National Railways to the position which they attained under his direction will stand out as a supreme achievement of national enterprise and public service."

The greatest tribute was provided by the workers of CN – fifteen bronze plaques in his honour in railway stations across the country. "Labour also saw to it," added Fairweather, "that those who led the attack on him [McGibbon, Hackett, MacMillan and Hanson] suffered defeat in the next election." The *Winnipeg Free Press* said, "The country is in his debt for a service of value not to be estimated." The *Winnipeg Tribune,* while admiring his magnetism, leadership and generosity, said, "His very qualities of greatness were in a sense his undoing. What Sir Henry lacked, other men – his board of directors, the government at Ottawa – should have supplied, namely a curb." The *Montreal Star,* which had been hostile, said, "He was a great railwayman. He was a great politician, but he was not too good at counting his small change."

CN suffered a blow in 1933 with the death, at the age of forty-six, of Ned

Brooks, who had made such a promising start in introducing diesels to Canada. His death, and the Depression, brought work on diesels to a halt, and apart from the purchase of switchers CN would not resume it for a decade and more, by which time U.S. railways were well in the lead.

Thornton would surely have loathed the next three years. For the first year, the burden fell on Hungerford, who responded with a frugality that reduced expenses without making much dent in deficits. "During the depth of the Depression the attack on Canadian National was accentuated," recalled Fairweather. Called "Mr. CN" because he appeared so often against Beatty's campaign to take CN into the CPR, Fairweather was one of the best champions of public enterprise CN ever had, while insisting that personally he was a "private enterprise man." A remarkable, eccentric, egotistical man, he had a keen mind and a forceful personality and saw the defence of CN as a duty. His chief weapon was publicity and whenever Beatty suggested a CN line be abandoned, Fairweather would make sure the threatened places sent telegrams of protest.

"In our defence of the system," Fairweather said, "it took all the ingenuity of Walter Thompson and myself to maintain a glimmer of hope. I invented two concepts which were designed to offset attack. They infuriated our attackers. The first concept was 'negative capital.' The second was a 'distress' budget. 'Negative capital' I used to describe the huge debt with which the system was burdened and which apart from the government takeover after World War I would have been written off through bankruptcy. I resurrected the study I had made of United States railways west of the Mississippi which showed that every line had gone through bankruptcy – some of them several times. I proved that if they were still burdened with the capital shucked off in this fashion they would be showing deficits instead of profits. We worked this idea for all it was worth. The distress budget concept was meant to show Canadian National management was making a mighty effort to meet the exigencies of the Depression."

But these, like the Duff commission recommendations, were stop-gaps when long-term policies were needed. With revenue 42 per cent below the average for the previous decade, CN's capital was shrinking at an alarming rate. "The public, and transportation people generally, undoubtedly have every confidence in Mr. Hungerford," commented *Canadian Railway and Marine World* in November, "but with the trustees unnamed and the appointment of a president not made, the affairs of the company at best can only be marking time. This is not good for the organization generally, and is bound to have an unsettling effect."

Legislation based on the Duff report – the Canadian National–Canadian Pacific Act, 1933 – took some time to implement because it was hard to find a chairman with "financial, administrative, and executive ability of a high order." The salary was modest, $30,000 a year, and tenure uncertain, but in the end the government convinced the chairman of the Board of Railway Commissioners, C. P. Fullerton, to assume the task as a public duty. A former judge of the Appeal Court in Winnipeg, he was sixty-four, a stocky, bald Nova Scotian of high principles and limited business experience. Two days before Christmas 1933 and almost seventeen months after Thornton's departure, Prime Minister Bennett announced his appointment as a "temporary management for a temporary situation."

When he joined CN in January 1934, Fullerton gave notice he would be no figurehead, and the *Winnipeg Free Press* feared he had been given power "beyond the reach of Parliament's will to maintain the CN as a going concern." The other trustees, both Conservative party supporters like Fullerton, had been members of the executive committee of the board under Thornton. J. Édouard Labelle, fifty-one, who agreed to serve for $6000 a year, was a dapper, punctilious Montreal lawyer from a family of railway contractors stretching back to the Intercolonial. Frederick K. Morrow, forty-eight, of Toronto, who declined any fee, was one of the best businessmen of his generation, the president of the Tobacco Products Corporation and director of a dozen companies.

Hungerford was elevated to the presidency, though the position was a shadow of what it had been, and he continued to do what he had done as vice-president – run the trains. Fullerton took charge of everything else: the legal department, finance and accounting, publicity, medical, colonization and agriculture, land and property, hotels and steamships. Any expense above $25,000 had to be approved by the trustees. "We are on trial," Fullerton said. "Every man should solicit business, should give everything in him to achieve success."

Despite his mandate to cooperate with the CPR, Fullerton turned out to be firmer than Thornton in opposing the rival railway. The CPR had been proceeding on the "bland assumption," he said, that where public and private railways are fighting for a diminishing market the private railway should be given a monopoly. "The underlying idea apparently is that the money of a shareholder has a sacred quality denied that of a mere taxpayer.... I desire to state that the trustees, individually and as a body are for many reasons opposed to amalgamation and unification." CN supporters were delighted. The *Ottawa Journal* reported that the new chairman said things that needed to be said: "Judge Fullerton is not speaking as a politician with a party theory or prejudice, nor as a railwayman with an axe to grind. He speaks as a public servant. As one anxious only for Canada." The Toronto *Telegram*, showing unwonted friendliness since Thornton's departure, said those who feared secret plans to join CN with the CPR could rest easy.

Though CN was costing taxpayers more than Canada's total bill for unemployment relief, Fullerton had difficulty finding anything to cut. "The measures which are open to us to secure a substantial increase in our gross revenues are limited," he admitted. "We ourselves can do little to expand the trade and commerce of the country.... It is our definite policy to seek out every possible means to economy, consistent with safe operation and reasonable service to the public. Even if there is a return to prosperity we shall continue this policy...." The accounting department had been slashed by a third, the investigative department, or police force, by a sixth to 540 men and women, and with immigration at a low ebb, the offices of the Colonization department in Europe were closed. The ten-year-old CN broadcasting network, which had been losing $300,000 a year, was sold to the government for $50,000, which used its staff and equipment in the spring of 1933 to create the nucleus of the Canadian Radio Broadcasting Commission, forerunner of the CBC. It had ended its CN period with a range of quality programs that included school broadcasts, "Uncle Dick's Talks for Boys and Girls," the Toronto Symphony, Canada's first radio drama series, and historical plays designed to foster Canadian unity and directed by England's Tyrone Guthrie.

Morale was poor. "Unless the position of all railways in Canada materially improves within the next few years," Fullerton warned, "many experiments, presently unacceptable, may have to be tried." Fairweather, whose Bureau of Economics had been reduced by half, found himself "muzzled by the chairman, for what reason I know not." Fullerton apparently feared that Fairweather's attacks on the CPR would jeopardize the cooperation he was told to achieve. G.H.Lash, bitter at being fired, if only temporarily, from the publicity department, whose staff of fifty-five had included seventeen writers, wrote that a "species of czarism seems to prevail, and a great fear has gripped everyone within the organization.... There is no longer a morale. Only disorder and disintegration." One of the few initiatives was a personnel department to deal with wage agreements, employment and working conditions.

The year 1934 was somewhat better due to an increase in movement of automobiles, lumber and newsprint. Thanks to CN, grain shipments through Halifax had doubled. Otherwise business was half the level of 1928, and grain traffic little more than an eighth of what it had been in that bumper year, but there were harbingers of an economy on the mend. Speaking in Saint John, Fullerton was hopeful a reviving economy would put CN in the black: "With the reduction in operating expenses which we have effected, if traffic resumed at a rate similar to that enjoyed in 1928, the people of Canada will have nothing whatever to worry about as far as the Canadian National Railways are concerned. And there will then be no further talk about amalgamation."

Fullerton was not optimistic about cooperation with the CPR. Efforts to abandon thirty-six branch lines, totalling 2000 miles, were getting nowhere. "Admittedly there are routes which do not pay and probably will not pay for some years hence," he said, echoing Thornton, "but people bought their farms and settled because the railway was there and afforded them easy and economical transport for their produce and supplies. These people cannot be abandoned by the railway and left to fare as best they can, with the capital value of their lands greatly decreased."

The Joint Cooperative Committee always seemed to find reasons why further cooperation was difficult or impossible; combined savings for the year were disappointing. When a bill was tabled in Parliament to unite the express and telegraph departments, the CN trustees had second thoughts and had it withdrawn, to the CPR's disgust. Having competed for decades – since the CPR challenged the Grand Trunk in the 1880s – the two railways had a natural reluctance to pull together, or when they did each sought an advantage. Agreement on transcontinental passenger pooling would have to wait while the railways argued over whether CPR's Windsor Station or CN's Bonaventure would be used, CN's plans for building a new Montreal terminal having been sidetracked yet again.

Urged on by an impatient Bennett, Fullerton ordered Hungerford to hasten cooperation. Beatty, for his part, had no more faith in cooperation than he ever had, though he paid it lip service when he suggested that unification was really only cooperation writ large. The CPR's annual report for 1934 described Beatty's aim as a "partnership between public ownership and private ownership, with the added advantage of a private operation free from political control." Manion opposed it. "We have made three great blunders in the past," he said, referring to the original decision to build too many railways, their nationalization and finally the era of Thornton. "Surely we are not going to be hoodwinked into the fourth and greatest of them, that of amalgamation with the Canadian Pacific."

The only change in the "railway problem" in twenty years had been the hundreds of millions added to CN's debt, said Manion, who argued that only increased earnings through increased trade would mend CN's fortunes. "The Canadian National railway is now being efficiently and economically operated," he asserted, "and it could not be more economically operated if the debt or part of it were wiped out." When asked why the government did not at least write off the accumulation of government loans, Manion replied, "As none of the capital or interest has ever been repaid, it would make no material difference to either the country or the railway if this were done. It would merely clear the railway picture."

"It is said that it is simply a matter of bookkeeping and will effect no useful purpose," Fullerton replied. "I disagree with this view. There are many reasons, one of which is the disheartening effect upon the management and the employees who must face year after year an insurmountable burden of debt. Recapitalization would paint a more realistic picture of CN's assets, improve the appearance of the balance sheet, and above all improve morale." Fullerton was exercising an independence that did not enhance his popularity in a government that had no more wish than the Liberals to shoulder the CN debt. "Let me say once for all," he declared, "that today the Canadian National Railways are just as free from having to consider matters from a political angle as any railway in Canada, and it is the intention of myself and my fellow trustees that this shall remain so."

Not that the trustees always saw eye to eye. "The task set the trustees was not always a pleasant one," Fullerton admitted. On one occasion Labelle complained directly to Manion that Fullerton had made a decision to purchase Alberta coal without his knowledge. Nor were they popular with employees, who grumbled about arbitrary decisions made behind closed doors. Hungerford himself was heard to complain of being a "glorified clerk." Accused of aimless penny pinching and the deadlier sin of not knowing how to run a railroad, the trustees laboured under restrictions that did not endear them to the rank and file.

The Bennett government, long on promises, short on solutions, had lost popular support and in the autumn election of 1935 Mackenzie King's Liberals returned to power and resumed the game of musical chairs with their choice of minister of railways and canals. "I felt I wanted in this position," King said, "someone who had not been actively identified in the controversy between the CPR and the Canadian National, and, at the same time, one whom I knew to be opposed to amalgamation of the railways, and one whom I believed had the confidence of the railroad employees."

His choice was Clarence Decatur Howe, a Massachusetts-born civil engineer who had moved to the Lakehead to make his fortune designing the grain elevators that dotted the Prairies. As an MP from the blue-collar riding of Port Arthur, and the cabinet's sole engineer, Howe was better equipped than most railway ministers, even if his practical experience had been confined to teaching a course on railway construction at Dalhousie University and tinkering with model railways as a boy. As an unrepentant capitalist, Howe also began to mould CN into more of a business and less of a governmental agency for national improvement, a process that has been going on more or less ever since.

The trustees had been tested for two years and found wanting, and Howe had his own plans for the "most important public utility in Canada." According to King's diary for October 28, 1935, Howe thought the Conservatives had done "everything possible to sabotage the National Railways" and regarded the board of trustees as a "miserable affair, and even the previous government had come to so regard it. He thinks we should get rid of it altogether." Howe believed the trustees had been "responsible to no one ... a sort of enforced absentee landlordism ... apparently without policy, and so far as public relations are concerned is even without a voice."

But just as it took a year to put the trustees in place, it would take a year to replace them, for Fullerton refused to resign, protesting that no one had questioned his efficiency and his five-year contract had three years to run. "When I was asked for my resignation," he said, "my first impulse was to give it, as, no more than any other man, do I have a desire for carrying on my work in other than an atmosphere of friendliness, appreciation and confidence. On reflection, however, it was borne in on me that to yield on a matter of this nature, no matter how great the temptation to do so, might be, would be, to betray a trust."

In the spring of 1936 Howe introduced a bill to discharge the trustees, "restore management by experts in the railway business" and elect a board with two thirds fewer directors so as to reduce regional pressures. When Howe launched an attack on Fullerton which even King found excessive, contending that as CN chairman Fullerton had usurped the president's duties though he "knew nothing of actual railway practice," Bennett angrily defended his appointment of the man he had sometimes criticized himself and demanded Fullerton be given a chance to defend himself. For good measure, the former prime minister called Hungerford incompetent, a "railway master mechanic" out of his depth in the president's office. "We cannot lift this tremendous problem out of the morass of politics," Bennett added, "unless we endeavour to see that those charged with responsibility are free from pressure."

Fullerton acquitted himself well before the Railway Committee. "When all the factors respecting the railway are taken into consideration," he said, "it is my confident claim that the railway is more economically operated, that its efficiency as a transportation system is greater, and that it is better equipped, from the standpoint of prospective profit, to deal with business expansion than it ever was before." His regime had certainly not been all negative, though some of the improvements did not appear until after he had departed. There were, for example, the first streamlined locomotives in Canada, delivered in 1936 for service between Montreal and Chicago. Built by Montreal Locomotive Works and bearing the CN numbers 6400–6404, they were big Northern-type engines jointly designed by CN and the National Research Council, streamlined not so much for speed or looks as to keep smoke out of the cab crew's eyes. For the first time in years CN hotels were making a modest profit and the Hotel Bessborough in Saskatoon had finally been opened in a gala in which shy Sam Hungerford was made an honorary member of an Indian band.

The depleted Canadian Government Merchant Marine reported a profit too little and too late to save this seventeen-year experiment with a national merchant navy. When it competed with CN trains in hauling lumber east from British Columbia via the Panama Canal, the CGMM had been of questionable value to the railway, and at all events most of the sixty-three ships had been sold. By 1933 the CGMM had been reduced to service to the West Indies and a ten-ship service from Montreal to Australia and New Zealand. In June 1936 the last ten ships were sold and the CGMM died largely unlamented, though some believe it never had a fair trial. The Canadian National (West Indies) Steamships service continued as before.

Afloat or ashore, times were hard. Two thirds of the CN system – 14,000 miles – failed to earn operating expenses, leaving the profitable trunk lines in southern Quebec and Ontario and between Winnipeg and Vancouver, Winnipeg and the east, and Montreal and Halifax to take up the slack. Passenger trains were losing out to motor cars, and receipts were down 50 per cent from 1928. The trucking industry, unhampered by a railway rate structure designed to move lumber, grain, coal and other heavy bulk at low cost, while making up revenues by charging higher tariffs for more valuable and less bulky commodities, was capturing railway business on the shorter hauls. A second advantage for truckers was that they paid only part of the cost of highway upkeep, while railways assumed the entire cost of their right of way.

As minister of transport, his new title, Howe was committed to devising a policy that would rationalize all modes of transportation – railways, highways, waterways and airways. "It is not too much to say that transportation is Canada's greatest problem, it always has been and always will be," he said. "The very economy of our country depends on cheap transportation, and at the same time the vast expanse of country, thinly settled, makes cheap transportation difficult."

On October 10, 1936, Howe replaced the trustees with a board of directors, and Fullerton departed to a law practice and an early death two years later. Reflecting the view that CN was hard on its leaders, who inevitably found themselves caught between the public servants of Ottawa and the mammon of St. James Street, the Montreal *Gazette* said of Fullerton, "He did his best in the fulfillment of his duties, some of which were thankless and brought the inevitable criticism. He was at all times forthright in his opinions. His public life all through was honourable."

To assure continuity, some directors were appointed for three years, some for two and others for one. King, with his usual ambiguity, advised his new minister to "avoid political appointments, but to keep party forces in mind," but Howe did exactly what he meant to do in the first place and sought competent businessmen "equal to the board of any other corporation in the country." He chose James Y. Murdoch of Toronto, president of Noranda Mines Ltd.; Robert J. Moffatt, former managing director of the Saskatchewan Wheat Pool; and Donald H. McDougall of Stellarton, N.S., a metallurgical engineer and company president. Two newcomers in particular were to contribute a great deal to CN over the next two decades and outlast two chairmen. One was Herbert J. Symington, K.C., of Montreal, vice-pres-

CN inherited a mixed bag of locomotives, including "tea kettles" like the one shown here, lightweight engines suited to the road beds and bridges of the day. Almost all CN steam locomotives were smaller and lighter than those in the U.S. At the peak of steam power, in the 1920s, CN operated 3260 locomotives. By 1944 the fleet had been reduced to 2524. No. 647 dated from 1895 and survived in branch line service until 1927, the year the photo was taken.

One of the early acquisitions after CN was formed in 1923, locomotive 4100, weighing 327 tons, was a Santa Fe type used for "helper service" on heavy freights at Toronto.

During a pause at North Battleford, Saskatchewan, in 1915, David Blythe Hanna (the tall man in the centre) lines up with his inspection group and local railway officials.

Sir Henry Thornton visits train crew at Bonaventure Station, Montreal, in 1930. The locomotive is a Northern type.

A standard passenger train comes into Saskatoon hours late in a March blizzard, 1927. 5547 was a Pacific type. Passenger service was CN's show window, but freight accounted for most of its workload. Up to the 1980s CN was also in the parcels business, long before the days of couriers. The catalogue business of Eaton's and other department stores relied on CN Express for door-to-door delivery.

CN *Continental* passenger train crossing the Thompson River in British Columbia in 1927, at the peak of prosperity before the market crash of 1929.

Grain collection from Prairie elevators in the 1920s, Vegreville, Alberta. A flagman prepares to protect the level crossing. Stations were positioned every few miles, and the grain elevators, a few houses, a Chinese restaurant, general store and pool hall clustered around them.

Milk run became the derisive term for any train that seemed to stop at every farmyard. This train in northern Quebec in the 1920s was also placarded for dangerous goods, probably explosives.

ROUTE SHIPMENTS VIA

CENTRAL VERMONT RAILWAY

ROCKET

DEPENDABLE DAILY DELIVERY

ABOVE Canadian National Express wagons were the standard pick-up and delivery vehicle in 1926. The switch to motor trucks took place only a few years later.

BELOW Crates, boxes, barrels and sacks in organized confusion in Bonaventure freight shed, Montreal, 1925. Drays and trucks lined up at the open doors at the right, boxcars at the left. The chalk marks are the destination codes, being checked by the foreman, right of centre.

Central Vermont Railway, from the border south of Montreal to New London, Connecticut, connected with various U.S. railroads in New England. Rocket freight service was launched in 1933.

Self-propelled diesel-electric passenger car 15820 reduced the cost of operating on branch lines. To test its reliability, CN sent it, in 1925, on a non-stop journey from Montreal to Vancouver. It broke all records for speed on the transcontinental journey.

CN's No. 9000, seen near Montreal in 1929 and built the previous year by Canadian Locomotive Co. of Kingston, Ontario, was the first diesel road locomotive in North America.

The 5700, a classic Hudson type with shiny bell and cyclops headlight, was introduced in 1930 as part of Sir Henry Thornton's efforts to "beat the CPR."

BELOW The railways were the government's immigration agency for many years. Here a group from Hungary changes trains at Toronto in 1927 en route to take up CN land on the Prairies.

A six-wheel yard switching engine, or "yard goat," takes charge of a massive refinery tower, a "high-and-wide" load.

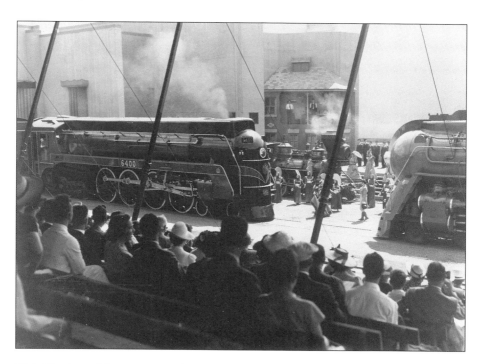

This Northern, No. 6400, was the product of wind-tunnel design by the National Research Council in 1936. No CN locomotive was more widely publicized. In 1939 it pulled the royal train carrying King George and Queen Elizabeth and it is seen here on display at the World's Fair in New York.

The SS *Lady Drake* at Bermuda, 1939. The red, white and blue funnel of CN (West Indies) Steamships was a familiar sight in many West Indian ports. They carried apples, fish, lumber and manufactured goods south, and molasses, tropical fruit and sugar north, as well as passengers in both directions.

As an extension of its rail services, CN operated rail car ferries. Here SS *Charlottetown* is launched in 1931 at Lauzon, Quebec, for service between Borden, P.E.I., and Cape Tormentine, N.B.

Sir Henry Thornton speaking on the phone from a moving train in 1930. At right in this photomontage a technician routes his call through wayside transmitters.

ABOVE Radio broadcasts picked up aboard the train, and on-board telephone service, were pioneered by CN in the 1920s. Headsets in this "Radio Car" brought in musical and variety shows from CN radio stations in major cities. The embryonic network later became the CBC.

This thirty-six-seat rolling restaurant was expensive to build and operate, but essential for long-distance train travel. In 1938, when this picture was taken, the car had been renovated with sealed windows and air conditioning.

In the roundhouse at Willow Park just outside Halifax, in 1934, a rare view of the brute force needed to manhandle steam locomotive parts.

The ritual of comparing watches carried out by engineer and conductor at Bonaventure Station, Montreal, in 1927 before an express train is given the signal to depart. The conductor's sleeve bears gold maple leaves and bars showing twenty-five years of service.

Judge C. P. Fullerton, former chairman of the Board of Railway Commissioners, ran CN for two years as chairman of a board of trustees appointed by R. B. Bennett as a "temporary management for a temporary situation."

Many CN communities had their own bands, and CN had its own "CN March." This band, made up of employees of the Transcona shops in Manitoba, was photographed in 1923.

S. J. Hungerford at the age of forty-eight. Rising from machinist apprentice, he became chairman and president of CN and one of the ablest railroaders in Canada.

This car with an open observation gallery was painted and decorated for the 1939 Royal train across Canada. King George and Queen Elizabeth used this balcony to greet thousands of Canadians at whistle-stops from coast to coast. In this photo they are seen at Mt. Robson.

In World War II women became a necessary part of the motive power maintenance staff. These engine wipers are attending to one of CN's most modern steamers, a bullet-nosed Mountain type built in 1944.

During the war years the gasoline-powered track motor car began replacing the hand-car. These Quebec railroaders are inspecting the right of way.

The war brought Victory bond drives and essential work stopped while the big V was formed outside Turcot roundhouse in Montreal.

The roundhouse at Turcot yard, Montreal, opened in 1905 by the Grand Trunk Railway, was the largest in the CN system, with a 100-foot turntable and stalls for fifty-six engines. Hundreds of railroaders worked, ate and slept on the smoky premises. The roundhouse is seen here in 1943, at the height of wartime activity, when it was servicing Northerns, Moguls, Mikados, switchers and other types.

ident of Royal Securities Corporation, who in his early years was a lawyer for Grand Trunk Pacific in Winnipeg and also for the Prairie provinces during the freight rate hearings in the mid-1920s. The other was the genial and hard-working Wilfrid J. Gagnon of Montreal, president of a family shoe factory, chairman of Dow Breweries and former Quebec minister of commerce. At King's urging, union members were given a chance to choose their own representative on the board, and B. L. Daly of Winnipeg, chairman of the Order of Railway Conductors, was elected. Each director received $6000 a year.

The seventh director was Hungerford, elevated to the combined position of chairman and president, though since he was sixty-five and ripe for retirement his appointment caused Murdoch to ask if Hungerford was up to the job. It was not the first time the question had been raised. Over the years critics had said Hungerford had difficulty withstanding pressure and was too willing to please. Maynard Metcalf, his assistant for twenty-four years, was often frustrated by Hungerford's caution at the annual meetings of the parliamentary committee. "As a real professional, he knew all the answers to the questions posed by members of the committee, but he seemed at times obsessed with the idea that a categoric answer should at all costs be avoided. It is no exaggeration to say that I could have cried to see my boss dodging straightforward questions even to the extent of answering in poor voice and holding his ear as if hard of hearing." Murdoch wanted Hungerford retired, but neither Howe nor two of the members of the board's executive committee, Symington and Gagnon, agreed. Hungerford stayed and Murdoch resigned.

As his vice-president, Hungerford appointed a man not unlike himself. Norman B. Walton, a native of Palmerston, Ontario, who had begun his career, as did so many vice-presidents, as a clerk and stenographer, had become Grand Trunk superintendent at Edmonton, general superintendent of CN's western division in 1924, chief of transportation in Montreal and finally vice-president of operations. Justifying Howe's faith, Hungerford in 1936 began to improve the company. The 15 per cent salary cuts made during the worst of the Depression were reversed. Though he refused to carry on Brooks' pioneering in diesels, arguing that diesels might be useful as yard engines but were uneconomical as mainliners, he ordered more and stronger Northerns to pull heavy freights from Montreal to Toronto and Detroit or the *Ocean Limited* from the smoky old Bonaventure Station 841 miles to the shiny new terminal in Halifax with a maximum speed of 85 miles an hour. To combat a serious shortage, he ordered 3000 boxcars and fifty of the latest all-steel passenger coaches. Both CN and CPR introduced ice-based air conditioning on name trains and it became common to see men humping 100-pound blocks of ice into compartments under sleepers and coaches.

In his determination to shake off the trustee years, Hungerford uncharacteristically ignored tradition and seniority by polling upper and middle management on how to improve the company, urging everyone to "feel absolutely free to advance any suggestion that may occur to him." The answers, a flood tide of enlightened ideas percolating up through the bureaucracy after five years of Depression and the public shaming of Thornton, provided an illuminating profile of CN's strengths and weaknesses.

They varied from the general passenger traffic manager's recommendation that CN should, like the CPR, have top businessmen rather than regional political appointees on the board, to a comment from a freight agent in Halifax that the muddy red of CN rolling stock was lifeless compared with the CPR's colours and "soon fades into a very dingy and dirty colour which gives a bad impression and is very poor advertising."

There was concern about poor morale, one respondent blaming Beatty's campaign for amalgamation or unification "with its mis-statements, half truths and veiled criticism." Morale varied from region to region, or even town to town. Fifteen years after CN took its final form, many retained their old loyalties. A crew coming in from the West was still apt to call itself a Canadian Northern crew and refer to men coming up from the Maritimes as an Intercolonial crew. Toronto complained that CN public relations had played second fiddle to the CPR during the trustee years and a veteran passenger manager in Montreal, reflecting ingrown CN-CPR antagonisms, said CN should discontinue pooling trains "in order to halt erosion of prestige and avoid injury to morale." In Regina CN was said to be always highly regarded and an anglophone agent in Quebec City said CN was more popular than the CPR but warned that CN should start recruiting French Canadians. "There is an undercurrent of opinion in this province which occasionally breaks out in print that French Canadians are persona non grata on the CNR and in federal employment generally."

Taken together, the answers coming to Hungerford's desk reflected an impatience to modernize, conditions having changed so much that many old regulations were now merely irritants. It was time to dump the sacrosanct seniority rule, as stiff as anything in the army whence it came, and establish a merit system. It was at this time that the marketing, or traffic, department began to rebel openly against the operations department, which had insisted, since railways were born, on being cock of the walk so that everything had to meet operations priorities rather than customer needs.

The debt load, two thirds of which had accumulated before CN was born, bothered employees at all levels. The most frequent and most embarrassing question heard by a Toronto claims agent was "When is the CNR ever going to pay its way?" This, said an employee in Vancouver, "had the effect of keeping the national railway constantly in the public mind and in an unfavourable light and subject to adverse comment or attack." Employees agreed that capitalization should be brought in line with the value of the property, or at least in line with CN's ability to pay, which Thornton had tried to achieve under the Board of Audit Act of 1925, arguing that CN's debt should only be that money which had actually been used to improve the property, and that funds paid to cover operating deficits before CN was formed should not be called capital. The bookkeeping in transferring the debt to the government would have been daunting, and when the Duff commission recommended the $2.5 billion debt be written down and Fullerton got auditors to draft a plan in which government advances to cover deficits would be written off and no interest charged on advances for capital purposes, Prime Minister Bennett could hardly have reacted more sharply if Fullerton had had his fingers in the till. "Almost incredible," Bennett called Fullerton's suggestion. "We must insist that the railway company's reports shall give a true picture of the real situation, and that the annual report as issued will enable anyone perusing it to understand exactly what the Dominion of Canada has invested in its railway enterprises."

Now it was Howe's turn to battle the monster. He found it stupid that deficits representing no tangible property were added to capital, creating spirals of interest charges and deficits. "When a company shows an operating loss at the end of the year," he said, "its shareholders do not add that amount to the capitalization of the firm, but that, in effect, is what has been done with the Canadian National Railways."

The year 1936 brought an improvement in business across the country and gave Howe his opportunity to rationalize the government practice of loaning money to meet deficits. "We are going to give CN a chance as a business to go out and build," he said. "We are going to give it the same chance that any other business firm in Canada has." It did not quite work out that way, however, and his Capital Revision Act of 1937, while eliminating duplication of liabilities and losses on their separate books, was a half measure to revise bookkeeping between government and the railway. It wrote off $900 million in government loans made to cover deficits, forgave unpaid interest, and converted government loans into equity capital worth $270 million and cancelled $247 million of the stocks declared worthless in arbitration proceedings after the Grand Trunk and Canadian Northern were nationalized. However, long-term debt would continue to haunt CN, as we shall see.

As minister of transport, Howe was planning a national airline in addition to his responsibilities for railways, waterways and harbours. Since 1930 CN and the CPR had owned part of James Richardson's Canadian Airways, which Richardson was wrestling into the black after three years of red ink, and in September a committee recommended that it be owned jointly by the government, CN, CPR and private interests, which Richardson fully expected to be part of.

Richardson's suggestion that the government interest be limited to 40 per cent was rejected by the cabinet, which wanted control. "Clearly, an air service will be a competitor with the railways," King wrote in his diary November 26, 1936. "To have left it as a purely private concern means a duplication of all sorts of facilities for connecting with railways, ticket agencies, etc. and also possibly make the railways an even greater liability, as was the case with the truck lines, privately owned, which should have been captured at the very outset by the two transcontinental [rail] systems." Richardson, who had made the first constructive effort to consolidate the small scattered airlines in the country, was squeezed out. The CPR would soon be squeezed out as well.

When Howe declared the government and CN between them must hold more shares than CPR, Beatty argued that the government and its railway were really one and were consigning the CPR to a minor role which he could not accept. Insisting that CN was separate from the government, Howe urged the CPR president to reconsider, but Beatty withdrew from the negotiations, leaving Howe to his vision of a government-controlled airline. "The government has decided," said Howe, "that its agency of transportation, the Canadian National Railways, should be the means of organizing this company, just as it was used as the means for operating such shipping as the government owned, and the means of operating other government transportation facilities." In return for guaranteeing deficits, the government expected the airline to provide service, as CN had done, with little or no profit.

The bill to establish Trans-Canada Air Lines received royal assent on April 10, 1937, with CN as the sole stockholder, responsible for providing, for a fee, such corporate functions as chief executive, secretary, treasurer, public relations, sales, etc. Hungerford became president of TCA as well as CN and brought in his two best directors, Symington and Gagnon, but since CN knew nothing about running an airline, Howe went headhunting in the States and hired the former president of United Airlines and the Boeing Airplane Company, Philip G. Johnson, as vice-president of operations. Johnson was supplied with an office in the CN Express building on McGill Street and a small staff recruited from CN and left to the task of planning the airline's future. The CPR and Richardson's Canadian Airways, left out in the cold, joined forces in what was to become Canadian Pacific Airlines in 1942.

Having failed to become partners in the air, CN and CPR cooperated only slightly better on land. They joined the government in a program to hire 10,000 unemployed to do maintenance on the tracks but made little progress in harmonizing rail operations to save money as required by the 1933 CN-CPR Act. The CPR president continued his unification campaign but, free from the shackles imposed by the trustees, Fairweather was able to trail Beatty around the lecture circuit and confute his arguments. Accounts of CN's liabilities, said Fairweather, had been distorted by "people desiring to give public ownership a black eye." From 1923 until well into the Depression, CN had paid for its operations, as well as municipal taxes totalling more than $6 million a year, and had covered all other items except for interest on invested capital, usually having something left over for that as well. "This view of the Canadian National may be a little startling," Fairweather said, "but it is true."

Beatty argued that the public need worry no longer about the old bogey of railway monopoly because highways and airlines now guaranteed ample competition, but in the clash of ideologies, private versus public ownership, Beatty's call for unification was rejected by both ends of the political spectrum – the unions and the Conservatives. CN autonomy won the day, if for no other reason than that unification would mean politically hazardous layoffs, tearing up tracks and abandoning communities. A Senate committee dodged the unification issue and merely asked the reluctant railways to make an effort to cooperate to reduce costs. Some cooperation was achieved in joint research, and in Vancouver the CPR closed its own hotel so CN could open the controversial hotel across the street, leased to the Hotel Vancouver Company, in which CN and the CPR held equal shares. At Beatty's suggestion, a joint committee of CN and CPR vice-presidents looked into the abandonment of duplicate lines, especially in western Canada, the closing of ticket offices and the sharing of stations, but little progress was made. Rivalry between the two railways was still strong. When the CPR tried to start up a trucking service in the Abitibi region, CN, jealous of its rights, opposed the application on grounds this was CN territory. When Howe wanted CN to be purchasing agent for both railways when the government decided to start buying rolling stock as a wartime measure, Beatty objected and said the government should provide the equipment to the CPR direct.

By the time CN decided that pooling of passenger services should be extended across the country, the CPR responded with a more ambitious plan: a pool of both competitive and non-competitive services – passenger, mail, express, stations and ticket offices. The Joint Cooperative Committee agreed on neither plan, and in the uneasy months before World War II, CN rejected further pooling so as not to interfere with the war effort, though the passenger pools between Quebec City, Montreal, Ottawa and Toronto were continued.

A poor wheat crop in 1937, accompanied by a break in the gradual economic improvement, caused a round of layoffs which was followed by improving conditions in 1938 and the beginnings of federal cyclical budgeting, in which government undertook to spend in bad times and pay off deficits in good.

By 1939 CN had endured four disparate business philosophies. From the careful stewardship of D. B. Hanna it had been swept up in the heady enthusiasm of Sir Henry Thornton and plunged into the penny-pinching receivership of the trustees. Under Howe's guidance and Hungerford's low-profile management, it had made modest progress in the late 1930s and economy was no longer the sole consideration in a country embarking on its great experiment in social responsibility for the health and welfare of its citizens. CN had survived the stress of melding five railways, survived the Great Depression and attacks from politicians, and Sir Edward Beatty, now old and ailing, had given up his campaign to bring CN under the CPR banner. The public ownership of CN was assured.

On the brink of war, Hungerford told Canadians CN could meet the demands of the conflict, and during the next six years it was to prove its value to a degree that Laurier, Borden, Hays or Thornton could not have foreseen. The little-used tracks that had caused so much controversy in peacetime would become essential to Canada's war effort.

8

CN
AT WAR

S THE ONLY MEANS of transporting mountains of materiel and thousands of soldiers over long distances with the speed demanded by war, the railways were as vital as the armed forces. They carried three quarters of the country's long-distance freight, with the waterways accounting for most of the rest. Even without wartime gasoline and rubber shortages, roads were too primitive for trucks to play a significant role outside of towns and cities.

With so much of its 26,000 miles of track running through northern country whose mines must now replace foreign minerals blockaded by war, CN had a surplus of transportation to offer. Whereas in World War I only the CPR had run from sea to sea, now there were two additional transcontinental lines, the former Canadian Northern and Grand Trunk Pacific-Transcontinental routes operated by CN.

No longer the tethered giant of the Depression, CN had an opportunity to achieve its finest hour, though when war was declared in September 1939 the initial call on CN was undramatic, consisting of a quick transfusion into government service of fifty officials to deal with problems new to civil servants. R. C. Vaughan, vice-president of purchasing, supplies and steamships, became chairman of the Defence Purchasing Board, forerunner to C. D. Howe's Department of Munitions and Supply. Starr Fairweather, director of CN's department of research and development, established a research organization in Ottawa as one of Howe's advisers, and Walter Thompson became chairman of Canada's Censorship Board and later Director of Public Information, to be succeeded when his health failed by his deputy at CN, G. Herbert Lash.

Employees of CN's land and survey department were seconded to acquire sites for airfields, army camps, munitions factories and the 100 depots of the Commonwealth Air Training Plan, and the superintendent of reclamation and scrap was drafted to rescue hundreds of thousands of tons of metal for war production. Half a dozen CN people hired by the Dominion Transport Controller, T. C. Lockwood, who had come from a steamship company and knew little of railways, tackled the twin threats of congestion and freight car shortage with a system of permits that ensured cars were used efficiently. "I sometimes wonder how they did it," said Jack Cann, who was then a maintenance engineer working out of Montreal. "On the main line west of Montreal trains stretched for ten miles, caboose to engine, caboose to engine."

Efficiency in terms of average speed and load size had doubled since 1920, but CN needed new equipment. All but 6 per cent of its 2540 locomotives were old and the railway prepared for war by ordering twenty-five Northern-type locomotives, 4765 boxcars, 500 flat cars and 100 refrigerator cars. Before the new equipment arrived, however, CN had its first wartime test.

With America neutral, it was difficult to transport troops to the east coast on CPR tracks because they ran through the state of Maine. Moreover the CPR terminated at Saint John rather than Halifax, departure port for most of the expeditionary army. The army would have to be moved over the all-Canadian routes of CN, and in forty-eight hours in December 1939 the Canadian First Division was brought to Halifax in twenty-five trains and loaded on troopships.

By year's end, with the war four months old, CN traffic had increased by 25 per cent, but only with the fall of France the following spring did Canada's war begin in earnest, symbolized by the National Resources Mobilization Act of June 1940. "The very surplus of transportation that has contributed to our railway problem in peacetime will be our salvation in time of war," said

Howe. Eleven thousand troops were sent to England from Halifax that summer in a closely-timed operation complicated by the incoming tide of mothers and children fleeing the bombing of Britain.

CN trains were also moving $7.5 billion in securities and gold bars brought from the Bank of England to Halifax on warships and liners, met at dockside by George A. Shea, chief of the CN investigation branch, and G. E. Bellerose, head of Canadian National Express, assisted by the Royal Canadian Mounted Police. Four bullion bars to a box and 200 boxes to a car, the gold was piled in sealed and guarded baggage cars timed to arrive in Montreal between midnight and dawn, when streets were empty and easily policed. The bullion went to the Bank of Canada vaults in Ottawa; the securities were deposited in Montreal at Sun Life Assurance. CN Express earned a million dollars for its work.

For an industry dedicated to transporting people and freight, conversion to war footing was relatively straightforward, the main difference being the size, type and urgency of the load, but as a crown corporation CN was expected to assume many burdens. Because of gas rationing, for example, it was called upon to carry traffic that would otherwise have gone on motor vehicles and acceded to a government request to run eight commuter trains a day for 20,000 workers in war plants in central Canada.

When Howe was whisked from the Department of Transport to run Munitions and Supply in 1940, he asked CN's help in building an arms industry and CN shops across the country began to turn out guns and vehicles of war, and one shop, at St. Malo, Quebec, was completely turned over to the government. The long-neglected Prince Rupert Dry Dock and Shipyard, built before World War 1 and the only shipyard in North America operated by a railway, was modernized to construct four minesweepers for the Canadian navy and eleven 10,000-ton freighters.

The liners *Prince Robert*, *Prince David* and *Prince Henry*, which had never been able to fulfil their intended roles on the West Coast, vindicated Thornton's decision to have them so built that they could serve as armed merchant cruisers. They joined the Canadian navy and *Prince Robert's* first success was the capture of a richly laden German merchant ship off the South American coast.

Revenue rose 25 per cent in 1940, cutting the deficit to a third of what it had been in the 1930s, and the tell-tale operating ratio at 81.82 per cent was the best in the history of the system. "The outlook for 1941," said Hungerford's annual report, "is for a further substantial increase in traffic, and the directors are hopeful the property will earn its fixed charges and will not require any appropriation by Parliament on deficit account." Whatever else might be said of war, it was providing the volume of traffic CN needed to pay its way.

The railway had never been confronted with so many challenges at once. Fairweather, back from Ottawa, set his R&D department to increasing the volume of freight carried per train, the fuel efficiency of locomotives and the utilization of rolling stock. Hundreds of ships were steaming into Halifax Harbour to load, and a single ship required 500 to 700 boxcars, or a dozen or more trains. The transformation of Halifax from a backwater to a major port was creating a bottleneck that began at Moncton where two lines converged – the old ICR and the National Transcontinental. East of Moncton, over the narrow Isthmus of Chignecto which connects Nova Scotia with New Brunswick, there was only the CN, most of it single track. Adding to the congestion at its western end was the Prince Edward Island rail ferry traffic, while from eastern Nova Scotia came trains of steel and coal from Pictou county and Cape Breton. Traffic grew so heavy when troop trains came through that freights loaded with cargoes for waiting ships were wasting hours in sidings, otherwise known as "the hole."

CN's initial response was conventional. In the biggest renovation since the Intercolonial Railway was built in the 1870s, the Moncton yard was enlarged to take an additional 2000 rail cars and the Halifax yard to accommodate another 600. Miles of new sidings were built and twenty old ones extended. Fairweather suggested double-tracking, but because it would take too long to install and steel was scarce he turned to a cheaper solution, a signal system known as Centralized Traffic Control (CTC), which in theory was 75 per cent as effective as double tracking. CTC had been used over short distances in the States and in a joint CN-CPR project at Wolfe's Cove, Quebec City, but had never been tried over anything like the 185 miles between Moncton and Halifax that Fairweather had in mind.

Calling the project "too speculative," Hungerford said the bottleneck would probably develop on the Halifax docks, not out on the line. Only after German submarines in the Gulf of St. Lawrence shut down normal shipping, and as many as fifty trains a day were needed on the single line to Halifax, was the CTC system allowed to demonstrate its efficiency. Installing double track would have taken years; CTC was installed in six months in 1941 on the worst bottleneck, 100 miles of hilly and twisting single track between Moncton and Truro, and the great army and air force staging camp at Debert, which housed 24,000 people at a time.

Under the old system, which consisted of "blocks" of up to a mile in length on which only one train was to proceed at a time, signals, train orders and timetables were designed to keep trains a safe distance apart, so that when a superior train ran late, a freight might have to wait in a siding for a long time before it got the message to move. To solve such problems the dispatcher in Moncton, at a CTC console shaped like an eleven-foot U, had a view of illuminated diagrams and an automatic recorder which showed the location of all trains. A key feature of CTC was its light signals – red, yellow and green. Train meetings could be timed so closely that neither might have to stop, giving passenger trains an average saving of an hour and freights two hours or more, and it became common to see twenty trains whistling down the line to Halifax with only two miles between each train. CTC increased safety through interlocked switch signals and worked so well it was put into operation around Montreal, where 170 miles of single track was controlled from a single tower. Stella Wellard, who worked in the Moncton dispatcher's office throughout the war and thirty years after, recalled how CTC revolutionized traffic control from the days of the block system with telegraph operators clicking out train orders. "They never had an accident all the time I was there," she said.

Not that CTC solved everything, for, as Hungerford had predicted, a bottleneck developed on the docks of Halifax, which was handling more overseas traffic than any other port in North America. When freight jammed up around the Ocean Terminals, trains backed up to Truro, and with war plants turning out guns and vehicles to replace the losses at Dunkirk, and export traffic already tripled, the congestion was as serious as Fairweather's solution was imaginative. There was obviously too little room for expansion on the narrow Halifax peninsula, so Fairweather took to the water and found a way to bypass material and manpower shortages at the same time. Recruiting old men who had created Nova Scotia's wooden ships, he built a hundred 400-ton wooden lighters and a lighterage pier with four tracks on Bedford Basin on the approaches to the city. Within six months ships could be loaded without having to tie up at the terminals, and those already docked could be loaded on their off-side as well as the pier-side.

Across the CN network, problems of increasing tonnage and limited facilities were solved in radical ways. Faced with carrying things of outlandish size – tanks, ships' funnels a block long, tugboats – underpasses had to be dismantled and switches removed from trackside. Fuel was a problem. With CN consuming 22,000 tons of coal a day, it was hard to maintain reserves when there were strikes in the U.S. mines. In western Canada, fuel for CN's growing number of oil-burning steam locomotives became such a problem that the railway decided to sink its own wells through its subsidiary Cannar Oils Ltd., which drilled near Vermilion, Alberta. "This experiment wasn't entirely successful," said Walton, "but at least we tried."

Having built from Senneterre, on the old Transcontinental line, to the copper deposits of Rouyn and Noranda in northwestern Quebec, CN pushed more lines into mining country, becoming a partner in extracting the minerals that the world had usually got from other countries – tin, chrome, tungsten, molybdenum and mercury. When Swedish iron ore was cut off by the Nazis, the railway supplied an ore dock and a branch line from Atikokan, Ontario, so the Steep Rock mine could be worked.

But it was in the wilderness of northeastern Quebec in 1941 that CN performed its most demanding service. At Arvida, the Aluminum Company of Canada (Alcan), producer of half the aluminum for Allied aircraft industries, was running short of the essential ingredient, bauxite mined in British Guiana. In peacetime, bauxite had been brought by ship through the Gulf of St. Lawrence and up the Saguenay River to Port Alfred, but Berlin radio was already gloating that Canada's aluminum industry had been put out of action by U-boats which had sunk two dozen ships in the St. Lawrence. To avoid the submarines it was decided to land the ore at Portland, Maine, and bring it by rail on the rickety, 300-mile single track between Montreal and Arvida, built decades earlier by Canadian Northern for the forest industry.

The line was in no condition for heavy traffic, but to keep Alcan producing enough aluminum daily for 200 warplanes, 500 tons of ore along with coal and other supplies were needed every day. Walton gave the job of improving the line to his assistant, Scottish-born Frank Simpson, who brought in crews from the Prairies to supplement French-Canadian crews and had storage yards built so bauxite could be moved up from Maine by stages. Powerful Santa Fe engines were borrowed from other CN divisions, each hauling sixty coal cars, one of which could carry fifty-two tons of raw bauxite at a speed of twenty miles an hour, which was as fast as they could go given the light rails, sharp curves, hills and heavy engines. It took two days to cover the 300 miles.

J. B. Vaillancourt of Chicoutimi, whose duties as a CN telegraph operator had exempted him from military service, recalled life as a young man in one of the lonely outposts every ten miles or so, where his task was mainly to maintain contact between the trains and the dispatchers. "It was just you and the moose out there," he said. "And the bears who stole food from me. I was alone and young, and, walking in the woods, I was scared of every noise at night. The only intelligent sound was from the telegraph. All those little stations have disappeared now."

The first winter was terrible. Between Christmas and New Year's Day blizzards filled the cuts and the snow froze hard. Word came down the line from Arvida that bauxite reserves were so low the pot rooms would have to shut down, stopping the flow of aluminum to plants building Spitfires, Liberators and Flying Fortresses. It took a week to get the first ore train into Arvida behind a vanguard of snowplows, and though the ore was frozen solid it arrived in time to keep the pot rooms open.

In the spring there were new woes. The overloaded roadbed began to collapse at a dozen places and a Santa Fe went off the track, closing the line for a week. Ten trains were backed up for days while engineers shored up a trestle threatened by the spring freshets and four trainmen were killed when two ore trains collided. Passenger services had to be suspended to keep eighteen ore trains moving every day on what the transport controller described as the "most congested line in Canada." In two years CN hauled 60,000 cars of bauxite, earning a profit of $4 million.

Though railroaders could claim exemption from active service, there were now enough CN people in the navy to man six destroyers had they all been kept together, or to form five army battalions or ten air force squadrons. Ken Leathem of Ottawa, who went to work as a locomotive fireman in July 1941 after release from the army because of an injury, said CN was so short of men that he wrote his application at 3 p.m. and was working his first shift at midnight. Priority traffic put his freight in the sidings so often he would start work at 7:45 a.m. and not get to his destination until well after midnight.

"The thing I remember," said Leathem, "was the sense of what a job everyone had to do. We had to move an enormous amount of material. We had to get that stuff down to the ocean ports and into boats and get it to hell over to England and France or wherever if we were going to win the war. If you had to work a couple of hours longer you didn't bitch about it. When you consider the amount of traffic we had, there were very few problems. I suppose there were a lot of times when we worked sixteen-hour days, maybe more, but then you'd just go and clean up, get some food into you, and then go to sleep until you got back up and got at it again."

His friend Frank Lapointe said the rolling stock was old: "They'd brought out a lot of stuff that had been stored for years. Some of the engines were antiques. Breakdowns were pretty frequent, but we tried to do the best we could. It was real busy. The freight trains were running, the passenger trains were running, the troop trains were running. Freight and passenger cars were coming all the time from the west. Everything was crowded." As a result of this great increase in traffic and the loss of trained staff into the armed forces, work-related fatalities tripled midway through the war from about fifty per year to 150.

"Rail technology was not as good as it is today," recalled Jack Cann. "There were serious derailments due to small things like one wheel getting off the track and tripping everything else up." The worst accident of the war occurred on CPR lines on December 27, 1942, when a troop train plowed into the rear of a passenger train at Almonte, Ontario, killing thirty-six and injuring 200 people. Almost miraculously, given the tremendous amount of traffic, there were no comparable accidents on the CN system during the war.

Douglas V. Gonder, later a vice-president but then a young locomotive foreman in charge of CN's biggest roundhouse, at Turcot, Montreal, had 450 machinists, boilermakers and others working at thirty pits. He remembered a confidential letter warning of sabotage and holding foremen personally responsible for the locomotives under their care. "We had to watch everything. For instance, a bar of soap thrown into a tender full of water would make the engine foam and cause breakdowns on the road. But we had little sabotage. Some agents came ashore on the Gaspé from German submarines, including one fellow who had plans to blow up the bridge at Matapedia, which would have knocked out trains to Halifax, but they were discovered. At Turcot we had quite a few Italian boys and all of a sudden I lost several of my best men. They just didn't show up. They had been incarcerated for the duration because someone questioned their loyalty.'"

On July 23, 1941, the sixty-nine-year-old Hungerford retired as president, having worked on the railways for fifty-five years. The demands of war required a younger man and R.C. Vaughan was brought back from Ottawa. To emphasize that he, and not Hungerford, was running things, he was the first to call himself chief executive officer as well as president. Within fourteen months Hungerford stepped down as chairman and Vaughan assumed both titles. Since TCA now needed a full-time president, Howe persuaded Symington, the CN director, to take the job.

Though Hungerford had headed one of the world's biggest railways, his retirement went largely unnoticed by the press. "Hungerford," quipped a Toronto colleague "is the best known Unknown Man in Canada." He was a railroader's railroader with a modest explanation for his rise from machinist's helper. "I never refused a job in my life," he said. "I just tackled everything that came along." Like many long in power, he found it difficult to leave and stayed on at McGill Street as chairman of the CN subsidiary National Railways Munitions Ltd., which built naval guns at a new factory employing 1350 people, many of them women, at Point St. Charles. Hungerford occupied an office adjoining the CN boardroom until the end of the war. "Eventually, like old soldiers," said Metcalf, "Mr. Hungerford just faded away without so much as a farewell dinner in his honour."

At the age of fifty-seven Vaughan emerged from two decades of obscurity into one of the biggest jobs in the country. Lacking Hungerford's operating experience, he wisely appointed Norman Walton, vice-president of operations, maintenance and construction, to be his executive vice-president. That he lacked the salesmanship and charisma of Thornton made little difference in wartime, for there was more than enough business for all and CN's duty was simply to help win the war.

Vaughan had come up through the ranks in typical railroad fashion, starting as a teen-aged messenger in Toronto, working his way through business college and rising from clerk and stenographer until at the age of twenty he was secretary to Hanna of Canadian Northern. The railway tradition of male secretaries provided an entrée to the top as nothing else did, and Vaughan became executive assistant to the Canadian Northern general manager at the age of twenty-six and vice-president of purchasing and stores, first at Canadian Northern and then at CN.

No vice-president had appeared at board meetings as often as Vaughan, whether to describe a $20 million order for rolling stock or to boast of saving $300 on a $42,000 order of envelopes. As vice-president his job was to buy the right material, anything from pins to steel bridges, at the right price at the right time, and almost all CN purchases were conducted through his department, where he was known as Honest John, a loyal if unimaginative company man. "He was not lavish with praise, and somehow seemed to leave the impression that he could have done better himself," said an assistant. "His subordinates came to recognize a whine in the tone of his voice as a sign of dissatisfaction." No one knew more about railway coal and no industry consumed more; he bought one out of every five tons produced in Canada and ran the Rail and River Coal Mine in Ohio, inherited from the Grand Trunk.

In 1941 CN moved the largest tonnage in its history, 20 per cent more than in 1928, the previous peak year. Passenger traffic had doubled and the *Ocean Limited* was leaving Montreal for Halifax with seven sections. Locomotives had to be kept going with a minimum of cleaning and repair and No. 6028, a Mountain, set a wartime record by running 18,353 miles in one month, averaging 592 miles a day hauling the *Continental Limited* across Ontario despite poor-grade coal, fewer mechanics and maintenance personnel, and bigger trains.

"It has been a matter of pride to railwaymen," said Vaughan, "that in the first two years of the war they have carried the troops, the munitions, the supplies, and the products of farm and factory along with vast quantities of material for construction, without a tie-up of any kind due to shortage of facilities, to labour disagreements or to any other cause." Within weeks of his speech, Japan's attack on the United States would stretch CN resources to the West Coast as well as the east.

With the Japanese invasion of the Aleutians in 1942 threatening Alaska and British Columbia, CN undertook the task of building a 2000-mile military communications network through the wilderness to communities that had neither telegraph nor voice contact with the rest of British Columbia. From Vancouver to Prince Rupert the lines passed over rivers and canyons and through a 500-mile wilderness where there were no settlements at all. The work was dangerous, there were drownings and one man lost his life when a ledge crumbled above the Thompson River. Having recruited a thousand men to cut and plant 24,000 poles and string thousands of miles of wire, CN then trained people to operate the system for the army's Pacific Command.

In the same region, Prince Rupert had thrown off its peacetime slumber when CN began building ships at Prince Rupert Dry Dock and Shipyard. Now it got another windfall when the American army, which had originally planned to ship 75,000 troops 1000 miles to Alaska by sea from Seattle, discovered it could send them faster overland via CN and Prince Rupert, which cut a third off the journey. The war tripled Prince Rupert's population to 20,000 and made it the thriving town Charlie Hays had in mind when he created it. Docks, warehouses, an air base and barracks housing 3500 U.S. soldiers sprang up, and four daily troop trains and countless freights from Chicago and Seattle kept the rails burnished. To protect the line from attack, CN fashioned an armoured train hauled by No. 9000, one of the two pioneer diesel locomotives it had built in 1928. Hung with steel plating, it was kept in readiness at a secret base to dash into battle with three steel boxcars and four flat cars carrying guns, searchlights and soldiers. Since No. 9000 did not function well in warpaint, fortunately it was never needed.

At the same time the American army was building the 1671-mile Alaska Highway between Fairbanks and Dawson Creek, British Columbia, north-west terminus of Northern Alberta Railways. Early in 1942 this Peace River farming community 500 miles northwest of Edmonton was transformed into a base camp, and instead of a few trains a week, eight or nine a day arrived with soldiers, construction workers, food, portable toilets, earth-moving machines and knock-down houses. Barracks, dormitories, office buildings, hospitals and huts sprang up along mudpacked streets and wooden sidewalks, and the population increased from 800 to more than 5000.

Built to haul farmers and wheat, the NAR with its second-hand sixty-pound rail, poor ballast and drainage was ill-equipped. Heavier rail had to be laid and engines borrowed from the NAR's owners, CN and the CPR, to triple the size of the fleet to forty, but even then there were traffic jams as far south as Edmonton. Nor was this the sole burden on the Northern Alberta Railways. Two months after Dawson Creek became a construction camp for the Alaska Highway, work began on a pipeline to carry oil to Alaska from Norman Wells in the Northwest Territories, and the town of Waterways, near Fort McMurray, the Mackenzie River terminal of the NAR northeastern line, became the railhead. Day after day trains rolled into Waterways with steel pipe, food and a total of 2200 American soldiers. All these activities in northwestern Canada brought CN an unexpected one million tons of traffic.

Traversing farming lands, the northern forests and the mineral deposits of the Canadian Shield, and serving virtually every manufacturing centre and port, CN had become Canada's biggest war industry. "Just a few years ago there was a feeling in some quarters that the railroads were back numbers, rapidly being superseded by road transport," said the *Ottawa Journal.* "This we know now was a misreading of the times." "Every Canadian," said the *Winnipeg Tribune,* "has reason to be grateful for the foresight of railway executives and the loyalty of railway employees who through the years of depression insisted on a high standard of maintenance when the temptation was to let the systems run down."

Wartime CN-CPR cooperation suffered a lapse in 1941 when the public railway complained that its privately-owned rival was receiving a disproportionate share of public business in eastern Canada, where CN's track mileage was two thirds larger. Alistair Fraser, the Nova Scotia-born former CN lawyer, who was now vice-president of marketing, or "traffic" as it was called, raised the matter in 1941, assisted by a handful of pro-CN MPs, but they received little support. Hungerford, with his dislike of controversy, refused to have anything to do with the issue and when Vaughan, who was more tenacious, raised it again in 1942 when he took over, the new minister of transport, P. J. Cardin, more or less told CN to fight its own battles and C.D. Howe reminded Vaughan that the war was too serious to worry about competition. At all events both railways had all the freight they could handle and were carrying hundreds of thousands of men and women of the armed forces to camps or seaports. Ten hospital cars were adapted from sleeping cars at Point St. Charles, hospital cots replacing the lower berths. Mobile jails were built to transport prisoners of war to camps in northern Canada. A mess-hall-on-wheels was devised with seating for fifty-four people rather than the normal thirty-six. Locomotives dating from the Boer War were rebuilt so well they were able to haul heavier loads at faster speeds than dreamed of by their original designers. Gondola cars, cabooses, passenger cars and 5000 boxcars were rebuilt, and to make up for a shortage of passenger coaches, old ones were remodelled to seat 120 people rather than the usual seventy-two.

The R&D department squeezed more use out of every piece of equipment, and the serviceability of freight locomotives – the percentage of total hours they were available for use – was increased by 15 per cent. CN's 2500 locomotives steamed a record 90 million miles in 1942, many of them averaging 375 miles a day. To stretch CN's 90,000 boxcars further, the government removed restrictions so that the weight of the average load could be increased by 35 per cent.

Two thirds of Canada's war production was going overseas – guns, ammunition, tanks, aircraft, ships and thousands of new vehicles, which were stockpiled in a dozen depots until convoys became available on the East Coast. With the Panama Canal closed by U-boat activity, B.C. timber that formerly came east by ship was carried by rail 3000 miles across the little-used northern routes. More than 2500 flat cars were marshalled to carry the wood, and since much of it was destined for England, the railways bettered by two thirds the time a ship would have taken from Vancouver.

In 1942 traffic exceeded the 1928 record by 50 per cent, and because of greater efficiency achieved it with reduced staff and 25 per cent fewer freight cars. CN had brought the operating ratio down 17.3 points since 1923, compared with the CPR's 9.4 point reduction, though of course CN had more slack to pull in. CN's operating ratio of 77 per cent was the lowest in history.

Every minute of every day, seven days a week, CN was moving an average of 138 tons of freight – 72 million tons in 1942 compared with 54 million moved by the CPR. Where one passenger travelled in 1939, three were going by train in 1942. The *International Limited* from Montreal to Toronto and Chicago often ran six sections, and on the eve of a holiday weekend CN might take 5000 jostling passengers out of Toronto Union Station in half an hour.

To avoid congestion and spread traffic over the week, the federal transport controller eliminated special weekend and holiday fares that had originally been introduced to stimulate traffic. Donald Gordon, chairman of the Wartime Prices and Trade Board, objected that this was not only inflationary but favoured the railways at the expense of the citizen, but the special fares were eliminated anyway, reducing weekend civilian travel without cutting the overall revenue that Vaughan was intent on preserving. Vaughan was anxious to make the most of these high-revenue years. "I would like to see one big year of net earnings," he said, "so that if unification should ever be discussed again we would have a figure to be used as indicating the potential value of Canadian National Railways and its ability to produce net earnings provided it can obtain the necessary gross earnings."

Under the stimulus of war, CN's earnings demonstrated what the railway could do. Deficit had been replaced by surplus and the railway was now paying off government debt as well as interest to public investors. The debt was further reduced when Canada, in exchange for munitions and supplies to Britain, was able to secure a large proportion of Grand Trunk preference stocks and bonds held by investors in the U.K., clearing the way for another CN recapitalization after the war. "Before the war our excessive railway mileage was a matter of concern," Howe told the Commercial Travellers Association in Montreal. "That mileage has proved to be no longer excessive. Our new productive capacity makes it unlikely that railroads will ever again be spoken of as a problem."

In July 1943 the controversial terminal in downtown Montreal, under fitful construction for fifteen years, was finally opened to replace the Bonaventure Station a few blocks away, which became a reception depot for men and women home from the war. In its first year 35,040 trains and 6.5 million passengers passed through Central Station, a squat, rectangular, utilitarian-looking building with none of the grandeur of Union Station in Toronto. Billed as "one of the most modern station buildings in the world," it had an innovative women's centre, "a peaceful haven where women passengers may rest and be comfortable," and twenty-one large bas-reliefs in the concourse executed by Charles Comfort to depict Canadian life, industry, recreation and culture. At the opening ceremonies, broadcast across Canada by the CBC, Vaughan promised that the rest of the multi-acre site, the choicest real estate in downtown Montreal, would sprout a hotel and office buildings after the war. Turcot Yards in west Montreal, too small for freights that ran to as many as 100 cars, would be enlarged and a branch constructed through the northern reaches of Montreal to the east end to eliminate a detour around the city of over 100 miles resulting from the three-mile gap along the waterfront inherited from predecessor companies.

At sea the CN vessels that had been sailing as armed cruisers were converted into specialist ships for the invasion of Europe. The *Prince David* and *Prince Henry* became mother ships for twenty-ton landing craft and did service off the Normandy beaches on D-day and in the Mediterranean. *Prince Robert* became an anti-aircraft cruiser on convoy duty. They were sold at the end of the war and never returned to CN service. The Lady boats of the Caribbean had a sadder war, and the *Lady Rodney*, which became a troop transport, was the only one to escape harm. *Lady Somers* had been in naval service only ten months when she was sunk by enemy action in the Bay of Biscay in the summer of 1941, all her complement being saved. *Lady Hawkins* was on civilian service when she was torpedoed off Cape Hatteras in January 1942 with the loss of all but seventy of her 300 passengers and crew. *Lady Drake* was torpedoed in May 1942 with the loss of twelve people south of Bermuda. In December 1944. *Lady Nelson* was torpedoed at St. Lucia and lost seventeen passengers and crew, but she was repaired and converted to a hospital ship.

"I was on one of the hospital trains," recalled conductor Mel Humble of Sarnia, Ontario. "Soldiers coming home from the war with no legs or arms, all shot up. One train was bringing back the dead from overseas … twelve cars, all black with no windows, filled with caskets."

By 1943 14,000 employees were in the army, navy and air force, 500 of them in the army's Railway Operating Group, which helped run the bomb-battered railways of England and landed in France after D-day to repair rolling stock, switches and communications, sometimes under enemy fire. "We used to work an average of about eighty hours a week," said Earl Harrison of Burlington, Ontario, a fireman and the son of a CN stationmaster. At Bruges in Belgium Canadians rebuilt 1000 railway cars a month to get the Belgian railway running.

At home, men were kept on after retirement age, but even so 2500 more workers were needed. When an attempt to recruit men from Newfoundland failed, CN turned to women to fill jobs traditionally occupied by men. A few became ticket agents, others worked in dining cars as chefs and waitresses, and telegraph boys were replaced by "messengerettes," uniformed girls between sixteen and nineteen who were allowed to work only in daylight hours and safe parts of town. Whereas women had been 15 per cent of the telegraph department before the war, they now exceeded 30 per cent, but the biggest change was the hiring of 460 women as turret lathe operators, welders, crane operators, blacksmith's helpers, oilers and labourers. Sally Amero, who weighed 127 pounds and was five feet tall, went to work in the St. Henri freight shed in Montreal pushing heavy equipment. Phyllis Lee of Saint John left a stenographer's typewriter to become a freight porter, earning better pay than she could make in the office.

Before the war women had been employed as stenographers, clerks or telegraphers and only eighteen women worked in non-office jobs, all but one as coach cleaners in Montreal, Halifax and Detroit, the eighteenth being Annabelle Cooper of the Grand Trunk Western in Battle Creek, Michigan, who was the railway's first woman crane operator. "I don't know what we would have done if the women had not come to our rescue," said vice-president Walton. In 1944 there were 903 women working in blue-collar jobs at CN and its subsidiaries, though they still were not employed in the elite running trades, the people who actually operated the trains. At Stratford, Ontario, Mrs. L. Gould was the only woman blacksmith in Canada; the other women at CN there ranged in age from eighteen to fifty and included thirty-four labourers, thirteen machinist's helpers, five painter's assistants, two plumber's assistants, two electrician's assistants and one sheet metal worker. "You felt you were part of something important," recalled Stella Wellard of her days in the dispatcher's office in wartime Moncton. "It made you feel you were working for a big system, coast to coast, and not just a little corner drug store. If anyone asked 'Where do you work?' I'd say with a kind of pride, 'I'm with CN.'" Most women left the railway when men came back from war, but Alice Gordon at Sarnia liked being a labourer, or "yard man," so much that she stayed until mandatory retirement at sixty-five, though she felt she had to outwork the men. "I was shovelling coal one time in the middle of a bad snowstorm and there were these men in the roundhouse waiting for me to give up and call it quits. By the time I was through shovelling I was black from head to foot and almost on my hands and knees, but I was bound I would finish the job before I'd let those old fogies see me give up."

Coal was crucial. CN burned millions of tons a year and no major town was without its glistening black pile, prey to spontaneous combustion. Though Nova Scotia production had increased 20 per cent, consumption had doubled and distribution became such a problem that in 1943 Quebec and the Maritimes suffered a coal crisis which the transport controller called "the worst we've ever experienced." CN hauled coal to New Brunswick from as far away as Indiana, but even so half a dozen train services had to be cancelled. Part of the problem was the German submarines that had frightened colliers out of the Gulf of St. Lawrence, leaving such inadequate alternatives as two small rail ferries plying between Cape Breton and mainland Nova Scotia. Seeking a solution, Fairweather discovered a safer route through the Bras d'Or Lakes, Strait of Canso and Northumberland Strait to Shediac, the fishing port near Moncton. Large ships were scarce but shallow-draft vessels were available. "It was fun improvising," Fairweather said. "I learned that idle pulpwood handling gear was available from a bankrupt pulp and paper plant. A bit of ingenuity could modify the grabs to clam shells suitable for handling coal." Within a few months the coal crisis was over.

Traffic jams were not solved so readily. "Our terminals, passing tracks and sidings are full of cars containing essential materials," the transport controller wrote in the hard winter of 1943, explaining the decision to curtail passenger services, "and the railroads are experiencing tremendous difficulty in being able to move them to destination, with the result that in some sections of the country we are unable to deliver full supplies to essential war plants. We have a heavy accumulation of freight at the head of the lakes going eastbound, and a large accumulation of freight at all essential terminals in Ontario."

Nevertheless, 1943 was CN's most profitable year to date. "Few Canadians realize," said the *Ottawa Journal*, "that Canadian National Railways, once called Canada's White Elephant, is today Canada's biggest business, earning more gross revenue, employing more workers (over 100,000) and paying out more in wages than any other Dominion enterprise, public or private. From being what pessimists a few years ago denounced as a 'threat of bankruptcy' the National has become a going concern, with operating and earning achievements little short of colossal, and financially as solid as Gibraltar." Said the *Vancouver Sun*, "The very excellent thing in the whole situation is that intrinsically the CN was so sound that it was able to respond to the added demands of the troubled times in a way that makes us all feel proud of it." The *Winnipeg Free Press* denounced those who would have sold CN to the CPR, though Sir Edward Beatty was dead and his successors would not resume his crusade. "How inadequate are seen to be the repeated efforts by interested parties to effect amalgamation. What poor service was rendered to Canada by the attempts to sabotage the CNR," said the *Free Press*.

By 1944 CN's war effort had reached its peak, with 102,000 employed in railway and telegraph service plus another 5000 in the hotels and other subsidiary companies. The railway was carrying twice as much freight and four times as many passengers as in 1939 and freeing itself from dependency on the public purse. "In each year since 1941," said Vaughan, "owing to the large volume of business available, we have been able to pay all interest charges, including interest on government loans. In addition we have handed to the government in cash nearly ninety million dollars, after setting aside substantial reserves for deferred maintenance of roadway and equipment, etc."

Canadian consumption of goods and services had risen by 40 per cent in five years; manufacturing production doubled, imports doubled, exports quadrupled. These conditions had allowed CN, for the first time, to overtake the CPR in traffic density. Given an equal amount of traffic per mile the public railway showed it could equal or better the private railway, but freight rates and passenger fares remained frozen, and even before wartime controls were lifted increased costs were beginning to reduce the surpluses CN had been making since 1941. A cost-of-living bonus was followed by increases in monthly and hourly wage rates. Coal prices doubled. The purchasing department was paying so much for supplies that the company ran a campaign to acquaint employees with how much things cost in relation to CN's earning capacity. It said 485 tons of freight had to be hauled one mile before CN made enough margin to buy one ton of coal.

No passenger equipment had been built since early in the war and the long-suffering public, which had been patriotically docile, began to complain about CN-CPR pool trains between Ottawa and Toronto, where traffic had increased 300 per cent. "I have come into some of these cars when the air was so heavy and filthy you could cut it with a knife," wrote an MP for Toronto. "It was not fit for human existence. If the same type of accommodation was supplied to animals, a prosecution for cruelty would be in order." Vaughan said the offending coaches must belong to CPR, but did pull in twenty air-conditioned coaches from elsewhere to placate the angry MP.

CN's 97,542 freight cars and 2560 locomotives were too few for the work to be done. So much grain was awaiting shipment that community halls and rinks on the Prairies had to be turned into makeshift storage depots. "We are short of passenger cars, locomotives, boxcars, flat cars, gondolas and experienced men to keep the railways operating," said transport controller Lockwood on March 20, 1944.

The shortage of locomotives and freight cars began to ease only late in 1944 when CN took delivery of another seven Northern-type engines, 4762 boxcars and 1500 freight cars of other types, such as flat cars, hopper cars and gondolas. It also took delivery of engine 6060, the first of twenty semi-streamlined Mountain types called Bullet Nosed Bettys because of their conical snouts. They were painted in olive-green CN livery and assigned to such prestige runs as the *Continental Limited* and the *International Limited*, and one of them, No. 6078, set a record from Toronto to Sarnia of two hours and fifty-eight minutes with an average speed, including water stops, of 58.7 miles an hour.

Railways everywhere cite large and indigestible figures to explain and justify their existence, and in the business of mass transportation there is perhaps no better way. Thus a few months before the war ended CN distributed a pamphlet, *Five Years of War,* full of statistics that took some imagination to comprehend. Since September 1939 the People's Railway had carried 132 million passengers, equal to ten times the population of the country, of whom 4,381,000 were armed forces personnel who required 116,940 coaches in 6540 special trains. Three million people had kept CN's twelve hotels overbooked, and the telegraph division had stayed open around the clock tapping out 55 million messages. The figures rolled on ... 36 million tons of coal burned ... 50 million tons of grain carried ... an increase of 133 per cent in the movement of manufactured goods.

Since the first war bride special left Halifax in April 1943, many thousands of women and children had been brought to their new homes. The biggest task remaining was to bring the troops home, and in 1945 CN transported 208,000 men and women on 600 special trains, in addition to sections added to regular services. One ship alone, the *Queen Elizabeth,* required sixteen trains, dispatched to Montreal at the rate of one an hour and equipped with telephones so people could call relatives. The *Lady Nelson,* the senior hospital ship, made twenty-five crossings with 13,000 wounded and sick who were brought home in 125 hospital trains.

Overall, CN had carried twice as much freight and four times as many passengers as it did in peacetime. A quarter of the pre-war CN work force had joined the armed forces, and of the 21,165 who enlisted, 842 lost their lives and 100 were decorated for gallantry. "The railways have been the backbone of this country's war effort," said the minister of transport, Lionel Chevrier. "In pre-war days there was considerable loose talk to the effect that our railways had been overbuilt ... were ruining the country. May I state here that our railways were the means of saving our country. They made possible our industrial war production." In ordinary times a Liberal minister making such a statement would have heard rebuttal from the opposition. Because of the war, CN was enjoying an unusual respite from politics.

9

THE PERILS OF
PEACETIME

FEARING UNEMPLOYMENT MORE THAN INFLATION, the government dropped price and wage controls in 1946 and encouraged demand for consumer goods and new homes. Instead of sliding into recession as after World War I, the economy soared into five years of prosperity and at first it seemed the railways would prosper too. Certainly they were moving more freight, but there had been no increase in general freight rates for twenty-eight years, inflation was cutting into the value of assets and reserves the war had built up, and a railway's complexity and size made it impossible to reduce expenses fast enough to counter inflation. Canadians were shipping more goods but more of it by truck; people were travelling by car. As a result CN and the CPR suffered a decline in revenue, with the latter's earnings on rail operations the lowest in decades and CN sliding back toward the dreary deficits of the 1930s.

The lack of a comprehensive national transportation policy was never more apparent. "We face new problems," president Vaughan told a parliamentary committee. "Traffic receipts are falling off, operating costs are increasing, and our big problem is how to meet our heavy fixed charges." Despite efforts to reduce debt interest during the war, it was twice as high as the CPR's.

Rolling stock, tracks and buildings had been worn and battered in fifteen years of Depression and war. Boxcars, flat cars and tank cars had to be replaced and special cars purchased for hauling the automobiles people were buying with their fatter incomes. The physical plant was run down – the shops at Point St. Charles, the freight sheds in Edmonton, the yards in Vancouver and countless stations had not seen paint for years. The handsome Grand Trunk headquarters on McGill Street could no longer hold all head office employees, who were dispersed around Montreal in a score of rented buildings or in noisy offices under the viaduct carrying the tracks out of Central Station. As CN's biggest terminal, serving the mineral, timber and industrial developments of the north and connections with the United States, Turcot yard, which had been extended twenty years before, was now inadequate.

The time had come to convert to the more efficient diesel locomotives, for while American lines had been doing so for years, Canada remained in the steam age. Having introduced main line diesels in 1928, CN had lost the initiative to the States, which nine years later produced the Burlington Zephyr, the first streamlined diesel in regular service, and by the end of the war there were 3000 road diesels in service in the United States, specializing in long western hauls. Under the direction of executive vice-president N. B. Walton, the first two units of a fleet of eighteen 650-hp diesel locomotives had arrived in Prince Edward Island in 1948 to begin the complete dieselization of that province's lines. Otherwise, apart from a hundred small yard diesels, CN had only eight road diesels for experimental mainline hauls in Quebec and Ontario.

Neither CN nor CPR had a strategy for country-wide dieselization and Vaughan worried about the capital expense. Steam engines should not be scrapped too quickly, he argued, and Fairweather agreed that the potential of steam had never been fully exploited, combustion being so poor that too much fuel was wasted. The technology had not changed for a century, apart from such innovations as superheated steam. "I believed that if engineering research had been directed to radical changes in the steam locomotive it would not have become obsolete," said Fairweather. "Efficiency had been overridden by rough and ready simplicity." His R&D department tried to increase thermal efficiency to equal the diesel locomotive, but the savings proved disappointing and Fairweather decided that diesels were the answer.

"I convinced Vaughan to make the change," said Fairweather. "I chose Prince Edward Island for demonstration purposes partly because it was an isolated area and partly because smaller locomotives would meet operation needs." The steam engines on the island were so old they would have to be replaced anyway, and diesels would ensure long-term savings because of the high cost of importing coal. Fairweather claimed to have inspired CPR to dieselize by regions, and if so he may have regretted it. While CN dieselization in P.E.I. was bogged down for two years because the new diesels were defective, CPR's subsidiary on Vancouver Island, the Esquimalt and Nanaimo Railway, became the first region in Canada completely dieselized.

CN having made money during the war, Vaughan believed money could be made in peacetime as well and led a campaign by the Railway Association of Canada, the industry's lobby and research group, to win freight rate increases on coal and grain. "I am trying to put the Canadian National Railways on a sound basis," he said. "We want to show a satisfactory financial statement and we do not want to feel we are a burden on the government."

Talk of amalgamating the two great railway systems of Canada was seldom heard any more, except in the Telegraph Department, where it made practical sense in many towns where the offices of CPR and CN could be seen in the same block. Canada was unique in having two large competing telegraph services. Though they were slow to merge their telegraph services entirely, they began the process in 1947 by uniting sales efforts against competing telephone companies such as Bell Canada. The first step was to pool new business obtained in leasing private lines – about 20 per cent of all business – while still competing for public telegraph messages.

Cooperation between CN and CPR on pooled trains on the Ottawa-Toronto and Montreal-Toronto routes was good for both railways, but CPR was capturing the lion's share of transcontinental traffic, leaving CN with a top-heavy proportion of people travelling short or medium distances, precisely the traffic most vulnerable to automobile and bus competition. Vaughan was concerned at the 30 per cent drop in passenger revenue since the war, and though CN was transporting 20 million travellers a year, they earned the railway less than ten cents in a dollar compared with seventy-five cents in the dollar earned by freight.

TCA was carrying 300,000 passengers a year who might otherwise have travelled by rail, and Vaughan admitted that CN would have no more chance against airline travel than 19th-century stage coach proprietors had of blocking the railway. Besides, TCA was family, though by 1948 Howe had begun to break the symbiotic ties by appointing Gordon R. McGregor, the airline's former general traffic manager, when Symington retired as president.

CN could and did challenge the highway transport industry, which in 1946 siphoned off $40 million in revenues that might have gone to CN. Federal and provincial subsidies were building so many highways that Vaughan urged the government to regulate trucks as it regulated railways, which under the Railway Act and Transport Act, administered by the Board of Transport Commissioners, were controlled right down to weeds on the right-of-way, whereas trucks, which came under provincial jurisdiction, were hardly regulated at all except for size and weight.

While a double-track railway and a three-lane highway cost the same to build, the railway could carry eight times as much traffic at less cost. Except on short hauls, highway transport was three to five times more expensive, and railways continued to dominate long-distance traffic in grain, steel, wood, coal and other such bulk. Coal brought in three or four times more revenue than grain under the low Crow rate, but grain, which accounted for almost 50 per cent of freight out of the West every year, was also the railway's greatest test when it was called on to make 20,000 boxcars available for the annual harvest, almost a quarter of its whole fleet. Since 50 per cent of the fleet was over thirty years of age and 15,000 cars might at any time be in the U.S. and 7 per cent out of service for repairs, CN put in an order for 5100 new freight cars, including 4200 boxcars with a capacity of 50 tons, 25 per cent greater than those in use.

The postwar export business was brisk, Canada being one of the few countries capable of trade, and though the silk market was gone, a victim of synthetics, efforts were made to restore business with the Orient. In 1946 CN reopened in Hong Kong and established an office in Calcutta, though these shut down again due to unsettled conditions, and CN did not regain a firm grip on Far East trade for another twelve years.

The United Nations Relief and Rehabilitation Agency (UNRRA) became one of CN's biggest customers. The London staff was restored to pre-war level, and from Cockspur Street the European general manager directed activities in Liverpool, Glasgow, Antwerp and Copenhagen which embraced freight, express, passenger service, industrial development and public relations. In Paris, CN was back in its rue Scribe building, which had been occupied by the Gestapo, the Luftwaffe and finally by the Allied press corps, though CN's representative, A. L. Regamay, a Swiss, had somehow managed to collect rent throughout it all. Hôtel Scribe was still operated by Société des Hôtels Réunis under the forty-year lease which, as CN secretary W. H. Hobbs said with considerable understatement, had a "somewhat troubled history." The lease had usually produced some profit, though there was often trouble getting the money out of the country, and Vaughan declared that CN had no business owning property in France and decided to sell, only to change his mind when Hôtels Réunis agreed to a higher rent. "We undoubtedly have a very valuable piece of real estate in one of the best locations in the world," he said.

Some 100,000 immigrants arrived in Canada every year, and the railway resumed its pre-war policy of settling them. Roy Liddiard of CN in London attended evening meetings throughout southern England to interest people in going to Canada. "We had an arrangement with the Cunard Line in competition with CP ships and there was great competitiveness between CN and CPR," Liddiard said. "We were fighting each other to get emigrants on our railways at Halifax, Saint John, Quebec City, Montreal and points west." Overseas freight revenue tripled between 1946 and 1949 and CN Express, which was separate from the freight department, had arrangements with steamship companies to set aside space so goods could be loaded onto trains at Halifax or Montreal an hour or so after arrival. Competition with the CPR was intense.

Apart from trying to winkle higher rates out of the government, there was little the railway could do about either inflation or the largest item of expense, the cost of labour, which was half CN's total outlay. Railroaders wanted their share of the new national prosperity. During the Depression a person was lucky to have a job, and during the war the government had kept the lid on, but in 1946 the Brotherhood of Railway Employees (CBRE) demanded an across-the-board increase of thirty-five cents an hour. The threat of the first national rail strike in Canadian history began to emerge when the union refused to drop below twenty-two cents and conciliation failed, and though the government gave them only half of what they asked for, Vaughan grumbled that the government had driven his wage bill up by 7 per cent and took the occasion, along with the CPR, to demand a rate increase, the first in twenty-eight years, starting the postwar seesaw of wage and rate demands.

The U.S. had boosted its freight rates but this was such a sensitive issue in the West and the Maritimes that the Liberal government hesitated to follow suit. Denounced as greedy and discriminatory to the West and the Maritimes, the railways' application became bogged down in public hearings and regional politics. By the time, a year and a half later, the Board of Transport Commissioners approved an increase – 21 per cent rather than the 30 per cent asked – inflation had wiped out much of the gain. "The railway industry," said Vaughan, "is still hobbled by the economic skirts designed a quarter century ago, while most other industries have been liberated from such controls." The delay in approving increased rates began a time lag of a year or so every time the railways tried to get an increase, which caused considerable difficulty in revenues and costs.

Though carrying almost as much freight as during the war, CN needed the higher rates, for in 1948 it had a $33 million deficit, a mirror image of the $35 million wartime surplus five years earlier. Part of the deficit was due to spring floods in British Columbia that had cut service to the coast for a month, and to a $2 million fire that destroyed the Bonaventure freight sheds in Montreal, but the main reason was inflation. "We are caught in the toughest kind of squeeze play," said Vaughan. "Our selling prices are frozen but our production costs are mounting in ominous fashion." New equipment was dear, a diesel locomotive costing as much as seven steam locomotives.

CN was now grossing more than in any other peacetime year, but expenses had climbed 75 per cent in a decade and deficits were the worst since the Depression. Nor did the postwar increase of north-south trade with the U.S. make it easier to run a 26,000-mile railway from coast to coast. Unable to cover interest on bonds held by the government and the public, CN once more tried to escape the treadmill of debt. "Our staff all dislike red ink figures," Vaughan told Howe, "and they have a decided adverse effect on the morale of our officers and staff because they feel that after expending every effort to operate efficiently and economically their efforts are, to an extent, futile, and also because in the final analysis we are judged not by the service we give but by the size of our deficit."

Dr. W. C. Clark, the deputy minister of finance, asked what the railway was worrying about. There was no danger that funds at favourable rates would not be forthcoming when needed. The only CN argument of substance, he said, was the effect of the debt on morale but he gave this little importance; whether CN reported a net income or a deficit had no effect on the public, who were always more interested in efficiency and courtesy of employees. Though Clark did not say so, CN's concern about its bottom line did not take into account the very real benefits it bestowed on the country by providing jobs and assuring a transportation service to areas the CPR had not found commercial.

The government did, however, form a commission, the third in thirty years, to study CN debt and the inequality of freight rates – the lower rates in central Canada, based as they were on the more intense competition there, having caused resentment in the rest of the country. The West had an abiding complaint known as "long and short haul discrimination," a practice that dated back to the opening of the Panama Canal and railway efforts to compete with the lower rate offered by ships at Vancouver. One example of this was steel, which cost less to ship by rail from Montreal to Vancouver than from Montreal to Edmonton. The Royal Commission on Transportation began work in 1949 under W. F. A. Turgeon, ambassador to Ireland and a professional diplomat who had served on previous commissions.

Tired of being reminded that its fixed charges were twice as high as CPR's and its average earnings per mile 10 per cent lower, CN in its submission asked that the government assume more of the debt burden. "We are always compared with a rich neighbour, namely the Canadian Pacific Railway, whose operating conditions are much different than ours," said Vaughan. "They have no lines to operate at a severe loss, such as we have." Renewing an argument made at the 1917 royal commission, he believed the value of CN service should be based not solely on profit but on its contribution to the nation. "Last year," he told an audience at the Canadian National Exhibition in Toronto in September 1948, "the railways of Canada hauled for each of you an average of about twelve tons of freight over a distance of something like 400 miles. That tonnage was made up of your food, your clothes, your fuel, and the thousand other things which you needed. The Canadian railways hauled it for you at the lowest freight rates in the world."

In the north country, CN supplied services that were losing money – in the wilderness of Quebec and Ontario, on the old Grand Trunk Pacific line from Red Pass Junction to Prince Rupert, and in the Gaspé. It had repeatedly been required by the government to take over the operation of small and unprofitable lines, the latest being the Témiscouata Railway, a pet project of Liberal MP Jean-François Pouliot, who had committed Prime Minister Louis St. Laurent during an election rally to the view that it was a national monument. This relic of the Victorian era, with a station appropriately named St. Louis-de-Ha-Ha, ran for 122 miles through farms and forests between Rivière-du-Loup, Quebec, and Edmundston, New Brunswick. The Témiscouata, which boasted seven locomotives, thirty-three boxcars and four first-class coaches, and had never paid a dividend, cost the government half a million dollars to buy and CN another million to refurbish, which it did with reluctance.

But this was a minor burden compared with the responsibility the government thrust on CN when Newfoundland became Canada's tenth province on April 1, 1949. The Newfoundland Railway and Steamship Service joined CN's Atlantic region as part of the confederation package and CN found its payroll swollen by 4169 people, a thousand freight and passenger cars the worse for wear, forty-nine locomotives and an organization that included the Newfoundland Hotel in St. John's, which required a million dollars in renovations, the telegraph system, a dry dock, and fourteen ships, steel and wooden, that served Newfoundland outports.

The longest narrow-gauge (three feet, six inches) railway in the world, the Newfoundland railway totalled 706 miles, of which 547 were mainline across rough country from St. John's via Gander, Grand Falls, Corner Brook and Stephenville to Port aux Basques with its steamship connection to North Sydney, Nova Scotia. Passenger service was provided by the *Caribou*, nicknamed the "Newfie Bullet" because it took twenty-seven hours and forty minutes to cross the island.

Since its beginning in 1878 as a private railway controlled by Americans who raised money in England, the Newfoundland railway had had a difficult history. The railway was only completed across the island when Robert G. Reid, a Montreal contractor, took over in return for operating rights and forest land on which he built a lumber and pulp and paper operation that became the Anglo-Newfoundland Development Company. Except in the war years, the railway lost money and it was spending $5.76 per mile to earn $4.64 when CN took it over from the Newfoundland government. The Newfoundland Railway and Steamship Service added $7.7 million to CN's operating revenues and $10.3 million to operating expenses. It was war-worn, and unless it were to become a poor relation, a refurbishing of rolling stock, replacement of bridges and an upgrading of salaries to Canadian standards was essential.

With the assimilation of the Newfoundland operations, CN was the only railway to operate in all ten provinces, as well as eleven states: Maine, 133 miles, Connecticut 80, Massachusetts 67, New Hampshire 124, Vermont 433, New York 44, Michigan 1,846, Indiana 191, Illinois 111, Wisconsin 8, Minnesota 276.

CN's communications services, with a total wire mileage of 186,700 miles, including 24,000 miles of pole line, were the biggest in Canada, running from the fishing hamlets of Newfoundland to the coves of Vancouver Island and far into the north. At 14 million telegrams a year, the volume of traffic was the highest in the company's history; the leasing of private teletype circuits to businesses was expanding and CNT was pioneering in the technological revolution of microwave transmission.

Water-borne operations ranged from passenger and freight vessels to car ferries and tugs. On the Pacific Coast the *Prince George,* largest passenger ship built in B.C., had replaced a namesake destroyed by fire and was used on cruises between Vancouver and Alaska. A car ferry plied between Vancouver Island and the mainland. On the Great Lakes, three rail-car ferries operated across Lake Michigan and two on the Detroit River. The Ontario Car Ferry Company, established by the Grand Trunk in 1905 between Rochester, N.Y., and Cobourg, Ontario, and still profitable in the 1920s, lost so much money in the postwar inflation it was closed down.

The CN vessels with the best future were the ferries in Atlantic Canada. The first major postwar addition had been the *Abegweit,* the largest icebreaker car ferry in the world. She replaced the *Charlottetown,* lost during the war, and along with the old *Prince Edward Island* ran from Borden to Cape Tormentine, N.B., to link the island with mainland Canada. She was launched in 1947, cost $6.5 million, was 372 feet long and 61 feet wide, and could carry 19 railway cars, 60 automobiles and 950 passengers on each 40-minute crossing of Northumberland Strait. There were four more ships under construction: the *William Carson,* to operate between North Sydney and Port aux Basques, the *Bluenose* for service between Yarmouth, N.S., and Bar Harbor, Maine, and two vessels for the Newfoundland coastal service.

These coastal ships were a separate operation from the Canadian National (West Indies) Steamships, CN's Caribbean fleet. While this service had usually lost money in its sixteen years, its operating profits after the war made it a bargain for the Canadian taxpayer in carrying out the terms of the 1925 West Indies Canada Trade Agreement. (It was argued that the subsidies demanded had the service been carried out by a private company would have been higher.) Vaughan had agreed the service was worth keeping after the war, and CN had purchased five war-surplus freighters, given them names starting with "Canadian," like the CGMM vessels, and ordered three fast diesel ships, each with accommodation for twelve first-class passengers and deck space for seventy inter-island passengers. The *Lady Rodney* and *Lady Nelson* were reclaimed from the navy and refitted. "The importance of this service," Vaughan told a Halifax audience, "is apparent in the fact that between 1940 and 1945 our vessels kept the West Indies supplied with flour and brought raw sugar to Canada. At one time during the war we had as many as twenty-two vessels engaged in the West Indian Trade."

Before long the CNS fleet began to suffer the labour strife that plagued all ocean-going Canadian merchant ships after the war. Whereas CN's coastal vessels were manned by members of the Canadian Brotherhood of Railway Employees, the biggest all-Canadian union with 40,000 members, CNS ships were manned by the Communist-dominated Canadian Seamen's Union. This was the time of Communist witch-hunts in North America, exacerbated by the Korean War, and the CSU gained the enmity of employers and non-Communist unions because of its political militancy. Apart from the *Lady Rodney* and *Lady Nelson,* eight CNS freighters were serving the Caribbean but due to dollar shortages in the islands, trade restrictions, and the fact that it cost 50 per cent more to operate a Canadian ship than one from a competing country, profits were tumbling.

The government, the companies and Frank Hall of the International Brotherhood of Railway and Steamship Clerks wanted the CSU ousted and replaced by the anti-Communist Seafarers' International Union of North America, based in San Francisco. In the spring of 1949 the Shipping Federation of Canada, which handled labour relations for companies including the CNS, began an exercise in union-busting. To organize the coup, Hal C. Banks, a tough SIU troubleshooter with a criminal record, was flown to Halifax.

The Canadian Seamen's Union reacted to the takeover bid by calling a strike centred on three CNS ships berthed at Halifax, the liner *Lady Rodney* and the freighters *Canadian Challenger* and *Canadian Constructor.* The Shipping Federation signed an agreement with the SIU, which devised an elaborate plan to take over jobs held by the CSU. During the night of April 7, 1949, a special train arrived on a siding with 200 strike breakers, including sixty SIU members, armed with pick-handles. In the chill of 3 a.m. next morning, protected by the RCMP and 100 CN police brought in from around the country, they rushed the CNS ships, broke through the picket lines and fended off the rival union until they were able to get the vessels to sea. By the summer most of Canada's deep-sea fleet was under SIU control, which was to bode ill for the future of CNS.

Incorporating the Newfoundland operations into CN was Vaughan's finale. He stayed on for a year after the retirement age of sixty-five and there is evidence he wanted to stay longer. He enjoyed the job and provided stable if uninspired leadership, and railway workers felt he was one of their own. "Employees felt free to come to him with their problems and to appeal to him for assistance in resolving them," said B. L. Daly, labour's representative on the board. "At his office he gave quick, crisp answers to questions, coming at once to the point and using no needless words," reported the Montreal *Gazette*. "He was a reserved man; he did not make friends quickly. But once he made a friend it was for life."

According to Metcalf, who was now vice-president and executive assistant to the president, Vaughan toyed with the idea of staying as chairman, as Hungerford had done, and installing his second-in-command, Norman Walton, as president for a year or two, to be followed by Metcalf once Walton reached retirement age. "One day," recalled Metcalf, "Mr. Vaughan said to me, 'How would it be if I continued as chairman and you became president of the company?' After seriously pondering the question I looked at him and said, 'Mr. Vaughan, do you think that would work?' To which there was no response. I am sure he felt, as I did, that it would not work for the simple reason that he was not a man who could be happy to sit on the sidelines and let someone else run the show."

The odds were against Vaughan's staying. Though he had been a careful manager, the deficit had quadrupled since 1945, and whatever favour he had enjoyed with Howe, now minister of trade and commerce and the second most powerful man in Ottawa, had degenerated into a series of arguments. So far as Howe and the new prime minister, Louis St. Laurent, were concerned, Canada was on the move, changing from a simple producer of raw materials to an industrial country, and CN, which was not only an industry but had to play its role in all industries, must modernize. Vaughan was of the old school, a veteran of the Canadian Northern and a railway culture that had its roots in the 19th century; during the war the average age of CN's senior officers had of necessity become high. "Mr. St. Laurent felt the CNR had become so ingrown, that it would never be any good unless it was shaken up," recalled Jack Pickersgill, who was then St. Laurent's aide.

Lionel Chevrier, the minister of transport, had his own candidate – J. V. Clyne, a conservative Vancouver lawyer and chairman of the Maritime Commission of Canada, but according to Metcalf someone on the board, probably H.J.Symington, objected and wanted Donald Gordon, who had controlled the cost of living and conquered inflation as chairman of the Wartime Prices and Trade Board. In Ottawa, such influential figures as Pickersgill and Norman Robertson, secretary of the cabinet, thought Gordon an excellent choice, and though Howe, who had sometimes tangled with Gordon, was not initially enthusiastic, he too agreed. Gordon had been invited to become vice-president of the World Bank and the CN job would be a chance to keep him at home. Clyne was appointed justice of the B.C. Supreme Court and said he hadn't wanted the CN job anyway: "I knew my good friend Donald Gordon wanted the position, and I thought he would do a better job in it than I would."

That was probably true, for Gordon knew more than he let on when he told reporters he "didn't know a damn thing about railways." At the Wartime Prices and Trade Board he had coordinated rail and truck hauls and studied the impact of freight rates. When approached to take the CN job, the six-foot-three, 240-pound Scot was back in his peacetime role as deputy governor of the Bank of Canada, a position he had achieved against considerable odds.

Born in the Scottish town of Old Meldrum, Gordon had had six years of schooling, interrupted with minding sheep and cattle, when his father, an impecunious watchmaker, brought him to Canada at the age of thirteen. (Donald Smith, better known as Lord Strathcona and a builder of the CPR, came from the same region, and when Gordon was little had been installed as chancellor of the University of Aberdeen, some twenty miles to the southeast.) Gordon's first job in Canada was in a box factory, where he helped support the family until the truant officer caught up with him. Upon leaving Manning Avenue Public School in Toronto at the age of fifteen, he got a job as a junior clerk in the Bank of Nova Scotia and subscribed to correspondence courses in commerce and banking from Queen's University in Kingston. At the age of twenty-three the bank's youngest inspector, he was described in a personnel report as possessed of a "good brain, temperament, judgement and forcefulness ... he is possibly a bit impetuous." He had a habit of asking questions that were hard to answer and of taking little for granted. At thirty-five his talents had won him the appointment of secretary of the new Bank of Canada in Ottawa.

Having served as economic czar during the war, at the age of forty-seven Gordon was pondering the offer from the World Bank when he was offered the CN presidency at $50,000 a year. There was speculation, given his financial training, that he was picked expressly to dig CN from its load of debt. Frank Hall said, "Organized labour hopes that Mr. Gordon and the government will as soon as possible grapple with the basic problems presented by the CNR's fantastic financial structure."

Subject to government approval, the choice of a president was really the prerogative of the board, and having groomed Metcalf, Vaughan was displeased that the new president was chosen solely by the government. "I had arranged with Chevrier and Howe that one of our vice-presidents would succeed me," he said. "My recommendations had the unanimous approval of the board. Imagine my surprise when I picked up the Montreal *Gazette* and found that Donald Gordon had been appointed."

Vaughan agreed to chair a meeting of all seven directors on October 11, 1949, but left the boardroom when the question of his successor came up; Symington took over, saying he assumed everyone knew what they were there for, and after an awkward silence Gordon's name was proposed and seconded. Since a chairman, unlike the president, must be appointed by the cabinet, Symington and Howe arranged the details over the telephone that afternoon and Chevrier rose in the Commons at the end of the day to announce that Gordon was CN's president and chairman.

Canadians, or at least their newspapers, had never held Vaughan in higher regard than they did at his departure. For his war work he was made a member of the Order of St. Michael and St. George and the *Montreal Star* pointed out he had never sought attention but had gained it by sheer efficiency and devotion. The *Ottawa Journal* said, "It was not his fault if operational costs outstripped freight and passenger rates and left the CN with deficits."

He was undoubtedly better at avoiding strife than his predecessors, and if he lacked Thornton's magic he had nothing of Thornton's self-aggrandizement and fatal itch to go too far too fast. "He seemed always concerned about not rocking the boat, not making changes," recalled W. J. Smith of the Canadian Brotherhood of Railway, Transport and General Workers. Though the nature of the job invited contretemps, it was only three days before he retired that Vaughan's one glaring mistake was revealed. Ironically, it involved coal.

For decades as vice-president of purchasing Vaughan had bought coal on the futures market and stored it in great black mountains at the Lakehead, Coteau in Quebec, and other locations. Coal for operations in the Maritimes and the West was purchased from local mines. Ontario and Quebec, having no coal of their own, bought mostly from the United States, where it was cheaper, a practice that had brought Vaughan under fire in Nova Scotia during the Depression. Next to wages, coal was the second biggest operating expense and in 1948 CN bought seven and a half million tons, two thirds from the United States.

When the directors met that autumn, there was labour trouble in the coal fields of the United States and Vaughan's successor as vice-president of purchasing and supplies, E. A. Bromley, recommended the normal reserve of three months be increased so as to assure four and a half months' supply by the end of 1949. The board had approved, but in June 1949 Vaughan had second thoughts. Extra stockpiles were expensive, there was pressure from the government and the banks to limit American purchases, and Vaughan expected prices to come down. He had been through this exercise successfully so many times he had no hesitation in taking it upon himself to reverse the previous decision and lower the stockpile to the usual three months. "In the spring of 1949 CN had over $70 million tied up in inventory and we did not want to borrow money on that account from the government if it could be avoided," Vaughan explained.

For the rest of 1949 a combination of strikes, walkouts, bad weather, and floods and slides in open-pit mines disrupted U.S. coal production. Instead of dropping in price as Vaughan had expected, coal supplies became dearer or dried up completely, and by the end of 1949 CN reserves were closer to thirty days than the four months originally projected. "It was a guess each year," recalled Norman J. MacMillan, who was then vice-president of the law department, "and this time the guess was wrong." On December 28, Norman Walton announced that the coal shortage would force the railway to cut passenger service as of January 9.

Though diesel locomotives were still regarded as adjunct to steam locomotives, the coal crisis had focused attention on their relative virtues, including the lower cost of diesel oil. However slow to embrace dieselization, Vaughan set the program in motion, though it fell to "Dieseling Donald," as the newspapers came to call Gordon, to carry it through.

10

RAILWAY
PEOPLE

RAILWAYS, like other creations of the industrial revolution, were hierarchical and very demanding of employees. Being a crown corporation, CN might have been somewhat less so than private railways, but like them it had inherited 19th-century military attitudes. "As with the army, so with the railway," said an editorial in the December 1920 issue of *Canadian National Railways Magazine,* "certain conditions are essential to the formation of the close-knit organization, the mechanism that drives forward as a unit to success. One essential is unquestioning obedience to orders. We have to assume that the officer who gives them knows why, and that it is in the best interests of the organization of which he commands a small part that they be carried out."

The railways created their own "culture" – their own way of doing things – in a remarkably short time in the mid-1850s. The need for discipline and strict timing became obvious when trains began running in opposite directions on a single track, so to avoid disaster trains were run according to the Uniform Code of Operating Rules (since 1990, the Canadian Rail Operation

Rules), which train crew had to learn like a catechism.Despite these safe-guards, Canadian train accidents of various kinds killed nearly 600 people in 1907, including almost 300 employees. After World War I the toll decreased rapidly. By 1940 the total was 275 and it declined to 180 in 1970.

Conductor James Garrett, who joined the Grand Trunk in the late 19th century, recalled that safety equipment was virtually unknown in that era of wood-burning engines. "The air brake was undreamed of and handbrakes were the thing," he told *Canadian National Railways Magazine* when he retired in 1923. "There were many ways in which a minute's carelessness could result in a serious mishap."

The conductor had full responsibility once the train was under way, his only communication with the cab being the communication cord, to which the engineer could respond with the whistle. A change of orders was relayed in a message clipped in a wooden hoop shaped like the figure 9. A telegraph operator at a distant station would hold up the hoop to the speeding engine and a crewman put his arm through it and hauled it aboard.

A railway, like an army, depended on timing and the telegraph. Morse operators, scattered along the line in station after station, kept track of a train from start to finish of its journey. The famous railway watch, which appeared about 130 years ago and was checked every three months by an authorized inspector, was the "pocket deity" because its accuracy was critical in keeping on schedule. On passenger trains or fast freights the engineer might be reminded by the dispatcher that he was running half an hour late and was expected to arrive on time or have a good reason why not. On steam trains, which had no speedometers, an engineer would time the train between mile boards on his "turnip" or pocket watch. Only in 1964 did CN become the first Canadian line to break tradition and switch to a CN-designed wrist watch.

Employees could be dismissed for breaking one of a dozen rules on fighting, insubordination, failure to carry out train orders and regulations governing train movements, failure to properly report company revenue, and so on. Drunkenness was covered by the famous "Rule G." A discharge was not necessarily final, however, for the training and seasoning of men in the running trades was a long and costly business. In August 1923 CN adopted the "brownie point" system devised by G.R.Brown for New York Central and used by the ICR and Canadian Northern. Under the Brown System of Discipline one demerit point was equal to a day's suspension. Penalties ranged from one or two points for failure to punch a time clock to sixty for a serious matter which meant dismissal. In Quebec a yard foreman with twenty-five years of service was given thirty demerit points and barred from pass privileges because he loaned his pass to a friend. Previously, this would have brought suspension or outright dismissal, and since he had eleven children to feed the Brown system was less harsh.

Brownie points were awarded for merit as well. In Manitoba a switchman got five points for discovering a bent axle and notifying a car inspector; a conductor got five for reporting a fault on a passing train not his own. An employee with demerit marks on his record could have twenty deducted after twelve consecutive months of good service.

In the 1950s, when 1200 people were being discharged every year, of whom 40 per cent were reinstated, Donald Gordon wondered whether the Brown System had outlived its usefulness. Apparently nothing better had been devised for the hazardous running trades, however, and the Brown System is still in use, though its punitive aspects have been mitigated by retraining programs.

Since they appeared in Canada in the late 19th century, unions have had an increasing influence on discipline, as on other working conditions. Basing their campaigns not only on wages but on social justice, railway unions were among the first unions to appear in this country, following the pattern of growth in the U.S. Railway work was dangerous and hours were long and, for non-operating trades such as baggage handlers and clerks, wages were low.

Experience was the only way to learn, and seniority was paramount. Older men got the best jobs, and the running trades were the elite, paid by the mile. Locomotive engineers made the most money, followed closely by conductors. Most spent their careers on freights which ran on twenty-four-hour schedules as opposed to the more predictable schedules of passenger trains, which a conductor or engineer might get as a reward for seniority. Considerably down the pay scale were firemen, brakemen, station agents and telegraphers, boiler makers, signal maintainers, porters and so on.

The 1931 census suggests that almost 5 per cent of Canadians claiming gainful occupation were railway workers. They constituted a quarter of all Canadian union members. Sixty per cent were Canadian-born, 20 per cent were immigrants from the United Kingdom or its possessions, and the rest were mostly sectionmen or track workers from Scandinavia, Germany or eastern Europe. Though Quebec held a quarter of Canada's population, it was under-represented in railway work, with less than 20 per cent of the total workforce on all railways in Canada. Only 5 per cent of railway workers were from the United States, and many of these were porters, who numbered more than 1650.

Recruits were apprenticed out of grade school to learn on the job, fourteen being a common starting age, and it helped if you had a relative on the railway. Alex Walker, who grew up in Richmond, Quebec, recalled that his apprenticeship had begun at ten years of age when his father, a car foreman, used to take him to visit the roundhouse. At thirteen friendly crew members showed him how to fire an engine.

An apprentice must have good health, sight and hearing, enough education for average literacy – and a railway watch. Many were hired as call boys to go around on bikes and wake people for their shifts. "On the railroad there was no night or day," said one veteran conductor. "You never knew from one day to the next what you were going to do," said another. "I might go to work at five o'clock in the morning or I might go at midnight."

"Three twenty-five a.m.," exclaimed Alex Douglas, an engineer out of Thunder Bay. "What time is that for anybody? Who would go to work at three twenty-five in the morning? But the job had its good points. If you wanted off you didn't go and ask the boss. You just phoned the crew office and asked if they had spare men available and when they said yes, you would book off. So it was different from your average work."

Freight duty was a particular burden on mothers, who had to fill the role of both parents when the men were away for days or weeks. When the men were working out of their home base, life was almost as difficult, for wives had to juggle their domestic routines to irregular hours. "It could be one o'clock in the afternoon, or the middle of the night," said Jean Humble of Sarnia, Ontario, whose husband, Mel, worked for CN for thirty-seven years. "He went to work on railway time, standard time, and when the city went on fast time our son Peter went to school on fast time. I was on everybody's time! There was a lot of laundry. Overalls and smocks and things to wash. Those railroad caps had to be starched and they're hard to iron so I made a little form to fit in the top of them so they would always be standing up. There were nine years in a row when he was never home for Christmas. There was not much social life. It was a job and you had to put up with it."

A youngster might start as an engine wiper, or if he was a bit older, a switchman, like Cliff McCammon, who worked in the maze of tracks at

Saskatoon when he was twenty-three years old in 1949. The switchmen, armed with kerosene lanterns for signalling, worked in crews of three, with a switch engine, engineer and fireman. A night's work for Cliff might involve checking a string of cars to make sure they were properly coupled and the brakes were off and then moving them downtown before picking up a string of empties. It was easy enough to get caught between two cars or make a mis-step in the dark. "It's worse in the winter," he said, "with twenty-five pounds of clothing on your back and working around icy steel. It depends on your luck – some are lucky and some aren't."

Once a young man became a fireman he could begin to learn the loco-motive engineer's duties, the meaning of train orders and how to work the throttle, brake valves and whistle. There were nineteen signals, standard throughout North America, ranging from two long, one short, one long, which was sounded a quarter of a mile from any of Canada's 32,000 level crossings, to the six short blasts that meant the conductor was asking the engineer to increase steam heat in the passenger cars.

Each steam locomotive was different, its driving wheels balanced for it alone, its boiler and cylinders custom-made. "I was a steam man," said Frank Fagan of Moncton, who served for thirty years as fireman and engineer. "I never had much use for diesel power, though I've got to admit it was a much easier and cleaner job. A steam engine had some life in it. You took pride in them, how they worked, how they looked, polishing them and keeping them clean. You take a nice high-wheeler, those 6000 Mountains and 6200 North-erns with white rims on them, it was something! Diesels look to me like something that's half dead. Years ago they assigned engines and the engineer hated to lose that engine. Those old drivers took a pride in their engine and kept it well greased and oiled so it didn't have to go in for repairs too often."

One thing the steamers had in common was the panting sound made by the two exhausts, a soft exhaust coming through with a hard following right behind it. According to D. V. Gonder, who worked up to a CN vice-presidency from the shops, a steam locomotive produced forty distinct sounds – from a gentle hiss in repose with the stack blower open just enough to keep the smoke from backing into the cab, to the thunder and whistle of an engine in full flight with smoke trailing back, "her tail over her back," as they used to say.

The cab of a steamer was rarely comfortable. Curtains were often the only protection against the weather. You were hot on one side and cold on the other, and if you got too close to the fire box you risked getting burned.

There was no toilet. If the fireman and the driver were at loggerheads they might end up blowing the fire right up the stack, which would halt the train until the fire was built up again.

The fireman was expected to apply the principles of combustion to use only as much coal as necessary but above all to keep the boiler hot at all times and under all conditions. He was responsible for the water in the boiler, for keeping watch out of his side of the engine, for checking order boards at stations for warnings of stormy or foggy weather ahead, and for calling out train orders with the engineer, and when Centralized Traffic Control came in was responsible for calling out the colour of the lights ahead – green, yellow or red. Having learned all these things, however, it would be years before a fireman got to sit permanently in the right-hand seat of a cab and join the Brotherhood of Locomotive Engineers.

The Fireman: Lorne Brisbin of Belleville, Ontario:
"The first thing you'd do after you stowed your lunch pail was to check your firebox to see there were no bad leaks and your water glass wasn't leaking and there was oil in your lubricators. Then you'd climb up on the tender and check your coal and water. It wasn't uncommon to put eighteen tons of coal through in a day or a night. You'd get a chance to get a cup of water, sit down for a minute or maybe eat half a sandwich. You would know when to put on more coal by the steam gauge – it moved very slowly but when it was ascending you didn't need any more coal. You could tell too by the colour of your fire. You needed a nice, white, bright fire, incandescent almost. When it started to die down it would get red. When your fire started to get oily and dirty looking you were firing too heavily.

"When you fired a locomotive you knew where every grade and every pimple was. To this day I can go from Toronto to Montreal in a night passenger train and without looking tell just where I am. A fireman ran into a variety of problems. There could be tubes leaking in the boiler, or poor coal, or the way the engineer drove the train.

"There were engineers that we fireman thought were real artists. They could run over the road and keep a swing on the train where others just wouldn't use the right valve cut-off and throttle setting and the engine would be almost choking itself. It would not be running free, so you were burning more coal. The engineman had to learn how to control the cut-off. It was just a case of listening and getting the feel of it.

"The diesels came in when I was still firing. I wasn't an engineman very long then before I became a supervisor. In the steam days with a Northern we were running seventy-five or seventy-seven cars, depending on the tonnage. Maybe up to eighty. Empties would be up in the hundreds. But with diesels you were consistently handling a hundred or more. I saw one train recently, it was 12,000 feet long."

The Locomotive Engineer: Alex "Beaver" Douglas of Thunder Bay:
"I fired from 1951 to 1956 and then I rode as an engineer and held the running most of the time as an engineer. It wasn't too hard because the skills of a firemen were a little tougher than they were for an engineer. You had several types of mechanical stokers and all the gauges you had to operate were more complicated than it was to run an engine. When you moved to the engineer's seat you were well seasoned with engines.

"There were two sets of train orders on the freights, one for the conductor at the tail end and one for the engineer at the head end. We read the train orders to each other. We would consult about everything. We made big money at times, but there were times we didn't because we were paid by the mile. If you were 'in the hole' – on a siding for a meet – and you had to sit there for three or four hours you would not make money. You would try to get the best meet you could and there would be arguments with the dispatcher as to why he put that meet there and not at the next town. Thirty or forty miles an hour was a fair average, and fifty miles an hour if you were working the main lines. An engineer could make more money than a superintendent.

"I loved steam more than diesel, but then I liked repairing a diesel better. I used to patch up a lot of diesel units on the road. I got concussion and burnt all the hair off one side of my head at Atikokan one morning – a crankcase explosion, took the valve covers right off and blew them flying. It blew the brakeman right over the handrails of the engine. But I was always known to patch up an engine. If Beaver couldn't fix it, it couldn't be fixed.

"We had tough times, but we had a lot more good times, and we made a good dollar. I wouldn't change it. I like CN. CP is a good railroad too, but CN was a good company to work for. I used to figure that every time I went to work I owned that engine."

The lad who set his sights on being a conductor would first become a brakeman, as he was called on a freight, where he wore overhauls and coupled, uncoupled and switched cars, and learned the paperwork a conductor must handle. When he got promoted to a passenger train he was called a trainman and wore a uniform. Railroaders who dealt with the public were required to wear uniforms, which promoted a sense of responsibility and loyalty, as well as a sense of security among the passengers A trainman wore silver buttons to distinguish him from the conductor, who wore gold buttons and gold braid.

The Conductor: D. J. Cryon of Sarnia, Ontario:
"I was hired out of Stratford as a brakeman and made my first trip August 15, 1940. Coming out of the Depression, I didn't have enough education to go into the professions so I considered myself lucky to have a job on the railroad. The pay was twice the money of chaps working in factories, but I found it hard on social life for women, because you worked the craziest hours and went when they called you, so you couldn't make any plans. We were away for Christmas and New Year's more often than we were home.

"We worked by mileage. I think it was forty-three hundred miles a month we were allowed to make. After that you had to book off until the end of your month. The wife never knew when you were coming home unless you were on a passenger train. The passenger trains, they were like a regular job, you knew what time you were going to work and usually what time you were coming home.

"The hours were long. In many instances you'd work eighteen hours at a stretch. Most of the men tried to slug it out and work all these hours so they could get back home. Your work orders could change from the time you went out. I worked a lot of single track out of Stratford and maybe the train ahead of you was in trouble. There'd be no way of getting around that train to carry on. Or a train might come from the opposite direction and you had to watch the order board at the stations to determine whether you could go through, or pause or slow up to get different orders, or stop. So you never knew, really.

"Maybe on a cold winter night your train would break in two. Freight trains are like roller coasters. Early on they never had the sliding equipment that gives with the pull of a train. You might have an eighty-car train and you'd run down a grade then start up another and the slack might break a weak knuckle, the coupler that holds two cars together. The train would break in two. The hose bags would part and the brakes would automatically go on. The darn thing would never break near the engine or back near the caboose and you'd have to carry a seventy-five-pound knuckle slung on a broomstick and replace it. Before they got radios or walkie talkies, which were terrific, we would light fusees so the engineer could see back in the darkness or fog.

"We never knew what was going to happen when we went out to work. I guess that's why I packed a pretty big bucket of food, always four or five meals. Carried it in a club bag. I became a full-time conductor in the late 1950s. As a conductor you had your own caboose, but the old ones could be pretty rough, no springs, and old coal stoves bolted to the floor. The new steel cabooses were great, though. Some of the boys had linoleum on the floor and curtains on the windows. Sometimes the brakeman or the conductor would be a good cook and do a roast. You had your own bed clothes. A home away from home. In the final year I was a passenger conductor. I never regretted my thirty-nine years of railroading but I don't miss it now I'm retired."

At the centre of it all was a dispatcher, a spider in a web of telegraph and phone lines. In a busy place like L'Assomption, one of half a dozen subdivisions around Montreal, dispatchers on a typical day might issue 150 separate train orders and over 100 clearances for trains to proceed.

The Train Dispatcher: Jim Munsey of Edmonton, Alberta:
"It was like a chess game. You issued train orders based on the timetable, told trains where to meet, where to wait for other trains, which trains to pass, which not to pass. You tried to set it up so they met with a minimum of delay and no risk of collision. You didn't have radio communication in those days. You couldn't afford to make a mistake. There was a lot of stress and strain.

"It was to my advantage to know every curve and grade and every engineman. Some were gamblers, some were cautious. So when the chips were down you could figure which guy would go and which would hang back. You had to know your engines because some steamed better than others, and who the fireman was, whether he could keep heavy steam up. All this counted and if you got out and rode with them on your days off you learned these things.

"When you delivered orders to a station for a train on the line, and it passed that station, it was gone until the next station. And if you made a mistake on those orders there was no way you could get hold of him to tell him to stop. He was headed for disaster. It's a terrible thing to live with if you're responsible for somebody being killed. I can remember dispatching out of Winnipeg when the Korean War was on and there were troop movements mixed in with all the freight traffic. I remember working from midnight till eight a.m. and then going to bed and having nightmares. I had a recurring dream. I was a teamster with a twenty-horse team trying to handle all the lines between my fingers.

"One dispatcher missed a train order and there was a head-on collision. He turned grey in a matter of days. I remember another chap right here in Edmonton discovered he had issued what we call a lap order, giving two trains the same authority on the same track at the same time. But it was on the prairie and they saw each other coming and stopped. A dispatcher set up trains out of Jasper and forgot about one of them and in effect had a lap order, a big heavy westbound freight and a little way freight out of Jasper. They all jumped off.

"The way most of us started, the station agent gave us the fundamentals of keeping a station – selling tickets, billing freight and express, learning operating rules and telegraphy. You got promoted to operator, who worked in essence for the train dispatcher, you listened, you practised, and you got thrown into heavy jobs where you had to sink or swim.

"The major change came with the diesel, and automatic signals where the light tells you to go, slow, go fast, or stop, followed thereafter by radio communication. Now they have bigger trains moving at sixty miles an hour there is a tremendous challenge in the engineman's job to know how to handle the train so he doesn't tear it all apart. You've got to think two miles ahead all the time."

Most railway travellers have had the experience of suddenly coming across a small gang of men miles from nowhere standing beside the tracks. These sectionmen, or maintenance-of-way men, responsible for a section of track, had to carry out their work of ballasting, laying new ties and track and securing it with bolts, tie plates and rail anchors in all weather, without interfering with train schedules.

The locomotive engineers might be the aristocrats of the road, said section foreman Fred Rolfe of Halifax, "but they don't move without us." Before modern machinery, twenty men, ten to a side, formed a tong gang to remove old track and put in new, under a foreman who kept them working in unison with his singsong: "Pick her up, boys. Move her east. O... K." And the tongmen set down the rail.

Many were immigrants and CN was a supporter of Frontier College, which offered education to section and construction gangs as well as loggers and miners. Founded early in the century by Alfred Fitzpatrick of Pictou County, Nova Scotia, Frontier College recruited as many as forty college students each year to serve as CN labourer-teachers and give classes at night after work was over. The idea was to sound out the men as to their interests and teach appropriate lessons. On one section a gang of Italian immigrants might want to learn English or French, or perhaps math or farming, or even take a course in poetry as was occasionally the case. The labourer-teacher was expected to work as hard as the rest and be one of the boys. In a season Frontier College might teach 3000 men, helping to keep the gangs together and reduce expensive turnover.

To change and service steam locomotives repair shops were sited at division points every hundred miles or so where the firebox was cleaned and the engine oiled and repaired if necessary. As one veteran shopman put it, "I always felt excitement working in the shops, getting the big brutes ready for the road."

The Locomotive Foreman: Jacques Gauthier of Montreal:
"I went from Montreal to Taschereau, a division point on what had been the Transcontinental line in northern Quebec, in March 1949. I was single at the time, twenty-five years old, and working nights as assistant foreman in the shop, and the shifts were twelve hours, seven days a week, starting at eight p.m.

"We had sixty-five to seventy men, half of them carmen to look after the cars. Every thirty days a steam engine had to be washed out. You had to damp the fire, remove the plugs and wash the interiors, the tubes, the hoses, the boiler to make sure all the accumulation of rust was taken out and the tubes cleaned of dust. The netting that prevented hot cinders flying out to set forest fires had to be kept in good condition. And then you had the way freights to Noranda, Parent and Cochrane every morning and passenger trains to take care of. They were constructing the line to Beattyville so every Monday morning about eight work trains set out.

"There were days off but you were subject to call all the time. We had a movie in an old garage once very three months, *Rin Tin Tin* and things like that, so I organized sports. I had three peewee hockey teams and three women's broomball teams. That's all I had to do in my spare time. If you do those things it's easier to do your job.

"I became locomotive foreman at Fitzpatrick, near La Tuque. It had a nice big yard for 100-car trains and a roundhouse that took care of twelve locomotives. It was well organized, built to carry all that grain the Transcontinental was supposed to carry. In 1952 we got our first diesel, so I could see the day coming when my job would be abolished by the new technology so I took a night course in diesel locomotives, electricity and mechanics. I became a master mechanic."

Black workers were porters and that was usually their only niche, until the mid-1960s when union and company began to upgrade them. They had first been hired by the Pullman Palace Car Company in the 19th century and by the 1930s about a quarter were U.S.-born, about the same number came from the West Indies, and the rest had been born in Canada. They preferred working for CN because it paid them more than the CPR and worked them far fewer hours per month than the Pullman company had. The Grand Trunk in the early days had a policy of hiring black workers as waiters on name trains out of Montreal, but in 1926 they were replaced on CN's *International Limited* by white waiters, which vice-president Hungerford told the Canadian League for the Advancement of Coloured People was due to complaints about service from passengers rather than "any feeling of prejudice against the employees as a class." The men were not fired, but became porters.

The Sleeping Car Porter: Leonard Dixon of Montreal:
"I was born and went to high school in Halifax. My father was a porter and my two brothers. In all the industries in Halifax there were no blacks. As a person of colour, the only job you could apply for in CN was sleeping car porter. They made that quite clear. If you applied for a labourer's job they would direct you to the sleeping-dining car department. There's two college graduates I know who graduated from Acadia University. The only jobs they could get at the time was working on the railway as sleeping car porters. One went on to become a school teacher; the other moved to Montreal and ran the Black Community Centre.

"I joined CN in 1939, served in the army from 1941 to '45, rejoined the railway and retired in 1983. As far as I was concerned it was a good place to work. You were making more pay than a waiter and the waiters were all white. They treated you good. You had a pension plan. The majority of blacks that sent their kids to university were sleeping car porters.

"In the 1960s I was promoted to in-charge porter, which meant a route where they wouldn't have a conductor. The highest position I attained was platform inspector and customer service supervisor."

Albino Paolucci of Montreal, who filled many roles at CN in his forty years and became a sleeping car conductor and supervisor, recalled that in 1964 it was decided to employ black porters as conductors. "I started training them," he said, "and it came out very well, though there was friction from some of the white guys who thought these coloured guys were taking their jobs but the coloured guys had thirty and more years of seniority and the ones complaining had five or ten years."

In the heyday of passenger travel, Paolucci, as pantryman, cook, waiter and trainer of waiters, had been one of those responsible for the meals, the gleaming silverware and white tablecloths and careful service on name-train dining cars. "Everything was cooked from scratch," he said. "You had coal stoves – later oil – with two big ovens, a warmer and a grill for steaks, chops or fish. We had a steam table for vegetables, stew, gravy. Everything was platter service, hot plates to bring to the table. The rolls used to be hot, too. I'm talking about the years up to 1948."

"It was always first class service," recalled Pat Bennett of Moncton, a dining car inspector. "The meats and fish were always fresh. We had really good food. The cooks used to bake their own pies on the train, do huge roasts and twenty-five-pound turkeys. They had maybe a foot and a half clearance between the stove and the cupboard. And hot? Those fellows must have lost twenty pounds a trip. They deserve a lot of credit, those fellows in the olden days."

11

FAREWELL
TO STEAM

DONALD GORDON'S WELCOME TO CN in mid-December 1949 was almost as chilly as the weather. In an industry that revered seniority and officers who had paid their dues of apprenticeship, a banker parachuted in by Ottawa caused understandable resentment. When R.C.Vaughan, whose candidate had been ignored, met Gordon at Central Station, he climbed into the front seat of his automobile with the chauffeur and put Gordon in the back to make small talk with the vice-president of the law department. "So you're Norman MacMillan," said Gordon to the CN lawyer who would one day succeed him. "I hear damn good things about you."

They lunched at the Mount Royal Club, where Gordon was soon calling Vaughan "Charlie." At CN headquarters both smiled for the cameras, but according to MacMillan "there was no rapport at all." Years later Gordon confirmed that Vaughan had been no help to him and Vaughan for his part, having launched a second career as director of various companies, complained that his attempts to get a better pension were ignored.

As chairman of the Wartime Prices and Trade Board, wielding powers possible only in wartime, the big, bluff Scot had become a household name. Now, as a newcomer to railroading and the youngest president in CN's history, he would have to prove himself again. "You have a right to expect of me that I show leadership, imagination and energy in the development and betterment of the system," said Gordon, and proceeded to demonstrate all three, as well as candour, choler, humour, arrogance, and a habit of changing his mind without apology. The first test of his mettle was not long in coming.

On the eve of taking office, Gordon learned that the U.S. coal strike he had been hearing about threatened Canada and within nine days CN would have to shut down a quarter of its service. "There was an explosion," recalled E. A. Bromley, vice-president of purchasing and stores. "No one had told him." This was no way to run a railroad, especially when the CPR had prudently cached enough coal for normal service. "I sweated blood for three months after that," said Bromley. "I got off to a bad start with him. I was brought up under Mr. Vaughan and he and Vaughan didn't see eye to eye."

When people accused Gordon of using the strike to kill off unprofitable passenger services, Vaughan, to his credit, shouldered responsibility for the decision that had left CN with hardly a month's reserve of coal. Having gambled on prices going down, he did not exactly apologize but did tell Parliament that in thirty years of buying coal he had never seen such labour trouble and bad weather all at once.

"They started to use up all the coal in the big supply docks at places like Belleville, Coteau and Lindsay where they had stored coal for years, and some of it had deteriorated badly," said Lorne Brisbin of Burlington, Ontario, who was then a young locomotive fireman. "It got so bad we had to cancel local passenger trains and little way freights." Despite emergency supplies from Nova Scotia, on January 9 CN was forced to cut services in one of the coldest, stormiest winters in years. Not until March 6 was Gordon able to assure Canadians that CN had enough coal to get full service back on track.

That was only the start of Gordon's ordeal. A few days later the man he was depending on to teach him railroading, Norman Walton, executive vice-president in charge of operations, died of a heart attack. The operations department directed the movement of trains, construction and maintenance of roadbed and track, maintenance and manufacture of rolling stock, the express services, and the supervision of ferries and barges. The *Montreal Star*, in a eulogy that describes many railroaders, said: "It was Mr. Walton's great gift that he was able to make trains run under all conditions and circumstances. He left the centre of the stage to others. He sat behind his desk making the system run smoothly all over Canada and the United States."

Barely a month after taking office, Gordon had to choose a successor to the second most important officer in the railway. Unlike his predecessors in the president's office, he knew nothing about the workings of the operations department or what sort of talent was needed. His rapport with the fourteen vice-presidents, including eight at head office, who were standing back to see what he intended to do with their railway, was minimal. Lacking other means of reaching a decision, and used to the ways of the civil service in Ottawa, he turned to the embryo personnel department. "Gordon asked for the papers as to who should succeed Walton," recalled George Lach who later headed the department. "There were no good personnel files, there was nothing, and from that moment he became convinced that we had to do a better job in thinking ahead about managers and where they were to come from."

Gordon upset people by ignoring seniority and choosing Stanley F. Dingle, who was the same age as Gordon and had spent his thirty years at CN in white-collar jobs, never getting "grease on his elbows." He had never been a vice-president like the other three candidates, but as Walton's chief of transportation he had been in the right place at the right time. "I suppose I was the youngest vice-president," said Dingle. "I was only forty-nine. I started as clerk-stenographer with the Grand Trunk Pacific and got my training with the top operating men. I wouldn't have given it up for any university training, but mind you I took night school classes at the University of Manitoba. I worked up by writing shorthand for top operating men in the West – that's where I got my background."

One of Dingle's tasks was to tutor a boss "who didn't speak the language" and who made a virtue of his ignorance by taking nothing for granted in an industry that had developed middle-age spread. "What's a rail anchor?" Gordon would ask. "What's a coupler?" To learn how trainmen coped with cold weather he went into the Quebec countryside on a snowplow during a January freeze. "He never tried to bluff anyone," said Bromley. "He could absorb information like a sponge, [with a] tremendous ability to grasp and summarize."

March 1, 1950, the year Gordon called the worst in his life, brought the death of his wife, Maisie. "It was an appalling period," said Norman MacMillan. "I think he cursed the day he had ever taken on this job. It was difficult for people to go in to see him and it was not a very happy ship at first."

Three weeks after the funeral he had to face the annual command appearance before the Commons Railway and Shipping Committee that had brought Sir Henry Thornton to his knees.

Though the hearings were a strain, Gordon proved tougher than his predecessors when the Conservative opposition used his appointment to attack the government for putting an Ottawa mandarin into CN headquarters. Gordon gave as good as he got, and when asked for reams of minutiae on how the CN purchasing department operated, informed them that bureaucracy, as well as red ink, was destroying managerial incentive and suggested sarcastically they set up shop at CN headquarters in Montreal. Though CN had earned an overall surplus only six times in its twenty-seven years, it had always managed to pay operating costs, Gordon pointed out, but deficits, whatever the cause, were seen by the taxpayers as failure. With fixed charges at 10 per cent of revenue – twice as high as the CPR's – he promised to persuade the government to reduce debt to reasonable levels – perhaps to $17 million annually, which was more or less in line with CPR debt.

In May Gordon began the obligatory presidential pilgrimage, travelling five thousand miles through floods in Manitoba, where CN performed rescue work, and rock slides in the Rockies. The latter were sometimes so bad the western vice-president, J. P. Johnson, fearing CN would lose its line down the Fraser Canyon, once cabled his superior at head office a demand for money to shore things up, adding, "Do you wish the Fraser River and the Canadian National Railway to run down this beautiful canyon, or just the Fraser River?" Jack Cann, later a vice-president of operations but in 1950 a young district maintenance engineer based in Kamloops, remembers that between November and April his bulldozers and draglines pulled thirteen locomotives out of the Fraser Canyon because of washouts, slides, and a head-on collision at Canoe River on November 21 which killed twenty-one people and resulted from a dispatching error.

Traditionally a railway president travelled like a prince in what the public calls a private car and the railways call a business car – private cars being those used by government officials and businessmen like Timothy Eaton. In the 1920s CN maintained a fleet of eighty: four for the prime minister and cabinet and two for the governor general, one for the railway commissioners and seventy-three for railway work. The president's car, *Bonaventure*, was comfortable enough, with bedroom, dining room, bathroom, secretary's room, steward's room and kitchen, but had no frills. "Gordon had no time for all that nonsense," said J.A. "Jim" McDonald, a tall red-haired former CN telegrapher who had become a Rhodes Scholar and economist and had been lifted from Fairweather's department to write Gordon's speeches. The other travellers were Gordon's secretary, Walter Smith, and Dingle, who had his own car and retired each evening when the big Scot with a big capacity showed signs of lifting a few convivial glasses and singing *Road to the Isles* in what he called a "jollification." Gordon was what was known as a social drinker and colleagues say his physique was such his excesses did not disrupt his work. "During my entire service under him I never saw him touch a drink during working hours," said Fairweather, a teetotaller. "I never saw his judgement impaired by a hangover. He would go on the wagon for a month from time to time to prove that he could."

Those were years when movie stars and prime ministers – even the sedate corporation lawyer "Uncle Louis" St. Laurent – had their pictures taken in engineer's cap and bibbed overalls at the throttle of a steam locomotive. Gordon, though a self-described ham actor, had a more serious purpose. "He got the feel of the railway and he got it through hard work, but I had to explain things to him," said Dingle, who spent 40 per cent of his time travelling the rails. "We had over 100,000 employees, and 90 per cent of them were under my jurisdiction. I was on call twenty-four hours a day. I received a copy of the crew's train orders and I'd hand these over to Donald and explain what it all meant, and of course he had a lot of savvy. He worked hard and he played hard. I'd go to bed and he'd keep on – but every morning, six o'clock, an inspection car would pull up alongside and we'd be on it. He never missed an appointment."

Grudgingly accepted when he first appeared, Gordon was warmly welcomed by the end of his spring tour across the country. "Once the shock waves diminished over the fact that a non-railroader was driving the railroad," said McDonald, "there was a sense that a new page was being turned. He was getting a lot of favourable press."

Gordon displayed poor judgement that summer, however, in his first encounter with the unions. Seventeen non-operating unions, representing all unionized employees except the Big Four of the running trades – locomotive engineers, firemen, conductors and trainmen – were demanding better wages and the five-day, forty-hour week enjoyed by railroaders in the United States. The Board of Transport Commissioners had authorized a freight rate increase and the non-operating unions wanted a share, complaining they not

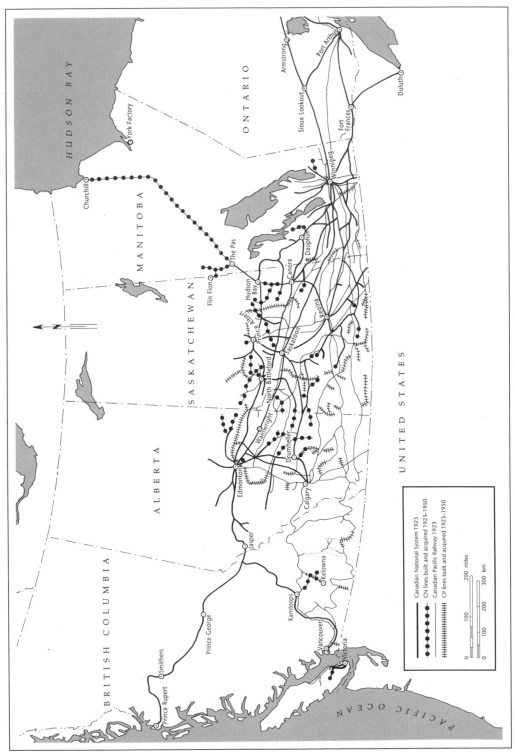

The competition to build branch lines. CN and CPR lines in western Canada, 1923–1950.

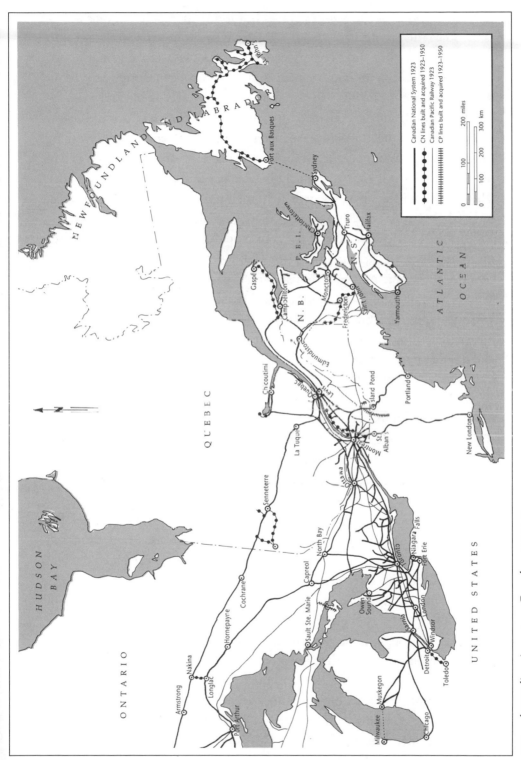

CN and CPR lines in eastern Canada, 1923–1950.

only made less than the running trades but less than people in other industries. Since this would have meant eight fewer work hours a week and a 20 per cent increase in hourly wage rates, CN and the CPR were resisting.

There had been no improvement in hours of work in thirty years. Management excuses of inability to pay were no longer acceptable and management-union relations had changed since the war. "They had one old fellow who represented the locomotive engineers in the West," said Dingle, recalling his early days in Winnipeg. "He'd come strutting down from the union hall in his bob-tailed frock coat and square bowler hat and go in to see the boss. They'd put their feet up on the desk, light their pipes, and make a verbal agreement, shake hands on it, and that was that. That didn't happen any more."

In the 1950s railways could not – or would not – meet union demands unless rate increases kept pace and what followed came down to a confrontation over how much the government would pay to keep CN trains running. "The wage and labour negotiations have reached a critical stage," Gordon wrote in June. "The breaking point may be upon us at any time and we will have to determine whether or not to fight this one out. It is a very trying time and a rather nerve-wracking experience."

When negotiations bogged down on August 8, Gordon and W. A. Mather, president of the CPR, took a hand, meeting with the two most powerful union leaders. The British-born Frank Hall, fifty-seven, who represented 90,000 workers, was vice-president of the International Brotherhood of Railway and Steamship Clerks; A. R. Mosher, a sixty-seven-year-old Halifax freight handler, was president of the homegrown 34,000-member Canadian Brotherhood of Railway Employees (CBRE).

The CPR, being less sensitive to public opinion than CN, usually took the lead in union negotiations, but since Mather was not a good negotiator and happened to be away, Gordon, despite his inexperience, presented a "final offer" – including a forty-four-hour week. A forty-hour week would have to wait until it became general across the country since only about a quarter of the industries CN served observed it at the time. "If you force this issue to a conclusion through imposing on the Canadian public the disaster of a strike," Gordon warned, "then we predict you will live to regret it." To the unions this was an obvious threat, though Gordon insisted he was merely warning of the possibility of compulsory arbitration.

"Usually," Gordon said, "it's the union that makes the statement and puts management on the defensive. This time, let's take the initiative ourselves." Against advice from MacMillan, who had a steadying effect on his mercurial boss, Gordon reverted to his wartime method of coaxing Canadians to accept edicts from his Wartime Prices Board. On August 15 he went on national radio to ask employees to refuse to strike. Union leaders were outraged to hear him appealing directly to the rank and file in the midst of negotiations.

A mediator, W.A.Mackintosh, vice-principal of Queen's University, found an "almost complete lack of confidence between the parties to the dispute." Other complications were the number and variety of unions attempting to bargain as one (there were over 200 separate collective agreements at CN) and the low level of the bargaining. The public, having no experience of a major railway strike (though the unions had come within hours of one in July 1948 before the government intervened) believed the government would step in. But Ottawa did not repeat its intervention of 1948, Vaughan having complained that it had settled the dispute at the expense of an intolerable CN wage bill.

On August 22, 1950, at 6 a.m., Canada's first national railway strike began, involving 80,000 CN and 58,000 CPR freight handlers, clerks, telegraphers, sleeping car and parlour car employees, electricians and waiters. The Toronto and District Trades and Labour Congress took Gordon's side and said the government was to blame, but generally the man once hailed as a benefactor when he ran the Wartime Prices Board was under heavy fire. "Donald rationed food, now he's rationing hours," said a picket sign. Strikers in Montreal who demanded his dismissal were echoed in Parliament by the leader of the CCF. "I believe his period of usefulness as president of the CNR has come to an end," said M.J.Coldwell of the man who had been barely eight months in the job.

The strike lasted nine days until Ottawa – where fifty MPs in CN's Chateau Laurier Hotel were having to make their own beds – legislated the strikers back to work on August 30. The unions got most of their wage demands and the forty-hour week, which started June 1, 1951, and once adopted by CN spread across Canada. Some 23,000 people had been thrown temporarily out of work in other industries, but because of the postwar proliferation of trucks the strike had had less impact than feared. It did, however, set a precedent for government intervention, weakening the unions' strike weapon.

"They were ready with everything that moved on wheels," said Metcalf, now a vice-president and Gordon's executive assistant, "and they got a lot of traffic, some of which the railways never got back." The strike had proved, were proof needed, that the monopoly the railways had enjoyed for a century was over. Though they were carrying twice as much freight as twenty years earlier, much of it was long-haul timber, coal, ore, grain and other bulk; lighter, more lucrative freight, hauled over shorter distances, was being scooped up by trucks, which, though they charged as much as or more than railways, were handier for short hauls and door-to-door delivery.

Not that railway business was bad. In Gordon's first year the deficit – $42 million in 1949 – was reduced to a manageable $3 million, but CN had been bouncing too long between lean years of excess capacity and financial stringency and boom years of equipment shortages and inflated capital costs to be optimistic. With the loss of monopoly, the old theory that the more volume carried the better was being questioned. While refraining from disturbing such a sacred cow as the Crow rate, whereby the bigger the crop the less relative profit for the railway, CN blamed regulations in general for high operating costs and studied ways to provide faster trains, better service, more competitive pricing and aggressive selling to compete against the highways.

The railway was in poor shape to serve the expanding economy of the 1950s. Half its passenger coaches, a quarter of the freight cars and three quarters of the locomotives were past their normal life span of thirty years. "On the freight side we were always short of equipment after the war," said Dingle, who was pleasantly surprised when he stalked Gordon for 1,000 boxcars and was told he could have 5000. "Quit trying to be president," Gordon told him. "Your job is to tell me what you need to run a railway, not what you can get by with. It's my job to decide whether we can afford it." From his vantage point as vice-president of purchasing, Bromley observed that Gordon "had the happy facility of being able to get money."

With his appalling first year past, Gordon began to enjoy the novel experience of directing a big company. "He took a bag of work home with him every night," recalled a newcomer to the president's suite, Lloyd Morgan, who became Gordon's executive secretary. "He didn't rubber-stamp anything that was submitted by an officer. For that reason it took him longer to do the work, but he did it at night. Every day was a rush. He always wanted things done fast."

He gained respect for his grasp of detail and could detect a flaw in a column of figures at a glance. Going over accounts one day he found an expensive item simply headed "for water" and, knowing that CN had its own supply, he asked what it meant. No one seemed to know, and Gordon discovered that whenever CN water got low valves were opened to let in city water and often were carelessly left open.

Gordon could be dour, arrogant and aloof, though his friends said this was due to his poor eyesight and self-imposed work load. "If you made a blooper he never let you forget it until you had redeemed yourself," said W.T. "Bill" Wilson, vice-president for personnel and labour relations. "If you did something well, he never forgot that either." "I didn't have an easy time with him," said Bromley, "[but] he and Sir Henry made us proud to be working for CN. One time I was with him on the train and he'd had quite a few under his belt and he said, 'I don't understand why you fellows didn't crucify me when I first came to the railway.' 'Well, [replied Bromley] we quickly found that you were for the railway, and if you were for the railway we were for you.'"

Gordon was concerned at the condition of the railway, having found too much antiquated equipment and a passenger service that was bleeding money. With domestic spending and the Korean War generating boom conditions, he determined that the next few years were to be CN's period of "rehabilitation and reorientation."

Serving ten provinces and twelve states, its slogan "To Everywhere in Canada" was more than a copywriter's hyperbole. CN operated trucks, buses and urban trams, ships, ferry boats and stockyards, and held all the capital stock in Trans-Canada Air Lines. It maintained 5000 stations, 7000 bridges, 121,000 freight cars and 3600 passenger cars. The Blue Folder, CN's timetable of eighty-six pages, listed 1400 schedules. It was transporting yearly 80 million tons of freight, 24 million express parcels and 18 million passengers, transmitting 14 million commercial messages and accommodating three quarters of a million people in its hotels.

Knowing Ottawa as he did, Gordon took every opportunity to discourage political interference. When transport minister Lionel Chevrier proposed that the deputy minister, Jean-Claude Lessard, Thornton's protégé of the 1920s, rejoin CN as a vice-president and informal pipeline between government and railway, Gordon successfully resisted. He preferred his own Ottawa contacts and ways of dealing with the government. As long as the Liberals were in power, relations were usually equable and disputes limited to the Railway Committee hearings, where they were more or less expected.

Being a crown corporation and living in the shadow of a romantic CPR image, which had assured the private railway the lion's share of publicity since Donald Smith drove the last spike in 1885, CN had the more difficult public relations task, but Gordon had learned the importance of effective PR during the war. "It was a rare day that I didn't see him at least a couple of times," recalled Charles A. Harris, who succeeded W. R. Wright as director of public relations in 1959. Though he was accused of it himself, Gordon condemned management by crisis. "Instead of being on top of the total situation, watching the symptoms of weakness and checking defects as they develop," he lectured Dingle, "we seem to struggle from one headache to the next, grappling with yesterday's problems. Under these conditions it is not surprising that we are more often the victim than the master of circumstance."

The head of this giant enterprise had to be a Jack-of-all-trades: hotelier, ship-owner, architect, financier, labour negotiator and good-will ambassador. "I have made decisions," Gordon boasted, "involving the purchase of a bus line, an electric railway, the sale of a coal mine [Rail and River in Ohio, sold because of dieselization], the sale of timber limits, the placing of orders for new ships and railway equipment running into the many millions, plans for railway coordination with the St. Lawrence Seaway, plans for dieselization, recapitalization procedure, wage negotiations, freight rate applications and so on ad infinitum."

Like his predecessors, Gordon deplored the low tariff for grain, which accounted for 40 per cent of all freight moved in the West and a quarter of the total freight of the nation. The Crow rate was half the rate charged for grain in the States, and a fifth to a quarter the rate charged for coal, the most lucrative bulk traffic, and meant higher costs were passed on to customers in other industries. But for the Prairies the statutory rate, controlled by Parliament, remained an article of faith ensuring independence from central Canada.

"The present freight rate tariff is a structure of unbelievable complexity," said Gordon. "Millions upon millions of words have been spread in one investigation after another and the record is replete with special pleadings, grievances, complaints, confusions and misunderstandings. I am not prepared to say that we can ever achieve a freight rate structure in Canada that will please everyone. But I do claim that an equalizing of competitive conditions will bring that possibility far closer to reality as well as giving the railways a chance to develop."

The dilemma resulting from its inability to compensate for rising costs by raising prices, as other industries did, could be seen in CN's discouraging deficit in 1951. The company was moving more freight but so much was low-rate pulpwood, grain and minerals that revenues were overwhelmed by expenses. Nurtured by provincial governments' refusal to collect highway taxes proportional to use, trucks were skimming off short-haul, high-value freight.

Gordon simply wanted railways and trucking to compete on an equal footing and found comfort in the Turgeon royal commission on transportation, which completed hearings that spring. Turgeon called for rate equalization across the country, which was subsequently written into the Railway Act. The government also subsidized rail freight crossing the "traffic desert" of northwestern Ontario.

Despite railway claims they were losing money on the Crow rate, it had not as yet been an undue burden. Turgeon did, however, recommend removing other burdens that had little to do with operating efficiency. Railways should be permitted to abandon money-losing branch lines, he said, and CN be allowed to reorganize its finances, since 1937 had been largely an exercise in bookkeeping. Meantime the debt load had swollen to $1.5 billion, twice that of 1923, and twice as high as the CPR's debt. (The latter's average earnings per mile continued to be almost 10 per cent higher than CN's.)

Two thirds of CN's debt was owed to the government and the rest to people who owned securities, some of them for Grand Trunk construction in the 1850s. In an effort to balance debt and equity, the secretary of the cabinet, Norman Robertson, met with CN and government officials in an atmosphere, as Gordon said, of "discord and futility." Dr. W. C. Clark, the boyish-looking deputy minister of finance, opposed CN with an argument that recapitalization would merely shuffle debt from CN to the treasury, a cosmetic exercise that would make CN look so much better it would drive up wages and freight rates. "Until it is made clear by way of instruction from the cabinet that his [Clark's] immovable prejudices are irrelevant to the task of the committee," said Gordon, "I can see no hope of making progress."

But progress there was, and the CN Capital Revision Act of 1952 reduced debt by half, though it offered limited safeguard against deficits and was only a partial recognition of the burden, psychological and fiscal, of the debt. "The present attempt at recapitalization may not be the last word," conceded the *Winnipeg Tribune*, "but at least it is a beginning toward correcting something that has needed correcting for a long time."

By giving back IOUs in exchange for stock the government became a proprietor rather than a creditor and the debt, in effect, became an investment rather than a loan, with interest to be paid only when CN earned a surplus. So that CN could finance projects without every dollar automatically hatching new fixed charges, the government undertook to purchase preferred shares of stock, an annual injection of $30 or $40 million in equity that was one of the best things in the act.

Gordon was overly optimistic: "It brings to a close the struggle for fair play which began on that day in 1919 when the system was created by statute of Parliament. The windows of our financial structure have been washed at last and all the cobwebs cleared away. From here on, we who work for the railway can at least see daylight and the people outside can see just how efficiently we are operating. If we can continue to operate as we have in the [recent] past, and if we can keep our costs in proper relation to our earning capacity, we should not have to show a deficit again."

Gordon was confident the proportion of debt to investment would henceforth be much like that at the CPR. Since 1946 the growth of CN traffic had reflected increases in gross national product, and Gordon anticipated that so long as freight rates, wages and prices were in balance, CN would be able to cover depreciation, debt interest and taxes. Profit, on the other hand, would depend on whether the Board of Transport Commissioners authorized rates that more than covered operating costs.

Over the next ten years CN would spend over $1.7 billion (five times that in 1990s dollars) on motive power, freight and passenger equipment, rails, right of way and marshalling yards, the biggest single expense being diesel locomotives (also called diesel-electrics because of their generators and electrical transmissions) and their requirement for better tracks, dispatching and signalling.

CN had scores of yard diesels for shunting when Gordon arrived, though only two dozen road diesels, the first generation ordered in 1948 for use between Montreal and Toronto and Chicago and Port Huron. As steam locomotives were retired, coal would be the first casualty, and CN had to proceed carefully to avoid the problems of England, where the fate of coal communities had become an issue that delayed switching to diesels. CN was moving 60 per cent of the country's coal production, its biggest single revenue producer, and as a crown corporation had to consider the political impact on Cape Breton and Springhill in Nova Scotia and on the Alberta foothills. But with dieselization sweeping the United States, and steam engines harder to acquire, neither CN nor the CPR had a choice. CN began the first of two five-year renewal programs in 1952, putting big road diesels on routes calculated to provide the best return on investment. By the mid-1950s, CN was operating 1105 diesels, which hauled half of its freight and passengers.

Some 2700 engine drivers were taking diesel instruction. "There was a tremendous educational process," said Alex Smail, then a roadmaster in northern Ontario. "There was some suspicion this was some kind of gas buggy that would flunk sooner or later, but resistance broke down when the driver sat in that nice clean warm environment on a comfortable seat. It was not hard to teach people to run the diesels, but maintenance people who had worked on steam engines became redundant."

Though the diesel cab did not quite resemble an airplane cockpit as it does now, it was a great improvement over the steamer in comfort and convenience. Instead of the array of heavy controls, throttle, reverse lever, airbrakes, valves, water gauge, sander, etc., there was a neat control panel, with one lever controlling the generators that fuelled the electric motors driving the wheels, one for forward and reverse, and the other two for braking. There were convenient buttons for the horn and bell, and sound-proofing that cut down track noise and the roar of the power plant behind the cab. There was protection from the weather and a toilet at the back of the cab, which the steamers had lacked. There was also a "dead man's pedal" which slowed the train if the engineer's foot came off it; this safety feature was sometimes nullified by drivers who jammed the pedal down with their lunch boxes to ease their legs.

Though a diesel locomotive cost more than a steam locomotive, running costs were half as much. Unlike most steamers, diesels could double in passenger and freight service when necessary. Diesels – often two or three units linked together – could haul more freight than steamers, were faster to start and stop, needed no coal docks, water stations or ash pits and required fewer people to serve them. Though diesels were not necessarily faster than steamers, time could be saved because of fewer stops. Diesels could haul a 100-car, 10,000 ton freight train 500 miles before refuelling, whereas steamers needed coal and water every 125 miles or so. The diesel did as much on one tank-car of oil as a steam locomotive on eight cars of coal. The railways anticipated they could make significant savings from eventually eliminating firemen and bypassing division points where steamers had to stop and refuel. While admitting whole trades would become redundant, Gordon insisted that communities and the human factor had been kept in mind. "We did not go bull-headed at it just for the sake of dieselization," he said.

Despite the comfort of the shiny new cabs, old-timers hated to see their drafty, dirty, beloved steamers die, and when a diesel broke down they chuckled to see a Northern steam up to save the day. Each steam locomotive felt different, with its own quirks, they said, but diesels were robots.

"For the older engineers it was a terrible change," recalled Alex Douglas of Thunder Bay, a young fireman at the time, "but for us it was a very easy transition because we had General Motors men who rode with us. The engineer had to stay with the throttle but the fireman got to know the whole diesel unit and how it worked. So that gave us a big advantage in repairing and keeping those units on the road that the older engineer did not have." Diesels required less "shopping," or overhauling, and cost 25 per cent less to maintain because standard parts could be purchased, as with automobiles, whereas replacement parts for a steam locomotive had to be custom made.

Starting from the east and west coasts, diesel conversion spread inward to central Canada, and the first passenger train to "go diesel" was the *Ocean Limited*, hauled by a gold, green and black newcomer between Montreal and Halifax in 1954. The Montreal-Toronto passenger service to Vancouver changed to diesel the following year and the *International Limited* from Montreal and Toronto to Chicago in 1957. Newfoundland was converted, as was the Central Vermont, the Duluth, Winnipeg and Pacific, and the Grand Trunk Western. Retired steam locomotives were often given to museums or towns along the CN line or dismantled for scrap.

On many counts, 1953 was Gordon's most fulfilling year. He had married again (to Norma, daughter of vice-president W. H. Hobbs). The railway was earning a modest surplus, and a strike that might have been more serious than that of 1950 was averted with a compromise settlement with the Brotherhood of Railway Trainmen. The diesel program was on schedule. The promising intermodal system known as piggybacking, wherein CN's loaded highway trailers were shipped on flatcars, had been inaugurated between Montreal and Toronto, a road-rail collaboration that was eventually extended throughout Canada. The overnight service improved door-to-door deliveries by combining the long-distance speed of trains with the local convenience of trucks.

Because railways had been created to populate and serve the country in an era when there was no competition, they had little marketing policy, so Gordon ordered a study of the most visible and least lucrative service, which he called the "mobile hotels featuring Waldorf service at steakhouse prices."

He was dismayed that ninety-two Canadians out of a hundred were using cars or buses, while coaches designed for ten times as many passengers were rattling over branch lines with half a dozen. The *Continental Limited* consisted of seventeen cars and a staff of twenty-seven, and to keep it running every day in both directions sixteen identical trains were needed.

The challenge from the automobile had been masked during the war, when train travel was high, but with three million automobiles now on the roads, passenger service was in the red. "Rear end" traffic – sleeping cars, parlour cars and dining cars – was a financial drain: bedding alone on the 366 sleeping cars had to be sufficient for a city of 20,000. To provide meals the railway had to operate 93 dining and 27 café cars and employ 263 chefs, 330 waiters and 110 stewards.

The TCA North Stars were claiming ever more passengers and under the presidency of Gordon R. McGregor, "our rich relative," as Donald Gordon called the airline, had doubled seating capacity in five years to become the ninth largest in the world. Though there was less symbiosis now as the two organizations, one an industry of the future, the other rooted in the past, inched toward divorce, TCA was paying its nominal parent for rent, medical service, communications and interest on capital stock.

People were the most demanding and least profitable of all commodities, said Gordon, and the future for passenger service was unpromising. It had become a fine question whether people were abandoning the railways or the railways were abandoning the people but to lure them back with faster trains would need tremendous capital investment. Caught between the Canadian romance of railway travel and a public disinclination to use the trains, Gordon was loath to invest but prevented by the government from cutting. The more the equipment deteriorated the more passengers stayed away, but both railways nourished lingering hopes of luring people back.

"CN shared to some degree with the CPR and all the major North American railways the illusion that passenger service was vital to the railways' future," said Jim McDonald, who at one time or another served as vice-president of both Canadian railways and the Penn Central. "The CEOs, the first thing they looked at in the morning was the behaviour of the 'varnish' or first-class passenger trains. They did not recognize that a whole generation had grown up that had never travelled by train. Since the days when Hanna decided passenger service could not pay, it had rarely if ever been exposed as the burden it was on net income."

Inasmuch as they believed in the future of passenger service at all, the CPR saw it as luxury travel, put on a second transcontinental train and ordered 173 stainless steel cars, some of them domed. "We thought about that," Dingle recalled, "but whereas CP's Windsor Station could accommodate them, we could not at the time put dome cars through Central Station because of their height." CN took a less expensive approach and bought 260 coaches whose only luxuries were rotating seats with reclining backs. "I managed to convince Gordon not to buy deluxe equipment but he felt that a second transcontinental train was worth a try," said Fairweather. "I predicted it would lose millions. The last analytical study I made before retirement proved this to be true." The trade journal *Canadian Transportation* complained that the CPR was making CN look amateur: "Please, please Mr. Gordon can't we show [the CPR] our tail lamps just once?"

Gordon had no wish to compete train for train as in the Thornton days, but in 1955 CN made its own bid for passengers by introducing the *Super Continental,* which, together with the *Ocean Limited,* cut sixteen hours off the trip from Halifax to Vancouver. Incentive fares encouraged travel in off-peak periods, as did the first year-round, all-inclusive package in Canada. CN promotion included a museum train of pioneer locomotives and coaches which travelled the country reminding people of their railway past.

While no subject was likely to stir politicians more than passenger complaints, in 1955 a headline controversy swirled around the most-discussed hotel manager in Canadian parliamentary history. The story began when Jack Pickersgill, then secretary to the cabinet, arrived at the Fort Garry in Winnipeg to find the CN hotel had no record of his reservation. What was worse, when Prime Minister St. Laurent arrived next day the manager, a Conservative, failed to greet him. Pickersgill complained privately to Gordon, making unfavourable comparisons with CPR hotels, and was surprised when the press printed stories that the manager, Robert Pitt, had been demoted to a smaller hotel, the Prince Edward in Brandon, Manitoba.

The Conservative opposition blamed political interference, but Gordon insisted it was purely an internal matter. When an elderly Conservative MP, J.M. Macdonnell of Toronto, doubted his word, Gordon made an angry desk-thumping scene such as the Commons had not witnessed for years. "I have been accused of giving in to political interests and I deny it," he told the Railway Committee. "Do you think that Jack Pickersgill or anybody else could scare me into removing the manager of a hotel?" When he ceased shouting, the Liberal majority shelved the business on the sensible grounds the committee should not get involved with CN staff.

"I am not becoming discouraged," Gordon wrote, "although I admit there are times when I suffer a considerable degree of impatience. The organization is so large and there are so many things to be done that one almost despairs of getting results." The marketing department had limited influence with the operating department which controlled the trains. Customers were tired of inconvenient passenger schedules, and Gordon began to give marketing a bigger role. "It was then," recalled Walter Smith, "that the marketing people began to tell customers, 'Hey, if you want a train at nine in the morning, you'll get a train at nine in the morning ... if it is worthwhile for us.'"

Otherwise railroading at CN had not changed much since 1923 when Thornton introduced the methods of the Pennsylvania Railroad. Born of the industrial revolution, railways had adopted rigid military traditions to ensure that trains ran on time and safely, and once a safe way of operation had been found there was a reluctance to try anything new. The typical railroader had begun at the bottom and through industry and ability had made his way up the ladder. While the system produced capable people, they tended to a traditional, rather narrow outlook. Even rationalizing the corporate structure was a ponderous operation.

"I am concerned," said Gordon, "about what seems to be a continuing process whereby each department considers itself a separate unit and makes its plans without due regard to their influence and effect on the system generally. It is of fundamental importance that we make some serious effort to break down the Chinese walls which appear to me to be resolutely defended by each department of the railway."

Gordon began to modernize CN department by department. Technical changes were vetted by Starr Fairweather, who controlled the capital budget. "He was not popular but he had one of the best analytical minds I have ever encountered, and people who worked for him respected him," said Jim McDonald. "Like Gordon he believed in an independent management and welcomed a strong president. He himself did not expect to be president and told me one time he probably could do just as well being the president's right arm."

If an indicator of a progressive railway is its research, Fairweather's R&D department compared favourably with any similar railway organization in the world, though this in itself was faint praise, perhaps, railways not being famous for research. In new laboratories in Montreal, chief chemist E. T. Hurley, who had been hired away from the National Research Council, was breaking ground in the acquisition, manufacture and use of the equipment and materials CN bought in such abundance, testing everything from locomotive efficiency to laundering. "We set up our own standards," said Hurley, "and you wouldn't believe what we ran into and rejected. A lot of people in the supply business, not all by any means, were playing games with the railway, a heck of a place to make a fast buck. There was monkey business in the quality of materials supplied, a bad thing both for safety and for the life of the material. We were finally even ruling on the quality of conductor's uniforms."

Seeking new blood, Gordon presented the R&D department with two academics who were to have great influence on CN. One was a young economist, Dr. Robert Bandeen, who would one day become president. The other, who was to replace Fairweather, was Dr. Omond M. Solandt, head of the Defence Research Board in Ottawa, who brought scientific rigour. "R&D, I discovered, was really defined as everything Fairweather thought was not being done well," said Solandt. "He knew more about the railway than all the other vice-presidents put together."

Projects that R&D was working on when Solandt arrived included costing and pricing, business forecasting, industrial development in half a dozen cities, lead and zinc properties in New Brunswick, and technical research into piggybacking, lubricants, refrigeration, paints and wood preservation. R&D was responsible for the corporate budget because, as Solandt explained, "in the early days the accounting people were bookkeepers and there wasn't anyone there who had the education and background for financial planning and forecasting, so Starr just took it on."

A knowledge solely of railway operation was deemed no longer sufficient for a railway officer and on the advice of Fairweather and W. T. Wilson, vice-president for personnel, Gordon founded the Staff Training College with the aid of the School of Business Administration of the University of Western Ontario. In April 1953 forty-four men from virtually all regions and departments were selected from 100 recommendations of superiors. The six-week course could hardly produce an all-round railroader but it did give the men (at first no women were included) a chance to see each other's problems and make friends with co-workers across the nation. The first session was held in a freight shed in Montreal but thereafter courses were held at Bishop's University, Lennoxville, Quebec, where students would not be distracted. Every summer fifty men were chosen until a core of a thousand graduates was built up and courses were no longer necessary.

"I think it was successful but not necessarily because it made for better managers as such," said George Lach, who succeeded Wilson as vice-president of personnel. "What it did first of all was expose the talent that we had not recognized. Secondly it built up a network of relationships because you had fifty people who had lived with each other for six weeks, coming from all branches of the railway, so that the channels of communication through the whole company were multiplied. Thirdly it gave the CN people a new vocabulary of production management and marketing and an awareness that there was literature on subjects they had not been aware of. We checked as best we could the benefits of these courses and found, generally speaking, that the more effective members of the courses were promoted. What we never established to our satisfaction was whether men were selected because they were going to be promoted or whether they were promoted because they had taken the course."

From the universities an annual quota of fifty engineering and law graduates had been enlisted and now the program was extended to graduates in commerce, economics and the liberal arts. "It seems to me that training in those fields makes for development of superior managerial talent," said Gordon. "The old order – recruiting juniors for office boy and clerical jobs – had much to commend it, especially in the days when few individuals ever dreamed of a university education. Now ever-increasing numbers are enrolled in our universities. We cannot expect young graduates to have the experience and maturity of those who have come up the hard way. However, one of the most useful assets which the average graduate develops is the ability to acquire knowledge."

The old order was changing in other ways. As a government corporation and the railway with the northernmost tracks, CN was expected to transport minerals and wood out of the north. In Quebec it built a fifty-five-mile line from Barraute, a zinc producing region near Amos, to Beattyville. Some 500 miles northwest of Winnipeg it laid a 144-mile line through muskeg, permafrost and rock from Sherridon Lake to Lynn Lake, where nickel, copper and cobalt had been discovered a decade earlier. On a snowy November 10, 1953, Donald Gordon walloped in the ceremonial spike, appropriately made of nickel, with eleven blows, missing on the first two. His eyesight had always been poor. "I noticed all the small children were gathered there to laugh and I didn't want to disappoint them," he said.

On the West Coast, CN built a forty-six-mile line through the Coastal Range from Terrace to Kitimat to serve the Aluminum Company of Canada smelter 350 miles north of Vancouver. Another line was built between Hillsport, Ontario, which lay on the CN transcontinental route 280 miles east of the Lakehead, and the new copper mining community of Manitouwadge twenty-seven miles away. Gordon cautiously drove the last spike – of copper – using a pneumatic spike driver instead of a hammer.

In Montreal the steel skeleton of the twenty-one-floor hotel beside Central Station was growing, as were arguments over who should manage it. The ubiquitous Fairweather, who headed the Terminal Development Committee, favoured leasing it out. "There was a difference between operation of a hotel chain for public acclaim and running it for profit," he said. "Our chain of hotels was in some sense a show window similar to our dining car service – not expected in themselves to be profitable … an invasion of the hotel market in Montreal should be judged by free market economics, a field in which we really had no experience."

Since it was to be a convention hotel that needed contacts in the States, the Hilton Hotel group, with twenty-five hotels in the U.S., was chosen to manage it. The first of many controversies arose when the Hotel Association of Canada, whose executive included Robert Sommerville, general manager of CN Hotels, objected that American management would be a "reflection on Canadian ability and reputation."

There was much discussion about the hotel's name and when someone suggested the Queen Elizabeth, Dick Wright, director of public relations, volunteered to consult External Affairs in Ottawa. When word got out, 200,000 French-speaking Montrealers signed a petition circulated by the nationalist St. Jean Baptiste Society to christen it Chateau Maisonneuve after a founder of the city. But by now a letter had come back from Buckingham Palace that the Queen had graciously agreed, as the formula went, and despite outcries from her francophone subjects, it was too late to change. If anyone was to be offended, it would not be the Queen.

When Montreal became headquarters of the International Civil Aviation Organization and the International Air Transport Association, C.D. Howe made sure the International Aviation Building was built on CN land by Central Station. MacMillan, who had done most of the planning, was still wondering what to do about the other six acres when William Zeckendorf swept into town from New York City. As head of Webb and Knapp, Zeckendorf had turned the mean streets of Manhattan into the UN building and Rockefeller Center, and since he promised to draw up plans at his own expense, Gordon gave him his blessing to develop the hole in the ground that had been an eyesore since the departure of Mackenzie and Mann.

The year 1955 was a hopeful one for CN as for the country. Production, employment and consumption had been growing virtually every year. From a crushing deficit of $29 million in 1954, CN had rebounded to a surplus of $11 million, dramatizing the extent that earnings could oscillate from year to year with shifting levels of traffic.

The following year the company again carried a record volume of traffic. Freight trains were moving 60 per cent more tonnage with 12 per cent fewer locomotives and 6 per cent fewer cars than in 1928, the best pre-war year. Though expenses rose to new heights, the result after payment of fixed charges was a healthy surplus of $26 million on which none of the recently introduced income tax for crown corporations was payable because of losses in prior years. As it happened, the 1956 surplus was not only the largest of the Gordon years – it was the last.

Nearly 800 miles of track were replaced that year, 270 track extensions, spurs and industrial sidings were completed and work was begun to install Centralized Traffic Control (CTC) on 4000 miles of single track across the country. Never had the railway been so involved in change and adjustment, the greatest being dieselization with its profound impact on operating procedures, train size, maintenance, employment levels and labour relations. The replacement of steam locomotives, begun in the late 1940s and completed in 1960, transformed the railway more than anything that came before.

PRAGMATISM
AND PUBLIC
ENTERPRISE

THE ROLE OF A GOVERNMENT-OWNED RAILWAY in a mixed economy and a changing society had never been easy. There had been a time when participation in regional development and other government policies had been an acceptable quid pro quo for the railways' monopoly in land transportation, but by the 1950s highways had cut into rail revenues and reduced the social need for trains to serve all but the most isolated areas.

Nevertheless, the government still expected CN to serve public policy. The latest example was the Hudson Bay Railway, which CN had completed and operated for the government, running the *Muskeg Special* from The Pas to Churchill and hauling grain in season with the government paying the deficit. The route had never fulfilled the expectations of its western backers or the government, but this did not stop the Diefenbaker government ordering CN in 1958 to take full responsibility for it, deficits and all, on the questionable premise that since CN had built its own branch line from Sipiwesk on the HBR to the mines at Moak and Mystery Lake, the People's Railway should take over the whole thing.

It was the sort of challenge Thornton had been ready to take on. Gordon was harder to persuade. In reviving the question of whether CN was dedicated to public service or profit, Gordon opted for profitability. "Canadian National can best serve this nation," he said, "if it is free to act, in its management philosophy and its operations, as an efficient business organization." He believed running CN as a business would avoid the need for the financial aid that attracted government interference and annoyed the taxpayer. Gordon wanted the debt removed once and for all. Weary of complaints that the CPR, through its taxes, was supporting the public railway, he wanted CN judged as the CPR was judged – on ability to make money, or at least to break even.

Gordon envied the CPR its freedom from the scrutiny of politicians, press and public. "You get delegations all the time at Ottawa to the minister of transport or the prime minister in respect of layoffs and other things," Gordon complained. "You never get delegations in respect to CPR matters. We get hell if we try to reduce expenses on the Canadian National but the Canadian Pacific does not because it is a private company."

CN was no "experiment in socialism," Gordon said. When an MP urged that the People's Railway make coal purchases to benefit Nova Scotia mining communities, Gordon replied that CN had no mandate to subsidize coal or any other industry and whether it bought Canadian or American coal depended on the price. When it was suggested that a profit-making crown corporation was a contradiction in terms, Gordon argued that CN was less a crown corporation than the offspring of a shotgun marriage between public finance and private enterprise. Ignoring the railway nationalization policy of Sir Robert Borden, Gordon added that public ownership was so foreign to Canada that only the CCF (NDP) consistently favoured it, overlooking the fact the Conservatives – despite their subsequent hostility to state enterprise – had produced four crown corporations: CN, the Bank of Canada, the Canadian Broadcasting Corporation and the Canadian Wheat Board.

The relationship between government and a crown corporation is never more touchy than when a new government appears, and the longer a party has been out of office the more difficult the transition. Thus in 1957 when the Conservatives were returned after more than twenty years in opposition, CN found itself obliged to teach new MPs that electoral success did not mean a turn at patronage. Gordon himself gave a blistering lesson to one honourable member from Montreal who demanded control of all CN purchases and hirings in his constituency. Otherwise, apart from attempts to secure inside information about tenders for ties – old-fashioned pork-barrelling that CN brushed off – relations at first were amicable, particularly with transport minister George Hees.

"In theory," Hees said later, "the president or chairman of a crown corporation is independent, but all presidents know they must come and get the government's okay for their actions because they are spending the people's money." But in 1957 Hees, like his cabinet colleagues, was new to the corridors of power. Gordon described him as a "babe in arms" so far as railroading was concerned and persuaded the new minister to leave the Liberal-appointed CN board intact. Prime Minister John Diefenbaker was less than pleased. Appointment to the CN board was a political plum, and sometimes a consolation prize for not getting a Senate appointment. "We always wondered what the difficulty was between Diefenbaker and Gordon," said corporate secretary Ralph T. Vaughan, "and we pinned it down to the time Gordon had his slate of Liberal board members reappointed and Diefenbaker had not been in office long enough to get advice."

Moreover, the economic boom was over and the surplus of $26 million that CN had proudly brought to the Liberal government had collapsed into a deficit of $30 million. Wages had doubled in a decade and people were paid the same amount for a day that their fathers got for a week in 1914. Long-distance truckers were cutting into railway business as never before, in one case hauling beef from Alberta to Montreal. The Trans-Canada Highway, the completion of four pipelines, and TCA and Canadian Pacific Airlines had reduced the railways' share of the transportation dollar to fifty cents.

Though the St. Lawrence Seaway, which opened in 1957 to draw Atlantic shipping 1500 miles into the heart of the continent, did not hurt the railway as much as originally feared, it did take a share of grain and lumber destined for Europe, iron ore and newsprint for the States, and U.S. coal bound for central Canada. It also forced CN to move forty miles of main line back from the St. Lawrence between Cornwall, Ontario, and Cardinal so the terrain could be flooded.

A more complex problem was the century-old Victoria Bridge, which carried a hundred trains a day and had to be altered so ocean freighters could pass. CN was there first and must have priority, said Gordon. Not so, said Lionel Chevrier, who was now in charge of the Seaway Authority, since water-borne navigation was historically senior to railways as everyone knew.

"We quickly reached a point where both of us obdurately refused to concede anything," recalled Chevrier. The unedifying picture of two crown corporations fighting over who would pay brought Hees in to arbitrate.

The Victoria Bridge was one of Fairweather's last tasks, and after frustrating complications the aging wizard of R&D settled for an arrangement that combined highway approaches, a railway diversion or "shoofly," and two lift spans so that when one span was open the other was closed and traffic could flow. "There would be little interruption of railway, highway or water traffic," promised Fairweather. "The cost of the lift bridge and the shoofly was borne by the Seaway."

Already a better railway since Gordon arrived, CN was putting a third of its investment into rolling stock and the rest into infrastructure, tracks, yards, real estate and Centralized Traffic Control. Freight cars were replaced at the rate of six thousand a year and to increase road-rail integration the piggy-backing of CN trucks was extended to commercial truckers, whose rigs, complete with cargoes, were loaded onto flatcars. To cut delivery from central Canada to the West Coast by twenty-four hours, a fast freight "highballer" service from Montreal and Toronto made second-morning deliveries in Winnipeg, third-morning deliveries in Edmonton and fourth-afternoon deliveries in Vancouver.

The western main line, which accounted for thirteen times more traffic than the branch lines carried, was in poor repair and Gordon approved a rehabilitation program that would permit the western route to carry, as it does today, the lion's share of CN traffic. To C. F. Armstrong, then in operations at Winnipeg, this was heady stuff: "Here was somebody suddenly saying, 'This is a railway here to stay, and I will give you the capital to get out there and build a mainline that some day will carry the traffic Canada expects it to carry.' It was marvellous. All of a sudden the railway was alive. It was an exciting challenge."

For better use of space, customers were offered discounts to ship entire carloads rather than less-than-carload (LTC) shipments. To avoid the expense of dispatching locomotive, crew and boxcars to fetch a small shipment on a stub line, CN took to sending a driver and a van for small loads. The express department, having followed the CPR into the trucking business, now had nearly a thousand trucks covering 20,000 miles of routes, some of them replacing former branch lines. The recently established department of road transport was supervising such varied operations as piggybacking, bus lines in the Niagara Peninsula and Oshawa, and automobile toll booths on Victoria Bridge.

Like dieselization, automation arrived at both major Canadian railways about the same time in the 1950s. "We had a hell of a time getting computers introduced," said Solandt. "When I came to CN, freight car accounting consisted of a huge office that looked like something out of Dickens – ledger keepers on tall stools. The only thing they lacked was quill pens."

Computers were first used to cut two thirds off the time needed to issue 100,000 bimonthly pay cheques (the running trades got paid by a complicated mixture of mileage and hours with formulae for overtime and deductions). Later, computers would keep track of freight cars, which normally spent 10 per cent of their lives in motion and the other 90 out on a lonely siding somewhere in Canada or the United States. "If you stopped to think about it, there was a problem," said Solandt. "A freight car goes into a siding on the Prairies with a load of Christmas goodies and there is no shipment out of that town till the following spring so the boxcar just stays there. That was considered good business." Computers would maximize revenue per car and change the economics of railway freight.

Automation was a godsend in the marshalling yards, where railways make or lose money by the speed with which they process trains. In the past, yards had been laid out on level ground and cars shuffled and banged about by yard engines to the detriment of rolling stock and contents. Then simple gravity hump yards had appeared – dominated by a hill up which cars were pushed by shunters to coast down onto their separate tracks – with the positions, contents and destinations of cars tabulated by hand. This changed as the company converted four major yards – Moncton, Montreal, Toronto, and Winnipeg – into automated hump yards where cars were sorted by electronically-operated retarders onto one of forty or fifty tracks. (Gordon had a simpler explanation. "The freight car goes over the hump and rolls down to kiss and couple," he said in his Scots burr.) The first CN hump yard, opened at Moncton in 1960, covered 830 acres. Montreal's, opened the following year at Côte-de-Liesse on the western outskirts of the city, was the largest in North America with 161 miles of track and a capacity for 10,600 cars.

As railways lost their monopoly, Fairweather had questioned the theory that railways were a "decreasing cost industry" – the bigger the volume the better – but it was a newcomer at R&D, Dr. Robert Bandeen, who revolutionized costing and weaned the industry away from seeking business at whatever cost. "He introduced 'regression analysis' to determine how you cost the use of the tracks, maintain the right of way, and how you apportion cost between freight and passenger service, that sort of thing," said Solandt. "Before that, costing had been rudimentary and hardly used at all in rate setting and this could be blamed for much of the decline of the railways. At the time I joined CN freight rates were set on the 'value of service' principle, which was really just what the traffic would bear."

To pay for modernization, CN cut costs, starting with a work force that accounted for 62 per cent of total operating expenses. Railroads were affected more than most other industries by new technology in the postwar years. The federal Department of Labour reported that during the 1950s staff reductions were 50 per cent for locomotive firemen, 23 per cent for section-men and express workers, 19 per cent for locomotive engineers and 10 per cent for conductors.

There were complaints that Gordon's new "professional managers" lacked "the human approach" – including the paternalism that kept people in jobs whatever the economic consequences to the company. Though the work force was reduced by a sixth from an unprecedented total of 131,000, one effect of automation was to bring more women into CN – as key-punch operators feeding information into the huge first-generation computers, as clerks storing magnetic tapes, and as programmers, like Edith Jennings of the data processing centre in Moncton. One of the more unusual jobs was that of spectroscopist, in the Montreal R&D laboratory, where it was the task of Linda Holmes to analyze samples of locomotive oil to determine, by the amount of metal in it, whether a locomotive was due for a checkup. Though women were denied the same opportunities for promotion, new technology provided jobs in the non-running trades where they were recruited. "Actually we were all in the same boat," said Belva Steeples, hired to run complex machines in the centralized duplicating plant in Winnipeg. "Everyone is new to this kind of operation so we all have a sort of common bond."

Due to a general shortage of skilled stenographers in the late 1950s, CN made a point of providing job experience for young women graduates from business colleges. But the rarity of women in many departments was illustrated by Martha Walker, who as secretary to the superintendent at the freight yard in Montreal was the only woman among a thousand men. The sole woman labourer on CN's work force at this time was Alice Gordon in Sarnia, who had managed to keep her wartime job. Though trained in Scotland as a nurse, she found "shovelling coal and lifting machinery like the rest of them" more lucrative.

One notable change began with Solandt's decision to promote Mary Mason. Traditionally, CN's senior officers had employed male secretaries, not only because there were few trained women available at CN but because railroaders travelled in business cars and had to take their secretaries with them. Solandt, accustomed to women secretaries in Ottawa, broke with tradition and chose a woman who had been with CN for many years and trained many of the male secretaries. "She automatically put me in touch with the railway because Mary knew every senior person in the company," said Solandt. "I would not be travelling as much as other vice-presidents, and if I travelled in a business car I would take my wife along as well as Mary."

After her appointment had shown the way, other women became secretaries to senior officers, and though none got the opportunity to become vice-president, as some of their male predecessors had, Mary Mason went on to become (in 1974) the first female secretary to a president. Women also began to appear in other jobs during the next few years, though the blue collar work they had done during the war was denied them by the company and the unions. There was still no room for women in the running trades. Mary Catling, the only woman among 273 men at the Calder diesel shop in Edmonton, became a mechanic but her great desire was to become a locomotive engineer. She took correspondence courses in motive power and applied unsuccessfully for eight years for a chance to train as an engineer. Marg Wilmot of Moncton, whose grandfather and father had worked for the railway, worked her way up from clerk stenographer to become an express supervisor for the Atlantic region. In Guelph, Ontario, Dorothy Lyon, who had joined CN during the war as a clerk stenographer, became the first woman ticket agent.

Year after year CN cut back its payroll, pruning a management that was a third again as big as the CPR's and a track maintenance force that was twice as big, but in another area where it might have saved money it was continually thwarted. "We had 130 branch line abandonments awaiting action," said Solandt, "and every one of them had been proven a real loser with no chance of success. On most of them, the total revenue wouldn't pay the fuel cost of running one train a year, but the government would not take them out." It was a rare community that did not regard its branch line as a status symbol the closing of which would harm real estate values, though there was less fear in the age of cars and trucks that communities would become ghost towns should the railway pull out.

CPR branch abandonments were double those of CN, but since the government railway bore most of the criticism, it began to study questionable branch lines in detail never before attempted. Since a branch might show a loss but be justified as a national asset, the railway tried to determine what the results of abandonment might be. One measure was the cost of highway service to the nearest railway station: if this proved greater than the loss incurred by railway, the branch line had to be retained in what the government called the "national interest."

"Profit should be only a secondary consideration," scolded a Conservative backbencher from Newfoundland, which justifiably feared it would lose its tracks, "and service should be placed above all else." But service to Newfoundland was costly. Spending more there on average than in any other province, CN improved and expanded phone and telegraph communications, modernized the Newfoundland Hotel in St. John's, kept a merchant navy of eight hundred men working the coastal shipping and purchased the Canadian-built car ferry *William Carson*. A sister ship of the *Abegweit* that operated between New Brunswick and P.E.I., she carried passengers, cars, trucks, buses, cattle and 800 tons of freight between the new docks at Port aux Basques and North Sydney. Even so, Newfoundland complained in mid-1956 that the "rail and coastal situation is really desperate."

Notwithstanding their tendency to blame CN for the sins and omissions of the federal government, Newfoundlanders were having to wait five weeks for freight from Montreal, longer than it took from Europe. "Quite frankly our problems in Newfoundland have reached a point where, in my judgement some special action is required," Gordon said. "Naturally we are disturbed that despite such expenditures we have apparently not been successful in achieving a standard of service that will satisfy local requirements." More freight cars were assigned, and with ten ships plying Cabot Strait the bottlenecks were unplugged in time for Christmas.

Commitments like Newfoundland devoured capital, but since they were decreed by the government to discharge its responsibility to provide adequate transportation for its citizens, CN was obliged to undertake them. There was, however, an obvious place where money might be saved – the pooling of services with CPR – which had never progressed beyond the mainline trains between Toronto and Ottawa, Toronto and Montreal, and Montreal and

Quebec. In an effort to improve cooperation, Gordon and Norris R. "Buck" Crump, his opposite number at the CPR, decided to investigate why the railways were running more trains than needed in some places and not enough in others. "Donald elected me to represent CN and Buck elected Ian Sinclair," said Solandt. "An excellent plan was worked out with two alternatives: either you trade off trains equally, or you pool finances as well as service. I took it to Donald and he said, 'Well, I don't know, go and discuss it with Buck.' So I discussed it with Buck and he said, 'Look, Omond, I hate to do it but I've got to say that as long as I'm here and am driven by a bunch of old railroaders under me, I have to say we will go on competing for deficits.' That explains why moves to get railways to amalgamate never got to first base."

There was cooperation in the CN-CPR telegraph departments, which for ten years had been jointly selling leased wire services in competition with Bell Canada and the provincial telephone companies. In 1962 they had introduced Telex, the "do-it-yourself telegram," which became one of their most lucrative products, and to meet the heavy postwar demand for commercial communications, built a trans-Canada microwave system in 1964 linking major cities.

The expansion of industry and aviation and the birth of television and computers had brought a fourfold growth to Canadian National Telegraphs since the war. Now contributing three cents in every dollar to overall CN income, it had long since graduated from a railway sideline into a modern communications system with six thousand employees. Two thousand "brass pounders" who tapped out twelve million messages a year in Morse code, binding the country with telegrams and train orders, and gossip when traffic was slow, had been displaced by automation and teleprinters feeding off half a million miles of circuitry.

CNT's far-flung services ranged from telephone systems in Newfoundland, the Northwest Territories, the Yukon and northern B.C., to the Pine Tree Radar Line in the north. The company pioneered telephone service to the Northwest Territories and purchased and modernized the Yukon Telephone Company. By the early 1960s it had connected Hay River on Great Slave Lake, Pine Point, Fort Resolution and Yellowknife with the south by land line and radio. Revenue reached record heights and to reflect the diversity of its services CN Telegraphs changed its name to Canadian National Telecommunications. "There was still a warm feeling of being in the CN family," said Dermot Daly, a senior manager. "Whether you were from telecommunications or from the CN passenger service it didn't matter. You were CN.

I think Donald Gordon had a lot to do with building up that spirit. But gradually as CN and CPR telegraphs merged that feeling disappeared."

The express department, which employed as many people as CNT, was holding its own despite the recession and boasted of handling "anything from elephants to plankton, Christmas trees to cut flowers and precious stones." Income from hotels was stable, due largely to the Queen Elizabeth–Le Reine Elizabeth, whose gala opening was celebrated on April 17, 1958, (anglophone guests being reassured that *Le* referred to the hotel rather than the Queen). Gordon was thankful there was none of the agitation of the previous spring when singing, shouting, sign-waving francophone students had appeared under his window on McGill Street to demand a Québécois name for the hotel and protest his blind assumption that the name Queen Elizabeth would symbolize unity between the two language groups. After the fuss of the year before, CN was at pains to make sure the hotel had a French flavour.

Special trains brought celebrities and travel writers and the master of the liner *Queen Elizabeth* radioed greetings from the high seas. Under an American manager, Donald Mumford, the Queen Elizabeth, whose rectangular facade did little justice to its inviting interior, became a popular and profitable convention hotel with a bilingual staff of 1400 and a capacity to seat 2500 people for a meal in the banquet room or 3000 for a meeting.

Hilton Hotels International, which had a fifteen-year management agreement under which the chain would receive 25 per cent of operating profit and cover any operating loss, was invited to suggest ways to modernize CN's other hotels. "They sent Mumford to the Chateau Laurier," recalled Ralph Vaughan. "He dined in the Canadian Grill, where the waiters all wore white coats and black ties [as on trains]. Mumford came back and wrote this remedy in his report: 'The guests aren't sick, they're hungry.'" Since Hilton could do a better job of running hotels than the railway could, it offered to buy all seven and Jasper Park Lodge. Railway hotels were no longer needed to support train traffic – which raised questions whether building the Queen Elizabeth was not something of an anachronism for a railway – but their sale to an American chain would have had such political fallout the offer was declined.

In the past, the railway attitude toward real estate had been that you never knew when you might need it so you kept it. But now, as one of Canada's biggest property owners, CN began to take advantage of downtown locations in towns and cities across the country. It invigorated the Maritime rail centre of Moncton by building an Atlantic headquarters and a new station and inviting developers to transform twenty-five acres into a transportation, business and entertainment complex. In London, Ontario, a station and office building were opened.

In Montreal, as Zeckendorf had promised, Webb & Knapp (Canada) produced a plan by architect Io Ming Pei for a forty-storey cruciform that would be the largest building in the country. CN being in no position to provide financial guarantees or equity, Zeckendorf needed signed tenants before funds could be raised to start building. Several prospects turned the New York developer down before the Royal Bank of Canada agreed to make the new building its headquarters. The complex, opened in 1962, included shops, restaurants and cinemas linked by underground passages, a unique refuge from Montreal's cold in winter and heat in summer, and was named Place Ville Marie to commemorate the first French community on the site of Montreal.

Mainly because of the recession, CN's finances worsened in 1958 for the second year in a row, almost doubling the deficit to $50 million. As well as the usual debt, CN was now facing "unrequited depreciation," which is to say it had overstated its assets by not taking accumulated depreciation into account until 1940, when it began to take depreciation for equipment replacement; it began to do so for hotels only in 1954 and for track in 1956. Up to then, like most other North American railways, it had kept assets at initial book value until they were replaced or retired. The government, as CN owners, presumably might have required depreciation accounting earlier than the 1940s though that would have required it to pay more in annual support funding. Something like $800 million was involved, so the government was not inclined to write it off. Unlike the CPR, CN was in no position to wipe part of this off by claiming against past payments of tax on profits, having no profits to claim against.

"I do not like to criticize my predecessors, for what they did in those years was accepted and recognized as being all right," Gordon told the Senate Railway Committee. "I assume that the thinking of the day was, in effect, 'it does not matter because we have no shareholders in the usual sense that are being affected by the payment of dividends.'"

Borrowing 70 per cent of the money needed for modernization, and faced with doubling deficit in five years, CN began to act more like a private company. Jim McDonald, who had graduated from presidential speech writer to assistant vice-president at R&D, had bold advice. "Strip off everything that cannot be made to yield at least out-of-pocket-costs," he told Gordon. "We must streamline the labour force and learn to live lean so that there will be a chance of accumulating in periods of peak business the surplus we need to carry us through less prosperous times."

With passenger traffic fetching less than nine cents in the revenue dollar, CN decided to halve transcontinental winter service to one train daily in each direction, combining the *Super Continental* and the older *Continental* between October and May. Studies had shown insufficient travel to support two trains, but when Gordon rode west he discovered that cutting service might deprive CN of a mail contract worth half a million dollars.

"I heard rumblings of discontent," he said. "I also heard that the CPR had been making statements to the effect that they did not intend to make any reduction in their transcontinental trains.... I began to be concerned about the undercurrent of criticism and general feeling of letdown that our contemplated action was producing. Moreover, I had constantly to correct interviewers from newspapers who kept referring to our decision to abandon *all* transcontinental trains. These highly inaccurate references I felt were seriously damaging our reputation in the passenger business."

Prime Minister Diefenbaker was furious. First Gordon had packed the board with Liberals before Diefenbaker had had a chance to say yea or nay, and now he was threatening Diefenbaker's own western turf. While assuring Gordon the *Super Continental* decision was entirely CN's, Diefenbaker made it clear what he expected Gordon to do. The railway's plans to reduce western service, he said, would be a "very damaging blow to our standing generally as well as being destructive to employee morale."

Gordon called a meeting of the board and reinstated the service before damage was done. Had CN had caved in to government pressure? Gordon insisted that his action had been simple common sense. Actually it was a bit of both, but Gordon justified his turnabout as common sense. "Cancellation of reservations has begun to appear," he said. "Its impact on our freight service was much greater than we had expected. When we did continue the double service that winter we obtained quite satisfactory results. The loss was not as great as we thought it would be."

Because a railway can rid itself of ships more readily than trains, Gordon had less difficulty in disposing of Canadian National (West Indies) Steamships – or what was left of it after the sale of *Lady Nelson* and *Lady Rodney* to the Egyptians in 1952. Canadian ships being half again as expensive to operate as those of other countries, the Canadian merchant navy, one of the biggest in the world at the end of the war, had been melting away as owners opted for flags of convenience. The eight remaining freighters in the CN fleet were carrying flour, fish, lumber, canned goods and a few passengers to the islands and bringing back raw sugar, molasses and fruit, and most years were unprofitable, though in 1956 CNS made its first profit in years.

This intrigued the Seafarers' International Union, which had become one of the strongest labour organizations in the country. Since they had cooperated to oust the Canadian Seamen's Union from CN deep-water ships, company-union relations had been equable, though CN had repulsed SIU attempts to extend jurisdiction to coastal ferries manned by the Canadian Brotherhood of Railway Employees.

Now the SIU was out to take over the work force "on everything that floats." It presented wage demands that would have created a large deficit and refused to consider a counter-offer that was considerably lower. The SIU might have lowered its demands in exchange for a foothold on CN ferries but Gordon was not prepared to accept either a 50 per cent wage increase or SIU control of CN's coastal fleet. SIU boss Hal Banks had demonstrated the thuggish traits that had given him a prison record in the U.S. and would eventually lead to his deportation from Canada for running the union for his own ends. Gordon called Banks to his office and warned him CNS would go out of business unless Banks changed his tactics.

For half a century, CN and its ancestors had carried the Canadian flag on the high seas, and perhaps Banks thought Gordon was bluffing. But when Banks called a strike involving eight CN ships and 222 seamen in 1957 Gordon had no intention of giving in. Carrying deficits on rail hauls was one thing, for in many parts of Canada there was no alternative, but incurring shipping deficits at the expense of the taxpayer was another. There were competing services ready and willing to serve the Caribbean.

Having dumped CSU in favour of the SIU in 1949, CN now shed the SIU, transferred registry to Trinidad and hired ninety-five Jamaican strikebreakers who were to be flown to Montreal. Two chartered planes were on their way with the Jamaicans one wintry Saturday evening when an alarmed Canadian government, under pressure from the labour movement, had second thoughts and ordered the shadowy operation stopped. The planes were turned back before they reached a point of no return, and the government found itself having to explain itself to Jamaican authorities.

To avoid winter freeze-up the five strikebound ships at Montreal were navigated to Halifax by their officers and a skeleton crew, and Gordon said the fleet must be sold. The three 7500-tonners, *Canadian Cruiser, Canadian Challenger* and *Canadian Constructor,* were bought by Cuba in 1958 and languished rusting at Halifax for some time before they were taken away. The other four, all of 4500 tons, were sold six years later to Spanish ship-breakers. In its thirty years CNS had carried nine million tons of freight, produced a deficit of $5 million and forged ties between the islands and Canada that have not been forgotten. From now on CN's seagoing would be confined to coastal waters, with a heterogenous fleet of thirty-odd ships, manned or supported by three thousand people, mostly coordinated with the rail movements of passengers, mail, express and freight.

Like so much of CN, the marine service had grown out of necessity and politics, the Newfoundland arm having been a Confederation promise, like the Prince Edward Island ferry service before it. On behalf of the federal government, CN ran ferries between North Sydney, Nova Scotia, and Port aux Basques, Newfoundland, between Cape Tormentine, New Brunswick, and Borden, Prince Edward Island, and between Yarmouth, Nova Scotia, and Bar Harbor, Maine. It operated tugs and barges on Lake Okanagan, summer cruises to Alaska aboard the *Prince George,* a so-called AquaTrain that carried freight from Prince Rupert to Alaska (shortening the distance of shipments from American ports by hundreds of miles), car ferries on Lake Michigan, and an Atlantic flotilla that navigated the year around through the fogs and treacherous waters of Atlantic Canada and up through the ice floes of Labrador. Loading anything from potatoes to travelling circuses, CN ships accounted for two million passengers a year and a million and a half tons of freight and ranged from coasters like the 170-foot *Petite Forte,* which carried passengers and freight to the outports, to virtual liners like the *William Carson.* Like branch lines, CN ships lost money but helped to glue the country together.

THE RAILWAY
PROBLEM

FTER TWO PROFITABLE AND ENCOURAGING YEARS, operating results had fallen back into the red in 1957, where they remained for six years at the lowest levels since the 1930s. Since there was no Great Depression to blame, some blamed the policies of the new Conservative government, though the decline had set in under the Liberals. Others blamed depressed export markets and a general fall in business spending. Donald Gordon, seeking reasons and remedies closer home, reached for a blank sheet of paper one June day in 1958 and scrawled at the top, *"What is the problem of the CNR?"*

Was the railway too much at the mercy of adversarial politics? Was it too big and dispersed for effective management? Royal commissions, parliamentary committees, editorialists and authors had long sought answers to these and other questions while CN went on with its business. In 1938, Lesslie R. Thompson, in a monumental study titled *The Canadian Railway Problem*, recommended a fresh start much as Drayton and Acworth had prescribed in 1917, including a permanent and self-perpetuating board rather than one picked every few years from the regions.

Debt problems older than CN cast their shadows. Operations dispersed across the country defied central control. There was the drain of having to run the Hudson Bay Railway for disgruntled Prairie farmers and finance the moribund Newfoundland transportation system as the price of Confederation. There was the perennial intrusion of adversarial politics and the old debate over the merits of public versus private enterprise, and whether nationalization had injected confusion into the business of railroading. As a crown corporation, CN was expected to be all things to all people – to make a profit while acting as a job-creating agency and avoiding the CPR's seasonal layoffs due to lack of work; to keep its shops open to prevent employee dislocation; and to construct or maintain uneconomic branch lines. There were those who said CN should not compete directly with the private sector – for example, by going into trucking – even though the CPR was allowed to do so.

More immediate problems were the rising prices and wages that had inflated the cost of borrowing for Gordon's billion-dollar rehabilitation project. As a yardstick of progress, he figured that if CN were carrying current traffic at 1928 efficiency, it would need a thousand more locomotives and 80,000 more freight cars and many more employees. Trains were hauling bigger loads and hauling them faster, but prices had increased so much that someone in R&D calculated that to buy a common lead pencil the railway had to haul a ton of freight two miles to pay for it.

The flow of commodities CN depended on most – ore, steel, pulp and paper, automobile parts, etc. – had declined and the investment in modernizing had proved too high for available traffic. Revenue that might have balanced increased costs was sucked away by trucks, forcing railways to rely more on bulk traffic from mine and forest, sectors notoriously sensitive to recession.

Passenger travel had declined by 50 per cent in two decades as travellers complained of fare increases, late trains and poor service in the dining cars, which had once been a joy of rail travel. Despite the purchase of hundreds of new coaches, sleeping cars and dining cars, the passenger department seemed powerless to arrest the decline, hampered by a tradition wherein its schedules were set not by itself but by Operations and its equipment was chosen by the Mechanical and Equipment Department.

On the Toronto-Ottawa run there was only one dining car for 200 diners. Linen had been removed in favour of "paper service" – paper napkins and covers – and CN had removed flowers as well, though the CPR, trying to merchandize the notion of old-fashioned luxury, kept them. Among CN's few vestiges of the glory days, the Montreal-Toronto trains offered an excellent table d'hôte dinner at $2.75 with a choice of halibut, lamb chops, salmon steak or turkey.

Apart from commuters, who produced no profit, CN was carrying only eight million passengers a year, a total that in 1957 included the last big movement of immigrants – 95,000 refugees from the Hungarian uprising who were brought inland in 300 special trains. There had been a time when the railways were Canada's immigration agencies, carrying on while governments changed and policies wavered. CN's department of colonization and agriculture settled 300,000 people in its thirty years, and though most of the revenue from overseas ticket sales still came from immigrants, they were now arriving in aircraft and settling in towns and cities. As part of its economy drive, CN cut the staff of "Col and Ag" in half, to about seventy people. The department was dismembered in 1961 and its work taken over by passenger and freight sales people. With planes replacing ships as mass carriers, the department was no longer needed and CN's European organization now concentrated on feeding freight into the Canadian rail system.

As a crown corporation CN had problems cutting staff. "There is a difficulty," Gordon wrote, "in making quick reductions. This calls for skillful management to keep our working force at a minimum and to select the proper timing for layoffs – gradual action rather than sudden adjustments." Nevertheless, CN executed one of the biggest cutbacks in its history with the loss of 11,000 jobs during 1957-58, while the CPR made a proportionate decrease.

"We no longer take men and use them as beasts of burden," said Gordon, "but we supply them with tools which take all the heartbreaking toil out of the business." Replacing men with machines, however, brought its own heartbreak, eliminating machinists, boilermakers, pipefitters and blacksmiths.

"The senior ones took their pensions but we had to retrain people and the craft lines of unions made retraining difficult," said Norman MacMillan. "One can't take a senior steamfitter and put him in the seniority listings of another craft. He has to start at the bottom. We couldn't get around it. We had to try to find a spot for the younger men and it was very difficult."

Two diesels could do the work of three steam locomotives and with fewer men. But what to do with firemen? Feeding coal to the fire, originally by backbreaking toil and later by mechanical stoker, was essential on steam locomotives. Now there was little for firemen to do but watch out the left-hand window, though they did have another role, for it was from the ranks of firemen that locomotive engineers were drawn after years of on-the-job training.

In 1956 the CPR began to get rid of firemen. When the private railway tried to embody its cutback in a contract, negotiations broke down and on January 2, 1957, the Brotherhood of Locomotive Firemen and Enginemen called a strike of its 2850 firemen, supported by more than 60,000 other employees. The strike against the CPR came to an end only when the government set up a royal commission under Justice Roy L. Kellock.

Kellock's decision killed the firemen's union but paradoxically proved a victory for the labour movement. In ruling that firemen were in fact redundant, he declared that firemen, and by extension all railway workers, had the right to share in the benefits of technology. As a result both lawmakers and railway executives dealt with technological change with more generosity, thereby reducing wildcat strikes in a period when changes were many.

Since the union insisted the CPR decision had no bearing on CN, the crown corporation now sought control over how or when firemen should be assigned to its diesels. "Unlike CPR there was no strike at CN," recalled fireman Lorne Brisbin, "but we ended up before a conciliation board chaired by Justice André Montpetit of Quebec. Eventually he handed down a decision that was almost a carbon copy of Kellock's except that our members were to be eliminated through natural attrition – there would be no new ones hired – whereas a bunch at the CPR, I don't remember how many, were wiped right off. There was a lot of criticism of our committee for not going on strike and it ended up with me losing my union job of negotiator. But I couldn't see the point. We had protected all our men. Looking back, I'm proud because ours was the first agreement I am aware of that protected people through attrition."

The firemen's union gave CN the right to stop hiring firemen for freight and yard service, and over the following years engineers with three decades of service retired in increasing numbers and firemen took their places. Firemen were phased out of freight trains slowly, and the cost of keeping them in passenger cabs proved heavy over the next two decades until all were gone.

The cost of wages and benefits in 1958 had reached 65 per cent of CN's expense dollar. Wage increases and the freight rates to pay for them were nagging twins that appeared every two years when labour agreements expired, but now the railways, acting in concert, were refusing to meet new demands until the government could assure rate increases. There had been a dozen since the war, rates had gone up by 150 per cent, and fearful they were getting out of control, the Diefenbaker government passed the Freight Rates Reduction Act, which rolled rates back and compensated the railways for losses.

At the same time, the fourth major royal commission on transportation in forty years was appointed under a Regina jurist, M.A. MacPherson, to study the "inequalities in the freight rate structure." MacPherson was expected to unravel the tangled skein of wages, freight rates and subsidies, though Gordon put little faith in the commission at first and permitted Solandt to appoint a junior staffer, Robert Bandeen, to guide CN's case.

Having asked himself what CN's problem was, Gordon took action, though on one of the money losers, grain, he made no progress. In the West he took the grain transportation issue to the public and politicians, demanding that something be done to increase grain rates and restore the deteriorating elevator and rail system that handled the crops. Apart from the fact a truck could make four daily deliveries to one or other of the 5000 country elevators, instead of the one delivery made before the war by a four-horse team with a tank wagon, the collection, storage and export of wheat, oats and other grains had changed little. Instead of sending trains down branch lines to call on small elevators, Gordon said, it would cost half as much to haul grain by truck to the major elevators, where trains could then pick it up in large quantities. Though there was some support for his plan, there was opposition from those who envisaged track being ripped out, jeopardizing the complex system of wheat pools and cooperatives western farmers had built up.

Within CN Gordon made progress. By temperament he believed that anything less than central authority would erode his powers, but he realized the railway was far too centralized. Having held the reins in his own big fists during his early years, he now promoted the vice-president of the legal department, Norman J. MacMillan, to executive vice-president in 1956. "It became a vertical division [of the company]," MacMillan said. "Donald at the top, me half an inch below, and the whole company split between the two of us at that point – Gordon financial, etc. and me operations."

For an organization as big and unwieldy as a railway, change for change's sake had advantages. As the biggest corporate employer in Canada and one of the longest railways in the world, CN had assets of $3 billion and 26,000 miles of mainline track – enough to girdle the earth at the equator – plus 9700 miles of secondary track, yards, sidings and spurs. Railways suffered from the effects of pyramids of power, creeping obsolescence and a way of doing things – a railway culture – that had its roots in the steam era. When the Uniform Code of Operating Rules was the railway bible, Gordon wanted less emphasis on the 19th-century preoccupation with operations and more on making the corporation profitable. He introduced a five-year plan to encourage better use of manpower, the old six-month forecasts for annual work-force requirements having proved inadequate. Efforts were made to close the gap between upper and middle management, which had appeared during the war. Marketing, which had been embedded in the Traffic Department, needed shaking up and an experimental sales campaign was begun in London, Ontario, with a separate organization responsible for research, sales planning, pricing and promotion.

The consulting firm Woods Gordon of Toronto declared that decentralization, popular in the States, was advisable. "Donald had no feel for organization at all," said Liberal party stalwart Walter Gordon, president of Woods Gordon. "He couldn't delegate. I told him right at the beginning, 'You can't run the railway with every damn decision coming to you.'" The CN president feared that decentralization would expand the top-heavy bureaucracy and add to administrative costs. Pushed by his senior people, however, he agreed to the Woods Gordon recommendation for decentralization.

"Regional offices should become much more autonomous and self-contained than they are at present," Gordon said, "and activities of head office departments should become concentrated upon staff or service functions in the broadest sense of these terms." No longer would the stationmaster double as freight salesman waiting for his customers to come calling.

The change would take time. Railroaders, like soldiers, worked on rigid departmental lines, communicating through layers of authority. Responsibilities were not always clear and headquarters was burdened with decisions better made elsewhere. "I remember Gordon getting upset at having to make a decision about painting park benches in front of the Nova Scotian Hotel in Halifax," said Walter Smith, his secretary at the time. "He had to make that decision because the hotel people and the operating people could not get together on who should pick up the tab." Too many people were reporting directly to Gordon, while down the street at the CPR only four were reporting directly to Buck Crump.

Listening to Jim McDonald, who tested the first decentralized area operation at Capreol, Ontario, the fork in the line where trains converge from Montreal and Toronto, Gordon decided that diesels had effectively eliminated the need for the "district," one of four levels of management. "The major thing had been the abolition of the steam locomotive because it could go only 120-odd miles without servicing," said McDonald. "That had formed the nucleus of the divisional headquarters with its superintendent, engineers, transportation officers and administrative staff. Diesels changed the whole pattern. Diesels, unlike steam engines, could go straight through from coast to coast in one run."

By 1960 steam travel had come to an end after a heroic career of 125 years. On April 25 engine No. 6043 made its final trip from The Pas to Winnipeg, where it was met by a hundred pensioners. This was the last CN steam train in regular service, though some ran on special excursions. The CPR retired its last steamer on November 6 of the same year. In place of the 2400 steam locomotives when Gordon arrived in 1950, the railway now operated 1736 diesel units with 300 on order, plus a fleet of self-propelled passenger cars.

On January 1, 1961, CN heralded the first reorganization in its thirty-seven-year history. It reduced levels of administration from four to three and halved the number of administrative centres. Instead of Atlantic, Central and Western regions with ten districts and thirty-one divisions subject to central control, five regions were established – Atlantic, St. Lawrence, Great Lakes, Prairie and Mountain (plus the Grand Trunk Western Railroad). These were subdivided into eighteen management areas or business units, each with defined objectives, each in effect a miniature railway responsible for its own results. Operations, sales, accounting and freight claims formerly coordinated at headquarters were delegated to area managers. As in the army, which had supplied many railway procedures, staff officers would provide specialized advice and services but the line officers, consisting of regional vice-presidents, general managers and area managers, would have final authority and responsibility.

Trainmasters, roadmasters, master mechanics, chief dispatchers and other supervisors began to feel the change, which embodied recommendations of Woods Gordon, though it took longer to sift through to rank and file. In the union halls and railway towns where jobs could be lost, freight handlers were worried by CN's intention to combine freight and express services, and the Canadian Brotherhood of Railway, Transport and General Workers convoked the first emergency policy meeting in its fifty-one years to discuss this radical alteration in command structure. "We can have our conditions altered on a piecemeal basis, as it suits the railway, or we can force them to work with us at the planning stage," president W. J. Smith told 235 local chairmen from across Canada. Determined to shuck off obsolescence, the union began the first major overhaul of freight handling rules in fifteen years and signed a collective agreement which improved job security for 20,000 clerical, express and freight shed workers while providing a flexible work force.

"The whole process of establishing the area system took years," said Frank Roberts, the first manager of the Champlain area, which included southern Quebec and the subdivision to Portland, Maine. "People who had been in no position to make decisions now made decisions. They had the authority to do it and that allowed people to grow in their jobs." Not that the area manager – "Mr. CN" in his community – had full authority, for he could not control policy or costs or publish schedules, key functions reserved for headquarters.

Customers benefited from the area system. Formerly a divisional manager had been an operations man with little contact with customers except when obliged to give reasons for delays, damage or poor service. Internal liaison was slow. A CN salesman might communicate with operations in writing, even though the customer was in a hurry. Now the area manager had replaced them both, responsible under one hat for sales, service and operations. "Instead of waiting for customers to come to us," said a manager in Nova Scotia, "we go to them to sell our services, tailoring them to meet any reasonable demand."

But decentralization was expensive, since many jobs were duplicated in the areas; nor were there enough trained people to go around. Stan Dingle, unwillingly elevated from a hands-on position in charge of operations to a lofty advisory post as system vice-president, disliked the change. "I did want to get rid of some of the detail at headquarters," Dingle conceded. "I was too tied up with things that should have been handled in the regions and was on call twenty-four hours a day, but I was sorry it happened. At no time did I figure the area organization worked properly."

Ron Messenger, later a vice-president but then a member of the operations staff as a trainmaster in the Rideau area in 1962, recalled, "The area organization brought a strong realization of what we were in business for. It brought interaction between the marketing people and the operating people. I certainly got a different perspective and I think we accomplished things the previous organization failed to do. On the negative side the new system was taken too literally because each of those eighteen areas followed the Noah's ark syndrome where they had one of everything and as a consequence a number of departments were not very effective and the structure was too expensive. But it was only ten years later that people started to say we really didn't need all this."

Fairweather, now in retirement, found another weakness: "The effort of a region became – to that region – more important than the results of the whole system." This was illustrated when an area stole boxcars from an empty train passing through so as to build up its reserve, upsetting the car distribution plans of head office. Public relations headquarters in Montreal complained that the Prairie region had gone off on its own and fashioned its own logo, featuring a teepee.

Reorganization was also a tonic. Jean Richer of Montreal, who followed Frank Roberts as manager of the Champlain area, found himself, while still a relative newcomer, in charge of 2000 people. "I became a fairly senior executive with tremendous power," he said. "I had my top operating man, top salesman, my accounting person, I had all the heads of everything except law and medicine, so you were really like the president of a small company. There was vibrancy and excitement though it was not all good. I think there were things I was doing that were good for my area but might not have been good for the whole system, and I don't think we developed the coordination where these kinds of conflicts could be ironed out."

It was typical of railroading at that time that few if any people from marketing were placed in charge of the areas. Looking back down the years from the CN presidential suite, Ron Lawless said the switch to areas had been a big step but turned out to be the wrong step because the emphasis had been put on geographical location rather than on customers. "We found ourselves," Lawless recalled, "with eighteen areas, or businesses, we were unable to coordinate." One reason was that they were reporting to the regional vice-president rather than head office, and the total view of the system became obscured. Gradually the areas started to disappear when it became clear they were not working properly – until eventually CN was back to regions, five instead of three.

Recognizing the value of "image," CN set out to demonstrate that the company had a purpose, knew where it was going and wanted the help of employees in getting there. The ambiguously named traffic department, which outsiders might confuse with operations, was renamed sales department and modernized to resemble the sales and marketing division of a large private enterprise.

CN changed its trademark at the urging of public relations director Charles Harris and his predecessor, Dick Wright, a Gordon import from Ottawa. The first public relations director who had not been hired from the media, Wright changed the approach to public relations and frowned on such traditional assignments as the "reindeer run," which meant calling on the media with a bottle or two at Christmas. "We had modernized and were getting no credit for it," Lorne Perry of Public Affairs and Advertising recalled. "We had hump yards, we had the dieselization completed, we had Centralized Traffic Control and our first computers, welded rail, and all those things, but the old corporate trademark and colours like forest green and muddy gold were reinforcing the idea we were an old-fashioned railway. The need for a new symbol led to a design program for train colour schemes and signs for stations."

Since 1923 the symbol had been a maple leaf and the letters CNR in a rectangle, a combination of the devices used by the Grand Trunk and Canadian Northern. For the new symbol, industrial designer James Valkus of New York was hired, along with a young Canadian, Allan R. Fleming of Toronto.

"Literal or drawn symbols were out," said Fleming, "not only because it is incongruous to see a maple leaf travelling by at seventy miles an hour but because a peculiar thing happens with a trademark. If you do, say, a literal drawing in 1944 of an object – even a leaf – that simply looks in 1954 like it was drawn in 1944. In other words the drawing retains the quality of the period in which it was done."

The symbol had to be bilingual, which meant it would drop the R for railway. Fleming worked with the letters C and N "night and day" and was on a flight to New York to consult with Valkus when he scrawled an acceptable version on a paper napkin. The result had the look of a cattle brand, showed the letters CN in a single, flowing line and symbolized the movement of people, materials and messages across the country. The next step was to get this futuristic trademark accepted in a conservative industry.

"I had a meeting with Gordon and MacMillan," said Harris, "because the management committee always took its cue from what Gordon said and if they saw him leaning one way or the other they'd all jump in on that side." Gordon was non-committal. MacMillan liked it.

Harris explained the logo at a conference of senior officers. "Well gentlemen, what do you think of it?" asked Gordon. One vice-president, followed by another, voiced doubt. Gordon said, "I like it!" And it soon appeared on everything at CN from boxcars to stationery, a "wiggly worm" as some called it, standing for Canadien National as well as Canadian National. As with so many railway innovations this design style spread across the country. "There had been nothing like it," said Perry who coordinated the project. "It was the beginning of a trend." CPR followed with a new logo seven years later. In the States the Grand Trunk Western got a flowing GT.

Diesel engines began to appear with diagonal black and white stripes and brilliant red-orange noses. These colours were useful for promotion, and orange, being a safety colour, was expected to reduce level crossing accidents. Seventy-five per cent of crossings across Canada were unprotected and only about 8 per cent had a safe separation by bridge or subway. (In 1960 a school bus and CN freight collided on a level crossing near Lamont, Alberta, with the death of seventeen children.)

As service industries vulnerable to Canada's cyclical recessions, both CN and CPR suffered from the sluggish economy in 1960 but as usual CN suffered more. Whereas CPR had to find $1000 per mile to cover fixed charges, CN needed $2500 and its deficit had climbed to $67.5 million, though operating loss, a truer gauge of the railway's efficiency, was only one tenth that amount.

Every dollar CN earned was going back into operations, and the operating ratio stood at 100 per cent. In comparison, the CPR was required to spend 85 cents in the dollar. "Our current figures show a continued downward drift in our revenue figures, and need to be reviewed most anxiously," Gordon told MacMillan. "We should try to establish once again why the CPR is able to control expenses by twice the degree we seem to be able to accomplish."

CN had 101,000 employees and the CPR 63,000. Since 1952 CN had reduced its payroll by 30,000 people, though still employing proportionately more than its smaller rival, partly because it kept more workers on in winter in order to give employment year-round. Layoffs were affecting long-term employees now as well as short-term. Louis Strabo, fifty-three, who had worked seventeen years in the motive power department at Transcona, Manitoba, said that during dieselization he had been laid off four times for short periods, but now he was faced with permanent layoff. "I have spent most of my working life with this company," wrote Strabo, "and have always served it faithfully and I gave extra effort when it was required of me in the war years and remained loyal to it when I could have earned more money elsewhere. Now when the odds of finding suitable employment elsewhere [are poor] … the company has seen fit to lay me off."

Since 1957 CN had been losing money on operations – the first time this had happened since the Depression – even before the fixed charges of debt were taken into account. By 1961 not even Gordon's job was safe.

14

HAZARDS OF
THE GAME

WHEN DONALD GORDON appeared before the Railway Committee in Ottawa in June 1961, trouble had been festering for months. Since September, when Prime Minister Diefenbaker had failed to renew his term as chairman, Gordon had been left dangling but had no intention of resigning.

Scenting blood, a noisy trio of Conservative backbenchers were trying to have him fired outright. None had shown much interest in railroading in the past, nor did they now, for they attacked Gordon personally, accusing him of arrogance, of ruining morale, of running CN like a dictator, and of hurting national unity by insulting French Canadians.

Diefenbaker undoubtedly could have silenced his aggressive backbenchers but seemed intent on getting Gordon out and it was only after the press chided him for trying to dump the CN chairman by sneaky methods that Diefenbaker disowned the "get Gordon" faction. "If the son of a bitch hasn't got the guts to fire me," said Gordon, "I am not going to help him."

"These malicious little men," said CN's old defender, the *Winnipeg Free*

Press, "have as their objective the replacement of Mr. Gordon by a more malleable successor, someone who will pay more attention to members of Parliament and less to the efficient operation of CN.... Not since another claque of Conservative backbenchers thirty years ago undertook to destroy Sir Henry Thornton has a distinguished public servant been subject to such a heartless campaign of character assassination."

The new minister, Leon Balcer, a wartime naval officer from Trois-Rivières, Quebec, insisted the delay in renewing Gordon's contract as chairman was simply due to the process of replacing Liberal directors with Conservatives and enlarging the board from seven to twelve. He wanted Gordon to stay but his influence with Diefenbaker was as limited as Hees's had been.

While Gordon was prepared to accept what he called the normal "hazards of the game," he would not stand for bullying. He got his chance to hit back at the June 19 meeting of the Sessional Committee on Railways, Air Lines and Shipping, which consisted in 1961 of eighteen Conservatives, seven Liberals and one CCF (NDP) member. Almost half of them came from rural ridings, where interest in railway affairs was highest, and for three days Gordon plodded, seemingly unperturbed, through the usual questions. Then he stood up and launched a twenty-five minute counter-charge:

> There has been a stream of irresponsible, uninformed and hostile and malicious statements made in the House of Commons and naturally carried in the press, over the radio and on television, all seeking to disparage Canadian National as an inefficient organization with incompetent management all of which will certainly disturb morale. This effort to undermine confidence and destroy respect for the management of the CN is a most serious matter and is against public interest as well as the individual interests of all employees. No organization can be expected to function properly if confidence in its leadership is steadily undermined.... The inevitable consequence of a campaign of this kind is to reduce the prestige of Canadian National in the eyes of its customers and this in turn will adversely affect its business and reduce its capacity to provide employment....

People believed CN continually fought with the unions, he said, but of 275 agreements negotiated in the past ten years 214 had been settled amicably and fifty-one through conciliation favouring CN. His relations with unions had improved and he appealed for support from union leaders.

"I have nothing whatsoever against Donald Gordon," said Frank Hall. "The CNR president is a hard man to deal with but actually he is paid to be tough. As far as I am concerned Mr. Gordon tries to get along with organized labour. If any railway employees are disgruntled it is not because of Donald Gordon." A letter from Charles Smith of the Brotherhood of Maintenance of Way Employees said, "During the past several weeks you have been subjected to a sustained and vicious attack.... As you know we have on many occasions criticized some of the decisions you have made and some of the results of policies adopted under your direction ... however we have never questioned your integrity and honesty of purpose.... Statements made in the House as to your lack of status with the employees are grossly exaggerated."

W.J.Smith, president of the Brotherhood of Railway, Transport and General Workers, which represented a third of CN's employees, testified that CN "is an efficient and vigorous enterprise serving the nation well, and compares equally with the best of railways on the North American continent. The criticisms of Mr. Donald Gordon as an individual to our knowledge are not warranted."

That Gordon had stood up for himself and for CN inspired an impromptu housewarming. Only a month earlier, three thousand employees had moved from 360 and 355 McGill St. and twenty other office buildings around town into the seventeen-storey building at the southwest corner of Central Station. (George F. Chadwick, manager of office services, who organized forty-five vans and 400 men to transfer 70,000 items of office furniture between six o'clock one Friday evening and eight o'clock Monday morning, called it the biggest single move by any Canadian business.) In the bright marble lobby at 935 de La Gauchetière St. West one morning in June 1961 Gordon received a heartwarming vote of confidence. Nearly 800 employees jammed the lobby to sing *For He's a Jolly Good Fellow* when he turned up for work after his Ottawa ordeal. "Just because I'm on time for work for once is no cause for a celebration," he grumbled, hiding pleasure under a growl.

With both unions and businessmen backing Gordon, and nobody on the horizon to take his place, Diefenbaker reluctantly reappointed him at a salary of $70,000 a year, making him the highest paid public servant, though his term was only for two years rather than the usual three, which Gordon called a bit of petty vengeance. Diefenbaker, when asked a decade later, insisted he had had only the highest regard for Gordon, adding, with somewhat more candour, "He could be overbearing and frankly the manner in which he spoke to some people could be offensive."

Appointed with Gordon was one of CN's more effective boards: Walter Koerner, the Czech-born Vancouver lumber company executive; Robert A.

Brown, president of Home Oil in Calgary; J. B. Sangster of Regina, president of a car dealership; J. R. Griffith of Saskatoon, a former railway union official; W. Gerald Stewart of Moncton, a lawyer; Walter Colquhoun of Sydney, N.S., a wholesale druggist; J.-Louis Levesque, a Montreal investment dealer; Guy Charbonneau, a Montreal insurance executive, G. E. Ayers, a Lachute Mills, Quebec, industrialist; Alex A. McBain, a Toronto investment dealer; and H. I. Price, a Toronto insurance executive and president of the Canadian National Exhibition.

CN has been compared unfavourably with the CPR in having few high-profile business leaders on its board. Whereas CPR directors were chosen for ability to bring in business, CN directors were patronage appointments chosen for their regional input and party affiliation. Ralph T. Vaughan defended the system: "Boards are sometimes wrongly accused of rubber stamping. Though a board was in no position to initiate a proposal, they could make counterproposals and compromises. I thought them useful because management sometimes gets insulated and inward looking, and whatever their background the directors were dedicated people and CN chairmen were emphatic about keeping them informed on labour matters, fuel contracts, contract bids, etc."

Though Gordon could hardly be described as a diplomat, he recognized Parliament's need to know where it was spending such large sums of money every year and usually did his best at annual Railway Committee sessions to answer those questions that did not interfere with his management of CN. He angered the parliamentarians, however, by refusing to divulge details of the sale of CN hotels at the Lakehead and Brandon or the financial arrangements over the Queen Elizabeth Hotel. He insisted these were managerial matters and publicizing them would destroy CN credibility in the marketplace. "No other executive officer that I know of in the country would stand for it or put up with it for a minute," he said. When Doug Fisher complained the smells in the washroom at Longlac, Ontario, left much to be desired, Gordon replied, "What sort of smells would you desire?"

Even at the best of times nothing took a greater toll on CN time and patience than these command performances in Ottawa's imposing Railway Committee room and preparations disrupted normal work for weeks. Lecturing the MPs on their duties, Gordon did not hide his conviction they were doing a poor job. They tried his short supply of patience by displaying technical ignorance or asking questions merely because they felt they had to say something at this rare opportunity to impress constituents.

"The committee should seriously examine just what it is trying to do," Gordon told them, and suggested they conduct hearings along lines of the CPR's annual shareholders' meeting. MPs should ask how CN was going to eliminate deficit, Gordon said, not whether a $3 lunch was served on the *Super Continental* or the Capreol restrooms were clean. Was management efficient? That was the crucial question. "And if you come to the conclusion it is not, for God's sake fire the lot of us. Take the general approach to it and let us work as a private enterprise corporation and manage it as such."

"It was an ordeal," conceded Ralph Vaughan, the Nova Scotia lawyer and journalist who became Gordon's special assistant before he was appointed vice-president and company secretary. "We'd have a big black book all cross-indexed with the annual report and boxes of material. Just the preparation was an awful strain on people all through the system. Gordon insisted on answering the questions on the floor, whereas his predecessor had often said 'I'll look into that.' The members felt we overpowered them with information, and we did. It was a contest. He would answer most of the questions except things that he felt were proprietary in nature: bids on contracts, the names and number of bidders, that sort of thing."

Gordon's bluster and efforts to run CN like a private corporation triggered inevitable conflict with the best-informed member of the committee, Doug Fisher, the socialist giant-killer who had defeated C.D. Howe in Port Arthur. The son of a locomotive engineer who had revered Thornton and was active in the union, the CCF (NDP) member for Port Arthur represented a vast constituency with more railroaders and division points than most. An articulate high school teacher, librarian and journalist, Fisher believed in CN's social role, and never let Gordon forget it at a time Gordon was trying to emphasize CN's commercial side. Since Fisher's arrival the number of railway questions asked in parliament had increased dramatically and as the most persistent of CN's critics he was, as he said himself, "out for Gordon's scalp," and his attacks ranged from Gordon's management style to his laundry privileges at CN's Chateau Laurier, which the CN president visited on his way to his weekend retreat in the Gatineau hills.

While others might applaud Gordon for having the courage to spend $1.7 billion on modernizing CN, Fisher noted that interest on long-term debt had doubled since Gordon became president. "We have a picture in the last four years that is a bleak one in terms of deficits," he said. "In view of these results and the fact you have had control for this length of time and have had a free hand in making changes and alterations why should we not have a complete lack of confidence in the management of the CNR?"

Gordon had a ready answer. The cost of labour and material had outrun savings made through greater efficiency; freight rates, frozen by the government since 1959, did not cover cost increases. CN rehabilitation, though expensive, had been a necessary investment to keep pace with other North American railways. Automation and diesels would save the taxpayer money. "If we had still been running steam locomotives today," Gordon said, "our business would have been away down because we could not have given service, and our expenses would have been way, way up over what they are today. So we had to make a managerial decision: are we winding up the railway or are we going to continue in the railway business?"

Physically the two biggest men in any room they happened to be in, Gordon in his banker's suit and shiny black shoes, and Fisher, in a red sweater, came close to blows more than once. When Gordon assured the committee that trucking companies CN had purchased in the West had made a profit, Fisher produced a crumpled, unsigned document that showed a loss, insisting the purchase had been a mistake. Gordon took one look and shouted it had been stolen from CN files; when Fisher refused to say who had given it to him and tried to reclaim it Gordon refused to give it up. The two stood glowering at each other. "I said to Gordon, 'Give it to him,'" recalled Ralph Vaughan, "and he thought I meant, 'Hit him!'" Before the meeting could be adjourned, it looked for a few tense moments as if the president of CN and the honourable member from the Lakehead would come to fisticuffs.

If drama between Gordon and Fisher produced sound and fury, it was a Quebec City lawyer, Gilles Grégoire of the Créditiste party, who stole the headlines late in 1962 – and single-handedly advanced the cause of Quebec separatism. With thirty minutes of artful questioning, the young nationalist made the CN president look like a racist in the eyes of French-Canadians and set off political repercussions in which the facts have often been distorted.

The Railway Committee had met in November that year and Gordon, sucking cough drops for a sore throat, tried to answer questions, supported as usual by Ralph Vaughan, who, as Gordon said, "will sit behind and whisper in my ear in order to keep me in a straight line." Grégoire asked a vague question about union membership and almost as an afterthought added mildly that he had another about the annual report. "I note," said Grégoire, "we have one president, seventeen vice-presidents and ten directors, and none of them is French Canadian."

In fact there were two Montreal French Canadians on the eleven-man board, J.-Louis Levesque and Guy Charbonneau, Wilfrid Gagnon having retired after twenty-five years of excellent service. A third director, G.E.Ayers of Lachute, was also a Quebecer. Although Grégoire spoke of the directors he really meant senior management, where his barb had more point. "Let's face it," Vaughan said later, "the whole company at the time was anglophone in outlook. I poked Gordon to warn there was a hardball coming at him but he thrust off my pencil and got into it."

Gordon, a bull who carried his own china shop as someone once said, professed difficulty in defining a French Canadian, a remark bound to upset French Canadians and give nationalists an opening for attack. Speaking no French, having little understanding of French Canada, and moving in anglo-phone society, Gordon was a victim of Canada's two solitudes syndrome. For Gordon there were no *French* Canadians, but only *Canadians* – Canadians who spoke English, Canadians who spoke French and Canadians who spoke both languages.

"Let me say quite clearly," said Gordon, "that the promotion policy of the Canadian National Railways has always been based on merit. The man who, by reason of experience, knowledge, judgement, education, or for any other reason, is considered by the management to be the best person for a job will receive the promotion, and we do not care whether he is black, white, red or French. We never ask questions of that kind in regard to promotion or employment and I think if we did we would be following a practice against the Canadian Fair Employment Practices Act which by law tells us that we must not discriminate because of race, national origin, colour, religion or age."

This policy had been enunciated five years earlier when the personnel department began to recruit from French as well as English universities. "Any bias against or in favour of the advancement of French Canadians to high administrative posts," said a company guideline, "is contrary to the company's best interests ... promotion to senior positions in the company should, in all cases, be based on ability...."

Lionel Chevrier, an MP for Montreal, assured the House that Gordon was not prejudiced but went on to suggest that something must be wrong when CN could find no French-speaking people for senior jobs. While failing to say why he had not corrected matters himself when he was minister in charge of railways, he asked why several men he knew personally had not been promoted to the top of the ladder. Why, for example, was O.A. Trudeau, who had retired in 1953 as general passenger traffic manager, never offered a vice-presidency? And why was Omer A. Boivin, a railroader for fifty years and general superintendent, not given the vice-presidency of the St. Lawrence Region? (Boivin, as it happened, had been offered the vice-presidency in an effort to improve morale in Quebec but had taken retirement.)

"How do you explain," asked Grégoire, coming back to the fray, but still confusing the board, which had French-Canadian members, with the administration, which did not, "that when we have a minister of transport who is a French-speaking Canadian you cannot find other French-speaking Canadians having enough merit to be members on the board of directors of the Canadian National Railways."

Gordon complained the MPs were distorting his words, unfortunately adding a statement which was in itself open to distortion. "As long as I am president of the CNR there is not going to be a promotion or an appointment made just ["just" was not in his verbal statement but inserted in the transcript submitted to CN for editing before publication] because a man is a French Canadian. He has got to be a French Canadian plus other things, and he has to be as able as the other fellow who has a claim on the job. There is going to be fair practice on the CNR as long as I am there. What you are arguing for is discrimination." He tried to lighten the atmosphere with a typical aside. "Even Scotsmen receive promotion in the CNR," he said, but he got few laughs. The damage had been done.

If he thought about it at all, Gordon had underestimated Quebec's growing pains. On the other hand, some of the Quebec MPs were out to score points and it was no hard task to bait Gordon into indiscretion. "Do you know the atmosphere in which these committee sessions are held?" Gordon asked later. "A question is thrown at you suddenly. You do not expect it and you are required to answer immediately."

This brief exchange aroused francophone Quebec more than any issue since conscription. Gordon's insensitivity as head of a public corporation for which Quebecers paid taxes prompted fifty of Quebec's seventy-five MPs, English and French, to present a resolution demanding equal treatment for French Canadians. The French press, municipal councils and even organizations not known for their militancy demanded Gordon's resignation. He was repeatedly quoted inaccurately as having said flatly that no French Canadians were competent to hold senior jobs. North America's biggest French-language daily, *La Presse* of Montreal, commented bitterly, "Let us sum up the debate by saying that a French Canadian will never be a vice-president of the CN unless he is more qualified than all the English-speaking candidates. It will not be enough for him to be their equal."

Gordon was burned in effigy that December more than anyone in recent Canadian history – in Trois-Rivières, Quebec City, at the war memorial in Ottawa, and on his sixty-first birthday in front of the gleaming new Place Ville Marie he had opened with so much pride a few weeks before. Five chartered buses brought well-organized University of Montreal students until 3000 people had joined the demonstration, which featured a pig-faced effigy of the CN president, though some of the demonstrators admitted to not knowing who Gordon was.

A delegation led by Bernard Landry, who later became a minister in the Parti Québécois government, was ushered to Gordon's seventeenth-floor office to stand before his teak desk. Lionel Côté, CN's general counsel, was ready to translate, but since the students were bilingual his services were unneeded and Landry emerged with hope that his generation could expect better treatment.

Since 1850 Montreal and CN and its ancestor companies had grown together. CN was among the top ten taxpayers in the city and employed close to 20,000 people. The Bonaventure freight terminal, the largest on the continent, handled more than two million shipments annually, and some two million freight cars a year moved over 500 miles of track in and around the city. Every year 50,000 CN passenger trains brought people in and out of Central Station, an average of 34,000 passengers a day, including 21,000 commuters. By 1960, however, CN had accumulated many French-Canadian grievances, ranging from hiring practices to English-only timetables and lack of French-speaking staff on dining cars running through Quebec from Montreal to Halifax. As early as October 8, 1923, the people of Ste. Marie Beauce in southeastern Quebec complained there were no French menus on CN trains. In 1937 Trois-Rivières protested appointment of a stationmaster who spoke no French. Mont-Joli threatened a boycott unless CN put up bilingual signs. In 1939 president Hungerford had ordered French-language instruction at CN but only one instructor was hired.

Opportunities for French Canadians had been improving, and francophones in such jobs as general counsel, regional general manager in Quebec, manager of industrial development, senior research analyst, etc. made up 13 per cent of management, but the fact remained there were no French Canadian vice-presidents. At Quebec City where 95 per cent of the 3800 employees were French-speaking, communications with head office were in English. Francophones were expected to give orders to fellow francophones – in English. A letter in 1961 from Yvon Alain of Donnacona, CN employee and Royal Canadian Air Force veteran, was typical of the frustration: "I have come to the conclusion that we French-speaking people, heirs to a universal culture, have no right to live unless we resign ourselves to earn our living in the other language. We are in the same position as any immigrant, we have to learn English and thus lose our cultural identity ... only the French Canadian is required to be bilingual."

CN was not alone in this. Conditions were similar at the CPR and other large companies. Pierre Delagrave of Quebec City, who had worked with Gordon's Wartime Prices Board and was hired by CN in 1958, said: "I think Donald felt they had to have a French Canadian and I was possibly the only available one he knew. In my experience no major corporations were looking for French Canadians at that time." As the biggest crown corporation CN made a handy scapegoat for French Quebec's resentment against all anglophone corporations – the pulp and paper, mining, banking, real estate, insurance and other companies that had run Quebec business since the 18th century. But Gordon took it personally. "It shook him," Vaughan recalled. "He was a sensitive man and he worried whether he had made a grave mistake and insulted the francophones and damaged the company. After that we started a major program for the use of French and development of French officers."

Gordon led a four-man committee of board members, including Levesque and Charbonneau, which ensured that French Canadians were recruited and promoted. While claiming that it found no discrimination as such, the committee conceded "that because the railroad industry in North America has been traditionally English-oriented it has looked to English language institutions for the recruitment of professional and specialist staff, and for the same reason has not seemed to offer a strong career attraction for French Canadians."

CN became the first crown corporation to use French as a working language (in the St. Lawrence region), produced the first bilingual timetable and increased French on operational signs and advertising. When the Liberals were returned in the spring of 1963, Gordon added Renault St. Laurent, the lawyer son of Louis St. Laurent, to the board and recruited Brigadier Maurice Archer, a French-Canadian engineer and former chairman of the National Harbours Board, as vice-president of R&D in succession to Solandt, who had resigned – partly because of incompatibility with MacMillan, Gordon's heir apparent.

"I became chairman of the bilingual committee," said Archer, whose role as the first francophone vice-president was sometimes awkward. "We'd meet once a month and I found that to become bilingual it takes at least a thousand hours; you can't do it in a three-week course. We tried to balance things, so we were also helping English employees learn French, but there was more opportunity for French to learn English in CN because the work was 90 per cent in English. We put bilingual signs on boxcars and stations but you had to be careful not to go too fast out west where they weren't prepared for it."

By autumn nearly half the French Canadians in senior jobs had been promoted or transferred to positions where promotion was possible. Typical of these was J.C. Crochetière, promoted from special assistant to the freight sales manager to assistant freight sales manager in Montreal. J.P. Blanchet was promoted from assistant area manager, Quebec, to general manager, real estate, at headquarters. French-speaking supervisors were becoming common, and Gordon's promotion of Pierre Delagrave to sales manager, passenger service, and then to vice-president (the second French-Canadian vice-president) put new life into the ailing passenger service.

To Thornton and R.C. Vaughan, passenger service had been a loss leader to attract freight. Delagrave, supported by MacMillan, believed it a potential money maker and convinced Gordon to give it one more try, based on better service, cheaper fares and better equipment. "The passenger department had become a 'second class citizen,'" said Delagrave, "but we got a little crew together and started to make our voice heard. The new spirit was unbelievable."

"The time has arrived to put up or shut up," said Gordon, recognizing the public's reluctance to see passenger service die despite its preference for cars and buses and planes. "We are going to be in the passenger business for a long time so we must face up and do something." There was a lot to be done. Though the passenger department was responsible for comfort and service, the crews working passenger cars came from the operating department. Some had not been properly trained and, at Delagrave's insistence, Gordon discontinued the practice of allowing people to be given passenger service jobs simply because of seniority. "The main thing," Gordon said, "is to smarten up supervision and smarten up crews."

"I found too little coordination when I took over," said Delagrave. "Getting to the train at Central Station was like walking through an Egyptian bazaar, what with the mail and express packages stacked on the platform. It took me six months to change this against resistance from people who thought things could be done no other way. There were conductors and stewards who had no training in service and public relations, men who knew only the operation of trains. I sat in the dining car for dinner once and asked for glass of wine and got a glass of vermouth! It wasn't their fault. They had not been taught. So we made a little booklet to explain everything, wines and so on, and gave three-day classes."

Though the CPR was abandoning passenger service, CN began to draw people back to the train. "I travelled from Vancouver to Ottawa on our own CNR," said Elizabeth McMaster in an Ottawa newspaper. "The last time I went over this route was shortly after World War Two. Everyone was looking for a tip. No one did anything to earn a tip. How conditions have changed. I travelled on three *Super Continental* trains and on each found every member of the crew eager to give friendly, courteous service."

Delagrave found that fifty different fares had evolved between Toronto and Montreal alone. Oddly, fares were lowest at the busiest times, and Delagrave reversed this to reflect traffic levels. When there was little business, as on weekdays, low fares were introduced, with higher fares at Christmas and weekends to take advantage of the captive market.

Delagrave recruited Garth Campbell, a transportation economist from Winnipeg who had been studying passengers at R&D, to develop an attractive fare system. "We wanted to give it a catchy name," said Delagrave, "and one night in the *Montreal Star* Eaton's was advertising a 'red, white and blue sale,' whatever that meant, but it sounded catchy and that's how the name of our Red, White and Blue fare plan was born." A pilot program was begun on the *Ocean Limited*, which had been losing money on its 840-mile run from Montreal to Halifax, a twenty-one-hour trip as costly as the three-hour TCA plane trip. Four hours were slashed from the running time, meals were included in the price of the ticket and passengers increased by 50 per cent.

Though bus companies protested the Red, White and Blue system was unfair, CN abolished first class and extended the new fare system across the country. Introduced by Delagrave September 16, 1963, in the nation's first coast-to-coast closed circuit press conference, it was the most progressive passenger service initiative in North America for years. A Red, or bargain, fare was offered on the 160 days of the year when travel was light; a coach fare on the *Ocean Limited* was cut in half. A white, or economy, fare covered the 140 days when half the travelling public was on the move. Blue fares, the highest, covered the remaining 60 days, the vacation months and holidays when travel was at its peak. "Provided we can get enough passengers going in the same direction at the same time," said Campbell, "the railroad offers a unique combination of low prices and comfort."

"Charlie Harris [director of public relations] did a fantastic PR job and between the two of us we transformed CN's image," said Delagrave. "Pierre was a breath of fresh air," said Harris. "He had ideas and he turned the place upside down. It was an exciting time and a treat for PR people to have someone like him running the passenger service."

Passenger revenue increased for the first time since the war, though undoubtedly many of CN's new passengers were people who had been abandoned by the CPR. Nevertheless, CN seemed to be solving the passenger problem and Gordon basked in unaccustomed praise for renewing what had long been regarded as a wasting asset. Another source of hope was the report of the MacPherson commission, which Gordon had at first derided. When the commission's report appeared, Gordon was about to issue a negative response until Bandeen, who had been working with the commission since 1958, pointed out that it was proposing precisely the breakthrough CN needed.

MacPherson would do away with restrictions that had been accumulating for decades and policies that forced the railways to carry passengers at less than cost and retain thousands of miles of unprofitable branch lines. Instead of fragmented, inequitable transportation policies spawned in the politics of an earlier age, it favoured a master policy embracing all modes of transportation, giving railways freedom to compete with all comers. If the nation wished railways to perform unremunerative public service, the government should pay for it, subsidizing branch lines and passenger service deemed necessary in the public interest. The report renewed Gordon's hope that CN would be allowed to reorganize its debt load once and for all, though it became apparent that the Liberals, with a minority government, would be unable to transmute the report into law in the near future.

Meantime, with his term drawing to a close in the autumn of 1963, Gordon had become a political liability. Liberal MPs from Quebec wanted a French-Canadian chairman. One MP, Yvon Dupuis, told Prime Minister Lester B. Pearson, "If ever Gordon's contract with the CN were renewed we may well expect such reactions that the very existence of our government would be at stake. His arrogance and lack of tact have destroyed his image." But even in Quebec Gordon had his supporters, and among the union leaders defending him was Paul Raymond, general chairman of the Association of Unions, a French Canadian who represented 80,000 CN employees.

After an emotional session with the directors, who vowed to resign *en bloc* if he were fired, Gordon had his chauffeur drive him and Ralph Vaughan to Ottawa, where he dined with Pearson at 24 Sussex Drive. At midnight, when Gordon returned to the Chateau Laurier, he gave Vaughan a mysterious message: "Mr. Pearson will phone you tomorrow morning at nine o'clock. He did not tell me why, he just asked me if I had somebody he could trust."

The next morning Vaughan reported to the prime minister's office for what he recalls as the following conversation: "'What I want you to do,' Pearson said, 'you write a letter from me to Gordon asking him to remain on for another three years. Then you write a letter from Gordon to say thank you Prime Minister, I would like to clean up some loose ends, like recapitalization and then I'd like to retire.'"

Vaughan took both letters to Pearson that afternoon and found him watching World Series baseball on television. "I now want you to write me a memorandum in French and English about what CN has done about bilingualism," Pearson told Vaughan. "I'm going to take the whole thing to the caucus tomorrow morning and we'll have it done." "That was the end of it," said Vaughan. "It was done."

The Gordon letter said: "I recognize that flowing from my appearance at the parliamentary committee [of 1962] was much criticism, distortion, misunderstanding and some public unrest. No one regrets more than I that this occurred." The work he had set out to do at CN should be finished "in about a year and a half, in which case I will, in good conscience, ask to be released from the duties which I have always done my best to perform in a way which would be of benefit to the railway and the country." On October 4 Pearson announced Gordon's reappointment and Grégoire, who had started the uproar the year before, praised Gordon's efforts to accommodate French Canadians. "I agree a big step has been made by this gentlemen and that it is only fitting that he now be given the opportunity to do what he failed to do in the past."

Fisher would have preferred to see Gordon go, for while he found CN more innovative than the CPR, he feared it would kill off railway towns in his northern Ontario riding. Since the introduction of diesels, both CN and CPR obviously wanted to eliminate division points to save money, but railway workers insisted the change be gradual with a minimum loss of jobs. "This tremendous change was going to lead to great diminution in the labour force of both railways, but particularly at CN," said Fisher. "They had brought Solandt in to lead research and there were all sorts of fife and drums about what a go-ahead company CN was, and how it was going to use science and technology, and yet the fact remained when it came to human relations it really wasn't doing a very good job at all."

In the steam locomotive era, the crews of enginemen and firemen changed twenty-one times on the run from Montreal to Vancouver and conductors and other trainmen nine times. But diesels required no change of crew every 125 miles, nor water tower, nor coal depots. To benefit from diesel efficiency, CN and the CPR had begun bypassing traditional stopping points in southern Ontario, and CN wanted to eliminate fifteen crew change stops in northern Ontario and run trains right through – until Fisher barred the way at Nakina.

A community in the bush north of Lake Superior, Nakina had been a railway town for forty years, founded in 1923 as a division point on the new short-cut through northern Ontario to Winnipeg. To create it, the whistle stop of Grant had been closed down, loaded onto flat cars – school, church, houses – and shunted eighteen miles down the line. Nakina had piped water, electricity, a sewage system, school, church, Legion Hall, two hotels, two cafes, workshops, a roundhouse and a thousand inhabitants who either worked in the bush or for CN. For the annual town picnic CN supplied old railway coaches, an engine and a crew and took the whole town twelve miles out to Twin Lake.

Nakina was a "home station," residence of engineers, firemen, trainmen and conductors, members of the 7400-strong Brotherhood of Locomotive Firemen and Enginemen, the 8900-member Brotherhood of Locomotive Engineers and 20,000-strong Brotherhood of Railway Trainmen.

On September 18, 1964, the CN assistant superintendent for northern Ontario notified the local chairmen that on October 25, "at the change of time-card," or midnight, CN intended to operate passenger trains numbers 1, 2, 9 and 10 through Nakina without stopping. By running straight through for 244 miles – five and a half hours – from Hornepayne to Armstrong, CN could save time and money, but for the local people this posed the threat of Nakina becoming a ghost town. Nor was Nakina alone. Changes were planned at Wainwright, 126 miles east of Edmonton, where the railway wished to run 266 miles without a halt between Edmonton and Biggar, Saskatchewan. Division 796 of the Brotherhood of Locomotive Engineers in Edmonton feared a return to the days "when engineers destroyed their health and neglected their families by practically living on an engine."

Nakina became the focal point, the symbol of solidarity, and since union leaders were taking no action a rank-and-file delegation from Nakina travelled to Ottawa to make their case. The government refused to intervene, reminding the men that a crown corporation must make its own decisions. The union men turned to their MP, who happened to be Fisher. "There is only one thing you can do if you want to get attention and stop the run-throughs and that's hit the brakes," Fisher told them. He advised them to recruit supporters across the country and promised to come to Nakina to help. "It's risky," he warned. "I don't think your union leadership would condone a wildcat strike. You would be breaking the law. You could face jail terms."

"I was never against the idea of the run-through," Fisher says, "but the railways were proposing changes piecemeal. It was my contention that they should publicize long-range plans for modernization and efficient operation rather than taking a little nibble here and a little nibble there. Both railways and government were ignoring the social costs."

Having failed on Friday, October 23, to persuade Parliament to debate the run-throughs, Fisher flew on Saturday to the Lakehead, where he failed to get an injunction to halt them. Saturday evening he raced the 200 miles to Nakina (killing a huge wolf on the road and smashing his windshield) just as the wildcat strike was starting at "change of time card." "We set up a little command headquarters in the hotel and I got on the phone and talked to contacts we'd developed across the country and we got it moving."

By Sunday morning calls of support were coming from all over northern Ontario and from Winnipeg, Edmonton, Wainwright, Vancouver, Montreal and Moncton. "I got exhilarated and then scared as the thing began to roll," Fisher said. "We knew by morning the strike was working and we had the company flatfooted. Then I knew I had the power."

Starting in Nakina, 2800 CN trainmen booked off sick and Fisher picked up the phone and called the minister of transport, Jack Pickersgill, at his home in Ottawa to warn him the strikers would tie up the whole railway. Fisher believed a government inquiry was the way to save the situation.

"To be fair to Fisher, I think he did the government a great service in that," said Pickersgill. "I have always felt Doug was not one of these people who look for ways to magnify problems to embarrass the government. His primary concern was the public interest.

"I was lying at home with the flu," Pickersgill continued, "but I talked on the phone to Prime Minister Pearson, and he said, 'Are you suggesting we appoint a royal commission?' I said, 'Not in the least, that would only infuriate Donald Gordon. Why don't we get Donald to ask the government to appoint a commission?' So I called Gordon and put the case. I said, 'Donald please don't give me an answer at once, think about it and call me back in a couple of hours.' When he called back he said he had drafted something and he sent a telegram asking the prime minister to appoint the commission."

On Monday Fisher was back in Ottawa to hear the prime minister's plan. CN would make no run-throughs pending the findings of Justice Samuel Freedman of Winnipeg, a one-man industrial inquiry commission. "For two or three hours I phoned across the country and got everybody back to work," Fisher said.

Some believed the wildcat strikers would have returned of their own accord and that Gordon gave in too readily to government pressure, but CN gained more than it lost by the action. The Freedman investigation gave the unions a voice that helped both management and labour through the difficult technical changes in the years ahead. Without it, similar wildcat strikes would have been likely.

According to Freedman, CN had been within its rights but he objected to the way it had ordered the run-throughs. Henceforth run-throughs should be negotiated rather than imposed, and both company and labour should have the right to take them to arbitration. When technological change was introduced, the company should shoulder the cost of protecting employees from adverse effects. Freedman added that the duty of the unions "involves a recognition that change is a law of life and that stubborn resistance to technological advance hurts everybody, labour included." Hailed by the unions as a landmark decision, the Freedman report bought Nakina two decades of stability before it was closed down as a divisional point, by which time it had built up its forest industry.

Though diesels had not yet produced the savings CN hoped for, economies in other areas improved CN's finances for the fourth successive year. CN reported a 20 per cent increase in passenger revenue for 1964, and though passenger operations were far from making a profit, Pierre Delagrave, with his Red, White and Blue fares, showed signs of turning the service around.

15

PURSUIT OF
PASSENGERS

A T A TIME OTHER NORTH AMERICAN RAILROADS were giving up on the unprofitable passenger business, CN in the mid-1960s introduced a new world of rail travel in an effort to woo people away from automobiles. Though the railway was losing $50 million a year on passengers, twice as much as the CPR, which had abandoned a hundred passenger runs, so long as there was a minority who would travel by rail and a majority sentimentally attached to trains even though they rarely used them, the crown corporation was expected to provide service.

Having introduced the popular Red, White and Blue fares, Pierre Delagrave embarked on more ambitious projects when he was appointed vice-president of passenger sales and services in 1964. As an earnest of the importance CN was giving passenger service, this was the first time freight and passenger sales had been separated and a vice-president appointed. Delagrave introduced the transcontinental *Panorama*, which clipped three hours off the time of the ten-year-old *Super Continental* on the run to Vancouver. Both were equipped with "Scenaramic" dome lounge cars from which passengers could admire the Rockies when they weren't playing bingo or enjoying "hospitality hour" (tea). Except those who wanted a grand view of the north woods, prairies and mountains, fewer and fewer travellers were willing to spend three days on a train between central Canada and Vancouver when they could make the trip by plane in a few hours. There were half as many sleeping cars on Canadian railways as in 1930.

In response to agitation for a better train between Montreal and Quebec City, CN purchased a second-hand Budd streamliner consisting of five gleaming steel cars, renamed it *Le Champlain* and put it in service in June 1964, cutting half an hour off the schedule. Advertised as a prestige train, *Le Champlain* offered piped music and sophisticated service in English and French.

CN added a non-stop passenger service between Toronto and Windsor, and a new train, the *Chaleur*, between Montreal and the Maritimes. Montreal-Maritime traffic had reached its peak, with CN running twenty sleepers every day (the CPR had only two) compared with the four sleepers it had used in 1925 and eleven in 1945. In addition, CN bought half a dozen "Skyview" bedroom-lounge observation cars for the fastest train in the Maritimes, the *Ocean Limited*, the average speed of which had been increased from thirty-one miles an hour in 1925 to forty miles. An hour and forty-five minutes had been cut off the *International Limited* from Chicago to Toronto and the Grand Trunk Western had introduced the fastest service available between Chicago and Detroit.

Since the mid fifties CN had purchased twice as much passenger equipment as its rival, replacing the old-style parlour car (swivel armchairs on either side of the aisle) with European-style reclining seats and adjustable footrests. Overhead luggage racks were replaced by baggage space at either end of the car. The new-style cars carried more passengers but whether they were more comfortable was a matter of opinion; at least they were electrically heated, ending the problem of leaky steam pipes in the depths of a Canadian winter. CN now had 1100 passenger cars, 40 per cent of them built before World War II. Delagrave planned to have 700 restored, with games rooms, offices for businessmen and "Camera Cars" with open platform for amateur photographers, and a bi-level train for transcontinental runs. He joked about including a swimming pool and bowling alley.

Though Delagrave was prepared to abandon unprofitable branch lines, he insisted there was a future for passenger service in the corridor between Quebec City and Windsor, the most travelled area in the country, and perhaps between Edmonton, Calgary and Vancouver. "What we had in mind," he said, "was a train that would leave Quebec City, come through Montreal, Ottawa and Toronto and on to Windsor. And another leaving Ottawa, stopping at Kingston and Toronto and then going to Chicago. This would mean the equipment that was costing you money twenty-four hours a day would be properly utilized. It's like airplanes, you know – you keep them flying because they are too costly on the ground. So that was what we were looking for."

One idea being informally canvassed was an international airport at Kingston, Ontario, rather than second airports, as planned, at Toronto and Montreal. By running fast trains to a Kingston airport from both Toronto and Montreal, the cost of one airport could be saved. All this was daydreaming, however. When Delagrave became vice-president, travellers in the busy Montreal–Toronto corridor had the choice of only three pool trains a day – morning, early evening and overnight – and the fastest took six hours. Convinced that much better service was needed to accommodate the six thousand people a day travelling between the two cities, Delagrave introduced the *Rapido* between Montreal and Toronto, the fastest diesel train in North America. "It will take us five years to know if we can make it," said Delagrave. "We'll know by then whether it is economic and if it is we'll stay with it."

At first the *Rapido* had been turned down by the operating and equipment departments. "They said it would be too fast, they could not operate it," said Delagrave. "Finally I grabbed an old file and went up to the president's office. I said, 'Donald, look, CN was running five-hour trains between Montreal and Toronto a generation ago under Sir Henry.' So I got my *Rapido*." Though Delagrave complained of lack of support from senior people in operations, he did receive support from conductors, enginemen and trainmen. "When we were doing trial runs," he said, "they would phone me privately and say, 'We did it in four hours and thirty-two minutes today!' They would phone me day after day."

Delagrave persuaded Gordon and the board to end the passenger pools that CN and the CPR had been running between Quebec, Montreal, Ottawa and Toronto. He pointed out that 60 per cent of pool revenue was generated by CN, and though pooling had saved CN money the CPR had benefited more, having been allowed into the lucrative central Canada passenger routes CN had dominated since the days of the Grand Trunk. Pools were a drag on CN initiative, said Delagrave, and since the CPR was fed up with losing money on passengers it should be allowed to withdraw.

The rival railways had developed different philosophies. After watching passenger revenue diminish by 50 per cent since the war, while automobiles claimed more than 80 per cent of intercity travel, Crump of the CPR decided there was no way passenger service could be made to pay. "By 1980," said Crump, "80 per cent of our population will live in urban areas. They won't need long-distance trains."

Gordon took the positive approach. Compared with cars and buses, railways were relatively non-polluting. They were safer, for there were years when highways were claiming five thousand lives and there were no passenger fatalities on the railways at all. They were efficient users of land and demonstrably the most efficient movers of masses of people. "There's been defeatism all over the continent about passenger traffic," he said. "That's why so much of it has been lost. There's a gambling element, of course. But the prospects offer a justifiable business risk. It's mainly the mass market we're after."

The CPR was happy to quit the pool, and on Saturday, October 30, 1965, a joint passenger service that had changed little in thirty years was scrapped. The next day Delagrave launched the *Rapido*. In Toronto a red carpet was rolled out and stodgy Union Station was brightened up with baskets of fresh flowers and new lighting. Mayor Philip Givens cracked a bottle of champagne and the train burst through a paper curtain that announced "CN's Rapido Fastest Inter-city Passenger Train in North America." Women were presented with flowers and a door prize was claimed by a CPR employee who had dropped by to see what the opposition was up to. In Montreal, Mayor Jean Drapeau and Donald Gordon saw the passengers off. Gordon gamely tried his hand at a little French – "En voiture!"

The *Rapidos* left Toronto and Montreal that Sunday at 4:45 pm, as they would every day except Saturday for years to come, making the non-stop journey of 335 miles in four hours and fifty-nine minutes, an hour and sixteen minutes less than the previous best schedule. A polite trainman in a new charcoal grey uniform settled you in wide, comfortable seats, and as the train sped through the dusk at sixty-seven miles an hour, red-coated waiters served consommé, roast beef and apple pie, all for the price of a $15 parlour car ticket. "We've considered the comfort of passengers," said Gordon, "which is a revolutionary thing in the railway business."

"All of a sudden, bang, we could do no wrong – almost," said Delagrave. "You can imagine how Donald and Norman felt. The *Rapido* became so popular and people were coming in such numbers they had to book a week in advance and passenger agents were overwhelmed with work." Not everyone was happy. For area manager J. H. Spicer in Toronto there had not been sufficient preparation. "Without any discussion with local passenger people, they made the decision to have reserved seats on coaches. We had a reservation bureau in Union Station with only four people to handle compartments and berths and had one week to adjust to handling reservations for every seat on the train. Holy Christmas! We couldn't get people trained, and Bell Canada couldn't put in phones fast enough. But we survived."

In addition to the *Rapido,* passenger trains between the two cities included the *Bonaventure,* twin diesel trains that left Montreal and Toronto at 4:50 every afternoon and made the run in five hours and fifty minutes, the *Lakeshore* morning and afternoon, and the overnight *Cavalier,* which left at midnight and reached its destination at the considerate hour of 7:30 a.m.

For the rest of 1965 stylish travellers between Montreal and Toronto had their choice of riding in CN's *Rapido* or the CPR's stainless steel streamliners, the *Royal York* and *Le Chateau Champlain,* which took almost an hour longer than the *Rapido.* Then early in 1966 the CPR withdrew from the Montreal-Toronto and Toronto-Ottawa routes and got government permission to terminate the *Dominion,* one of its two transcontinental trains, but there was so much public criticism it was obliged to keep the train for two more years. After Expo 67, the *Canadian* was the CPR's sole transcontinental.

CN's passenger totals continued to climb, though the railway continued to lose money. The *Super Continental,* attracting people who liked comfort, economy and better food than they could get on planes, cost twice as much to operate as it earned. The biggest losses, as always, were in the sleeping and dining cars, where services cost four times more than they earned. The *Rapido,* arguably the most convenient way to travel between downtown Montreal and Toronto, was popular, but progress was hard-won. Though operations people were well aware of the need for customers, passengers had never been their first priority. Old-style conductors had much more on their minds than the comfort of passengers.

Delagrave recalled that on trips to the yards at night he saw freights leaving an hour or two late so as to fit operating priorities rather than customers' needs and he was pleased when MacMillan launched a blitz to improve train times. He also rode the rails to make sure passengers were getting service. "One overnight trip was a very bumpy ride," recalled Garth Campbell. "They were changing crews at Belleville or Brockville and he put on his homburg and overcoat over his pajamas and went storming down the platform to catch the engineer coming off the cab. He sticks his hand out and says, 'I'm Pierre Delagrave. It's my job to get people on these trains. I just want to tell you if you keep driving the way you did tonight I'm wasting my time.'"

Though Gordon had announced that no new modernization projects were necessary now dieselization had been achieved, Delagrave was looking for something that would catch the imagination of the public. For Expo 67, the world's fair in Montreal, and Canada's centennial year, he wanted nothing less than a revolutionary jet-age train then on the drawing boards.

Since 1962 CN had been studying high-speed trains as a way to double passenger revenues in the Montreal-Ottawa-Toronto corridor. Three years later came word that United Aircraft Corporation was building a "train of the future," an aerodynamic lightweight "Turbotrain" powered by oil-fired gas turbine aircraft engines. Each train of seven gleaming white cars would have four engines, three for propulsion and one for power, air conditioning and lighting, and cost $2 million.

On paper it was a marvel, a low-slung, streamlined, tube of aluminum stretched over an aircraft-type frame. The *Turbo* was capable of speeds a third again more than the *Rapido* and carried more passengers. It was designed to bank on curves so passengers were not tossed about by centrifugal force. With power units and cabs at both ends, turn-around time was greatly reduced. In the operations and maintenance departments, which had to make sure trains ran safely and dependably, there was much shaking of heads. CN engineers had investigated turbine power at GM in Detroit and found it less effective than diesel, and they were equally sceptical when a McGill University professor tried to interest them in a coal-burning gas turbine. The *Turbo* was brand new and had never been tested, and its speeds were incompatible with level crossings. But Delagrave, regarded by veteran operations people as more salesman than railroader, was persuasive, getting MacMillan on his side and, eventually, Gordon.

In the six years since Delagrave had joined CN as a special assistant in the secretary's office, he had moved up quickly for one who had been a civil servant with no railway experience. As a vice-president, the slim, energetic, likable Québécois, who often lamented that his formal education had ended in high school, had shown himself to be one of the most forceful, imaginative and enthusiastic officials in the company. His innovations – the Red, White and Blue fares, a French-language version of the timetable, a convenient Tickets-by-Mail scheme, and the Car-Go-Rail scheme which later became Auto-With-You, allowing a passenger and car to travel on the same train – had won Gordon's support. In fact his influence with Gordon gave passenger service priority over the Operating department, a remarkable development at that time and one with inherent dangers, as became clear in the *Turbo* episode.

Though other vice-presidents did not share Delagrave's enthusiasm, he was convinced the *Turbo* would triple passenger revenue but must be acquired in time to carry the crowds to Montreal for Expo 67. The train would be a leap into the jet age, an opportunity to steal a march on the CPR and put CN on the map with the "most dynamic form of land transportation anywhere in the world." United Aircraft asked CN to make its decision by mid-summer of 1965 but Gordon decided the company should proceed cautiously; opinions were divided on the *Turbo's* viability, and a furthermore major investment of $10 million was required to guard level crossings against a train that could exceed ninety miles per hour. (It could travel at 120 miles an hour on dedicated track but this demanded welded rail, concrete ties and elimination of level crossings.)

Since Gordon was nearing the end of his tenure, he turned the project over to MacMillan, who in turn had Ralph Vaughan, the company secretary, guide the negotiations. "It was a good-looking train, there's no doubt about that," said Vaughan. "Delagrave wanted to buy it but I didn't want to. It had never been tested. What we did was lease it, based on reliability performance. As it turned out it was a godsend that we didn't sink a lot of money into it."

By autumn, no decision having been reached, Delagrave heard rumours an American railroad was planning to buy the *Turbo*, depriving Canada of the honour of having it first. MacMillan was sympathetic but was having difficulty reaching a decision. Delagrave became frustrated at what he perceived to be lack of support. "You know," he told the author twenty years later, "the railways never really wanted to be in the passenger business. It was a PR thing. I said unless you spend money on the line from Montreal to Toronto we're never going to make it. So I pushed and pushed this with MacMillan and Gordon. I said to Garth Campbell, 'If I don't succeed in getting this they're playing us for suckers.'"

Delagrave's increasingly urgent communications to MacMillan began to carry an unmistakable warning. Unless a favourable decision was reached he would quit. "I thought the idea was just getting lip service, which is why I left," he said. He resigned on December 3, 1965, a disappointed man. "I remember the day he resigned," said Vaughan. "He had gone to see Mac-Millan to go over the new program and it didn't gel."

Gordon was upset. "The next day," Delagrave recalled, "I went to shake hands with Donald and say goodbye and he said, 'Get out of here. I never want to talk to you again in my life.'" Delagrave became a vice-president at Domtar, the pulp and paper company, and years were to pass before the two met at a cocktail party and had an opportunity to repair their friendship.

Ironically, had Delagrave stayed he would have got his wish, for before the month was over CN announced its decision to lease a fleet of turbine trains. Committed to a *Turbo* service, CN asked the government for special funding and was turned down, but on January 26 Gordon put the question to the CN board and got approval to rent five train sets, four for service between Montreal and Toronto and a fifth for a Quebec-Montreal-Ottawa schedule. The decision had been influenced by CPR's withdrawal from the Montreal-Toronto run, which meant more CN trains were needed to meet the demand and CN would have to acquire more equipment since ninety coaches were too old. Moreover, if *Turbos* were going to be useful in Expo year a quick decision was necessary.

The Delagrave philosophy would live on, though he would be spared the embarrassment of watching the new train bedevilled again and again by mechanical problems. Addressing the Commons Transport Committee some months after Delagrave had departed, Gordon said CN was on its way to making money on passengers within the next five years.

Though passengers were far from paying their way, they were bringing in more revenue than at any time since the war and Delagrave had proved there was a demand for service – if only between Montreal and Toronto. CN's efforts to attract passengers had also demonstrated that in the age of airplane and auto, Canada had neither the geography, the population, nor the will to operate a profitable passenger service, but as a government corporation CN had to prove this without any doubt before it could go the way of the CPR and throw in the towel.

The new passenger vice-president, Jean Richer, was no Delagrave, having doubts about the future of passenger service, but he gave it his best effort. "You were a drain on the organization," Richer said later. "You could get good publicity by promising the *Turbo* and getting your picture taken – here was CN in the vanguard! – but I never really did believe in my bones that passenger service was viable. To be really viable, rail has to be a way of life, as in

England and France, but it never could except in the corridor between Toronto and Montreal, which you might extend as far as Quebec City and Windsor but that would be the end of it."

Richer, promoted to the vice-presidency of the Saint Lawrence region within two years, was succeeded by Garth Campbell, though by now the title had been downgraded to general manager. "We kept it going," said Campbell, "and by Expo year, 1967, our biggest job was just handling people. It was phenomenal." Some 18 million passengers rode CN trains, a 25 per cent increase over the previous year, as people flocked to Expo, where, among 130 industrial exhibitions, CN's "Time and Motion" drew a million and a quarter visitors. To handle the record number of passengers CN leased sixty-four coaches, sleeping cars and diners from the U.S. and became the first railway in North America to install a full-scale computerized reservation service. CN and CPR cooperated to run a "Centennial Train" which exhibited phases in Canada's development and was visited by nearly three million people across the country.

The two afternoon *Rapidos* between Montreal and Toronto, which had grown to fourteen cars on weekdays and eighteen on weekends, were augmented by two in the morning in addition to four conventional daily passenger trains in each direction and an afternoon *Rapido* between Montreal and Quebec City. On the Montreal-Ottawa run the noon *Bytowner* supplemented the *Gatineau*, the *Laurier* and other trains. Red, White and Blue fares were extended to the Grand Trunk Western between Detroit and Chicago, the first time such a system was used in the U.S.

"We think we are succeeding," MacMillan said. "We are very hopeful that we shall succeed completely and that we will be able to show a marked improvement in the financial results of the passenger business." Ian Sinclair, on his way up the CPR ladder to the chairman's office, had a different view. "I don't say they are wrong," he told the *Financial Post* on May 14, 1966. "I know they are wrong."

The *Turbos* were built at the Montreal Locomotive Works more or less straight from the drawing board, their performance studied only by computers that simulated runs over CN tracks. The turbines supplied by United Aircraft of Canada were Pratt & Whitney aircraft engines weighing only 250 pounds each. They burned more fuel than diesels but were expected to make long-term savings because two trains of seven cars could be operated in tandem, hauling as many passengers as three diesels.

Early in 1967 UAC said the *Turbo* would probably be ready by midsummer, but delivery dates began to lag until mid-November, too late for Expo, and in consequence CN lost revenue. In November CN personnel took their first ride on a *Turbo* and were favourably impressed, though the train was noisy. Only now was the train going into intensive testing, which would take the better part of a year.

When it finally did appear in public at its inaugural press run on December 12, 1968, the train had the misfortune to ram its red nose and sleek white body into a forty-foot tractor-trailer at a level crossing near Kingston. No one was hurt but the accident confirmed the operating department's fears about level crossings and was publicized on front pages across the country with photos showing the highway rig split in two and frozen meat flying through the air.

A few weeks later the service was discontinued because of electrical problems and the discovery that the train was poorly insulated against Canada's winters. "After that," recalled Vaughan, "we had trouble with the carriage system. Then one caught fire. They used to stall. Thank heavens we didn't buy them." The *Turbo* was one of the most imaginative, challenging and disappointing innovations in the history of CN passenger service and the odds against its success were heavy given the short time allowed for building and testing. Although it was frequently out for repairs before it settled down to reliable performance in the mid-1970s, it redeemed itself by covering the distance between Montreal and Toronto in four hours and ten minutes. Its times have never been equalled in Canada.

One of CN's more successful passenger ventures was its entry into commuter service in southern Ontario. Though CN had lost money on commuters for decades, the company responded favourably when Government of Ontario Transit asked it to provide service on CN track along the shore of Lake Ontario. The province wanted a commuter service for Greater Toronto and was prepared to cover the cost because the alternative was building ten highway traffic lanes.

The first GO (Government of Ontario) train, North America's most modern commuter service, pulled out of Union Station in May 1967. As the first custom-built commuter service in Canada – others having evolved as cities grew and using mostly existing equipment – GO covered sixty miles between Oakville and Pickering, gathering commuters from east and west of Toronto. The service, which ran every twenty minutes at peak periods, was extended to over 230 miles, embracing Oshawa, Toronto and Hamilton and all but thirty miles was operated by CN, which maintained track, supplied crews, and operated eight diesels, forty aluminum and steel alloy cars, and nine conventional rail cars. The government set fares, covered operating deficits and provided stations and rolling stock.

Another successful innovation was the *Tempo* service – light, inter-city trains designed for the same-day-return traveller. Consisting of a diesel with dual controls for operation in either direction and four or five streamlined coaches and a club car – the first coaches in Canada to be electrically air-conditioned – these trains were introduced in 1968 between Toronto, Windsor and Sarnia. To entice passengers after the excitement of Expo 67 was over, a Bistro car with a straw-hatted piano player was added to one end of the afternoon *Rapido*. At the other end an Executive Car was added with conference room, offices and other services for workaholic businessmen. Despite these efforts and more, passenger business tumbled by almost 20 per cent.

"They began to clip our wings after 1968," said Campbell. "You couldn't top Expo year, and MacMillan [who had succeeded Gordon as president in 1967] called me in and said, 'I'm going to take you out of the passenger business. You have been so successful – these were his words – that I want you to do the same thing in other parts of the business.' But I knew where the decision was actually made. There were guys in Ottawa who were on his tail. Transport Canada and Pickersgill had decided there was no future in the movement of people and Norm backed away. That's when he decided to take me out of the business. I was supposed to make a freight marketing plan, but that was not my bag at all. I ended up going to Ottawa to work for the Post Office."

"Little by little things changed," said Pat Bennett of Moncton, a veteran of the dining cars. "Services were cut, a lot of meals were pre-prepared and that reduced the crew. People today have no idea what the service used to be like. It's the old saying, 'If you don't use it you lose it.' How true that is."

Nevertheless CN's annual report for 1968 insisted its "experiments" had confirmed there was a market in populated areas like Montreal-Toronto, where it would maintain service while withdrawing from unprofitable routes. After Expo the CPR operated only the *Canadian* across the country, though CN continued to run two daily services, the *Super Continental* and *Panorama*, between central Canada and Vancouver and three daily trains to the Maritimes, the *Scotian, Ocean Limited* and *Chaleur*.

ABOVE The seat of power. This 1947 photo shows an engineer, goggled against flying cinders, at the controls of a 335-ton 6200 Northern type locomotive. His hand is on the throttle, controlling steam pressure upon pistons that turn the seventy-three-inch driving wheels. Above the throttle are boiler and air brake pressure gauges. Below are two brass handles for the locomotive and train brakes, and the reversing gear lever.

LEFT Getting up steam. In the decades before diesels made them redundant, firemen were the hardest workers on the trains.

Hand signals, like cabooses and steam plumes, have gone the way of the steam locomotive. This brakeman is giving a back-up signal to the engineer from the steps of a caboose in 1925.

The caboose was home away from home – utilitarian, rough riding, drafty, but with pin-ups, pictures, stove and cushions.

Northern steam locomotive 6124 being overhauled, a typical engine on mainline freight and passenger trains from 1927 to the end of steam in the 1950s.

A telegram usually began with a call to telephone operators at a CN Telegraph office. In 1946 sending a message was labour intensive.

Starr Fairweather, as vice-president of the research and development department, wielded immense influence in shaping CN for more than three decades. He is seen here (at centre) in the lab with president R. C. Vaughan.

A Northern type engine hauling fifteen heavyweight express, mail and passenger cars of the *Maritime Express*, leaves Victoria Bridge, Montreal, to cover the 840 miles to Halifax.

A freight train hauled by a Mikado type, flying the white flag that announced it was a special.

When Newfoundland joined Canada in 1949, the Newfoundland Railway was entrusted to CN. The trans-island passenger train was officially the *Caribou*, and unofficially the "Newfie Bullet." This picture, as would almost any picture, shows a grade and a curve in the same shot.

Starting in the 1950s, CN expanded north for two decades, building seventeen lines into resource areas, mainly mines. Here Donald Gordon drives the last spike on the Manitouwadge branch line, July 27, 1955, using a mechanical spike driver.

Opened in 1957, the Senneterre to Chibougamau line in Quebec tapped a rich mineral area. Donald Gordon, carrying a symbolic key and always ready to pose, has just tripped the signal lever to start the first official train over the line.

The Manitouwadge line under construction – a tractor train delivers supplies along the road-bed during the winter while the surface is hard.

To make a solid roadbed across a valley, a wooden trestle bridge is built. Side-dumping ballast cars are positioned on the trestle and a plow is dragged from car to car, pushing the ballast out the sides. It takes hundreds of trainloads to fill a valley, but the result is a maintenance-free crossing with no risk of fire.

Plain food fuels branch line workers in a converted passenger car. The hours were long and the physical demands high, but the pay was good.

BELOW Giant tracklayer on the Moak Lake line, 1957. Ties move ahead on one side of the flat cars and rails on the other and are put in position. The tracklayer rolls on the new track and other machines finish spiking and ballasting.

In 1952, to compete with trucks, CN began the trailers-on-flat-cars "piggyback" service between Montreal and Windsor. Then, trailers were backed on to flat cars in "circus-loading" fashion.

This train was known locally as the Moccasin because Cornwall, Ontario, Indians used it to carry their craft work to market in Montreal. In this 1958 photo at Coteau, Quebec, it is making its last west-bound trip to Brockville, Ontario, still handling express shipments in the head-end car.

Centralized Traffic Control revolutionized train operations. Machines like this one at Hornepayne, Ontario, 1957, replaced the train order system, which relied on the telegraph.

In 1955 CN re-equipped much of its passenger car fleet and launched an improved service between central Canada and B.C., the *Super Continental*.

In 1961 CN introduced its new symbol. The designer was Allan Fleming, left, of Toronto, who is shown with Charles Harris, director of CN Public Relations. In the background a diesel locomotive displays the controversial symbol.

Le Champlain, a train-set purchased from the Reading Railroad in Pennsylvania, about to cross the Quebec Bridge in 1967 near the end of its two hour and forty minute run from Montreal.

Planned to enter service for Expo 67, CN's *Turbo* was two years late. Although it broke Canadian speed records at 161 miles per hour on a special run, it never realized its potential. In the end, rising fuel costs made it uneconomic to operate.

Jack Pickersgill, minister of transport, shown with CN chairman and president Norman J. MacMillan when CN gave historic equipment to the National Museum of Science and Technology in Ottawa, 1967.

Completed in 1969 230 miles north to Dawson Creek, the Alberta Resources Railway connected with the Alaska Highway to open up the Peace River District.

Dr. Robert Bandeen, CN president, on a *Turbo* run between Montreal and Toronto when VIA Rail Canada was being formed.

Loading a unit train at Cardinal River, Alberta. The worldwide demand for metallurgical coal in the 1960s and Canadian demand for electric power led to a resurgence in coal transport. Unit trains can be loaded and unloaded without uncoupling the cars.

At Taschereau yard in Montreal, computers control the flow of cars through the sorting process, ensuring that each car is in the right train for its destination, at the right time.

A full-length intermodal train, carrying international containers shipped through the port of Halifax, crosses the Salmon River bridge in northern New Brunswick. In Montreal the load will be split between local delivery by truck and onward shipment by rail to Toronto, Chicago and western Canada.

Ronald Edward Lawless, a railway man all his working life, became president and CEO in January 1987, with the task of improving service while keeping the railway on its budgetary track. He is show here at the Monterm Intermodal Terminal in Montreal, November 3, 1988.

A little-known international route is CN's AquaTrain service connecting Prince Rupert, B.C., with Alaska, providing the shortest rail ferry route between the continental rail network and the Alaska Railroad.

ABOVE Although machinery has eliminated much of the back-breaking work from track maintenance, joining long sections of welded rail calls for a moment of brute force. Hinton, Alberta, is on a stretch of railway where tonnages are highest and concrete ties are the norm. In 1983, when this photo was taken, CN was double-tracking long stretches of its western main line.

Laura Bennett, filling what had traditionally been a man's job, as a foreperson at Malport yard, Mississauga, Ontario, in 1991.

BELOW Crews change at Kamloops, B.C., on a 10,000-ton trainload of potash bound from Saskatchewan to Vancouver, hauled by 3000-hp SD50 General Motors locomotives.

Taxpayers who didn't use trains were complaining they were having to subsidize people who enjoyed the luxury of diners and sleeping cars. CN began to substitute café cars for diners on its *Super Continental*, the labour-intensive diners being among the few restaurants in the world that cost a quarter of a million dollars to outfit but seated only forty people and served hardly more than a hundred meals a day.

Frank Roberts, who succeeded Garth Campbell as general manager of passenger sales and services, had orders to cut expenses – without making political waves, a difficult task, even among people who had no intention of using the train. Roberts recalled the odd opposition he sometimes encountered: "One western farmer told me, 'You people don't realize what the railway means to us. I never use the passenger train,' he said, 'but here I am in a small town on the Prairies in the middle of winter, a cold, miserable and lonely life, but if I want to get out of here tomorrow morning I can go down to the station and get a train the hell out of here.' There was comfort in having a railway station in town, even if you didn't use it."

Intent on maintaining a transcontinental service, the government tried to keep losses within reasonable limits. Since it was subsidizing transcontinental trains at the rate of $24 million a year, it recommended an integrated CN-CPR passenger service during the nine-month off-season, September to June. When that did not work it ran newspaper advertisements asking for suggestions from the public. Five years later the two railways were still operating their own transcontinental trains – and losing money.

Between Montreal and Toronto, the one area where CN hoped to make a profit, the *Turbo* had become a public relations headache, plagued with malfunctions which repeatedly put trains out of service. For over a year, between January 6, 1969, and May 25, 1970, *Turbo* service had to be suspended. Passenger reaction to the train had been generally favourable, but there was little reason to believe it could be profitable. The break-even point was 60 per cent and though the occupancy rate on afternoon runs averaged that amount, the morning service occupancy was only 30 per cent.

On February 1, 1971, the *Turbos* were taken out of service again after a gearbox failure in one train and a fire in the turbine of another and a problem of thermal cracks in the wheels. Some felt it was time to give up, but by September 1974 most of the problems seemed solved, CN leased three more, and for the next few years *Turbos* operated more or less as advertised though passengers complained of jolting rides. There were high points in the troubled history of the train advertised as the greatest leap forward in railway technology in a hundred years, and the highest was reached on Thursday, April 22, 1976. A train of nine coaches, newly painted yellow and blue and driven by John Shipman of Montreal, reached 140.6 miles an hour on a twenty-mile stretch of welded track east of Prescott, Ontario, breaking the Canadian record of 129 mph set earlier that year in a CPR test of an LRC (Light, Rapid, Comfortable) prototype. The occasion was a media trip from Kingston to Montreal and, recalling what had happened on a similar inauguration, CN had blocked off the five level crossings along the test stretch and the record was broken without disturbing the journalists' cocktail hour.

The *Turbo* had been a mistake. The people in CN's own operations and mechanical departments had not been given enough say in it. The track between Montreal and Toronto – with its 240 level crossings and rails pounded by freight trains – was inadequate. Operating difficulties had plagued the train from the start, but just as the service was stabilizing, some 200 modifications having been made, its poor fuel consumption, compared with a diesel, sealed its fate. The last two trains were withdrawn on October 31, 1982.

Research had begun in 1971 on a diesel-powered alternative, the LRC, a compromise between the futuristic *Turbo* and heavier, more conventional trains. It had a suspension system for banking at high speeds on curves and could make the run between Montreal and Toronto in four hours and thirty minutes or less, averaging about seventy-four miles an hour. A typical LRC train consisted of a dozen aluminum cars, each with a capacity for eighty people, and to develop it CN joined with Montreal Locomotive Works–Bombardier, the Aluminum Company of Canada and Dominion Foundries and Steel (Dofasco). A prototype was completed June 1971 but there were problems, including a defective axle, something that would plague the LRC for years to come, and the first LRC run came only in June 1982, five years after a new crown corporation, VIA Rail Canada, had taken over CN and CPR passenger responsibilities.

Both CN and the CPR had attempted to revive passenger service with attractive coaches, faster schedules and lower fares, CN running ads boasting that "Passenger travel is alive and well in Canada!" Passengers had failed to respond, and the CPR, cutting its losses, dropped out of the race. CN pressed on, but the effort was quixotic, though if it had not made one last big push it might have found it more difficult to get out of the passenger business in the end. The unions said CN had not done enough, the Canadian Brotherhood of Railway, Transport and General Workers charging that CN had adopted a deliberate policy to discourage rail travellers. That may have been true after 1968, but not before. Until the appearance of VIA Rail in Canada and Amtrak in the States, CN for many years had been virtually alone among North American railways in trying to reverse the decline and turn passenger service into a profitable business. Once they dropped out of the passenger business, CN and the CPR were left to do what North American railways do best.

16

A FUTURE FOR FREIGHT

B Y JANUARY 1966 CN was moving more freight than ever and inching out of a seemingly endless series of deficits in operations. The economy was buoyant and revenue was growing faster than expense but it would clearly take more than cost cutting and aggressive marketing to pay the interest charges which year after year made CN's results look worse than they were. In the autumn of 1963 Donald Gordon had allowed himself a year and a half to correct this before retiring. Those eighteen months having stretched to twenty-eight, Gordon now added an additional year.

Gordon had given up hope that the government would honour its promise to relieve CN of its debt load – he wanted Ottawa to shoulder two thirds, or about a billion dollars – the very idea having prompted editorials complaining that CN, having been recapitalized in 1937 and 1952, was going to the well once too often. The CPR, as usual, saw recapitalization as a threat, and Crump went so far as to tell the prime minister that it would have "serious implications for the continued existence" of his company, though precisely how he did not say.

Troubled by failing eyesight and saying that at his age a senior executive was best occupied "looking out the window and meditating," Gordon had turned over increasing responsibilities to Norman MacMillan, executive vice-president since 1956. Gordon had mellowed, charm and the soft answer replacing blunt words at the annual Transport Committee meetings, partly perhaps because Doug Fisher had retired from politics and there was no one to do battle with and less to battle about.

North-south traffic had increased as a result of the auto pact signed by Canada and the U.S., which created one large market for North American-built motor vehicles; CN was distributing the very vehicles that were robbing it of freight and passenger business. Its push into resource country was producing the long-distance bulk traffic North American railways handle best. Since the 19th century CN and its ancestors had advanced the northern frontier, since building track for specific purposes such as mineral exploration was one of the few ways a railway could be sure of earning its way. In Gordon's time the names along 700 miles of new northern lines were a history of post-war expansion Kitimat, Lynn Lake, Manitouwadge, Chibougamau. In Quebec a sixty-mile line had been completed to the zinc and copper mine at Mattagami, 400 miles northwest of Ottawa. A twenty-two-mile line had been built from Bartibog to Heath Steele, a mining region in northeastern New Brunswick. In Alberta a twenty-four mile industrial branch was built from Whitecourt to Windfall to reach a sulphur extraction plant in the gas fields fifty miles north of Edson. In northern Saskatchewan and Manitoba fifty-two miles of track had been opened from Optic Lake to Chisel Lake, and thirty-two miles from Sipiwesk to Burntwood River. Now work was being completed on the biggest project since CN was founded – the Great Slave Lake Railway.

This was one of the few results of Diefenbaker's dream of a "new Canada of the north," which he claimed would complete the east–west nation Sir John A. Macdonald had created. Though the Great Slave Lake Railway would help the north in general, its initial purpose was to serve Cominco's lead-zinc mine at Pine Point. Neither Cominco nor its parent, the CPR, wanted to build it themselves though they agreed to put up a fourth of the cost, which points up the disparate roles of the two railways. As usual when private enterprise failed to advance the frontier, the government stepped in and funded CN to build and operate the first line into the Northwest Territories.

From Roma Junction, 300 miles northwest of Edmonton on the Northern Alberta Railways, the Great Slave Lake Railway ran through the rolling, lightly-timbered upper Mackenzie Valley to the lake port of Hay River (population 3000), 377 miles north. Below Hay River a branch jogged off to the right for fifty-five miles to Pine Point's lead and zinc deposits. The ore was destined for Cominco's smelter at Trail, B.C., once there was a railway to haul it, highway costs being too expensive.

Apart from increasing CPR's profits the Great Slave Lake Railway hauled out grain and lumber and became the main supply line for Arctic oil exploration. By linking the Northern Alberta Railways to Hay River, the staging point for the Mackenzie River barge system, CN lowered the cost of shipments not only to Yellowknife but the Mackenzie delta and the Arctic coast. It brought settlers into the Mackenzie valley and traffic waxed four times heavier than initial forecasts.

At the same time, construction equipment was clanking through Alberta, Saskatchewan, Manitoba and northern Ontario. The Alberta government had commissioned CN to build and operate the Alberta Resources Railway, a 234-mile line north from the CN line near Hinton into coal and timber country. But the biggest rush of new business was in Saskatchewan, where the potash mines, half the world's reserves, had gone into production when deposits in New Mexico began to run down. CN had built a branch to the biggest potash deposit in the world, at Yarbo, near Melville on the main line, and had mobilized 1000 hopper cars and 850 boxcars to move it to market. In northern Manitoba a branch was built to the Hudson Bay Mining and Smelting Company seventy miles north of The Pas. In northwestern Ontario a sixty-seven-mile line linked Bruce Lake to Amesdale on the main line to haul iron ore to Thunder Bay, whence it went by ship to the Stelco smelter at Hamilton.

With the great postwar increase in north-south trade, a quarter of Canadian freight loadings were flowing to the United States. Two thirds of CN's freight came from mine, forest and farm, but in 1965 a dramatic increase in grain orders from Russia and China strained the railway's capacity. West of the Great Lakes, where grain trains had been part of the autumn scene for seventy years, the railways were moving a record quantity of wheat. The seasonal flow of export grain out of the Prairies is reminiscent of a watershed where springs become rivulets, then streams and finally a river. By August, farmers were trucking their grain to country elevators, whence the railways were hauling it to terminal elevators at the Lakehead, Vancouver, Prince

Rupert and Churchill. A freight car could make a full cycle from country elevator to terminal elevator and back in ten to fifteen days.

All this was regulated by the Wheat Board, which announced that CN would be expected to load 1176 cars a day five days a week. Over 12,000 boxcars and covered hoppers, which work like funnels, were allocated, and by September the railways were labouring around the clock to get wheat to the Lakehead and Churchill before the winter closed navigation, and to Vancouver and Prince Rupert throughout the winter. Had the railways been making money on grain, the sale of 100,000 carloads over and above domestic sales, would have been good news, but the Crow rate meant they were hauling grain at a quarter the rate American railroads were getting south of the border. Just how much CN and the CPR were losing depended on the bookkeeping. The MacPherson commission confirmed there was a considerable loss – albeit less than the railways were claiming – but no reform of the Crow was included in the upcoming National Transportation Act. As Gordon had pointed out when he tried to reform the grain haul in 1962, the system was obsolescent, discouraging the purchase of new rolling stock. Nevertheless, by mid-December CN had moved substantially more cars of grain than the year before and a letter from the United Grain Growers Limited in Winnipeg thanked the railway "for a job well done" on behalf of its 56,000 members.

The Lakehead had shown a creditable performance, but with potash, lumber, sulphur and other freight flowing through Vancouver there had been bottlenecks, with ships hanging at anchor for days with mounting expenses. Profiting from Vancouver's woes, the half-forgotten port of Prince Rupert, which had been built for Pacific trade, was proving its worth for the first time since the war, exceeding its target. For several years a small export traffic in lumber, minerals and grain had been flowing up the CN tracks to Prince Rupert and a Port Development Commission had been formed after Donald Gordon had assured the town that what was good for Prince Rupert was good for CN. Prairie premiers were urging the development of Prince Rupert and a CN study recommended Ridley Island, in Prince Rupert's fine bay, as a site for a bulk terminal now that Japan had become Canada's third largest customer after the United States and Britain. Gordon, in 1966, became the first CN president to visit the Orient, five years after having appointed a sales manager for the area, William H. Neale, after many years in which the company had no representative there. The volume of Pacific Rim trade passing through Vancouver had tripled in less than ten years – exports of pulp and aluminum, imports of everything from Japanese cars and bicycles and cameras to tulip bulbs.

Freight, as David Blythe Hanna had predicted after World War I, would always account for the bulk of Canadian rail business, though rolling stock had changed beyond recognition. In Hanna's day, freight equipment came in only half a dozen types: the ubiquitous red boxcars, flat cars, refrigerator cars which relied on ice, stock cars, coal cars and tank cars. Grain cars had been ordinary boxcars with waterproof roofs until C. D. Howe invented a dumper which gripped the cars and tipped out their contents so eight cars could be unloaded in an hour, instead of the three hours it had taken a gang of men to do the same job.

Now there were covered hopper cars for grain, cement and potash, fifty-two-foot gondola cars with covers which protected the cargo and allowed for fast unloading, rack-type bi-level cars to haul trucks, tri-level cars for automobiles, cars for auto parts, fifty-foot newsprint cars with yellow doors for identification, seventy-ton mechanically-refrigerated cars for the fresh produce traffic, insulated cars for heated service, special cars for aluminum ingots, for iron and steel, for brewery products, and fleets of special flat cars to carry piggyback trailers.

To speed the record traffic a CN project begun eight years earlier culminated in November 1965 with completion of the first coast-to-coast Centralized Traffic Control in North America. CTC, which had demonstrated its value in the Maritimes during the war, eliminated written train orders, hand-turned switches and long waits on sidings for passing trains. In Toronto, CN opened the fourth of its automated freight yards, which covered 1000 acres, employed 1500 people, sorted 5000 freight cars a day with push button consoles and control towers, and together with the yards at Winnipeg, Montreal and Moncton could handle 60,000 cars a day.

For decades trains had been growing longer as more diesel power was added. Once the National Transportation Act let railways merchandise bulk cargo movement as a package instead of having to quote rates for each carload, huge trains began snaking through the country like ambulant conveyor belts. These were the unit trains, 100 or more identical and permanently-coupled cars carrying a single commodity that might be coal, oil, potash, grain or whatever. Ideal for a system that is most efficient in long-haul movements of bulk, unit trains, like containers, assured the future of Canadian railways. Though most these days are seen in the West, CN's first unit train ran 340 miles to the Dofasco smelter in Hamilton late in March 1968 with iron concentrates from the Sherman Mine near Temagami. There were actually three unit trains involved, running on a seventy-two-hour cycle between an automatic loading dock at the mine and an elevated railway over the blast furnace bins at Dofasco.

The piggyback service had grown 125 per cent since it was introduced in the early 1950s as an experiment. The overnight No. 301 from Montreal to Toronto, hauled at seventy miles an hour by three diesel units, left Montreal at 12:15 a.m. five nights a week with between sixty-five and seventy trailers on flat cars. The mile-long train was the fastest scheduled freight in North America.

Since piggybacking had its drawbacks – transporting a whole trailer, wheels and all, cost a lot of space and weight – the next step was the container, which could be lifted right off a road vehicle and strapped to the flat car. So out of piggybacking developed the custom-built container that would revolutionize freight handling and give railways a new weapon in their battle with trucking. The system wherein anything from silk to lumber is packed into big metal boxes and transported in an intermodal flow of ships, trains and trucks without disturbing the contents was not new. Containers were used on the Camden and Amboy Railroad in 1848 and the Pennsylvania Railroad twenty years later, on British railways in the 1920s and by the U.S. army during World War II.

CN introduced containers in Atlantic Canada after the war, the biggest problem being standardization so that any container could be handled by any railway or truck – and by ships on the Newfoundland route. In the early 1950s CN introduced aluminum boxes for express freight, with containers twenty feet long by eight wide and eight high, strapped on flat cars and carried on fast freights to terminals where they were transferred to trucks for direct delivery.

By 1968 a new use had been devised for containers. In the past, when shipping lines confined their business to ports rather than reaching inland, merchandise was carried in vessels with hatches and holds, but now containers were a removable part of the vessel itself. Among the advantages were less handling, smaller crews of sailors and longshoremen, and greater speed and capacity. Where it had taken a week or more to load or unload a ship, now it might take a day or even half a day as twenty-five containers could be hoisted by a crane every hour and three cranes could serve one vessel.

The ship container revolution had begun in 1956 when an American,

Malcolm McLean, bought a fleet of ships and converted them to specialized vessels plying between New York, Texas and Puerto Rico. Container service had been extended to Europe and major companies like Manchester Liners, which had been sailing into Montreal with conventional vessels with cargoes carried onward by CN, began to gear up for the new container era. CN's vice-president of marketing, A.H. Hart, brought Rupert J. Tingley from customer research to study whether CN should also get into the new service. Canadian Pacific had ordered three container ships to go into service in 1970 between London, Rotterdam and Quebec. CN, with no ocean freighters of its own, would take another tack.

"All of a sudden the whole world got interested," said Tingley, a graduate engineer. "To say that the conventional shipping industry panicked was an understatement. They realized the economics were fantastic and companies operating into Canada like Manchester Liners said, 'Boy, we have to get into this.' So in 1967 CN was faced with the question – are we going to stay in the export-import traffic? For the next six months I was in Europe, Japan, Hong Kong, and it became apparent we just had to offer this service. In the past we dealt with the shipper and the receiver. But with a container you now had to talk to the shipping line because it was offering door-to-door service. It had come to my attention that CP had ordered equipment to handle Manchester Liners traffic so we went down to see them and Hart laid it on the line. We secured their traffic from Montreal to Toronto to Detroit and Chicago and that was a real breakthrough."

CN established a Container Development branch and Ronald E. Lawless, general superintendent of express services in the Great Lakes Region, Toronto, was brought to Montreal as system manager, Container Development, and the new organization assisted Halifax, Montreal and Vancouver design container terminals.

In November 13, 1968, the first of the deep-water container ships sailing to Montreal, the 12,000-ton *Manchester Challenge,* arrived at the new container terminal with 500 containers. From Montreal a CN train of specially-designed flat cars – Canada's first container train – carried 200 containers to Toronto, whence they were distributed through southern Ontario, to Detroit and Chicago, and as far west as Alberta. The *Manchester Challenge* was followed by the *Manchester Courage* and *Manchester Concorde* in weekly service from Manchester. The vessels were equipped for ice-breaking for year-round trips up the St. Lawrence.

The fast container vessels reduced costs and cut Atlantic crossings by half, to six and a half days. Since many of these ships would be too big to pass easily up the Seaway to the Great Lakes, CN had the opportunity to move their cargoes from the docks at Halifax or Montreal to central Canada, Detroit and Chicago.

Two thirds of Europe's tonnage came from the United Kingdom, and as a veteran of North Atlantic trade, soliciting business from shippers and manufacturers and working for twenty-five years with Manchester Liners in general cargo, CN was well positioned for the new business. The railway pioneered inland container terminals, which were, in effect, extensions of the docks where the container ships unloaded. In Toronto the CN express terminal, Conport, could handle 2500 tons a day. In Halifax CN joined the Nova Scotia government and Clarke Transportation in a consortium to build Halterm, a terminal run by Halifax International Containers Limited (Halicon). On July 16, 1969, container trade came to Halifax for the first time when the *Joerg Krueger* of Dart Container Line, a Canadian, Belgian and British consortium, inaugurated the Antwerp-Southampton-Halifax service with CN trains taking the containers to Montreal. By 1970 the Halifax container terminal was handling 50 per cent of the country's import-export container business and forty-foot containers made their appearance. The same year the Cast Line began running between Antwerp and Montreal.

On the West Coast, container ships arriving at Vancouver from Japan revived dreams of a "land bridge" whereby trains carrying hundreds of containers might speed from coast to coast, like the silk trains, eliminating the long haul via the Panama Canal. Unfortunately Japanese shipping companies that carried traffic directly between Japan and Europe showed little enthusiasm for the idea since land bridge traffic revenue would have to be split with other carriers. Nevertheless some land bridge traffic could be expected, in competition with American west coast ports.

"We had been growing slowly during the 1960s," said Bill Neale, CN's manager in Asia, "but suddenly there was a dramatic increase in the magnitude of business." CN opened an office in Hong Kong in cooperation with Air Canada and got a foothold in the Pacific Rim countries. In Vancouver, where the CPR had been top dog since the 1880s, CN began to compete on equal terms with its rival. Having doubled its traffic in five years, in 1971 CN delegated A.H. Hart to open a corporate office in Vancouver, which had become one of the ten busiest ports in the world, ranking second in North America after New York.

Lawless recalled that as manager of container development he had the opportunity of a lifetime: "We were in a unique position for growth. An exciting thing was happening in the company and I happened to be there to take it on. It was absolutely marvellous but I certainly did not think it was going to grow to what it is today."

CN laid claim to being the leading container operator, a claim soon disputed by the CPR. Advertised as a "total system" which transported goods from origin to destination, containers were the answer to the railway's need to move cargo at competitive rates and bulk intermodal railroading became the fastest-growing sector of the freight market. With the introduction of diesels, containers, unit trains and automation, CN had come to look at its freight service in a new way – as a vast conveyor belt between producers and consumers rather than a carrier of individual shipments in the closing days of a sunset industry.

Early in 1966 Gordon had begun to have second thoughts, as had most of his predecessors, as his retirement date drew near. "One day," said Pickersgill, "we had a discussion about this and I said: 'Donald you are not someone who is going to have a nice old age playing cards. If you retire at sixty-five you will be highly employable and you will get something interesting to do. At sixty-six that will be questionable. At sixty-seven no one would be interested. But I would be happy to recommend that you stay – on the board.' He thought about that, and one day he said to me, 'I want to go clean, I don't want to be hanging around.'"

On September 30, 1966, the prime minister announced that Gordon would retire at the end of the year. A month later the CN president began his farewell tour. In Newfoundland Premier Joey Smallwood said CN had brought about a "revolution" in the Newfoundland railway and ferry service by spending $179 million there in two decades. In the region where many Gordon-era innovations had first been tried out – including dieselization and Red, White and Blue fares – employees in Moncton gave him a twelve-foot boat, a sou'wester and oilskins. In Saint John he declared that CN now enjoyed "the best organization it ever had."

In the West, Gordon attended ceremonies demonstrating CN's program to rejuvenate city centres by developing, in cooperation with private enterprise, downtown railway property dating back to the 19th century. In Edmonton, he opened the twenty-six-storey CN Tower Building. In Saskatoon he turned sod for Midtown Plaza on the site of the old CN station and freight yards. In Montreal, the Place Bonaventure convention and trade centre, the biggest in the country, had been completed above the tracks south of Central Station. In Toronto CN set out to do what it had done for Montreal by revitalizing the downtown core. In collaboration with the CPR (Marathon Realty Company), a billion-dollar program was announced to transform waterfront railway property into a convention and communications centre.

Back from his adieus, on Friday, December 30, Gordon left his home on Edgehill Road in Westmount, stepped into his black Cadillac and had his chauffeur drive him to his office for the last time. Newspapers across the country reacted as if a popular statesman was departing. "Everyone in Canada is better off because Mr. Gordon has been president of the CNR," said the *Ottawa Citizen.* The *Montreal Star* said Gordon, like C. D. Howe, "had a quality of single-minded integrity that commanded public devotion." Even the French-language press paid respects. "If it is true that M. Gordon has shown a lack of tact in his relations with French Canada," said *Le Devoir,* "he is better known as a man whose achievements have deeply transformed a company which was encrusted with conservatism."

Gordon went on to a brief career as president of British Newfoundland Corporation (Brinco) for two years, raising money on Wall Street to develop the hydro-electric potential of the Labrador watershed. He died in his sleep of a heart attack at the early age of sixty-seven in the spring of 1969 and leaders of government, finance and industry attended his funeral in Montreal and supplied the press with the customary tributes due to the departed.

A quarter century later what are we to make of the man biographer Joseph Schull called "The Great Scot"? Though Gordon's reputation as a railroader may not have equalled the glory won as chief of the Wartime Prices and Trade Board, where he built an organization the envy of Canada's wartime allies, much depends on the yardstick, and even Doug Fisher, who had wanted him fired, admitted in later years that Gordon was a "moderately good president."

Arriving at CN at a time the whole industry was modernizing, he got credit for diesels, computers and the experiment in decentralization that doubtless would have appeared anyway. Though he presided over the layoff of thousands, CN was handling more traffic with 90,000 workers than it had with 130,000. There is no question that he created what amounted to a new railway, won it a reputation for research and corporate planning, and started it on the road to overall profitability. Apart from Thornton, no president had engaged in more morale-boosting, and even the "French question," as painful as it was, produced improved opportunities for francophone workers and better French-language service.

Not the least of Gordon's contributions was the new blood he brought into the railway, creating a team of managers with university degrees, in contrast to older generations who had gone into railroading in their teens and learned on the job. Though his manner was often abrasive, he won loyalty among colleagues and employees and the support of union leaders. His battles were usually with the parliamentary railway committee, and rarely with the cabinet, where for example he was not strong in campaigning for higher freight rates, though he was not averse to taking on the cabinet, as in 1961 when the Conservatives wanted CN to buy out the Canada and Gulf Terminal Railway because of election promises. The purchase made no sense, Gordon said, and the matter was dropped. He had won more independence for CN head office than any president before him.

Gordon's final year at CN was a good one, the railway having moved a record amount of freight and more passengers than at any time since the war. For the fifth consecutive year the financial position had improved despite a week-long strike in support of a 30 per cent wage increase to equal that given to the St. Lawrence Seaway workers. (An arbitration settlement awarded the railroaders increases of 24 per cent.)

Gordon's greatest regret was his failure to achieve the recapitalization needed if CN was to experience what he called the "smell of profit" that would spur people on to greater effort. His greatest pleasure, on the other hand, was to see the National Transportation Act passed (though some months after he left), sweeping aside a century of restrictions and opening the way to freer competition.

17

A NEW
DEAL

W ITH THE 1967 NATIONAL TRANSPORTATION ACT about to
revolutionize railroading, the government wanted a less
rambunctious president and a peaceful period of consolidation. Donald Gordon's years at CN had not been restful.

Having nursed the act through Parliament, transport minister Pickersgill
retired from politics and got himself appointed head of the Canadian Transport Commission (CTC), which replaced the Board of Transport Commissioners to regulate and "harmonize" rail, air and water transportation (trucking was largely controlled by the provinces). Though Quebec MPs said it was
high time a francophone headed CN, Pickersgill preferred continuity.

"I had the highest regard for Norman MacMillan," said Pickersgill. "He
had kept Donald Gordon out of a lot of trouble." Groomed by Gordon and
supported by the board MacMillan was appointed chairman and president
on January 1, 1967, at the age of fifty-seven. CN pay, though higher than any
in the civil service, was much lower than the CPR's; his salary was the same as
Gordon's – $75,000 – the same as Thornton's basic pay in the 1920s.

Though trained as a lawyer, MacMillan had come to regard himself as a railroader, which detractors called his Walter Mitty side. Otherwise he was a pragmatic careerist who accepted the fact that railways would always be woven into Canadian politics and always had been. He lacked Gordon's eminence and command of the podium, but thirty years at CN had taught him more about day-to-day railroading. Unlike Gordon, who regarded steam locomotives as dirty and uncomfortable, MacMillan romanced about steam, cowcatchers and Morse keys. "Gordon liked running the railway but he never did understand it," said MacMillan. "It was just a little too physical for him."

The son of a Bracebridge, Ontario, grocer who moved west to sell store equipment, MacMillan had been infected by railroading as a boy doing odd jobs around the station at Grand Beach on Lake Manitoba. He joined CN's law department in Winnipeg in 1937, went to head office in 1942, and seven years later, at the urging of H. J. Symington, the lawyer and CN director who had known him in Winnipeg, was appointed vice-president of the law department, a post that might otherwise have gone to Ivan Rand, who had been summoned from CN to the Supreme Court.

Gordon evidently found it easier to deal with a lawyer than with by-the-book railroaders, and MacMillan made himself so useful he was invited to move his office close to the president's. A study in contrast, the blustery banker and the circumspect lawyer made an effective team. "If he got into trouble we pulled him to hell out of trouble," MacMillan said. "He gave me a thousand laughs, would get himself all cranked up to do something and then he'd try it on me. I was the dog."

As senior law officer, MacMillan considered himself the corporate conscience and was one of the few executives prepared to stand up to the volatile new president. This was something Gordon needed, and six years later MacMillan was appointed executive vice-president, outranking Dingle and Metcalf, who had come up through the ranks in the railway tradition.

MacMillan was avuncular, a corporate politician, a stocky, balding, second-generation Scot with a well-developed sense of his importance to the company and a taste for French cuffs, skiing and duck hunting. He disliked public speaking, was never known to raise his voice and preferred to adjudicate different points of view rather than snap out orders. The press called him the quiet man of Canadian railroading and from the start he was upstaged by the flamboyant tenth president of the CPR, Ian Sinclair, another Winnipeg lawyer, who resembled Gordon in bulk and vigour but surpassed him in business savvy.

Like Gordon in his early days, MacMillan took too much on himself. In 1968 he had twenty-eight executives reporting to him directly. He was also briefly acting president of Air Canada, which CN still technically owned. Though he lacked Gordon's status in Ottawa, to the dismay of some of his senior officers he insisted on handling personally CN's relations with the Department of Transport, whose wishes reached CN either in the form of directives, formal ministerial letters or, more commonly, informal discussions. Unlike Gordon he rarely took work home, preferring to spend evenings at his basement carpentry bench. He came to the office at nine in the morning, took an hour and a half for lunch and worked until six-thirty because the phone stopped ringing at five.

Recalling MacMillan's circuitous style, Ralph Vaughan said the day United Aircraft people came to sell the *Turbo* MacMillan referred them to a committee of vice-presidents. "We thought MacMillan should have said from the start who would be in charge but he wouldn't," said Vaughan, "so I decided, rightly or wrongly, that I should be in charge because as secretary of the corporation I did not represent any special interest in the matter. Though it left me in a difficult position, I took over the negotiations and was the spokesman. I asked MacMillan later, 'Why didn't you indicate who would be in charge of this thing?' He said, 'I knew you would.' So he had not alienated any of the other vice-presidents. He could say, 'Vaughan took over.'"

MacMillan boasted he could turn the bottom line from red to black within four years; he was on the right track though it would take nine years. CN had been in the red so long that for ten years the section for profit and loss in the annual report had simply been labelled "deficit." If Gordon was haunted by the everlasting debt, MacMillan was prepared to live with it and was more concerned with keeping trains running on time and maintaining relations with Ottawa. He insisted there were no contradictions between CN's dichotomous roles as public service and competitive business enterprise.

After Gordon, MacMillan seemed bland. "He wanted to get along with Ottawa and would hold us back in many cases waiting for a more opportune time," recalled Keith Hunt, operations vice-president and one of the young Turks who made CN a lively place in the 1960s and '70s. One reason for MacMillan's caution was the pressure to reduce jobs. Nevertheless, said Hunt, when he needed money he got it.

"MacMillan was a bit of an enigma," said Jack Cann, whom MacMillan had singled out to build the vast Toronto hump yard, which the colourful westerner supervised from horseback. "He was a great guy for pulling strings, but when he gave me a job to do, he made it absolutely clear that I would run it and nobody was going to interfere. He would give one criterion, that you finish it on time and within budget. In effect he gave me $100 million to build the thing and we finished three months ahead and $28 million under budget."

Considerable growth was recorded during MacMillan's seven years as CEO. Year after year operations yielded a surplus and revenue increased from $1 billion in 1967 to $1.5 billion in 1974, partly because of annual increases in freight tonnage but also because of the momentum generated during the Gordon era and the new people he had brought in. They were now moving into senior positions to fashion the most versatile and imaginative management team CN had known.

Of those on their way to the executive suite, Charles F. Armstrong came up through R&D, the forcing house for executive talent, which he joined in 1953 with a degree in commerce. John Gratwick, who joined R&D in 1960 from the Air Ministry of his native England with a degree in science, became one of the most innovative people in transportation. Donald P. MacKinnon, who had studied mechanical engineering and business administration, became corporate secretary.

Others came up from more workaday departments. Ronald E. Lawless started in express at the age of seventeen, and after service in the RCAF became manager of express and intermodal systems, rounding out his practical education in railroading with university extension courses. Keith Hunt took a degree in electrical engineering after an initial exposure to CN in 1940 as an apprentice electrician, the first apprentice hired in six years because of the Depression, and serving in the air force. John H. D. Sturgess, a civil engineer from England, joined the engineering department in 1958 and eventually moved up to become senior vice-president. Yvon H. Masse, a graduate in electrical engineering, became chief financial officer.

There had always been a railway tradition of son following father, or even grandfather, as in the case of Jacques A. Gauthier, a Montreal area manager who had been brought up in the station at St. Estelle, Quebec. Mary Mason's father had been a chief clerk in the days when they were virtual rulers of their departments. After World War II people whose fathers had worked up from apprenticeship began to join CN from university to infuse a mixture of family tradition and academic knowledge. Jack Cann, whose father had been pipefitter and shop foreman in Winnipeg, joined CN in 1939 as a chain man, got a degree in civil engineering, and worked up to vice-president of operations. "People did not get slotted as they had in the old days," commented Cann. "I started in the engineering department and under the old system would probably have remained in the engineering department." John C. Gardiner, whose father had been a passenger department manager, emerged as vice president of marketing. G. M. Cooper, whose father had been a comptroller, joined the law department and became secretary of the company, to be followed by Howard Pye, whose father had been general purchasing agent. President Vaughan's son, Peter, was CN's chief medical officer.

MacMillan's first task as president was to implement the National Transportation Act, which began a new deal by striking down old regulations born of monopoly and called for an "economic, efficient and adequate transportation system involving the best use of all available modes of transportation at the lowest total cost." MacMillan likened it to a supermarket because, he said, it encouraged the most efficient intermodal combinations – road and rail, rail and air, water and rail – or all four together. It was seen in the States, which had nothing like it until the Staggers Act surpassed it thirteen years later, as a model of transportation legislation.

In the past, 90 per cent of non-statutory freight had carried common tariffs, interpreted by clerks whose arcane talents were seen by other departments as black magic. Rates were regulated by bureaucrats whose bibles were Canadian Freight Classification, which pigeon-holed every article that might conceivably be shipped, and the Class Rate Tariff, the product of years of negotiation between the railways and Ottawa. Since the war there had been a dozen "horizontal" or across-the-board rate increases which had, nevertheless, only chipped at the walls of outdated policy.

Though it was to take three or four years before the full effects of this partial deregulation were felt, in essence the railways no longer needed to seek Ottawa's permission to change prices. "Agreed charges" became the norm, in which the customer guaranteed a certain volume of business in return for a specified rate, which could be either above or below the traditional tariff.

It used to be said that CPR kept CN efficient and CN kept CPR honest. Though competition had largely narrowed down in recent years to availability and quality of service, the two still performed a balancing act between competition and cooperation, vying for freight and transcontinental passengers while joining forces for labour negotiations, rate increases, appeals for subsidies, safety issues and the loan of equipment. The new act now recognized their practice, which had become entrenched, of sitting down together to devise common tariffs. "The law now allowed this, " said John Gardiner. "I met with my counterpart from CPR, sometimes in the Windsor Hotel where we would not be bothered by phone calls. All the rates had to be published for the protection of the shipping public, so shady deals in the back room were impossible."

Regulation, for years a whipping boy, was no longer an excuse for poor results, though the new freedom was not always productive. When the railways jointly announced higher rates for express and less-than-carload traffic the potential 20 per cent increase in revenue was lost as clients switched to trucks. Statutory grain, a third of all freight, remained untouched despite a MacPherson recommendation "the Crow" be reviewed. Despite railway complaints that the spider web of branch lines was outdated, the government imposed a long-term freeze on abandonment of Prairie lines; if the CTC, however, considered a branch line necessary for the public good the government would pay the railway a subsidy equal to deficit.

In passenger service, the routine of having to file for abandonment before being able to claim the 80 per cent subsidy was not only awkward but put the railways in bad light with the public. It automatically made the government a hero each time a petition for abandonment was denied and a service saved. Moreover, since railways still had to pick up 20 per cent of their losses, the act discouraged investment and did nothing to revitalize the Canadian passenger train.

The CPR, which had once run the best passenger service on the continent, had read the future and pulled out with the alacrity permitted a private company. Passenger service being a drain on public coffers, Pickersgill wanted CN out of it as well, even in the 700-mile stretch between Quebec City and Windsor that contained half the nation's population. "With the sparse population between Montreal and Toronto there is no way you can run a passenger service and charge fares that would pay for it," he said. "Why should you lose money on passenger service to serve Montreal and Toronto? Any government that did so would lose votes in Halifax and Vancouver and places in between."

Sometimes when the railways filed for abandonment, abandonment was what they got. One of the first victims was the *Caribou*, or "Newfie Bullet," which meandered across Newfoundland every day during summer and three times a week when the snows swirl down White Bay into Gaff Topsail. Its usual consist was two diesel units, four sleepers, a diner and three coaches and since taking it over CN had quickened its narrow-gauge gait by several hours. The Newfie Bullet now made the 549-mile run across the island in something less than twenty-two hours but was losing so much money CN might have done better by keeping it home and giving passengers free taxi chits.

Few trains have earned more affection, so there was anguish in July 1968 when the CTC gave CN permission to replace the Bullet with buses. For months train and bus ran side by side until the uproar died down, as such things finally do, and on July 2, 1969 the Bullet made its last sad run and all that was left were the four mixed trains that carried freight and passengers .

The fate of the Newfie Bullet was an augury of things to come. Across the nation the railway share of the passenger market had declined to 3 per cent as the mania for the versatile, convenient automobile eclipsed the railway mania of the 19th century. Though MacMillan was quoted in the Moncton *Transcript* of September 18, 1969, as saying CN would be in the passenger business for a "long time to come," CN to all intents and purposes would be out of rail passenger service within a decade.

In the freight department there was reason for optimism. While it was true the railway share was shrinking as trucks took more business, railways were carrying more freight than ever because there was so much more of it to carry. Moreover, CN was finally getting to grips with real costs, a nagging problem on all railways whose size and organization made it difficult to discover whether they were making or losing money on a given service. Using computers, CN was able to trace accounts to a level of detail where costs could be pinpointed and managers held accountable. The express department, the courier service of its time, had operated under conditions that had made it easy to show a profit, using passenger trains but paying disproportionately low fees for services received from other departments.

Computers were also being programmed to take the guesswork out of locating the 100,000 CN freight cars scattered across the continent. "When I first went to Montreal in 1957," said J.H.Spicer, "a conductor would write out his train journal – the list of cars he was responsible for – and mail it to Montreal, where there was a book for every car on the system and some poor clerk would have to look up boxcar 677 or whatever and make a note of what moved on that particular train on that date and put it back on the rack. By the time all this was done three weeks had gone by."

A computer-based system called TRACS, an acronym for Traffic Reporting and Control System, was gradually coming on line – it would take seven years – to update information on car movement twenty-four hours a day. When fully operative TRACS would monitor 2500 locomotives, 120,000 freight cars, 20,000 containers and 3000 piggyback trailers by means of trackside electronic scanners reading sensitized information stuck to the sides of rolling stock. Essentially an all-CN creation, it linked trains, dispatchers, sales and freight offices and sped trains by eliminating paperwork. "The idea came from the computer people, from operational research, and a general acknowlegement in the operating department that we needed it," said Charles Armstrong, chief of transportation.

The next step toward an integrated system was a nationwide chain of 100 Servocentres, which wrapped express, carload freight, piggyback, containers, telecommunications and passenger reservations into a handy package and eliminated the need for the 1200 agencies. W.H. Bailey, then assistant vice president at R&D, introduced something which is commonplace today – customer research and a determination to reform the "have a cigar" school of salesmanship. "We had to get away from that," said Bailey. "Customer research changed the whole thing."

"We found we weren't getting our share of the market because we didn't know enough about it," recalled J. Frank Roberts, who was in charge of market development in the early 1970s. "We had newsprint, automobiles, grain, potash, coal starting to move from the foothills of the Rockies to Japan – and we really did not have a handle on them. So we started looking at segments of the freight business. We appointed a market manager to learn everything he could about pulp and paper, for example, something we had never done before."

The new breed of manager was backed by platoons of researchers, market forecasters, equipment planners, pricing managers, costing specialists and salesmen for grain, ore, coal, automobiles and a new product, sulphur, produced in Alberta's foothills as a by-product of natural gas and stockpiled in yellow mountains awaiting shipment to half the world for use in fertilizer and chemicals.

MacMillan chose Jim McDonald, vice-president of the St. Lawrence region, as vice-president of production, a new term at CN for better management, but because he had no staff and little control over marketing and transportation he had little chance of success. "I was to be responsible for all matters affecting production, the services the company produced and sold," said McDonald, "but I used to have a terrible time explaining what vice-president of production really meant." J. H. Spicer recalled, "Jim and I were good friends but it was awkward for him and awkward for me. I was in charge of the operating department and when he came down to talk about improving productivity in the operating department, the major part of the railway, he was right in my hair." Within the year McDonald, who had contributed so much in the Gordon years, accepted an offer from the Penn Central where he became an executive vice-president before he went on to become a vice-president at CPR.

The promotion of Robert Bandeen to vice-president of corporate planning and finance, two functions R&D had dominated, was more successful. The tall, husky, prematurely balding son of a southwestern Ontario Scots farming family, with a Ph.D. in economics and statistics from Duke University, North Carolina, Bandeen had joined the research and development department in 1955 as an assistant economist. His work with the MacPherson commission alerted his superiors to his capabilities.

Working with Solandt to introduce modern corporate planning, Bandeen had brought in statistical costing, sniffed out internal cross-subsidization, which caused hidden "horrendous" losses, and demonstrated the necessity of finding the real rather than imagined costs of doing business. CN, like other railways, had suffered from revenue-ton-mile-syndrome. In a shotgun approach to freight, the railways had believed if revenue per ton-mile was greater than the previous year then all was well. But analysis was now showing that while low rates attracted freight, the returns might be so low it would have been better not to carry it.

Impatient for change, Bandeen had a clear idea where CN should be going. Infrastructure must be pared and track used solely for mainline, high-volume operations, which meant that feeder branch lines, particularly in Saskatchewan, Ontario and the Maritimes, must be abandoned and traffic brought to main lines by truck. The heavy work force must be pared still further. Freight must be marketed with the flair with which passenger service had been marketed.

MacMillan recognized Bandeen's talents, but the two differed too much in personality to form the sort of effective team Gordon and MacMillan had made. "MacMillan and I worked very closely together," said Bandeen, "but I never knew whether he really wanted to use my ideas. It got so it was becoming more and more difficult because I was trying to do then what I eventually did as president, segegate the areas where there were problems and find solutions. We finally got in the position where MacMillan believed I was being unduly critical, and perhaps I was.

"MacMillan felt that if I stayed around I might become a candidate to succeed him. Not that we didn't get along personally, but he felt I was the wrong person to head CN at that time. He represented the thinking of perhaps the majority of senior officers. I wasn't even forty at the time and to be president you should be in your sixties. One day he came in and said, 'Well I've decided that for your future you had better learn something about administration.'"

Bandeen thought it "irresponsible" that a person with no operating experience should be given such a job, but in the spring of 1971 he moved to Toronto as vice-president of the Great Lakes region, which covered Ontario from the Ottawa Valley almost to Thunder Bay. A man whose staff had consisted of one secretary was suddenly in charge of 13,000 people and 7000 miles of track which carried 150 freight trains every day. Within a few weeks he discovered other reasons for his move. "Oh yes," said MacMillan, "we're going to give you our American railways as well."

Bandeen would also become president of CN's biggest U.S. subsidiary, the Grand Trunk Western, which was in trouble, as Bandeen had been pointing out to all who would listen. It had not shown a profit since 1955 but though transborder traffic would probably have been much the same whether CN owned GTW or not, CN kept the subsidiary despite annual losses of around $10 million and indications that half a dozen American lines were interested in buying it. Whether as reward or penance, Bandeen had the task of putting it right. "They threw me in to sink or swim," said Bandeen.

The GTW, which ran from Detroit to Chicago and served Pontiac, Kalamazoo, Battle Creek, South Bend, Grand Rapids and (by Lake Michigan ferry) Milwaukee, had become the major transporter of automobiles in Michigan. Though most of its 1320 mainline miles were in that state, it also served Illinois, Indiana and Wisconsin. Automobiles were 50 per cent of its business.

Reversing the usual practice wherein American firms lord it over subsidiaries in Canada, the GTW was controlled from Montreal, and being a neat, self-contained railroad in comparison with its sprawling parent, it served as a training ground for Canadian executives, leaving Americans with no hope for promotion.

In 1969 complaints from one of the CN's biggest customers, the Pontiac division of General Motors, became serious enough to fetch MacMillan to Pontiac with a ten-man delegation to promise improved service. The next year, the Grand Trunk Western's troubles came to a head when a 100-day strike at General Motors contributed to a deficit of $30 million, which was worse than the deficit of the parent company, debt and all.

MacMillan made Bandeen the designated troubleshooter and sent him to Detroit to turn the subsidiary around. "On August 3, 1971, I arrived in Detroit on one of the hottest days of the year to take over as president," he said. "There was no air conditioning, the window was open and my desk was covered in soot. I had no executive to speak of. People were openly hostile to the idea of yet another imported president from Canada. It didn't take long to figure out that the basic problem was an awkward, demoralizing management structure. Each department head reported directly to his counterpart in Montreal. Poor communications, inappropriate decisions made by people remote from the realities of the situation and the lack of a cohesive management team in Detroit made it virtually impossible for things to work smoothly."

A holding company, Grand Trunk Corporation, with Bandeen as president, was formed to run the Grand Trunk Western and consolidate its income statements with those of CN's smaller U.S. companies, the Duluth, Winnipeg and Pacific Railway Company, which ran 167 miles from Duluth to the Canadian border and had been prospering, and the Central Vermont Railway Company which connected Canada with the eastern U.S. and was profitable by fits and starts. Each would retain its identity but the old Grand Trunk line from Island Pond, Vermont, to Portland, Maine, would remain CN's Berlin subdivision, having no corporate identity of its own.

The Grand Trunk Western was given an American management and much-needed autonomy. John H. Burdakin, a graduate engineer of the Masschusetts Institute of Technology, was hired away from the bankrupt Penn Central, where he had been vice-president and general manager, to become GTW's senior vice-president with the task of mapping the future. The GTW continued to lose money though not nearly as much. The holding company, Grand Trunk Corporation, on the other hand, began to show a profit.

Bandeen had been less than a year out of head office when his career changed abruptly. "I was working very hard," he recalled. "I had been thrown into the Great Lakes region and then given the American lines a few months later. I had to recruit a new senior staff in Detroit and was spending three days a week travelling – Washington, Detroit, Vermont, Duluth – and wasn't following much of what was going on in Montreal.

"I hadn't seen MacMillan in months and I was in Washington or somewhere one Thursday when I heard he wanted to see me in Toronto next day. I got a flight back Friday morning and went to lunch with him. 'I have only a year and a half or two years to go,' he said, 'and I think it would be good if you came back to Montreal.' I was really starting to see the American thing going fairly well and everything was coming along nicely. I said, 'I'm not interested at this time because I'm finding this fascinating.' He told me to think about it."

Bandeen tried to find out what was going on, but apart from hearing the board had turned back the budget to be reworked, an unprecedented occurrence in his experience, he was none the wiser except for hints that his budgetary expertise was missed. Bandeen, in the tradition of the R&D department, had been preparing the budget for years and had devised his own routine for squeezing it down to size. When he received a proposal from the regions he would cut it repeatedly until the protests grew so loud he was satisified extraneous fat had been cut.

The next Friday MacMillan repeated the routine. "He came back to Toronto and after lunch he asked if I had reflected. I said, 'I have and I am still of the same opinion. I think I'm more useful here to the railway than I would be in Montreal. I just don't want to go to Montreal.' He looked across the table and said, 'You either go to Montreal or you quit.'

"One thing I had criticized MacMillan for was not being decisive. Now my belief he was not decisive went down the drain. So that's why I spent only one year in Toronto and came back to Montreal."

In 1972 Bandeen became responsibile for finance and administration, as one of four executive vice-presidents in an unusual oligarchy introduced by MacMillan that caused much talk at the water cooler. In 1971 there had been only one, J. W. G. Macdougall, a fifty-six-year-old Nova Scotia-born CN lawyer who had that year taken over the role ("the whole running of the railway") that MacMillan had filled under Gordon. To prepare, Macdougall had spent three years as vice-president of the Atlantic region, where he also resolved the latest round of problems – press and politicians were upset by the unending layoffs – that had been arising between the railway and the Maritimes since the ICR became the CNR.

Within a year, Macdougall, who had been MacMillan's heir apparent, was jostled by three other executive vice-presidents. Besides Bandeen and Macdougall, there was Pierre Taschereau, who had joined as a lawyer after the war, left in the 1960s to join the Canadian Transport Commission in Ottawa, and was now in charge of CN corporate affairs, which included personnel, labour relations, public relations and law. And there was J. H. Richer, vice-president for passenger, express and non-rail services. Was the cautious Mac-Millan merely presenting a wider choice to the government and board, or did this new arrangement mean, as many suspected, he wanted to remain longer himself?

Operating profit had increased sufficiently to pay down some of the debt, which was alarmingly close to $2 billion. Admiring Canadian Pacific's successful diversification into forest products, minerals, oil and real estate, MacMillan planned to diversify, undeterred by the troubles diversification had caused the bankrupt Penn Central and other American railways.

The hotels, ferries, communications and coal mine CN had inherited were connected with railroading in one way or another, and the railway had avoided the diversification into unrelated products that the CPR had pursued. Railroading, rather than forestry, mining or shipping, still had CN's undivided attention. Having laid 1600 miles of track since World War II, CN had a total of 32,590 miles, including 8445 miles of double track. During the next few years it would become the leader in North America in continuous welded rail, called "velvet rail" because of its smooth ride. Thirty-nine-foot rails were welded into quarter-mile lengths in the shops and then welded into a continuous band of steel. CN also became the first railway in North America to use concrete ties throughout the system. Although they were twice the price of wooden ties, they could be more widely spaced so that fewer were needed. They were also supposed to have much longer life, though structural problems developed in eastern Canada that necessitated more replacement than expected and there were wear and tear problems in the West as well.

Another innovation was the Transportation Training Centre at Gimli, a small town sixty miles north of Winnipeg, where aspiring drivers could learn on locomotive simulators. "We found," said Keith Hunt, who got the simulator installed, "it shortened the time required to train an engineer more than anyone thought possible and assisted veteran engineers to better handle the bigger, tougher, high-speed trains, the unit trains where the braking system is harder to handle."

MacMillan believed CN should acquire pipelines, as well as unit oil trains – the "pipeline on wheels" it was running – and a task force investigated the costs of constructing pipelines for coal, ores, potash and sulphur. With other companies CN established Gas Arctic to study bringing natural gas from the north. There was talk of using unit trains in a joint CN-CPR venture over a 1210-mile route from Trout River, Alberta, to Aklavik. The study found that a railway with the same capacity as two forty-two-inch pipelines could be in operation within a decade, but the climate and permafrost terrain would be formidable and the cost high ($10 billion) and the project was droppped.

Following the CPR lead, CN had purchased eight trucking companies. As well as a one-third interest in Halterm container port at Halifax, it was part owner of a Dartmouth "Autoport" for storing and trans-shipping vehicles. As real estate developer it had been responsible for Place Ville Marie and Place Bonaventure in Montreal and was involved in developments in Toronto, London (Ontario), Moncton, Campbellton, Saskatoon, Vancouver and Prince George.

CANAC Consultants Ltd. was formed in 1972 from a pioneer consulting group of CN and Air Canada specialists established four years earlier to solve transportation problems and introduce technology to foreign railways and governments. It was both lucrative and educational and within a decade CANAC had completed 300 projects in forty-five countries. A domestic version, Canalog Logistics Ltd., concentrated on such projects as how to move millions of tons of steel and construction supplies into the far north.

MacMillan believed in diversity. Though he was criticized for being too cautious, it was MacMillan, as executive vice-president, who had backed Delagrave's *Rapido* and *Turbo* and CN's most obvious totem, the CN Tower in Toronto, which, until the project was renewed, stood for many years as the sole result of the billion-dollar 190-acre Metro Centre project CN and the CPR had announced jointly in December 1968.

The original plan had called for a downtown core a quarter mile wide and a quarter mile long between Front Street and Lake Ontario with commercial and residential sections. The two railways were to share costs fifty-fifty but the project ran into the anti-development movement. The CPR abandoned the tower project to CN. "We had to drop our original plan and develop a piecemeal one, one piece here and one there," said Maurice Archer, who moved from the vice-presidency of R&D to supervise the Toronto project. CN went ahead on its own with the tower that was to be twice as high as anything else in Toronto and 400 feet taller than the Empire State Building. The concept had grown from a relatively simple communications tower to serve radio and TV stations, which were having trouble with their signals, to a structure that could bring in money as a tourist attraction. .

As MacMillan's sixty-fifth birthday, in April 1974, approached, there was speculation as to his successor. Though Macdougall, whose management style resembled MacMillan's, was second in command and the most obvious choice, other candidates were mooted: Bandeen, Richer and Taschereau, even Archer and Alex Hart, who was now senior vice-president looking after CN interests on the Pacific Rim.

For political reasons the prime minister's office wanted the posts of chairman and president split, one English, one French, which narrowed the permutations. Richer and Taschereau were French. Bandeen and Macdougall were "English." Nor did a duo of lawyers, Taschereau and Macdougall, fit the bill.

Since the more important position was president and CEO, Bandeen and Richer made it clear they were not interested in being chairman. Only thrice in CN's history had the jobs been separated – 1920-22, 1933-35 and 1941-42 – and the split had never worked because of ambiguities and personality conflicts. Nor would it work well in future, despite a reasonable start by Taschereau and Bandeen, either because the chairmen knew little of railroading or because their appointments, like those of directors, were political.

As a result of his successful overhaul of Grand Trunk Western, Bandeen's reputation was high. The ministry seemed in the mood for a strong leader, Jean Marchand, the minister, having suddenly announced that federal transportation policy was "in a mess" and in need of integration. Announcing a change of reponsibility that promised more political involvement for the railways than the MacPherson report had recommended, Marchand announced his ministry would take back the policy-making function from the Canadian Transport Commission. (The CTC had been given that power under the National Transportation Act expressly because it was seen as an independent body less subject to short-term political pressures than a government department under an elected minister.) Having decided the act was too competitive, Marchand recommended changes that would integrate all transportation and lump CN and CPR rail operations into one nationalized service. This was an idea whose time had definitely not come so far as CN was concerned. In 1974 the Trudeau government reversed its anti-passenger policy and began to talk of something that did eventually take root; they called it the Canadian Passenger Transportation Corporation, a government entity that would relieve CN and the CPR of the passenger burden.

MacMillan, who clearly would have liked to have stayed as had his mentor R.C. Vaughan, retired April 10, 1974 but remained as a consultant because his salary was deemed to have been too low to generate a suitable pension. To the disappointment of Macdougall and Richer, Ottawa made Bandeen president. With nineteen years in planning, finance and administration, and as a graduate of the research and development department which at times had virtually run the railway, Bandeen had qualifications no other president had possessed.

Taschereau was appointed chairman and he and Bandeen drafted a careful agreement on how they would work together. "I was to be the 'senior citizen,'" recalled Taschereau, "with a particular mandate to ensure good relations with government and the public. Bandeen would be operating head. By law the president was chief executive officer, but I did not want the administration to be entirely in the hands of the CEO so I reserved some jurisdiction over law, the secretary's office, linguistics, international consultants (CANAC) and pension investment." Taschereau was also acting chairman of Air Canada, and left CN in 1976 to become its fulltime chairman, a route Ralph Vaughan had followed earlier to become Air Canada president.

When the Trudeau government tried to replace Taschereau with the controversial Paul Gérin-Lajoie, a former Quebec education minister and expresident of the Canadian International Development Agency (CIDA), Bandeen successfully opposed the appointment. Instead, the government appointed General J.A. Dextraze, a Québécois and former chief of staff of the armed forces, whose railway experience had been limited to a directorship in the little Thurso and National Valley Railroad in Quebec.

Given Bandeen's personality and experience, there could be no doubt as to who was running the railway. The next eight years would be CN's most successful peacetime years since Thornton briefly turned things around in the mid-1920s.

18

IN PURSUIT
OF PROFIT

I N THE SPRING OF 1974 Dr. Robert Bandeen, at forty-three the youngest president in CN's fifty-five years, was impatient to lead the railway to
the profitability that Gordon had sought in vain.

The nation-building required of the People's Railway in the 1920s
had lost relevance in a 1970s world of cars, buses, trailer trucks, pipelines, jet
aircraft and television. "The People's Railway" was not a slogan often heard
anymore. CN would respect its social responsibilities like any corporate citizen, said Bandeen, but government ownership was no substitute for good
management. CN would serve the Canadian people best if a distinction were
made between services required to show a profit and those created for political reasons. If the government wanted CN to participate in nation-building it
should be paid.

Bandeen built on foundations laid by Gordon and had taken over when
there was a better chance of running CN like a business. Though no one person could shape all the issues in so large a company, Bandeen made CN more
entrepreneurial. He made senior managers more accessible, both to each

other and to subordinates. People used only to formal meetings were invited
to half-hour coffee sessions at eight o'clock every morning to discuss whatever was on their minds. He took French lessons and encouraged others to do
so in a company where francophones were no longer timid to communicate
in their own language at head office. "Nine tenths of the function of the CEO
of a large company is leadership," said Bandeen, whose appointment followed a pattern. As if by natural progression, charismatic leaders had followed low-profile administrators. Hanna, having fashioned the foundation,
was followed by Thornton, a man for the 1920s. Depression produced the
prudent Sam Hungerford and World War II a shrewd technocrat,
R. C. Vaughan, followed by Gordon and MacMillan.

Bandeen, though less intimidating than Gordon, was just as outspoken
and better informed. He set out to end the deficits in what was, technologi-
cally at least, one of the best railways in North America. "What used to
annoy the hell out of me," said Bandeen, "was that individual parts of the
company did well but we did not seem to be able to pull the whole thing
together. We had people with brilliant ideas, but the old tradition persisted
and I got tired of people saying CN was 'government,' inefficient and bureau-
cratic. Some of it was true, but it did not have to be."

Bandeen was helped by a demand for resources that started the railways
growing again. Every day 270 to 300 CN trains totalling 10,000 loaded cars
were each averaging 700 miles across the country. The railways were carrying
three times more freight than the highways, though with two million commercial vehicles now on the roads the gap was closing. Tractor-trailer rigs
were hauling twenty-ton loads at sixty miles an hour, changing the folklore.
Transportation songs that used to be all about railroaders now wove fables of
truckers and their CBs.

Trucking was only one of CN's problems. Among others, the question of
state versus private ownership had never been resolved. What was the proper
balance between private and public enterprise? How to measure viability in a
crown corporation caught between the profit motive and commitment to
national development. These questions had began at birth when the government failed to heed the words of Drayton and Acworth. In 1917 the two royal
commissioners would have shielded the People's Railway from the winds of
Parliament, the pressures from the cabinet and the minister of railways, and
made it solely accountable to a body one step removed, the Board of Railway
Commissioners. But for better or worse the CN Act two years later left it up

to whatever government was in power to decide CN policy, and the People's Railway, for better or worse, was fated to account directly to the politicians, even after the Duff commission in 1932 recommended that independent auditors report to Parliament on CN's behalf.

Gordon had tried to assert CN's independence. Bandeen, if anything more uncomfortable than Gordon under the government umbrella, would advance the largely perceptional independence Gordon achieved to something more substantive. "I wanted to prove we could run effectively on a commercial, free-enterprise basis," said Bandeen. "I spent much time establishing that we were not part of the government." Otto Lang, Trudeau's new minister of transport, proved to be an ally. The socio-economic role was downplayed in favour of commercial self sufficiency. "We swing like a pendulum, from one extreme to the other," mused Bandeen. "In CN, hopefully, the swings are getting less frequent and less wide."

In a time of inflation and recession, Lang agreed that the government should not impose obligations unless it paid for them. Nor should CN be subjected to "day to day variations of the whim of the minister or in response to immediate demands of a particular member."

This in itself did not abolish all political interference. Bandeen in Montreal might speak of behaving as if CN were the next thing to private enterprise, but local politicians were still capable of pressing regional representatives to do things not in CN's interests – ranging from old-fashioned patronage down to changing the shift of a constituent who did not like night work. "I had to lay down the law to our officers that they were not to talk to politicians," Bandeen said. "If a politician approached a regional vice-president, or anyone else, they were to refer them to me. I wanted all political contact to go through me. I didn't mind taking anybody on."

Prohibited from selling shares as private corporations did, for a dozen years CN had generated capital internally through depreciation and sale of preferred stock to the government. It had battled inflation by increasing productivity through automation and reducing the work force. It was carrying more freight but earning the same per ton-mile as twenty years earlier.

The interest on debt was the boulder of Sisyphus that kept rolling back when pushed up the hill. Even in prosperous years CN had seldom covered interest with operating surplus. In the mid-1970s debt was climbing again. "You hated to be kidded by your neighbors when the annual report came out every year," remembers J. H. Spicer. "CPR was making money but here was

CN with another fifty million down or whatever. You knew you had a good operating company and you wondered what the hell was the problem."

The government began to toy with the idea – which Bandeen favoured – of selling shares in CN on the public market, but nothing came of it. On one hand CN was paying tremendous interest while sustaining large losses on grain and passengers. On the other it was taking in large amounts in subsidies. It was not that CN was incapable of making money, as operational surplus had shown year after year. There was just no way of keeping it to improve the company. But before seeking another recapitalization CN decided to make a psychological breakthrough by achieving an overall profit. No longer would the railway go hat-in-hand to Ottawa to say, "We are losing money, please help us."

First there must be fundamental change. The question had to be asked, was CN too large and too dispersed for effective management? The semi-autonomous geographical areas of the 1960s had not been a great success. Eighteen "miniature railways" were too difficult to coordinate, caused expensive duplication, and were unsuited to unit trains because of the multiplicity of areas of command. Under this "functional-geographical" scheme, each region had lumped freight, passenger, express, marine or whatever into a balance sheet showing overall revenue and expenses. Bandeen now had the opportunity to attack the problem at its roots and in 1976 CN followed the CPR's lead of several years earlier. It scrapped its area system in favour of autonomous "profit centres" (not all of them profitable) designed to avoid the cross-subsidization that had masked unprofitable operations. The six new divisions were CN Rail; CN Trucking and Express; Grand Trunk Corporation; CN Telecommunications; CN Marine; and Passengers, Hotels and Tower.

Corporate headquarters, with the chairman, president, some corporate vice-presidents, and finance, public relations, personnel and labour relations and purchasing, became a holding company, an idea Bandeen had developed at Detroit in the early 1970s, exercising control through budgets and the approval of decisions developed at the division level.

To get the new system running, Bandeen gathered a senior team of people he had worked with in the past. W. D. Piggot, one of the old guard who had joined CN as a timekeeper in 1929 and lately been vice-president of the Great Lakes region, became vice-president in charge of the transition. Spicer took over planning and administration and Radcliffe R. "Rad" Latimer headed CN Rail, the largest and most profitable division despite the drain of the Crow rate, the Hudson Bay Railway, Newfoundland and the under-used branch lines. The forty-two-year-old Ontario-born Latimer was an MBA from the University of Western Ontario who had worked in marketing at CN. He had also been executive vice-president of the Algoma Central Railway in Sault Ste. Marie and with the White Pass and Yukon Corp. of Vancouver, whose railway in Alaska and the Yukon was reputedly the first in the world to offer an integrated road, rail and ship container service in 1955.

"The whole attitude toward departmental responsibility changed, with more onus on managers of various branches to produce and be held accountable," recalled Gordon Trainor, a general manager of CN Hotels. "Before that, it had never been clearly spelled out."

"As far as the railway part of CN was concerned, the reorganization did not change things very much," said Latimer. "We had really got things rolling at the time MacMillan left. I think decentralization – the profit centres Bob set up – meant more to other parts of CN than it meant to the rail division."

CN Telecommunications was making money. In 1972 it had helped launch Anik I, the domestic communications satellite. The stage had been set for more merging with Canadian Pacific, and in 1979 CNT came under the control of an integrated management as CNCP, the newest telecommunication company in Canada as well as the oldest, dating back more than a century to the iron telegraph wires of the mid-1800s.

The labour-intensive CN express department, with 5500 people who handled eight million items every year by rail and road, was losing money to specialized highway services. CN withdrew from unprofitable routes to concentrate on regions of large population, which brought complaints from communities in the West and the Maritimes. The CN trucking division, which now accounted for 4 per cent of the nation's trucking, was showing a modest profit. In 1976 it contained thirteen separate companies, employed 2000 people and operated 3500 tractor trailers, tankers and delivery trucks.

CN's eight hotels were in the doldrums with too few of their 4000 rooms occupied to produce a profit, but the CN Tower, which opened to the public halfway through 1976, looked promising. With its 1815-foot elevation it became the prime tourist attraction in Toronto, and a national symbol, and by year's end a million visitors had passed through the turnstiles of the world's tallest free-standing structure to visit three observation decks and a 400-seat revolving restaurant.

The Atlantic coastal services were consolidated under vice-president

John Gratwick as CN Marine, a separate CN business with a large government subsidy. Its 3400 employees moved two million passengers a year on ferries to Newfoundland, Prince Edward Island and Bar Harbor, Maine, and on the Saint John-Digby service it had taken over from the CPR.

In 1976 CN made its first overall profit in twenty years – $11.8 million as compared with a $168.1 million deficit the previous year, a breakthrough resulting from cost control and higher freight rates following a two-year freeze the government had requested to control inflation.

"The railways were bleeding from every pore for lack of revenue and this was the first time we had gone to the brink with Ottawa on rates," said Latimer. The railways had sought a 25 per cent rate increase, the government would agree to only half, and the railways appealed to the courts and won. "The economics of the increase had been soundly based and there was a real revenue requirement," said Latimer. "The government huffed and puffed but after a while they approved it."

By and large, CN had entered a period in which Ottawa allowed it to manage its affairs with little interference. To some extent this was a sign of the times – railways were not the political lightning rods they had once been because they did not loom so large in the national psyche.

Having demonstrated that it could be profitable, CN now sought the recapitalization that Gordon had wanted so long. Despite opposition from the CPR and the Conservative party, the 1978 "recap" went far beyond those of 1937 and 1952 in making CN self-sufficient. The government converted $800 million of debt to equity – the amount lost during the years of unrequited depreciation – decreasing debt-to-equity ratio from 60 to 40 per cent, which was in line with other first-class North American railways. At the same time it required CN to pay a dividend of 20 per cent of any profits and ceased advancing loans and equity, compelling CN to raise capital on the international market like any private corporation. For half a century the federal government had covered deficits and lent money to assure CN's survival, and the rare times there was a profit CN had handed it over to the government. Now cut off from borrowing from Ottawa, CN had a healthier, arm's-length relationship.

Moreover, CN had shed passenger services. It had been operating forty-six routes compared with the CPR's thirteen, eleven of which were local RDCs (rail diesel cars). CPR's sole remaining transcontinental was the *Canadian*, daily both ways between Montreal-Toronto and Vancouver, whereas CN ran only the *Super Continental*, though in two sections in summer. On average, passengers were paying half of what it cost to carry them. The transcontinentals, which cost the traveller with sleeping accommodation almost as much as an economy air fare and accounted for only 12 per cent of all passengers, gobbled 40 per cent of the federal subsidy. *Turbos, Rapidos* and *Tempos* between Quebec City and Windsor were more cost-effective, carrying 60 per cent of the country's rail passengers while claiming only 20 per cent of the subsidy. In addition CN ran two conventional trains daily between Montreal and Halifax and several elsewhere, as well as RDCs.

In the war between rail and highway, highways had won. With eight million automobiles on the roads, and billions spent on highways, good roads being notable vote catchers, so little had been spent on railways that passenger service was given a starvation diet until revived by the world oil crisis of the mid-1970s. CN found Ottawa's suggestions to combat the crisis impractical, including one that CN and CPR go back to operating passenger trains on a fifty-fifty basis, not only in the Quebec-Windsor corridor but across the country. Since CN already operated two thirds of the national passenger service, it rejected the idea. "I went to see Bandeen," recalled Garth Campbell, back at CN as vice-president of passenger marketing. "'The only way we are going to beat Ottawa is to have the public on our side,' I said. 'Let's give this thing a new image.' In my experience, any time we went to Ottawa we were the enemy because the railway was brooking no interference from the civil service." CN added six trains to the Quebec-Windsor corridor and introduced a blue and yellow colour scheme and a marketing slogan – "VIA CN" – which prompted one cynical wag to predict that CN would "end passenger service with a preposition."

In a manoeuvre that derailed the government idea that the two railways run a national passenger service in concert, CN proceeded on its own to hive off its passenger services. According to Campbell, Transport Canada was not pleased. Here was CN making improvements again in passenger services with no explanation as to how these might improve operating results.

By 1977 what had begun as a slogan became a CN subsidiary, VIA Rail Canada, which would operate passenger trains. In 1978, eight years after Amtrak was established in the States, the government turned VIA into a separate crown corporation (as it had Air Canada the previous year) to operate both CN and CPR passenger trains. Garth Campbell became vice-president of Marketing at VIA and Frank Roberts, who had orchestrated cuts in CN passenger services a few year earlier, was president and CEO.

"This time," said Roberts, "I've been appointed to revitalize passenger service – one authority, VIA Rail Inc., with the necessary financial support from the government to ensure [it] has its proper place in the future of Canada." CN and the CPR, for a fee, would supply the track and run the trains but VIA owned the rolling stock, most of it aging equipment purchased from the two senior railways. Despite an encouraging increase in passengers, an inevitable deficit caused Jean-Luc Pepin, minister of transport, to cut VIA by 20 per cent three years after it was born and nine trains were eliminated, including the *Super Continental.*

In 1978 CN achieved the best performance in its fifty-six years by earning a net after taxes of $136 million, which allowed it to pay a $27 million dividend to the government. Paradoxically, CN was criticized for its new solvency as it had been criticized previously for its losses. Some felt a crown corporation should concentrate on the public good rather than profits. Politicians found it harder to explain CN layoffs to constituents when the People's Railway was showing a profit. "The government was not ready for that," recalled Bandeen. "All the years we made money after that, never once did anybody in Ottawa say that was a good thing. It had become easier for Ottawa to deal with a deficit than with a profit. If there was a profit government opponents would be screaming that we were charging too high a rate or that we fired people that should have been kept on staff."

Relieved of passengers, CN tried to relieve itself of the losses suffered annually in Newfoundland, where, despite containerization and other measures, traffic remained too light. In 1977 a federal commission recommended abandonment of the railway. Since this was politically risky, CN offered to return it to provincial ownership but the province refused. So CN rail, intermodal, express and bus services were integrated into a separate operational division, TerraTransport, where they remained a financial burden.

On the West Coast, on the other hand, business was brisk due to the explosion in trade with Pacific Rim countries. The oil crisis and labour trouble in the Australian coal fields had opened a market for western Canadian coal and by the mid-1970s tonnage flowing to Vancouver through CN's Mountain region, which included Alberta, British Columbia and western Saskatchewan, had doubled in a decade.

Where five or six trains a day had run in each direction there were now sixteen long trains of sulphur, potash, lumber and grain or consists of seventy 100-ton gondola cars with coal travelling to Vancouver from Grande Cache in northern Alberta. Capacity would have to be increased by 25 per cent, particularly between Edmonton and Red Pass Junction in the Rockies, where the parallel tracks originally laid by Canadian Northern and Grand Trunk Pacific had been long since reduced to one. With much aging track, a huge injection of cash was needed. To make matters worse, a bottleneck was developing at Vancouver, where 2000 ships were arriving each year to discharge containers crammed with racks of silk dresses or automobile parts, or to take on grain, sulphur, potash or coal. Transportation was feast or famine – sometimes as many as 600 freight cars backed up awaiting ships or a dozen ships swinging at anchor awaiting boxcars or dock space.

CN was profiting from the trade boom with the Far East, having extended marketing from Japan and Hong Kong to South Korea, Taiwan, Australia, New Zealand, Singapore and as far as India and Pakistan. The port of Vancouver had improved its infrastructure as it became one of the busiest in the world, second in North America after New York, and to take pressure off the Neptune Terminal the federal government built a terminal at Roberts Bank, south of the city. But the whole area had become the end of a funnel, fed through mountain passes prone to bad weather and rock slides by CN, the CPR and BC Rail (the former Pacific Great Eastern). In addition the Burlington Northern came up from Washington state.

Meantime, 500 miles to the north, Prince Rupert, which the Grand Trunk Pacific had created to serve the Orient, was begging for traffic at the end of under-used if badly under-maintained track. Though some grain was flowing through its lone and aging elevator and the lumber trade was picking up, a year might pass with only fifty ships entering a port that had the advantage of being closer to Japan than Vancouver by a day's sailing. "We believed we had a major role to play in the development of Prince Rupert," said Ron Lawless, vice-president of freight marketing at a time CN was a prime liaison between Canadian coal companies and Japanese steel factories looking for metallurgical coal. "I remember we spent a morning in Japan with a slide show talking about Prince Rupert and were able to demonstrate it could be a viable port because it had the room and, given the right circumstances, CN could upgrade the track into Prince Rupert and provide a first-class service for coal, grain and petrochemicals."

By the end of the 1970s the federal and B.C. governments, CN and BC Rail and the Japanese trading companies were working together to develop the north east B.C. coal project, one of the biggest industrial projects in the province's history, dedicated to supplying a quarter of Japan's metallurgical coal from the Peace River field and the new terminal town at Tumbler Ridge, B.C., where Nemoto Plaza was named after the president of Japan's Kokan Mining Company. The federal government built a state-of-the-art coal terminal at Ridley Island in Prince Rupert Harbour and in 1982 Lawless, by then president of the CN Rail division, signed a fifteen-year contract, the biggest single such contract the company ever negotiated, to carry the coal to tidewater.

A modern grain terminal was built at Ridley Island by the Alberta government and other grain organizations across the Prairies to expand West Coast capacity to export wheat, barley and canola (rapeseed) by 20 per cent. Grain farmers had been prospering, with high prices and good markets, though their resentment of central Canada had not disappeared. Meantime, a royal commission on grain rates had confirmed in 1979 what the railways had known for years: CN and the CPR were losing huge sums of money on grain. Carl Snavely, the American economist of the Commission on the Costs of Transporting Grain by Rail, put the loss at $150 million annually. The Crow rate, he said, contributed to railway inefficiency and should be scrapped.

A second commission, the Grain Handling and Transportation Commission, which investigated the needs of Prairie communities, came to the opposite conclusion and would extend the Crow rate to other agricultural products. Chairman Justice Emmett Hall of Regina would eliminate only a third of the thousands of miles of branch lines built by Thornton and Beatty and recommended that CN and CPR be encouraged to upgrade deteriorating tracks. (In line with another recommendation, CN in 1981 took over the CPR's half of the Northern Alberta Railways, which moved grain from the Peace River region, effecting an operational saving.)

The railways had mustered allies who believed that only compensation for grain could save the rail networks. Producers of coal, potash, sulphur and forest products were concerned about the ability of the railways to carry their products. Beef producers could not compete with eastern producers, they said, because easterners paid lower freight rates for feed. The government finally seemed convinced that the benefits of compensation for export grain would outweigh political risk. Nonetheless getting rid of "the Crow," the oldest freight rate in the world, would prove a long and sometimes acrimonious process. The province of Saskatchewan, farm organizations such as the National Farmers' Union and the Saskatchewan Wheat Pool opposed the change, as did the NDP and, to some extent, the Conservatives. Don Mazankowski, who would later become transport minister, declared that "most people in western Canada put little trust in the railways," and while he agreed the railway should be compensated by the federal government, he said the Crow rate should remain.

Not until the end of 1983 would the Western Grain Transportation Act be passed, under which the government made up the shortfall by paying the railways a "Crow benefit" of more than $600 million annually. In return the railways agreed to invest heavily in expansion and modernization over the next decade, aided by government funding for branch lines and purchase of grain hopper cars. For the first time in decades grain would become a paying proposition.

CN was now more of a wholesaler of transportation than a retailer. Eighty-five per cent of its revenue was coming from about one hundred of its biggest customers, such as General Motors. The notion that a railway was meant simply to haul goods from one point to another, making whatever profit it could under outmoded regulations, was outdated.

Nevertheless return on investment at 7 per cent, Bandeen argued, was below acceptable commercial standards, even for a railway. To cushion the jolts of a cyclical economy he sought diversification, which had been limited by deficits and government insistence that CN put its money into renewal of rolling stock and infrastructure. "Monuments" like the CN Tower had come under attack as being foreign to railroading, but during the next decade 13 per cent of CN net profit would come from growth outside the railway proper. Real estate and the Tower brought in money, as did CN Communications. CN Exploration, the company's oil and gas business, was formed to manage two and a half million western acres of mineral and oil rights inherited from Canadian Northern. Unlike the CPR, however, CN would concentrate on acquisitions allied to railroading – which Bandeen called a "transportation conglomerate."

A criterion for diversification was whether the project augmented existing services. CANAC was marketing services on five continents and bringing in millions. In the United States, in 1980, CN had purchased the Detroit, Toledo and Ironton Railroad which took CN almost into Kentucky and provided access to the south through Cincinnati. In Quebec, in 1975, it had purchased the sixty-year-old Canada and Gulf Terminal Railway (Chemin de fer de Matane et du Golfe) which Gordon had turned down when the government tried to get CN to buy it for political reasons. Now it was not the government but CN itself, for business reasons, buying the line.

The importance to CN of the south shore Gulf Terminal, which ran thirty-six miles from Matane and Mont Joli, was that it connected with CN tracks and provided a jumping-off port at Matane for a rail ferry to the north shore. Pulp and paper, iron ore, and aluminum industries had grown up there in the past decade and CN wanted access to the ports of Baie Comeau, Port Cartier and Sept-Îles. It acquired 49 per cent of the Compagnie de gestion de Matane (Cogema) and launched the rail ferry *Alexandre Lebel*.

In a bolder initiative in 1975, CN had bought 18 per cent of Euro-Canadian Shipholdings of Bermuda, better known as CAST, which had been shipping its blue containers from Antwerp to Montreal since 1970. CAST, allied with Manchester Liners, was aggressive and flexible; having refused to join the North Atlantic Conference system, the rate-setting shipping cartel, it could undercut its competitors. CN's rivals complained that taxpayers' money was going into a maverick company fighting a rate war on the North Atlantic.

The Halifax *Chronicle-Herald* called CN's partnership with CAST the start of a "monumental transportation and shipping empire." It was to be nothing of the kind. CN, having twice got out of the shipping business, was not getting in again, but simply guaranteeing container traffic for its flat cars. There was strong opposition. CP, which held 60 per cent of the St. Lawrence container traffic and once handled CAST containers itself, was concerned that CN and CAST would get a stranglehold on container business through Montreal. The Seafarers International Union, which had failed to get members on CN ships, opposed the CN-CAST agreement on grounds that Canadian tax money was going into a foreign company that hired no Canadian seamen.

The CTC ruled there was no justification for killing the CN-CAST agreement, despite fears in the Maritimes it would divert traffic from Halifax, but the partnership was doomed anyway. By 1982 trans-Atlantic rates were so depressed CAST was in financial trouble. No everyone at CN agreed with the partnership, but for a while it appeared the government would permit the railway to take over the entire operation. But in the end CN bowed out, leaving CAST to its creditors and CN with a loss of $60 million. Bandeen, who had opposed withdrawal, maintained later that it was a mistake; CAST's eventual recovery and profitable alliance with the CPR would seem to bear him out.

Doomed to shrink in order to grow, CN had cut its workforce to 78,000 by 1978, a third fewer people than the early 1960s when dieselization and automation took hold. Nevertheless, more women were being hired than ever before, Bandeen being the first president to challenge the gender status quo. He had commissioned a study which showed that though a third of Canada's workforce was female, only 4 per cent of CN's employees were women and those, since blue-collar jobs had been closed to them again after World War II, were mostly confined to clerical work. "They make every operating job sound like you have to pull the locomotive all by yourself," one woman said.

Where women were employed in significant numbers as clerks, promotion beyond a certain level was rare, regardless of education or abilities. Many male managers, ensconced in an outdated culture, showed no inclination to accept women as equals or superiors. Spurred on by the government, CN launched a program of equal opportunity. Women were encouraged to seek railway careers, while men were counselled on their attitudes. Despite these efforts, the Canadian Human Rights Commission received dozens of complaints during the next few years, and CN was criticized as a corporate laggard.

The biggest complaint was a charge of systemic discrimination launched in 1979 by Action Travail des Femmes in Quebec. ATF, which CN had initially approached for help in finding women for blue-collar jobs, alleged that the railway's methods of testing applicants virtually ensured no women would be hired. In August 1984 a human rights tribunal upheld the charge. The company was given a hiring quota for the St. Lawrence Region in which women must make up one fourth of recruits for blue collar jobs, until their proportion reached the national average of 13 per cent.

By 1981, operating surplus had exceeded fixed costs for six consecutive years, which had never happened before, and Bandeen had turned CN into a profitable transportation system. Despite an unfavourable economy, CN that year earned a net income of more than $192 million on revenues of $3.7 billion, which enabled it to pay a dividend of $38 million to the federal treasury and have some left for capital investment and debt retirement – this despite the fact that the railway was having to pay out $370 million for unprofitable services such as grain, CN Express and TerraTransport in Newfoundland.

Cutbacks in staff continued, and among the 16,000 lopped from the payroll since Bandeen took office were some who called him "Dr. Band-Aid," because he could "cover cuts." Those who remained were working for a company that had pulled itself out of chronic deficit. Bandeen's original $75,000 salary, which had sometimes been surpassed by his vice-presidents, had been increased to $215,000, though it was still below the going rate at the CPR.

Bandeen was not, however, getting along with his board or with Ottawa, where his aggressive efforts to shape CN in the image of a private company had plumage of various hues. Some thought a crown corporation had no business competing with the private sector, or diversifying into businesses unrelated to transportation. Though the range of activities permitted by the CN Act was broad, when all was said and done many Canadians still expected the corporation to provide jobs, support their communities and generally exercise its vast purchasing power for the public good. There were those at the Ministry of Transport who insisted that corporate profits should go towards upgrading the railway rather than the purchase of other businesses.

These views were naturally reflected among the twelve directors appointed by the government from all regions of the country. By and large, the board in 1981 was one of the better ones, though Bandeen, like Thornton and Gordon, would doubtless have preferred the CPR's system rather than one based on patronage and regionalism.

Bandeen's departure appears to have been a mutual decision by himself and the board, and though he has not given any details, he volunteered that it was not an easy decision. It appears to have been influenced by the prospect of the presidency of Crown Life Insurance but also by pressure from some directors. At any rate, on January 25, 1982, he announced in a press release that he was quitting – thirteen years before normal retirement age. He left in April after twenty-seven productive years, eight as president, as CN hurriedly sought his successor.

When he took the job, Bandeen had said he planned to remain as president no more than eight years. The eight years were up, but people are rarely satisfied by such simple scenarios. Doug Fisher, still keeping watch on CN, wrote in his newspaper column, "The best explanation one can ferret out for the replacement of Bandeen as CN president is that he was too aggressive in dealing with the Ottawa establishment, including the transport ministry and the prime minister's office." It did not help matters that the CAST deal had soured and that a recession had set in, the first quarter loss in 1982 being the worst in the company's history.

The senior team Bandeen had gathered around him had dispersed. Piggot and Spicer had retired and Latimer, an obvious choice, was now president of TransCanada Pipelines. Among those mooted to succeed Bandeen was Ron Lawless, who had recently succeeded Latimer as president and chief operating officer of CN Rail. His work at the rail division was such that *Rail-*

way Age of New York commented, "During the Bandeen-Lawless era CN Rail has become the envy of nationalized systems around the world – and many private systems." Another potential candidate was Charles F. Armstrong, president of CN Holdings, responsible for communications, hotels and tower, express and other non-rail activities.

The railway that had been headed in its time by a judge, a banker, a lawyer and an economist would now be headed by a physician. To succeed Bandeen, the Trudeau government chose Dr. J. Maurice LeClair, fifty-five, of Sherbrooke, Quebec, who had served in Ottawa as deputy minister of health and welfare and secretary of the Treasury Board. Bandeen had hired LeClair in 1979 to succeed Spicer as corporate vice-president, and in his short time with the company he had won a reputation for financial acumen and his efforts to smooth relations with Ottawa.

With the departure of Gen. Dextraze at the end of his three-year term, the new chairman was Jack Horner, the Alberta Conservative MP who had turned Liberal cabinet minister before losing his seat. Horner, whose father had been a CN director in the 1930s, had served on the Transport Committee, where he had tangled with Gordon, but as he pointed out his appointment owed much to the fact that the West was becoming so important to CN.

When LeClair took office April 1982 few people expected business as usual. For one thing, there was concern CN's eighth president was less prepared than Bandeen to withstand political pressure. After several successful years the financial future looked doubtful. Recession had curtailed diversification. Now financially on its own, CN was facing the same rules as the CPR, but with a debt that stood at $2.3 billion.

The decade ahead would be difficult, with three cycles of commercial ups and downs and strong competition from American railways. Rescued from financial disarray by the deregulatory Staggers Act of 1980, they were now moving in on CN's share of transborder traffic, which contributed a third of CN's revenues.

The 1980s would bring mixed signals from Ottawa as to CN's role, regulatory reforms not in the railways' best interests, and a retreat from decentralization to a tighter, centralized structure. But above all, CN would change from Bandeen's diversified conglomerate into a multi-modal distribution system with few interests outside transportation – the freight railway, in fact, Hanna wanted in 1922.

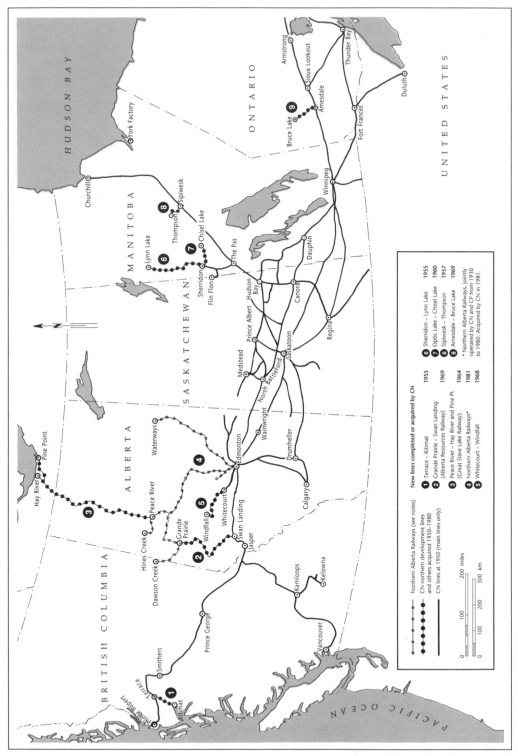

Expansion into mining country. CN lines in western Canada, 1980.

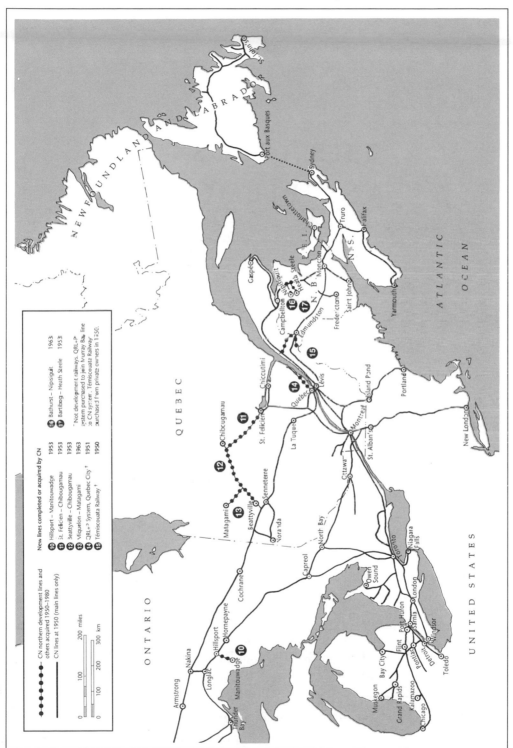

Expansion into mining country. CN lines in eastern Canada, 1980.

19

THE 1980S –
AN EPILOGUE

ROBERT BANDEEN'S ABRUPT DEPARTURE surprised the rank and file of a company struggling with recession. In the precipitous economic downturn of 1982 CN was to suffer a loss for the first time in seven years, a reminder that no matter how skillful the management the railroad responded sensitively to the ups and downs of the economy.

Prospects were brighter in 1983. The country shook off the recession, and the Crow rate was finally replaced by the Western Grain Transportation Act. After decades of heavy loss, the government began compensating the railways for the revenue shortfall on grain movement so that it became a paying proposition. By year's end CN had made a remarkable turnaround and a $223 million loss was followed by a profit of $212 million. Diversification resumed. In an attempt to strengthen Grand Trunk Western, Grand Trunk Corporation tried to acquire the bankrupt Chicago, Milwaukee, St. Paul and Pacific Railroad but the Soo Line, a CP Rail subsidiary, got it instead.

The election of a Conservative government under Prime Minister Brian

Mulroney in September 1984 had profound effects on CN. Out of office for almost twenty years and eager to shape the country in their own image, the Conservatives talked of selling crown corporations and using the proceeds to reduce the federal deficit. Government had no business owning a public enterprise competing with private companies, but so long as it did the government should control it. In the past, Tories, like Liberals, had exploited the crown corporation's assets and patronage potential, influenced management decisions for political reasons and used management on occasion as a scapegoat. Yet to people committed to private enterprise a crown corporation was an ideological embarrassment. During the next three years of Conservative rule, CN's competitive environment would alter – not always to its liking.

In a sense, the railways themselves precipitated regulatory reform when, to compete with American railways, they petitioned the Canadian Transport Commission in 1982 for permission to negotiate confidential contracts with transborder shippers. Before anything could come of their request, transport minister Don Mazankowski in July 1985 released a discussion paper lyrically titled "Freedom to Move," which went far beyond the modest changes the railways wanted and made shipper, rather than carrier, the beneficiary. Assuming that greater competition meant lower costs and better services, "Freedom to Move" would permit confidential contracts and create competition in areas where Ottawa believe no natural competition existed. While welcoming the philosophy, CN expressed reservations, but the legislation flowing from it, the National Transportation Act of 1987, went into force January 1, 1988, with few of CN's concerns reflected in its sweeping provisions.

Meantime, the financial picture was not promising. Debt was mounting rapidly, mainly because of capital expenditure on western expansion and lack of adequate compensation on the money losers, such as express services and the Newfoundland railway. A record profit of $242.0 million in 1984 had become an $86.3 million loss in 1986 and long-term debt had reached $3.36 billion. Interest payments were a million dollars a day, and an alarmed government imposed a debt limit of $3.5 billion.

The need for capital – $5 billion over the next five years – was pressing. Though half of that could be generated internally, the rest would have to be borrowed on commercial markets, which, however, would drive the debt-to-equity ratio to 50 per cent from the current 43 per cent. One solution, as Bandeen had suggested, would be to allow CN to raise equity on commercial money markets through share offerings, but this was rejected as politically impracticable. Nor was equity capital forthcoming, as CN had hoped, from the government.

Instead, the government diminished CN's anticipated cash flow by separating CN Marine from its parent and making it a crown corporation in its own right, Marine Atlantic. This was a blow because, though the ferry operation had been subsidized, CN's contractual arrangements with Ottawa had made it a money maker for the railway.

There was a further surprise in November 1985 when CN decided to withdraw from the trucking business, which had been losing money for twelve years. CN Route, as the trucking division was called, would be sold, but if no suitable buyer came forward it would be wound down to end chronic losses and trucking industry complaints of unfair competition. A year later, CN Route was sold for $29 million but it remained a headache long after the sale. The new owners declared bankruptcy two years later and the remaining employees lost their jobs.

The mid-1980s brought the first woman to chair the corporation. Elizabeth J. (Bettie) Hewes, an Edmonton politician, was appointed May 1984 by the Liberal government after Jack Horner's departure but was ousted by the Conservatives less than a year later. Maurice LeClair took over as chairman while remaining chief executive officer, and Ronald E. Lawless became president and chief operating officer.

CN Rail was no longer a separate profit centre. The corporation as a whole was once again a railway first and foremost – with a number of ancillary interests, to be sure, but rapidly discarding conglomerate aspirations. This was a giant step back from the decentralized, diversified company CN had been trying to perfect.

Of the two remedies chosen to reduce debt, one was traditional despite a new name: laying off employees had become "downsizing." The other remedy was to sell non-rail assets, a reversal of a policy that dated from 1923. With privatization high on their agenda, the Conservatives hoped private equity would be the white knight. At first, management opposed selling profitable non-rail units piecemeal, arguing that splitting them off would weaken CN salability. They felt that if CN were to be privatized, it should be left to market forces and the judgement of management to determine what its conglomerate nature should be.

Even now, however, the company's financial position made it a poor candidate for privatization. The issue had become not whether CN should be privatized, but who would buy it. Reluctantly, management began to regard piecemeal divestiture as a practical way to raise enough money to hold debt at a manageable level.

LeClair, who had been appointed during the Liberal regime, inevitably must have had difficulties in dealing with Conservative ministers. Nor did he and senior officers always see eye to eye on the social programs he was determined to develop, such as day care. Late in 1986, seemingly out of the blue so far as outsiders were concerned, LeClair resigned. Like Bandeen, he did not explain why. President Lawless assumed the mantle of CEO, and one of the directors, Brian Gallery, mayor of Westmount, Quebec, and a key figure in the Conservative Party's national fund-raising organization, was named acting chairman.

The policy of selling off parts of the CN empire continued. The remaining CN hotels went on the block and there was a pang at losing – and to Canadian Pacific at that – the noble Chateau Laurier, the bustling Queen Elizabeth and Jasper Park Lodge. Next to go were portions of CN Communications– two regional telephone companies and CN's 50 per cent share in CNCP Telecommunications and in Telecommunications Terminal Systems. CP Limited, which had an option to buy its partner's share, took full ownership of CNCP. As a result of these sell-offs, by the end of 1988 long-term debt had dropped from $3.4 billion to $2 billion in two years; debt-to-equity ratio had been trimmed from 52 to 37 per cent. With the economy booming again, profits doubled from 1987 to a record-setting $282.7 million in 1988.

Growing competition and downward pressure on prices as a result of regulatory reform tempered the good news. Studies comparing CN's administrative structure and costs with those of other North American railways revealed that CN, despite years of cutting down, was still burdened with unnecessary overhead and lower productivity. Almost a third of the railway's workforce held administrative jobs, compared with about one fifth in U.S. railways.

Efforts to reduce the payroll were met, as always, with protests. An effort to consolidate the administration of the Prairie and Mountain regions in 1985 had to be abandoned when politicians and the media in Winnipeg protested it would not only cost jobs in the Prairie region but destroy Winnipeg's historic role as a transportation centre. The closing of the Moncton shops in 1988 was even more controversial. No longer needing the shops, CN tried to work out an arrangement whereby General Electric would buy them for the manufacturing of locomotives. It required the approval of the seven shopcraft unions involved, but two unions rejected the proposal and the shops were closed.

The end for the Newfoundland railway came more peacefully due to Ottawa's financial support, the logic of the move and the province's acquiescence. Early in 1988, CN and the federal and provincial governments announced the railway would be replaced by an intermodal sea- and highway-based operation. For CN, the closure meant an end to statutory obligations and large annual losses. The second province to lose its railway was Prince Edward Island when the National Transportation Agency approved the abandonment of CN track in 1989. The provincial government protested but the money-losing railway had already been all but replaced by an efficient intermodal service and the province's demand for compensation similar to Newfoundland's fell on deaf ears in Ottawa.

When Lawless succeeded LeClair as CEO early in 1987, the first president with a marketing background focused attention where he felt it was most needed, customer relations. He had a firm belief in the container and intermodal systems, the fastest growing CN business. Convinced CN had to prepare better for its future, he established a Leadership Centre for two hundred top executives; unlike Gordon's staff training college, which had a business school curriculum, it would concentrate on internal problems and involve suppliers and customers as participants.

Otherwise, "downsizing" remained the well-trodden path to containing costs. Employees had never been very militant at CN, but in 1987 the unions called the fourth general rail strike in Canadian history, and within five days Parliament legislated the strikers back to work and referred the issues to binding arbitration. The company's viability, and the employment of its workers, obviously lay in keeping CN's costs as low as those of its competitors. The downsizing, however, had a cost, and the unions were concerned that the railways were cutting maintenance staffs too much.

Like all railways, CN had had its share of accidents, but, along with the CPR, it ranked among the half-dozen safest railways in North America. It had invested heavily in safety technology, such as electronic trackside devices to detect "hot boxes" and other flaws, and reset devices to brake a train automatically if the crew became disabled. So when a CN freight collided head-on with VIA's *Super Continental* near Hinton, Alberta, in February 1986, killing twenty-three passengers and crew, it was the worst accident the company had suffered in four decades, since a crash at Dugald, Manitoba, which killed over thirty people.

The Dugald crash was attributed to failure to observe orders. The Hinton crash was attributed to an engineman's failure to obey a red signal light. Calling the time-honoured "railway culture" into question, the enquiry criticized both management and unions for not correcting old practices, such as the crews getting insufficient rest before going on duty. CN launched a campaign that emphasized employee physical fitness, better internal communications and safer technology.

The railway continued cutting staff by 4000 jobs each year until by 1991 the total employed was 36,000, and there were more people on pension than there were on the job. Women had a firmer standing in the company now, one breakthrough having come in November 1984 when CN appointed Louise Piché assistant vice-president of employee equity. Piché become CN's first female vice-president when she was named to head human resources in 1990, a year in which women were one fifth of CN's new hirings – though 92 per cent of its workforce and 95 per cent of senior management were men. There were more women sales representatives since Yvette Dufresne had been appointed to work with a sales team of six men in Montreal passenger sales in 1966. Women were moving into the blue-collar work force again. Janet Wice of Hornepayne in northern Ontario, whose father was a locomotive engineer, had become the first female section hand in 1974 and was working to become a brakeman. Cutting down CN's size had reduced recruitment to a trickle, however, and because of union seniority many women newly hired as blue-collar workers were the first to go during layoffs.

As they entered the 1990s, Canada's railways were working hard to compete with trucks through intermodal operations, but some of the obligations they had undertaken in the days when they enjoyed a monopoly on transportation still haunted them. About 90 per cent of CN's traffic was still being carried on 33 per cent of its rail. The rest was costly overhead. Both major railways were dogged by low-revenue returns, less-than-effective marketing and what they described as the unfair advantages of trucking, which paid only half the cost of the highways it used. Truckers on the other hand replied that the railways, and CN in particular, had unfair advantages in government subsidy and such things as CN's $800 million recapitalization in 1978. The railway share of freight traffic continued to drop during the two recessions of the past decade and the deregulation of transport systems across North America.

After the sale of hotels, telecommunications and trucking, CN concentrated on railroading, though continuing to benefit from the contributions of such remaining non-rail units as CN Real Estate. With an active land sales program and redevelopment projects in Toronto, Winnipeg, Edmonton and Vancouver, real estate made the difference between profit and loss in 1990, contributing income of $95 million to offset a loss of $100 million on rail operations. Income from the non-rail units – CN Real Estate, CANAC International, CN Exploration and the CN Tower – allowed the railway to show a profit of $7.7 million for the year. It was clear that CN Exploration would follow hotels and telecommunications into the private sector.

While CN was withdrawing from businesses that had been part of its heritage, it was changing the shape of the railway itself. Although the National Transportation Act in 1987 retained some restrictions on rail line abandonment, CN itself began to solve the problem of over-extended, under-used track. Since the Staggers Act, large U.S. railways had begun selling some of their lines to independent owners, creating a thriving short-line railway industry. Adopting the same technique, CN sold lines in Alberta and Ontario, as well as the Grand Trunk New England line to Portland, Maine. It also began discussions with the CPR that it hoped would lead to consolidation of parallel trackage in areas such as the Ottawa Valley.

Even before free trade with the United States, traffic had been shifting from Canada's traditional, nation-building east-west direction to a more north-south flow, and by the 1990s CN was seeking a greater share of the U.S. market. CP Rail's acquisition of the Delaware and Hudson Railroad in January 1991 gave it access to the industrial U.S. northeast and threatened formidable competition to CN's eastern network. CN matched the CPR move with the formation of CN North America in late 1991– the integration of Grand Trunk Corporation units with CN's rail operations and marketing in Canada – and with the decision to build a larger tunnel under the St. Clair River between Sarnia and Port Huron, Michigan, to accommodate double-stack container trains.

The president of the CPR spoke of amalgamating the two lines – shades of Shaughnessy. But in most ways the times, indeed, had changed. In the mid-19th century, railway philosopher Thomas Coltrin Keefer said railways were more than economics. They represented social, economic and even moral progress that freed people from the bonds of nature. Above all they were steel bonds of unity. For that purpose the people's taxes had paid to build railways east and west. Now, however, railways intent on economic trends were looking south, not only to the border states but as far as California, for alliances involving the coordination of marketing, routing and information.

In its first seventy years, less than one human lifetime, CN has gone through prodigious change, technological, cultural, financial. Railways were the offspring of the industrial revolution, and in the information age many understandably think them a sunset industry. Lawless would not agree. As he told a U.S. rail shippers' group in May 1991, "Railroading is not yesterday's industry. On the contrary, it is the industry of tomorrow – or could be, provided it is seen that way by those who exercise such a strong influence over its destiny, and of course by railroaders themselves, who have such a long, rich history to build on. If we were to allow our railways to diminish or fade away, we would only have to re-invent them to achieve the most effective transportation system possible for the 21st century."

Lawless, a quintessential railroader, retired from CN in 1992, having stayed past retirement age. At CN, with its dual responsibilities as crown corporation and commercial enterprise, succession has rarely been a simple matter. The railway had to look over its shoulder even in periods when government involvement waned, and in recent years it had tended to increase. But even so there was palpable surprise among employees over rumours that the new president and CEO would be Paul Tellier, fifty-three, a bilingual senior federal civil servant and advisor to the federal government on constitutional affairs.

The chairman of CN being Brian Smith, a former B.C. cabinet minister, the appointment of Tellier, a lawyer, meant that for the first time since Donald Gordon held the combined post of chairman and president, the two top jobs were held by people with no railway experience. On the next rung down, however, there was a depth of experience, typified by John Sturgess, senior vice-president and chief operating officer and the man Lawless had groomed to succeed him. And as under Gordon and others brought in from outside, the railway had a life of its own beyond the executive suite.

It is tempting to imagine the CN of seventy years hence. While it is possible an entirely new technology will appear in the 21st century, it is equally likely that a national railway authority will have replaced both CN and the CPR to haul the bulk freight that has always been, since automobiles stole the passengers, the raison d'être of railways in this country.

APPENDICES

A BRIEF CHRONOLOGY

June 6, 1919 – Canadian National Railway Co. incorporated; president, D.B. Hanna.

1919 – Canadian Government Merchant Marine added to CN.

Oct. 10 1922 – Sir Henry Thornton, chairman and president.

Jan. 30, 1923 – Grand Trunk Railway formally joins CN.

Feb. 5, 1923 – CN headquarters to Montreal from Toronto.

July 1, 1923 – CN radio broadcasting begins.

July 1, 1925 – First CN silk train.

1925 – Crow's Nest Pass rate becomes statutory.

1927 – Maritime Freight Rates Act.

April 16, 1927 – Canadian National (West Indies) Steamships Ltd formed.

Aug. 6, 1927 – Toronto's Union Station opens.

1928 – No. 9000 first mainline diesel in North America.

1930 – CN pioneers two-way train phone service.

April 14, 1930 – CN extends Hudson Bay Railway to Churchill.

Sept. 1932 – Duff Commission on transportation.

Aug. 1, 1932 – Thornton resigns; S.J. Hungerford, acting president.

1933 – CN broadcasting network sold to government, eventually becoming the CBC.

Dec. 23, 1933 – Trusteeship; chairman, Charles P. Fullerton.

Sept. 10, 1936 – Board of directors replaces trustees;.

Oct. 1, 1936 – CN-CP Act of 1933 goes into effect; Hungerford, chairman and president. Demise of Canadian Government Merchant Marine.

1937 – Trans-Canada Air Lines (Air Canada) incorporated. First Capital Revision Act writes off deficits.

July 24, 1941 – R.C. Vaughan, president.

1941 – Centralized Traffic Control in Maritimes.

Sept. 1942 – R. C. Vaughan, chairman and president.

July 14, 1943 – Montreal Central Station opens.

1947 CN-CP Telecommunications pool marketing.

April 1, 1949 – Newfoundland Railway joins CN.

Jan. 1, 1950 – Donald Gordon, chairman and president.

Aug 22-30, 1950 – Strike of non-operating employees.

March 15, 1951 – Turgeon report on transportation.

1952 – Second Capital Revision Act.

1952 – Piggyback service between Montreal and Toronto.

April, 1955 – *Super Continental* introduced.

Jan. 1, 1956 – Uniform railway accounting adopted.

April 16, 1958 – Queen Elizabeth Hotel opened.

1960 – Steam trains end regular service.

1961 – CN reorganizes into decentralized areas. New logo. MacPherson report on transportion.

May 1962 – Red, White and Blue fares.

September 1962 – Place Ville Marie opens.

Oct. 25, 1964 – "Run-through" wildcat strike.

1965 – *Rapido* introduced between Montreal and Toronto.

Aug. 1966 – National rail strike.

Dec. 31 1966 – Gordon retires.

Jan. 1, 1967 – Norman J. MacMillan, chairman and president.

1967 – National Transportation Act.

Dec.1968 – *Turbo* inaugurated.

1968 – Great Slave Lake Railway completed. International Consulting Division formed as forerunner to CANAC (1972). Buses replace Newfoundland train service. TRACS (Traffic Reporting and Control System) introduced.

Dec. 19, 1968 – Toronto Metro Centre development announced.

1968 – Containerization.

1969 CN becomes part owner of Halterm, Halifax container terminal.

1971 – Grand Trunk Corporation formed.

Aug. 1973 – National rail strike.

May 1, 1974 – Robert A. Bandeen, president; Pierre Taschereau, chairman.

1975 – CN acquires part of CAST container line.

1976 – CN reorganized into profit centres.

June 1976 Toronto's CN tower opens.

1977 – VIA Rail Canada established as CN subsidiary.

Sept. 1, 1977 – Gen. J.A. Dextraze, chairman.

1977 – Air Canada becomes separate crown corporation.

1978 – CN's third recapitalization.

April 1, 1978 – VIA Rail Canada becomes separate crown corporation.

1979 – CN and CPR telegraph services combine as CNCP.

Dec. 11, 1979 – Ron E. Lawless, president CN Rail division.

1980 – CN purchases CPR's 50 per cent of Northern Alberta Railways.

Jan. 1982 – Bandeen resigns.

April 1, 1982 – Maurice LeClair, president and CEO.

Oct. 31, 1982 – Last *Turbo* run.

1984 – Repeal of Crow rate.

April 18, 1985 – LeClair, chairman and CEO.

April 18, 1985 – Lawless, president and CEO.

Dec. 31, 1986 – LeClair resigns.

Jan. 1, 1987 – Lawless, president and CEO; Brian O'N. Gallery, acting chairman.

1987-88 – Divestiture of CN hotels, Northwestel, Terra Nova Tel., CN share in CNCP, etc.

1988 – End of Newfoundland Railway.

Nov. 15, 1989 – B.R.D. Smith, chairman.

June 16, 1992 – Paul Tellier appointed president to take office Oct. 1.

June 30, 1992 – Lawless retires.

SOME HERALDS
& LOGOS

Pre-1919

1919-

(Grand Trunk)

(Central Vermont
Railway)

PRIME MINISTERS &
RAILWAY MINISTERS

Sir Wilfrid Laurier (1896-1911)	A. G. Blair
	Henry Emmerson
	George P. Graham
Sir Robert Borden (1911-21)	Francis Cochrane
	John D. Reid
Arthur Meighen (1920-21)	John D. Reid
	John A. Stewart
W.L. Mackenzie King (1921-26)	W.C. Kennedy
	George P Graham
	Charles A. Dunning
Meighen (1926)	W.A. Black
Mackenzie King (1926-30)	Charles A. Dunning
	T.A. Crerar
R.B. Bennett (1930-35)	R.J. Manion
Mackenzie King (1935-48)	C.D. Howe,
	P.J. Arthur Cardin
	Lionel Chevrier
Louis St. Laurent (1948-57)	Lionel Chevrier
	George C. Marler
John Diefenbaker (1957-63)	George H. Hees
	Leon Balcer
Lester Pearson (1963-68)	George McIlraith
	John W. Pickersgill
	Paul Hellyer
Pierre E. Trudeau (1968-79)	Paul Hellyer
	Donald Jameison
	Jean Marchand
	Otto Lang
Joe Clark (1979-80)	Don Mazankowski
Pierre E. Trudeau (1980-84)	Jean-Luc Pepin
	Lloyd Axworthy
Brian Mulroney (1984-)	Don Mazankowski
	John Crosbie
	Benoit Bouchard
	Douglas G. Lewis
	Jean Corbeil

GRAPHS

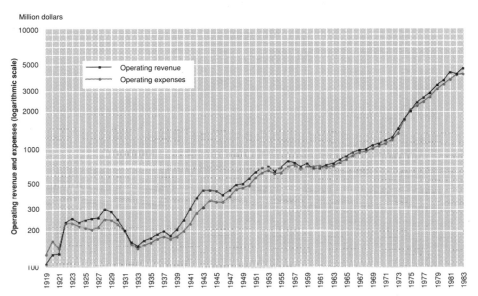

Above: Revenues and expenses. Below: Income, interest and the bottom line. Because accounting approaches have changed periodically, these graphs are an approximation.

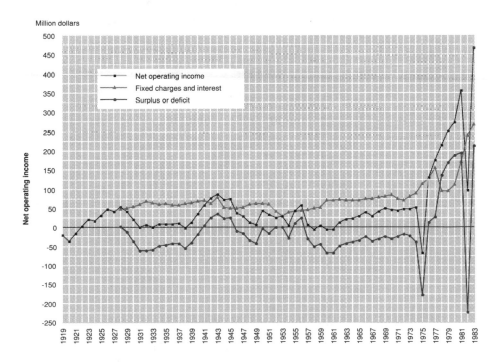

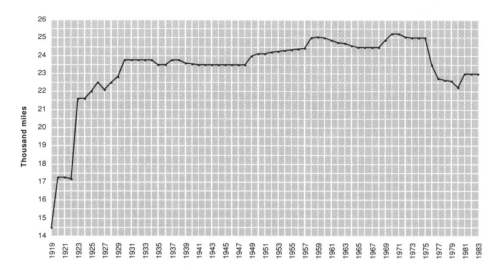

"First main track" operated by Canadian National, 1919–1983. There was also as much as 9000 miles of secondary track – i.e., double-tracking, sidings, yard track and spurs.

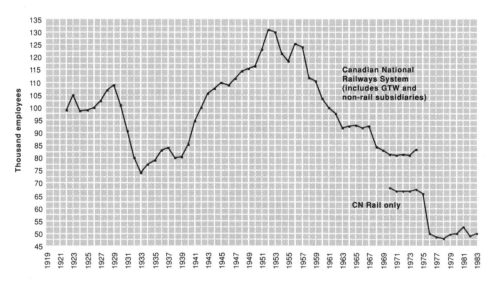

Number of employees, 1922–1983. As of the mid-1970s, CN was divided into various divisions, one being CN Rail, and the record-keeping changed.

NOTES

Apart from Canadian National Records (RG 30) at the National Archives of Canada (NAC), sources include, inter alia, Railway Branch records (RG 43); MG 32 Transport Ministers (Chevrier, Balcer MG 16 and 18); Manion (MG 27 III B7) Howe (MG 27 III B 20) Pickersgill MG 32 B 34); W.L. Mackenzie King letters; King diaries, microfiche; Department of Transport (RG 12); Canadian Transport Commission (RG 46), Dafoe Papers (MG 30 D 45); Donald Gordon Collection, Queen's University Archives, Kingston, Ont.; minutes of the Select Standing Committee on Railways and Shipping (SC); speeches in CN Library, Montreal. Quotations bearing a CA 1980-49 accession number are in Joseph Schull Collection, Oral History section, NAC. Unless otherwise identified quotes from CN people past and present and others are from taped interviews listed below and are in CN Archivist's Collection, Montreal, as is Starr Fairweather's unpublished autobiography from which his quotes are gathered.

Interviewees: Archer, Maurice; Armstrong, Charles; Bailey, W.H.; Bandeen, R.A.; Bennett, Pat; Bleakley, Jack; Bonenfant, Wilf; Brayshaw, D.W.; Brisbin, Lorne; Bureaux, Alfred; Burgeois, Gerry; Campbell, Garth; Cann, Jack; Carlyle, Jack; Cooper, G.M; Cronan, Bill; Cryon, J.D.; Daly, Dermot; Delagrave, Pierre; Dingle, Stan; Dixon, Leonard; Douglas, Alex; Duffie, Archie; Frank Fagan; Fielding, Gardiner, John; Graham; Fisher, Doug; Gauthier, Jacques; Gonder, D.V.; Gratwick, John; Harris, Charles; Humble, Jean; Humble, Mel; Hunt, Keith; Hurley, E.T.; Hutton, Frank; Lacombe, Doug; Lapointe, Frank; Latimer, R.R.; Lawless, Ron E.; Leathem, Ken; Macdougall, J.W.G; McDonald, J.M.; Messenger, Ronald; Morgan, Lloyd; Munsey, Jim; Neale, William; Noel, John; Paolucci, Albino; Perry, Lorne; Pickersgill, J.W.; Proulx, R.; Pye, Howard; Richer, Jean; Roberts, J. Frank; Schram, Bill; Steeves, Larry; Sergeant, Wilf; Smail, Alex; Smith, Walter; Solandt, O.M.; Spicer, J.H.; Tingley, R.J; Taschereau, Pierre; Trainor, Gordon; Vaillancourt, J.B.; Vaughan, Ralph; Walker, Alex; Webb, Vance; Wellard, Stella; Worracker, Richard;.

INTRODUCTION
p. 1 "Does the railway": Biggar, p. 6.

CHAPTER I
p. 5. "For half a century": Willison, "The Railway Question in Canada", Canadian Club of Montreal, 1921.
p. 8 "We want all the railways": *Manitoba Free Press*, Nov. 3, 1902.
p. 9 "The time is now": Calgary Board of Trade, Dec. 6, 1902, Laurier Papers, p. 68201.

p. 9 "We would hail": Van Horne in *Manitoba Free Press*, Nov.13, 1902.

p. 10 "Both companies": Canadian Northern Railway Arbitration 1918, p. 2603.

p. 11 "You know, we expected": Mackenzie, Toronto *Globe*, Nov. 3, 1904.

p. 12 "To those who urge": Laurier, HC Debates, July 30, 1903, p. 8396.

p. 12 "That mad route": Montreal *Star*, Jan. 23, 1904.

p. 12 "One of the": Montreal *Gazette*, Jan. 1, 1904.

p. 13 "entirely owned": Borden, HC Debates, 1904, 3559-.

p. 14 "Perhaps no more": *Canadian Magazine*, April 1906; National Transcontinental at first the name for whole line from Moncton to Prince Rupert, later was applied only to the Moncton-Winnipeg section, the remainder being Grand Trunk Pacific.

p. 15 "Thoroughly Canadian system": McBride, *Canadian Annual Review*, 1909, p. 587.

p. 17 "We have too much": Laurier, in *Robert Laird Borden*, p. 445.

p. 18 "If you were": Flavelle to Borden, June 28, 1915, in Bliss's *Flavelle*, p. 253.

p. 20 "the logical": Toronto *Globe*, Jan. 14, 1918.

p. 20 "On July 14, 1917": *Robert Laird Borden*, p. 650.

CHAPTER 2

p. 22 "It was fated": Hanna, *Trains of Recollection*, p 251.

p. 23 "The board must operate": Reid, "Trains", p. 258.

p. 24 " Not one of them": "Trains", p. 257.

p. 24 "We are still": HC Debates, April 1919, p. 1645.

p. 26 "There would appear": Shaughnessy Plan, April 16, 1921, presented to government.

p. 28 "Canada today": *Canadian Annual Review*, 1920, p. 320.

p. 29 "They could not have done": ibid, p. 230.

p. 29 "Parliament's attitude": ibid, p. 263.

p. 29 "The National Railway's": *Canadian Annual Review*, 1920, p. 323.

p. 30 "finest system": *Canadian Annual Review*, 1921, p. 381.

p. 30 "Though 1920": "Trains", p. 284.

p. 30 "great advertising": HC Debates, March 23, 1920.

p. 31 "It is a heartbreaking": Hanna "Trains", p. 280.

CHAPTER 3

p. 33 "one of the worst": Thomas to King, June 1, 1922.

p 36 "wisely and": *Canadian Railway and Marine World*, March 1927, p. 142.

p. 36 "your position": Geo.P. Graham, Oct. 5, 1922.

p. 36 "The future success": Hanna, quoted in *Montreal Star*, July 21, 1922.

p. 37 "I can recall no": King to Henry W. Thornton, Oct. 11, 1922.

p. 37 "I said he knew": King Diary, Aug. 25, 1933.

p. 37 "It is clear": Borden Memoirs, p. 1038.

p. 39 "Let it be": *Canadian Railway and Marine World*, Jan. 1923.

p. 39 "He is very simple": Flavelle to Dafoe, Oct. 24, 1922.

p. 39 "Unfortunately the Prime Minister's": *Canadian Railway and Marine World*, Jan. 1923.

p. 40 "I think the": Dafoe to F.S. Cahill, MP, June 11, 1924.

p. 40 "as long as": HWT to Dafoe, June 18, 1924.

p. 42 "On and on": *Saturday Evening Post*, July 6, 1929.

p. 42 "Because the CPR": HWT speech, Vancouver Board of Trade, Jan. 19, 1923.

p. 46 "The first three months": HWT to King, May 14, 1923.

p. 47 "Where are we today?": HC Debates, June 8, 1923.

p. 48 "I have reason": Thornton to Graham, Aug. 20, 1923.

p. 48 "He took the action": HWT letters of April 25 & May 31, 1923, kept King informed of the general intent, if not the details, of the Scribe purchase.

p. 49 "The unspeakable": *Montreal Star*. "Whisper of Death" series, July-Aug., 1923.

p. 49 "As long as": HWT to King, Sept. 10, 1923.

p. 49 "deliberate propaganda": HWT to King, July 29, 1923.

p. 50 "I have meant": King to Thomas, July 16, 1923.

p. 50 "what impressed me most": King to Thomas, July 16, 1923.

p. 50 "He tells me the most amazing": King Diary, Dec. 13, 1923.

p. 51 "Those off-hand statements": Hanna to Meighen, Nov. 13, 1923

p. 51 "A very influential section": *Canadian Annual Review*, 1923.

CHAPTER 4

p. 52 "Stand up for": *CN Magazine*, March 27, 1924.

p. 53 "In the very first year": *Saturday Evening Post*, June 6, 1929.

p. 54 "Last night": HWT to 2nd Lady Thornton, June 10, 1924.

p. 54 "I have visited": letter to 2nd Lady Thornton, June 10, 1924.

p. 57 "I am concerned": Flavelle to Meighen, June 12, 1923.

p. 58 "whose composition": HWT to King, April 22, 1924.

p. 58 "The committee": HWT to Dafoe, June 18, 1924.

p. 58 "It is altogether too": Graham to Dafoe, Jan.7, 1926.

p. 58 "All our friends": HWT to Lady Thornton, Dec. 23, 1924.

p. 60 "There appears to be": Sifton to Dafoe, April 24, 1925.

p. 60 "greater latitude": HWT visit is described in King's Diary, Aug. 24, 1925.

p. 61 "I have been": HWT to 2nd Lady Thornton, March 26, 1925, CN Archivist's Collection.

p. 61 "The whole railway": King Diary , Nov. 11, 1925.

p. 62 "We must always": HC Journals, 1924, append. 5, 226.

p. 68 "We are held": King to Veniot, Dec. 27, 1924.

p. 68 "Vote as your": HWT in Montreal *Gazette*, Apr.28, 1929.

p. 68 "The CN Railways": Vancouver *Province*, Apr. 3, 1927.

CHAPTER 5

p. 71 "The National Railways": (Beatty Letter Book) to W.R. MacInnes, Sept. 23, 1923.

p. 72 "After Beatty": HWT to the 2nd Lady Thornton, Aug. 7, 1925.

p. 72 "It is a peculiar": Beatty, in *Canadian Annual Review*, 1924-25, p. 114.

p. 73 "We do not want": HWT to Dominion Commercial Travellers Association, Montreal, Dec. 22, 1924.

p. 74 "slogans, radio, dogteams": Beatty to J.L. Counsell, Dec. 15, 1924, Beatty Letterbooks.

p. 74 "Beatty says": quoted in Millar-Barstow, *Beatty of the CPR*, p. 46.

p. 75 "As you are aware": HWT to Dunning, June 25, 1928.

p. 79 "We tried": Brosted, *CN Magazine*, July 1922; Hanna, "Trains", p. 333, describes how CN was responsible for CGMM traffic.

p. 76 "I am convinced": Thornton to King.

p. 81 "This is not bad": HWT to King, June 20, 1928.

p. 82 "He is certainly": King Diary, July 29, 1929.

p. 83 "I then moved": *Go West Young Man*, p. 161; Charles was surveyor and later chief engineer, Western Region;.

p. 84 "Sir Henry": *Monetary Times*, Sept. 27, 1929.

p. 84 *"esprit de corps"*: *Canadian National Magazine*, Feb. 1931.

p. 85 "joke of the financial world": quoted in Vancouver *Province*, May 15, 1930.

p. 86 "We agreed": King Diary, Sept. 10, 1929.

CHAPTER 6

p. 88 "He looked like Falstaff": King Diary, April 18, 1930.

p. 88 "Competition ever": Bennett speech in Montreal, June 26, 1930.

p. 89 "In the last six months" (Manion) and "I have served" (Thornton): Dinner in Montreal, Jan. 29, 1931, *Canadian National Magazine*, Feb. 1931.

p. 91 "...the present government": King Diary, April 22, 1932.

p. 93 "I wish it were true": Sessional Committee, June 16, 1931, p. 97-.

p. 96 "I had for two years": Beatty, Canadian Club, Toronto, Jan. 16, 1933.

p. 97 "I was a great deal shocked": Dafoe to D'Arcy Marsh, Dec.21, 1934.

p. 97 "The Canadian National has had": *Wall Street Journal*, Dec. 21, 1934.

p. 98 "Excepting in one or two": HWT to Dafoe, March 3, 1933.

p. 99 "At the present": Ruel to Manion, Jan 21. 1932, Manion Papers.

p. 99 "comes from the political": Beatty quoted in Miller-Barstow *Beatty of the CPR*.

p. 101 "deliberately and boldly": *Farmer's Sun*, Feb.2, 1933.

p. 102 "I feel": King Diary, May 11, 1932.

p. 102 "Thornton too": King Diary, May 11, 1932.

p. 102 "He was no longer": *Montreal Star*, Aug. 31, 1935.

p. 102 " rawest deal": Euler, quoted in *Border Cities Star*, Sarnia, Ont., Jan. 18, 1933.

p. 102 "He is not": King Diary, April 22, 1932.

p. 103 "get rid of him cheap": Manion to Bennett, May 30, 1932.

p. 103 "liquor, flowers": Why HWT should resign, June 29, 1932 Manion Papers.

p. 103 "He boasted": *Life is an Adventure*, p. 300;.

p. 104 *Winnipeg Free Press*, July 20, 1932.

p. 104 "...in this period": HWT to Manion, July 14, 1932.

p. 105 " himself to blame": King Diary, July 19, 1932.

p. 105 "He was often": Metcalf, p. 168.

CHAPTER 7

p. 107 "a splendid foundation": Manion Papers, Dec. 16, 1932.

p. 108 "Man for man": Lord Ashfield, quoted by Fairweather, unpub. autobiography.

p. 109 "I think anyone": Thornton to King, Jan. 13, 1933.

p. 110 "When he talks": Bennett to E.S. Busby, Vancouver, June 5, 1933.

p. 110 "Unite them": Senate debates, 1932-1933 p. 297.

p. 111 "Unquestionably": HWT to Dafoe, Jan. 21. 1933.

p. 111 "something phony": Dafoe to W.S. Thompson, Feb. 10, 1933.

p. 111 "I am too old": Hanna at Senate Standing Committee on Railways, Feb. 1, 1933.

p. 112 "It is sad": King Diary, March 14, 1933.

p. 112 "What Sir Henry": King, quoted in *Canadian Railway and Marine World*, for April 1933.

p. 112 "He was a great": *Montreal Star*, March 21, 1933.

p 115 "We ourselves": *Canadian Railway and Marine World*, p. 289, July 1934.

p. 115 "Judge Fullerton is not": Ottawa *Journal* and Toronto *Telegram* cited in May 1934 *CN Magazine*.

p. 115 "a species of czarism": Lash to Dafoe, June 4, 1934.

p. 116 "Admittedly there are routes": Canada's Weekly, Montreal, Sept. 6, 1935, p. 33.
p. 117 "We have made": Manion to Canadian Club, Toronto, May 1, 1935, quoted in *Canadian Annual Review.*
p. 118 "everything possible": HC Debates, 1936, pp. 2365.
p. 118 "responsible to no one": Howe to the Toronto Railway Club annual dinner, Dec.7, 1935.
p. 118 "When I was asked": Fullerton, Sessional Committee, pp. 352-4, Aug. 1936.
p. 119 "railway master mechanic": Bennett, HC Debates, 1936, p. 2200.
p. 122 "feel absolutely": Hungerford poll of managers, RG 30 V 219.

CHAPTER 8
p. 141 "I don't know": Walton, *CN Magazine,* April, 1945.
p. 142 "Few Canadians": *CN Magazine,* May 1944.

CHAPTER 9
p. 146 "We face new problems": Vaughan to Railway Committee, May, 1946.
p. 156 "Mr. St. Laurent": Pickersgill CA 1980-49-35.
p. 157 "I knew my good friend": J.V. Clyne memoirs, *Jack of All Trades,* Toronto, 1985, p. 140.
p. 158 "He seemed always concerned": Smith, CA 1980-49-32a p. 2.
p. 159 "It was a guess": MacMillan, CA 1980-49-36-38a;
p. 159 "In the spring": quoted in Montreal *Gazette,* Feb.20, 1950.

CHAPTER 10
p. 164 "Worse in winter": CN *Magazine,* Nov., 1949, p. 11.

CHAPTER 11
p. 173 "So you're Norman MacMillan": CA 1980-49-36-38a p. 7.
p. 174 "There was an explosion": Bromley, CA 1980-49-35a, 36a p. 1.
p. 174 "You have a right": *CN Magazine,* January, 1950.
p. 174 "It was Mr. Walton's": cited in *CN Magazine,* March, 1950.
p. 175 "Gordon asked for the papers": Lach, AC 1980-49.
p. 175 "It was an appalling": MacMillan CA 1980-49 36-38a.
p. 180 "If you force": Gordon quoted in *Maclean's,* Aug. 15, 1952.
p. 180 "Usually it's the union": "Big Donald at the Throttle", *Maclean's,* Aug., 1952.
p. 181 "almost complete lack": *Labour Gazette,* 1950. p. 1643.
p. 181 "I believe his period": HC Debates, in Toronto *Globe and Mail,* Aug. 31, 1950.
p. 181 "They were ready": Metcalf, CA 1980-49, 35.
p. 183 "If you made": *Reader's Digest,* "Unforgettable Donald Gordon", July 1974.
p. 184 "Instead of being": Gordon to Dingle, July 7, 1952.
p. 185 "The present attempt": *Winnipeg Tribune,* June 10, 1952.
p. 185 "Until it is made clear": Gordon to Chevrier, Jan. 11, 1952.
p. 187 "We did not go bullheaded": Sessional Committee, June 15, 1963, p. 93.
p. 190 "Please Mr. Gordon": *Canadian Transportation,* May, 1955, p. 60.
p. 190 "I have been accused": Sessional Committee, March 23, 1953, p. 105.
p. 191 "I am not becoming": Gordon to W.J. Parker June 16, 1953 Gordon Papers.
p. 191 "I am concerned": Gordon to Dingle, May 28, 1952.
p. 193 "The old order": Gordon to Metcalf, Aug. 10, 1955.
p. 193 "I think": Lach, CA-1980-49, 9.
p. 194 "I noticed": *Toronto Star,* Nov.1, 1953.

CHAPTER 12

p. 197 "experiment in socialism": address to Canadian Railway Club, *Montreal Star,* Dec. 11, 1951.

p. 198 "babe in arms": Gordon to H.J. Symington, July 9, 1957.

p. 199 "We quickly reached": Chevrier, CA 1980-49-43a.

p. 203 "Profits should be only": MP James McGrath, HC Debates Aug. 29, 1958, 4334.

p. 203 "Quite frankly": Gordon to Arthur Johnson, Deputy Minister Economic Development, Newfoundland, June 20, 1956 (RG 30).

p. 206 "Strip off everything": RG 30 v. 13065.

p. 207 "a very damaging blow": Diefenbaker, quoted in a Gordon Memorandum dated Oct. 31, 1958, Gordon Papers.

p. 207 "Cancellation of": Sessional Committee, 1959, p. 71.

CHAPTER 13

p. 210 "What is the problem": June 6, 1958, Gordon Papers.

p. 212 "We no longer": Sessional Committee, June 16, 1961, p. 132.

p. 213 "The time has come": Memo dated Oct. 31, 1960.

p. 215 "Donald had no": Walter Gordon, CA 1980-49-56.

p. 216 "We can have our conditions": W.J. Smith in *Montreal Star,* Jan. 21, 1961.

p. 220 "Our current figures": Gordon to MacMillan, Sept. 23, 1960.

p. 220 "I have spent": Strabo to NDP MP D. Fisher, March 6, 1961.

CHAPTER 14

p. 221 "If the son of a bitch": Grattan O'Leary, CA 1980-49 1&2.

p. 222 "There has been a stream": Sessional Committee, 1961, p. 291.

p. 222 "I have nothing": Hall et al, Sessional Commitee, June 19, 1961, pp. 317-18.

p. 223 "He could be": Diefenbaker, CA 1980-49, 21-27.

p. 225 "The committee should": Sessional Committee, May 6, 1959, p. 211.

p. 224 p. 227 "Let me say quite clearly": Gordon, Sessional Committee, Nov. 19, 1962, p. 59.

p. 229 "Let us sum up": *La Presse,* Nov. 20, 1962.

p. 230 "I have come": Alain to J.A. Lambert of CN, Nov. 21, 1961.

p. 231 "The time arrived": Gordon put this more colourfully in an interview with *Reader's Digest,* Nov. 1966, when he said, "If we can't get rid of our passenger service before we all have long, white beards, then we'll do our damndest to make it pay.".

p. 233 "If ever": Dupuis to Pearson, Aug. 29, 1963.

p. 234 "I recognize that following": Gordon to Pearson, Gordon Papers, Sept. 14, 1963.

p. 234 "I agree": Grégoire, Sessional Committee, Dec. 1963, p. 338.

CHAPTER 16

p. 260 "One day we had": Pickersgill, CA-1980-49, 20.

CHAPTER 17

p. 277 "In a mess": Marchand, Canadian Labour Association, Ottawa, March 19, 1975.

CHAPTER 18

p. 292 "The best explanation": Fisher, Edmonton *Sun,* June 28, 1982

p. 293 "During the Bandeen-Lawless": *Railway Age,* New York, Feb. 22, 1982.

BIBLIOGRAPHY

Biggar, E.B. *The Canadian Railway Problem*, Toronto, 1917.

Bliss, Michael, *A Canadian Millionaire: The Life and Times of Sir Joseph Flavelle*, Toronto, 1978.

Canadian National Railways, A Synoptical History of Organization, Capital Stock, Funded Debt and Other General Information, 1962, unpublished, at CN Library.

Canadian National Railways, *Serving the Nation in the War*, 1942, and *Five Years of War*, Montreal 1945, pamphlets.

Clegg, Anthony and Raymond F. Corley, *Canadian National Steam Power*, Montreal, 1969.

Borden, Henry, ed. *Robert Laird Borden, His Memoirs*, 2v. Toronto, 1938.

Eagle, A. John, "Sir Robert Borden, Union Government, and Railway Nationalization", in *Journal of Canadian Studies*, v. 10, no. 4, 1975.

Fairweather, Starr, autobiography, unpublished, at CN Library.

Hanna, D.B., *Trains of Recollection*, Toronto, 1924.

Keefer, Thomas C. *Philosophy of Railways and Other Essays,* Toronto, 1972.

Lamb, W. Kaye, *History of Canadian Pacific Railway,* New York, 1977.

Cruise, Davidand Alison Griffiths, *Lords of the Line, The Men who Built the CPR,* Markham, Ont., 1988.

Love, J.A. and J. Norman Lowe, *Canadian National Coast to Coast,* Edmonton, 1986.

Manion, Robert J., *Life is an Adventure,* Toronto, 1936, New York, 1977.

Marsh, D'Arcy, *The Tragedy of Sir Henry Thornton,* Toronto, 1935.

Metcalf, Maynard Albert, *One Man's Word for It, An Autobiography,* Montreal, 1981.

Miller-Barstow, D.H., *Beatty of the CPR, A Biography,* Toronto, 1951.

Schull, Joseph, *The Great Scot, A Biography of Donald Gordon,* Montreal, 1979.

Regehr, T.D. *The Canadian Northern Railway,* Toronto, 1976.

Stevens, G.R. *Canadian National Railways,* 2v. Toronto, 1960, 1962.

– *History of Canadian National Railways*, New York, 1973.

PERIODICALS

Canadian Government Railways Employees Magazine, May 1919-Dec. 1921; *Canadian National Railways Employees Magazine,* 1922-1937; *Canadian National Magazine,* 1937-58, when it became *Keeping Track* and its French counterpart, *Au Fil du Rail.*

Canadian Transportation & Distribution Management, formerly *Canadian Railway and Marine World*, and later *Canadian Transportation*. .

CN Annual Reports, 1921-1992.

COMMISSIONS

Royal Commission to Inquire into Railways and Transportation in Canada, 1917. The Drayton-Acworth report.

Royal Commission to Inquire into Railways and Transportation in Canada, 1932. The Duff report.

Royal Commission on Transportation, 1951. The Turgeon report.

Royal Commission on Employment of Firemen on Diesel Locomotives in Freight and Yard Service on the Canadian Pacific Railway. The Kellock report, 1958.

Royal Commission on Transportation, 1961-62. The MacPherson report.

Industrial Inquiry Commission on Canadian National Railways Run Throughs, 1965. The Freedman report.

Commission on the Costs of Transporting Grain by Rail, 1976-77. The Snavely report.

Grain Handling and Transportation Commission, Grain and Rail in Western Canada, 1977. The Hall report.

INDEX

Index